Balancing Change and Tradition in Global Education Reform

Edited by
Iris C. Rotberg

ROWMAN & LITTLEFIELD EDUCATION
Lanham • New York • Toronto • Oxford

Published in the United States of America
by Rowman & Littlefield Education
A Division of Rowman & Littlefield Publishers, Inc.
A wholly owned subsidiary of The Rowman & Littlefield Publishing Group, Inc.
4501 Forbes Boulevard, Suite 200, Lanham, Maryland 20706
www.rowmaneducation.com

PO Box 317
Oxford
OX2 9RU, UK

British Library Cataloguing in Publication Information Available

Library of Congress Cataloging-in-Publication Data

Balancing change and tradition in global education reform /
edited by Iris C. Rotberg.
     p. cm.
   Includes bibliographical references and index.
   ISBN-13: 978-1-57886-146-0 (pbk. : alk. paper)
   ISBN-10: 1-57886-146-2 (pbk. : alk. paper)
  1. Educational change—Cross-cultural studies. 2.
Comparative education—Cross-cultural studies. 3. Education
and state—Cross-cultural studies. I. Rotberg, Iris C.
LB43.G56 2004
370'.9—dc22

                                                        2004002911

⊗™ The paper used in this publication meets the minimum requirements of
American National Standard for Information Sciences—Permanence of
Paper for Printed Library Materials, ANSI/NISO Z39.48-1992.
Manufactured in the United States of America.

To
Gene, with whom I shared the joy of exploring the countries
described in this book,
and to
Maya, Sam, Eva, Madeline, Tess, Emma, and Quinn,
who will be the best judges of the success of our school reforms

Conservatism makes no poetry, breathes no prayer, has no invention; it is all memory. Reform has no gratitude, no prudence, no husbandry . . . each is a good half, but an impossible whole. Each exposes the abuses of the other, but in a true society, in a true man, both must combine. Nature does not give the crown of its approbation, namely, beauty, to any action or emblem or actor, but to one which combines both these elements; not to the rock which resists the waves from age to age, nor to the wave which lashes incessantly the rock, but the superior beauty is with the oak which stands with its hundred arms against the storms of a century, and grows every year like a sapling; or the river which ever flowing, yet is found in the same bed from age to age. . . .

—Ralph Waldo Emerson (1803–1882)

Contents

Foreword

Mary Hatwood Futrell

Isaac Asimov, the science fiction writer, said: "It is change, continuing change, inevitable change that is the dominant factor in society today. No sensible decision can be made any longer without taking into account not only the world as it is, but the world as it will be." I believe that Asimov's statement describes well the transformation that defines education, not only in the United States but also in countries throughout the world. However, very few analyses bring together in one source information about the changes being implemented in a diverse set of countries, the policy deliberations that inform these changes, and the impact changes have on children's educational experiences. This book is an attempt to do just that by presenting an analysis of education reform in sixteen countries.

As I have visited schools throughout the United States and around the world, listened to educators and policy makers, and attended international conferences, I have become increasingly concerned about the widening disparities in educational opportunity among countries—and often within the same country. Resources in many nations are so limited that the countries are forced to choose between providing even a minimum education to their low-income and rural populations and strengthening educational quality for relatively few children. Because of the disparities in national resources, some nations are reforming their education systems, while others are still struggling to establish education systems. All, however, recognize the critical role that education plays in securing the future of the country and the quality of life of its population.

Industrialized countries have the resources necessary to provide both universal and high-quality education, and many have made significant gains in strengthening instruction and broadening access to upper secondary and higher education. Yet, increasingly, educational outcomes are not meeting expectations. There are common themes in the reforms described in this book—worldwide concerns about access, decentralization, choice, privatization, standards, tests, and accountability. There is no unanimity, however—either among or within countries—about the specific reforms to put in place: centralized or decentralized decisions about curricula and resources, public education or vouchers, standards that encourage critical thinking skills or directive teaching techniques, high-stakes testing or diagnostic assessments, education programs that are religious or secular.

Balancing Change and Tradition in Global Education Reform is a timely and valuable study, which presents a unique and comprehensive analysis of education reforms on a global scale. After reading this book, we see that education reform is not simply a national or regional effort but, in fact, a global movement. Only time can tell whether we are witnessing real change or the politics of words. Socrates cautioned 2,500 years ago: "Fellow citizens, why do you turn and scrape every stone to gather wealth and, yet, take so little care of your children, to whom one day you must relinquish it all?" For many children, that question remains unanswered. Others are fortunate enough to be given rich educational opportunities. But even countries with generally strong education systems are reexamining the assumptions and priorities on which these systems are based in order to assess their responsiveness to societal change and the relevance of their programs to the demands children ultimately will face in a global context.

This book describes attempts in sixteen countries to strengthen education both for the children who have not been well served (or not served at all) and for the children who have had an opportunity to attend good schools but whose educational experiences still might not be keeping pace with societal change. The book demonstrates in country after country the high priority given to education reform in the face of rapidly changing societies and global demands. It highlights how decisions about education will ultimately facilitate or impede economic growth, improvements in the quality of life, and social justice.

Preface

Iris C. Rotberg

A nation's priorities are typically reflected in its education system. As a result, when a country is subject to major societal shifts—political, demographic, or economic—it focuses attention on its education system and seeks to "reform" that system so it becomes more consistent with the changing societal context.

All of the countries represented in this book are reexamining their education systems in a fundamental way and assessing the trade-offs and consequences associated with their efforts. Each country's reforms, whether real or rhetorical, stem from its particular societal context and are molded by that context. In some cases, the context facilitates change; in others, it limits it. But in one way or another, the reforms in all countries must balance change and tradition.

Some of the countries in this book have undergone major changes in their political and economic systems. In others, demographic changes—increased ethnic and racial diversity of the student population or changes in the size of the school-age cohort—have contributed to a perceived need for reform. Many countries have proposed reforms in response to publicized educational successes in other countries or to changes in the global economy.

The reforms often represent a reaction to the country's existing education policies. For example, a country with a decentralized, flexible system like the United States attempts to institute more uniform and rigorous academic standards. Conversely, countries with traditionally centralized systems, like France, China, and Japan, try to institute changes designed to encourage more flexible and diverse teaching methods. Some of the school reform proposals result in a fundamental transformation of schools. Others do not move beyond political rhetoric into real changes in the education system.

Irrespective of the reasons for educational change, there is a consistency in the issues that countries address. All countries face decisions on resource allocation, the equality of educational opportunity across diverse populations, access to higher education, student testing and tracking, teacher accountability, school choice, and innovation. These decisions, in turn, have a significant impact on students' educational experiences and on the distribution of educational opportunities across different population groups in the society. What a country does also affects educators' working conditions and, therefore, makes a difference in the country's ability to attract and retain the qualified educators needed to maintain academic standards.

This book began as a reaction to the international test score comparisons. I have been concerned over a period of many years that these comparisons, frequently presented to the public with great fanfare, provide misleading information about the quality of education, given the enormous range of values, choices, and societal pressures in different countries. We have, therefore, missed the opportunity to highlight—to public officials, educators, and the general public—information beyond test scores that would be relevant to formulating education policy. This information includes the difficult policy choices about school reforms made by nations throughout the world, the trade-offs implicit in these choices, and their impact on the learning experiences of diverse student populations.

In focusing narrowly on test score comparisons, we also have missed the opportunity to emphasize the limitations of attempting to transfer education policies from one country to another. The education system represents a country's social and political priorities and often its historical antecedents. To the extent that the education system is a proxy for a country's social structure, it does not transfer readily to countries that are quite different in values, culture, and history. We hope this book will provide insights about the underlying value systems that form the basis for national education policies and the extent to which policies can be transferred among countries with different political and social systems.

Countries were selected for the book to represent both the diversity of societies and education systems and the commonalities in their educational problems and proposed reforms. The most difficult problem I faced in making these selections was deciding which countries *not* to include, with the knowledge that each country omitted represents an important loss of valuable information.

The authors included in this collection were selected to have "first-hand" experience in the countries they describe. They were invited to write essays that give the reader an understanding of each country's education policies and reforms in a political and social context. Thus, they were asked to go beyond structural or statistical descriptions of school systems and, instead, focus their analysis on the implications of the policy choices that were made or rejected. Authors had wide editorial latitude in drawing interpretations that they felt were appropriate.

Inevitably, the essays will raise as well as answer questions. The range of societal and educational issues in each country is too broad to address fully in one chapter. The authors, therefore, have had to make difficult choices in selecting the themes to emphasize; as a result, some important issues are not given the attention they deserve. In all countries, for example, minority populations face political, cultural, or economic environments that affect their educational experiences. In some cases, these topics are addressed. In others, the authors felt that the issues required an in-depth, comprehensive analysis that goes well beyond the scope of their chapters.

My intellectual debt begins with the colleagues and friends directly involved with the education systems described in this book: Chinese colleagues in 1981, recently emerging from the Cultural Revolution, who discussed their professional and personal hardships during that period and their efforts to rebuild the Chinese education system; South African educators who described the obstacles they overcame during the apartheid regime and the creative energy they experienced in the years of independence that followed; Japanese friends who shared their personal hopes and concerns as their children prepared for the university entrance examinations; and many others from each of the participating countries. I am grateful to colleagues at The George Washington University whose insights and suggestions contributed to the themes of this book: Mary Hatwood Futrell, the dean of the Graduate School of Education and Human Development; Ralph Mueller, the chair of the Department of Educational Leadership; and faculty and students in the education policy, international education, and teacher preparation programs—John Boswell, William Cummings, Elaine El-Khawas, Karen Foreman, Colin Green, Lisa Hansel, Ginny Hudson, Gregg Jackson, Jae Hoon Lim, Yas Nakib, Becky Skinner, and Jim Williams.

My experience in developing a course on international education policy with Jim Williams was invaluable as I conceptualized the framework for this book. Lisa Hansel's article, written while she was a doctoral student at The George Washington University, also provided pertinent comparative information about education policy in England, Germany, Japan, and the United States. Both the course and the article pointed out the need for bringing together, in one accessible source, current education policy deliberations in various countries throughout the world, written by "insiders."

I would also like to thank Tom Koerner, the vice president and editorial director of ScarecrowEducation, for his many substantive contributions to the conceptualization of the book and for the expertise and support that he and his colleagues provided throughout the preparation of the manuscript. I am particularly grateful to the contributing authors for their input to the overall framework of the collection, to which they generously gave their time in addition, of course, to their work on the individual chapters.

Randi Gray Kristensen, an assistant professor of English at The George Washington University, was a superb colleague whose editorial assistance and insights enriched the book's presentation and style. I would also like to express my appreciation to C. Ann Robertson, for her many important contributions to the book's quality and consistency, and to Mary Ann Kennedy, who was extremely helpful in providing a wide range of administrative assistance during the preparation of the book.

I

DRAMATIC POLITICAL/ECONOMIC CHANGE

1

China: Turning the Bad Master into a Good Servant

Kai-ming Cheng

> They must often change who would be constant in happiness or wisdom.
>
> —Confucius (551–479 B.C.E.)

A land of contradictions, China is the world's largest developing country. Despite its relatively developed coastal cities, most of the nation is still agricultural. According to the World Bank (2003b), the gross domestic income per capita in 2001 was US$890, which continues to keep China in the lower brackets of the world's economies. In 2002, although agriculture contributed to only 15 percent of China's economic output (World Bank, 2003a), 60 percent of China's population was rural (*People's Daily News*, May 19, 2002).

However, China supports the largest and, in many ways, one of the world's most effective education systems. In 2002 the system served about 319 million students, of whom about 122 million were in primary schools (Ministry of Education, Development and Planning Department, 2003). More than sixteen million students are in China's higher education system, which has become one of the world's largest systems of higher education.[1] On the qualitative side, China has demonstrated some highly effective educational practices that have achieved recognition in developed, as well as developing, countries.

China's experience, therefore, contradicts the widespread belief that a nation's level of economic development determines its level of educational development. One explanation is China's cultural heritage, with its long history of valuing education and scholars. However, that same culture also accounts for the conservative dimensions of China's education. This chapter describes China's education reforms during the past twenty-five years and analyzes how the reforms have built on the strengths of traditional culture and have overcome its negative characteristics.[2]

DECENTRALIZATION AND EXPANSION

Chinese education has been reformed substantially since the early 1980s, when China reconstructed its education system from the ruins of the decade-long disastrous Cultural Revolution that ended in 1976. It is necessary to understand the Cultural Revolution in order to appreciate the difficulties of the reform. The Communist Party began governing the nation in 1949. In 1966 Mao Zedong, chairman of the Communist Party, asserted that the society was still overwhelmed by bourgeois ideology, despite the rather thorough socialist transformation of the economic system. His position was that unless this ideology was completely overturned, it would undermine socialism. The political movements Mao then launched were designed to eliminate bourgeois ideology, along with economic incentives and individual interests in social institutions. He focused on culture and began with education. The result was that for the ten years of the Cultural Revolution, schools were first suspended and then replaced by institutions taken over by workers and peasants. School subjects were replaced by learning experiences directly related either to production or to class consciousness and class struggles. Textbooks were largely replaced by the writings by Marx, Engels, Lenin, and Mao. Universities were replaced by new institutions where only workers and peasants were admitted and where "study" completely merged with work.[3]

The Cultural Revolution became highly visible to the rest of the world when it evolved into nationwide political turmoil that caused an almost complete standstill of the nation's economy. It might seem ironic that in a country where education had been highly regarded, it became a blank page for ten years.

Beginning in 1978, economic reforms have led to new educational initiatives, which began in the rural areas where economic reform first took place. Rural farmers, for the first time in the socialist system, were allowed to keep most of their output, which gave them the resources and hope needed to seek a better education for their children. Traditionally, as will be discussed later, education has always been the means for social mobility—an opportunity to move away from the villages and a path to greater opportunity. The farmers were keen to resume that tradition.

In 1980 the central government quickly captured farmers' initiatives and adopted policies that permitted farmers to finance their children's education. The use of local initiatives would never have happened in the earlier years of socialism because all initiatives were required to come from the state. The new policy then evolved into a more general shift toward decentralization that continued throughout the next two decades.

For the first fifteen years of that period, reforms concentrated on the structure, financing, and administration of the education system.[4] Decentralization has led to new educational resources from local communities and from the nongovernmental sector. Basic education is now funded by the following mix of resources from the government, private contributions, and income generated by schools (Cheng, 1996, 1997):

- Salaries of teachers are financed by local revenues.
- Buildings and facilities are funded by donations, often with matching funds from the government.
- Other nonsalary expenditures rely on income generated by schools, for example, tuition fees and commercial or industrial activities carried out by the schools.

In order to increase resources from local governments, an education surcharge has been levied over other industrial and commercial taxes. There have also been unusual stipulations that local revenues collected at the township level should all be devoted to basic education and that expenditures on education were to see positive annual growth that exceeded growth in the economy (Cheng, 1996, 1997).

Although the details vary over the years, and sometimes across provinces, the net effect is that local governments and local communities are financing basic education, which is often taken to mean nine-year compulsory education. There have been similar developments in postcompulsory, vocational, and higher education. The net effect is that central funding has become minimal, and government funding in general contributes only to a small percentage of education expenditures. Decentralization might originally have been attractive to the central government as a means of reducing government funding, but it evolved into a national campaign to develop education with the enthusiastic support of the population.

At the height of the structural reform, from the mid-1980s to the mid-1990s, China was known for its spectacular achievements in the expansion of basic education. In a matter of less than ten years, China achieved almost universal attendance in primary education and above 80 percent enrollment in junior secondary education (grades seven to nine). This is an unusual achievement at China's level of economic development. That achievement, however, was made possible mostly by community and local resources. It is an example of how the traditional values placed on education mobilized the population not only to demand education but also to contribute to its supply.

DISPARITY AND DIVERSITY

The remarkable achievement in decentralization also brought about unprecedented diversity across the nation and, with it, unprecedented disparity. China has always been known for its culture of uniformity and conformity. In the broad sense, this is an inevitable reflection of the collective culture, in which individuals' behaviors abide by the expectations of the community.[5] Such a community might start with the family, but it extends to the broader society and to the nation. Hence, starting from very ancient times, rituals and morality have been given priority, and individual behavior is bound by relatively strict and rigid social norms.

This culture was reinforced by the socialist system that was established in 1949. China in the 1950s and 1960s followed a strict form of socialism, and its people led collective lives in the very extensive sense of the term. In particular, the economic development of the nation was dictated by one national plan (the Five-Year Plan). The goals of the national plan were translated into production target goals for the respective economic sectors, which in turn were translated into target goals for production units, such as factories and mines. In order to fulfill these goals, China practiced strict manpower planning, one of the most comprehensive in the world. The production target goals in the manpower plans depended on the supply of personnel at all levels and in all economic sectors. The manpower goals were then realized through meticulous planning in the education system. The purpose was to match the outputs of the education system to manpower demands.

In other words, the manpower pyramid in the economic sector was matched by the pyramid of student populations and graduates in the education system. In order for this match to be successful, the education system was planned not only in terms of the physical numbers of school places but also by preparing students ideologically to abide by national planning goals. In concrete terms, students at different levels were "educated" ("indoctrinated," as viewed by the West) to appreciate the need for national development goals and to willingly follow national assignments of individuals to specific study programs and future careers. Although this type of manpower planning was practiced in almost all socialist countries during those years, the Chinese practice was more likely to be implemented as planned, largely because of the national tradition of a collective culture.

The collective ideology was also reinforced by the reality of life in the workplace. In a way, there was no life beyond the workplace. Every individual belonged to a work unit and was indeed *owned* by the work unit. Through the work unit, the state supplied practically all basic living needs. Individuals received minimal "incomes" for purchases that were not supplied by the state.[6] Food, clothing, and industrial products, such as bicycles and electrical appliances, were rationed. Hence, individuals were made to feel that they were no more than part of the national machinery.

The socialist system treated the entire vast nation as one system and hence tried to mobilize national resources, physical and human, as one single pool. This had the effect of suppressing individual and local aspirations and left very little room for diversity. Because of the national planning ideology, disparity was never an issue either. What was in place was a national blueprint for national development, and any difference was no more than the division of labor within the nation.

Under such a system, education was no exception. All through the socialist era, until the reform started, there had been a uniform system of education throughout the vast territory. Not only was the structure uniform (in terms of duration at each level), but all schools were run by the state and received funding at the same "student unit" cost. Teachers received salaries on a single salary scale. There was one university entrance examination that dictated teaching and learning in schools. There was only one curriculum and, indeed, one set of textbooks for the entire country.[7]

Thus, the decentralization of education finance has changed the scene by creating a funding pattern dependent on local sources of funds: local revenues, local donations, and local school-generated income. All of these sources are highly dependent on the local economy. As a result, the funding method embraced by decentralization policies has inevitably produced large differences in funding among regions and communities and has substantially changed the amount and distribution of education resources.

Indeed, in a reform document issued in 1985 (*Reform of China's Educational Structure*, 1985), the central government set different goals for different parts of the country. For the first time in the history of the socialist nation, the central government divided the nation into three development zones, assigned different timelines for the achievement of universal basic education, and encouraged the development of local, and diverse, plans. Provincial, and even county, authorities were responsible for setting targets and deciding how to achieve these targets.

Decentralization resulted in variation in the duration of schooling. Despite the norm of 6 + 3 + 3 class years in the primary/junior secondary/senior secondary school structure, many less developed provinces currently opt for a 5 + 3 + 3 system, primarily because of the shortage of resources for an additional year of universal primary education. Many developed urban centers operate a system of 5 + 4 + 3.[8] There are also urban schools that have begun to operate a 3 + 1 system at the senior secondary level in order to enhance young people's employment opportunities.[9]

The real diversity in curriculum started in 1988, when local authorities were allowed to develop textbooks according to local needs and cultures. That diversity has been reinforced by the commercialization of these books.[10] At first, there were eight different sets of approved textbooks for all subjects; that number soon grew and evolved into a competition to develop local textbooks or even diverse textbooks within the same locality.[11] The proliferation of textbooks was followed by a mushrooming of local curricula developed by different local authorities. The variation in textbooks and curricula was antithetical to the culture of uniformity; teachers were confused because they were used to following one approach to teaching. Bolder steps toward diversity in quality, however, soon overtook these relatively minor confusions.

REFORM IN QUALITY

Since the mid-1990s, reforms in China's education system have revolved around the theme of "quality education," which refers mainly to basic education. This theme began as an appeal against the rigid examination system in basic education and was intended to alleviate the enormous, and many believed harmful, examination pressure faced by students. To meet the demands of the examinations, there has been widespread reliance on private tutorials that have taken up a large amount of students' time after school. In the final years of secondary school, a large percentage of students' leisure time, including evenings and weekends, is also devoted to examination preparation. The concern is that the resulting pressure is detrimental to the younger generation's development and distorts the purpose of learning.

The cult of examinations in China can best be understood in a cultural context. During the ancient dynasties, the civil examination system was the *sole* system of "education" and was designed only for the purpose of recruitment into government positions. Over a period of more than 1,000 years, that tradition has created a high value on "education" but has also contributed to the view that education is only a means for social mobility. The examination system started during the Shui dynasty in 603 A.D. (Huang, 1992) and, despite variations, maintained more or less similar characteristics over the dynasties:

- It was a fairly sophisticated system with a high level of security and validity in order to ensure that it was seen as a fair competition.
- The examination was based on writing essays, with the finalist sometimes interviewed orally by the emperor or his deputy.
- The essays were mostly about political ideas pertaining to governing the nation.
- The examination focused on the management of political affairs and social welfare, not on objective knowledge and skills.
- The essays were expected to be based on the thoughts of the ancient sages, taken from their classical writings.
- The emperor or other senior administrators assessed the quality of the essays in terms of their "correctness" rather than their objective accuracy.
- The system enjoyed the beauty of brevity. It was extremely low cost, relied on the commonly available *Four Books and Five Classics,* and required only self-study.

The civil examination derived its power from the fact that it was the only means of social mobility. It was an absolutely open system that created an opportunity for practically every person to become a senior official just by reading and writing. Success in the public examination has long been every family's aspiration and has served as the basis for the long heritage of valuing education. This heritage led, as described previously, to the nation's overwhelming support for developing education during the reform years.

An analysis of the examination system, however, also demonstrates that learning, in the sense of acquiring objective knowledge, is not a part of traditional Chinese formal education. A scholar in the traditional sense meant a literary man, with almost no reference to scientific knowledge or technology. This interpretation is also consistent with Gardner's (1984) distinction between cultures where human–human relations are emphasized as a matter of core competencies and cultures (mainly Western) where human–nature relations are central.

Although the imperial civil examination was abolished a century ago, the traditional conception of "education" has influenced contemporary schools in China. First, public examinations, which determine university entrance, have replaced the civil examination as the goal of education. Second, schools in China, in the contemporary sense of the term, began as a result of the colonial invasion and import of Christianity only at the end of the nineteenth century. The school curriculum, therefore, was modeled after Western curricula and included natural science as a symbol of modernization.[12] The Westernized curriculum was treated as if it had taken the place of traditional classics. Third, passive rote learning is still the most common way of learning.[13] Teaching has always been didactic. Students are generally expected to listen and to learn the material that is presented; innovation and creativity have seldom been part of school's agenda.

Thus, the very tradition that brought about the rapid expansion of the education system also contributed to its rather conservative practices. For this reason, there was a national call, starting in 1993, for "quality education," which was intended to reduce the emphasis on examination-oriented education. As mentioned earlier, the public examinations had become a matter of widespread social concern because student lives were overwhelmed by the pressures of examination preparation.

The goals and details of the quality education movement, however, were not prescribed and inevitably led to diverse interpretations. In contrast to the expansion of basic education, where there were quantitative enrollment targets, the "quality" reform could not be easily defined or measured. Moreover, the reforms were initiated at the school level, in contrast to the systemwide expansion of basic education. Well-known early examples include "Education for Success," whereby a junior secondary school in Shanghai admitted only primary school leavers with the poorest academic records.[14] By offering a range of opportunities, the school was able, in three years, to turn most of its students into academic achievers, who were then admitted to above-average senior secondary schools. Another example is "Education with Happiness," whereby several schools in major cities provided students with enjoyable learning experiences without compromising their academic achievement. "Swift Character Learning," a third example, enables children to read 3,000 Chinese characters within two years in early primary school, thereby easing the considerable difficulties involved in learning the Chinese language.[15]

The reform for quality education did not start with favorable responses, however. Although all stakeholders described the adverse examination pressure as intolerable, the actual movement to remove the pressure received only lip service. In reality, public examinations still carry high stakes and high currency. Formal education and entrance to higher education remain the only reliable method by which a farmer's child can leave the village and the only way a child from a poor family can escape poverty. The economic reforms, which gradually phased out political favoritism, have contributed to fair competition and have increased the importance of examinations as the main selection mechanism in a meritocracy. Thus, public examinations assumed even greater legitimacy as the society moved from a planned to a market economy and the state had less power over its citizens' futures.

The reform for quality education, however, took a positive turn in the last years of the twentieth century when a new approach began to bear fruit. First, the examination was reformed. Instead of trying to reduce the significance of the examination, as is typically done in other parts of the world, the Chinese education reform attempts to introduce new elements into the examination system: Instead of weakening the dominant role of examinations, the Chinese reformers try to make positive changes in them. The reforms both reduce the number of subjects and change the types of questions asked in the university entrance examinations. Students used to take examinations in six or seven subjects across science and the humanities. Since 2000 there has been a new type of examination known as "3 + x." Students are examined in the three mandatory core subjects: language, mathematics, and foreign language. In addition, they write either one or two integrated papers (the x), as selected by the provincial authority. Some provinces have chosen $x = 2$, and students write one integrated science paper and one integrated humanities paper, but others have chosen $x = 1$, where there is only one general integrated paper.[16] A typical subject for the integrated paper is the increase of private motor cars in China: The student's response requires knowledge of statistics, international comparisons, supply and production issues, urban traffic, social impacts, and pollution.[17]

The new approach to examinations has effectively suppressed direct cramming and instead has emphasized application of knowledge, rather than regurgitation of factual information. Teachers are no longer able to teach to the syllabi and marking schemes because the questions require students to demonstrate creativity. In the language paper, for example, students are encouraged to write poems and stories as alternatives to argumentative essays, and the marking schemes are designed accordingly. Students receive a basic score for the demonstration of core competencies, but a large portion of the score is devoted to diversity and creativity.

The changes in the examinations have reflected contemporary theories about learning that are based on the principle that knowledge is constructed through application and integration. Although the reforms are welcomed by the society at large, they have also caused concern among teachers who are used to teaching to a syllabus and preparing students to provide "model" answers. Some parents and students also worry because examinations have now become more precarious, for hard work at memorization alone will no longer guarantee high scores.

EXPLOITING THE CULTURE

The reform in the examination has been accompanied by a nationwide campaign to reform classroom teaching approaches and, therefore, students' learning methods. There is, for example, the suggestion from central curriculum developers to "return the time to the students," which advises teachers to talk less and allow students to participate more in classes. This teaching approach is inconsistent with traditional Chinese classrooms, where the students' tasks were basically to listen and do the work as assigned by the teachers. The teachers have responded to the new philosophy by designing a broader range of student activities, which have changed the learning environment and substantially increased student participation in many classrooms.

There is also a call for "multiple answers to a question" and "multiple solutions to a problem," which has effectively changed the teachers' role in the classroom. Teachers now try to explore alternative solutions and answers or alternative ways of presenting the same answer. This approach is used even in conventionally rather rigid areas such as primary school arithmetic.

Research has shown that these changes are widespread in different parts of the nation and are visible even at the grassroots level.[18] Thus, the deep-rooted, rather didactic teaching approach is changing in ways that can be expected to have lasting implications. These changes deserve research attention because attempts to reform education throughout the world have repeatedly demonstrated that changes in classroom teaching are among the most difficult to accomplish. Evidence to date suggests several aspects of the reforms that might have contributed to their success at the grassroots level.

First, the Chinese have been effective at launching mass movements. Although mass movements that are political in nature have basically disappeared, the methods of mass mobilization remain a strength in the system. The curriculum developers have fully exploited this tradition. The calls for "more time for students" and "multiple answers" are slogans or "sound bites" that are easily comprehensible by grassroots teachers. Yet such slogans have vividly crystallized contemporary thinking about teaching for the sake of effective learning.

Second, despite the reduction in central planning, China remains a highly organized society. Changes in classroom teaching are supported by other, related changes. The recommended teaching approaches are immediately reflected in inspections and teacher development programs.[19] As soon as a recommendation is given, there are widespread examples of model teaching demonstrated by reputable teachers available in videos, in published lesson plans, and often through the national TV system devoted to teacher development and transmitted by satellite. Thus, the central organization has full command of the education reform and is able to implement the approach in many parts of the nation.

Third, teachers' professional development is highly organized. Although China is still struggling with the formal qualifications of teachers and there is still a shortage of qualified teachers in underdeveloped regions, there is a fairly sophisticated and active system of continuous professional development, which is effective at reaching individual schools.[20] Typically, teachers in the same locality gather in weekly meetings, which are commonly used for disseminating professional information, for example, through demonstration lessons by experienced teachers or seminars on new curricula and innovations. These activities are facilitated by regular documents and materials circulated by the central or provincial authorities and in many cases supported by audiovisual materials. Many of these can be obtained through the teacher development satellite TV network. The central government subsidizes the installation of the network in remote areas.

Fourth, there is a general culture among Chinese teachers to believe in "the best method." They are positive, therefore, about learning from or imitating "good practices" and regard this modeling as a contribution to the reform. This willingness to apply existing models is rather different from approaches in many other countries, where reform is synonymous with innovation and innovations are expected to distinguish themselves by being different from the practices of others. In China, by contrast, whenever there is an innovation that is perceived as effective, dissemination is almost immediate, and teachers in general are open to changes.

Fifth, the composition of the leadership in education reform contributes to its apparent success. With few exceptions, decision makers in education reform are almost all experienced teachers. Contrary to the common belief that China is a bureaucratic state that is overwhelmed by political cadres, education professionals seem to have assumed leadership in the reforms. This is particularly true in the areas of curriculum design, teaching methods, and teacher development, which are often seen as apolitical, in contrast to more political issues such as funding and administration.

In short, the Chinese education reforms have adopted an approach that builds on traditional culture (such as the authority of examinations), inherited conventions (such as the organized nature of the teaching force), and, as the saying goes, "holding new wine with the old bottle." This is perhaps a result of Chinese pragmatism and a reflection of broader national reforms in the economy and the society.

LOOKING BEYOND

The previous discussion concentrates on basic education. Beyond basic education, the themes of the quality education initiative, such as improvements in learning methods, have yet to receive significant attention. There is little in vocational education, for example, that contributes to more effective learning. Indeed, there is generally a crisis in vocational education because of the changing economy and the reduced demand for occupation-oriented training. In higher education, where teaching and learning have always been an issue, attention is still very much on scale and structure. Curriculum design has received attention only recently and will require more time in order to bear fruit.[21]

Moreover, the reform in educational quality in basic education has demonstrated marked regional differences, perhaps even more severe than the differences in quantitative expansion. Thus, disparity in access to effective learning experiences is even more worrisome than disparity in facilities and general access to resources. In a way, the rapid changes in students' learning approaches in the more developed areas have better prepared them for contributing to a knowledge society. In the less developed regions, where education remains relatively conventional, students are less prepared for changes in the society and therefore are caught in a vicious circle.

In general, however, China has gone a long way in a relatively short period in terms of educational development and reform. Much of what has happened could not have been foreseen even ten years ago, and we can expect changes that are even more dramatic in the future.

NOTES

1. These data come from a presentation on August 22, 2003, by the Ministry of Education to a group of visiting scholars from Hong Kong.

2. Although comprehensive reform of China's education was officially launched in 1985, the first policy steps toward reform started in 1980. Many of the innovations, however, emerged as early as 1978, when the nation began its rural economic reform.

3. By the end of the Cultural Revolution there were over 30,000 "July 21 Universities," following Mao's statement on July 21, 1968, when he called for the replacement of universities by work-related learning institutions admitting only workers and peasants.

4. In 1980 the central government issued a document that endorsed farmers' initiatives in funding local schools. Full-scale national reform was launched in 1985. Details are available in *Reform of China's Educational Structure* (1985). Earlier discussions about the reform can be found in Cheng (1986).

5. Many observers in the West have also described this characteristic of Chinese culture. See, for example, Hofstede (1997), Hsu (1985), and Solomon (1971).

6. Incomes were not quite "salaries" as seen in other countries but, instead, something like "per diems" for purchases not supplied by the state.

7. Unlike the case in most developing countries, textbooks in China were guaranteed by the state: They were produced by the state and distributed to students at a minimal price. There was also a national exercise each year in order to guarantee timely printing and transportation. This process changed, however, when textbooks were commercialized as part of the reform.

8. The 5 + 4 + 3 system resulted from the view that student learning deserves less time at the primary level and more time at the junior secondary level. This model requires additional resources because junior secondary education is more expensive. It is affordable, therefore, only in the more affluent coastal urban centers.

9. In the 3 + 1 system students receive an additional year of employment-related training, and relevant certification, after completing senior secondary education in a general school. Thus, opportunities are created apart from admission into higher education.

10. There have been almost annual circulars from the central government against the local abuse of student book purchases as a means of profiteering. Textbooks were one of the convenient sources of abuse.

11. One of the eight sets of textbooks, for example, was the "coastal edition" developed in the province of Guangdong for "outward-looking" economies. Another example is a textbook for "affluent rural regions," developed by the province of Zhejiang.

12. The German system influenced Chinese education in the first decade of the twentieth century. Later, John Dewey had a profound influence on Chinese educators. In 1919, as part of the May 4th movement (a "progressive"

movement in the areas of education and culture), intellectuals called for "democracy and science" as essential elements of modern social development and as a way to strengthen China.

13. However, it should be noted that some analysts have reinterpreted what is conventionally known as "rote learning," in a negative sense, as an alternative mode of learning (Biggs, 1996).

14. This was No. 8 School in Zabei District, Shanghai.

15. This method was used almost simultaneously, yet independently, in Shanghai and Shantong in the early 1990s.

16. Students may still choose other papers on specific disciplines such as mathematics or history, but those are exceptions.

17. This was an examination item in the integrated paper in 2001.

18. The Shanghai Academy of Educational Research, for example, has made videos of over 2,000 classroom lessons in more than fifteen provinces, including villages in less developed regions. These videos show significant changes in the mode of teaching and learning in classrooms.

19. China began using education inspectors in 1986. The system is largely modeled after Her Majesty's Inspectorate, which existed in Great Britain, and is designed to ensure that schools operate according to national requirements. The inspectors, who review schools at different levels of education, are generally respected and seasoned educators who have retired from teaching.

20. A study describing this type of network at the local level can be found in Cheng (1996).

21. In 2001 the central government issued a major document that called for reforms in the quality of teaching and learning in higher education. The reforms include the use of English in teaching and the adoption of technologies.

REFERENCES CITED

Biggs, J. B. (1996). Western misperceptions of the Confucian-heritage learning culture. In D. A. Watkins & J. B. Biggs (Eds.), *The Chinese learner: Cultural, psychological and contextual influences* (pp. 45–68). Hong Kong: Comparative Education Research Centre; and Melbourne: Australian Council for Educational Research.

Cheng, K. M. (1986). China's recent education reform: The beginning of an overhaul. *Comparative Education, 22* (3), 255–69.

———. (1996). *Improving basic education in rural China: The case study of Zhejiang Province.* Paris: International Institute for Educational Planning.

————. (1997). The meaning of decentralisation: Looking at the case of China. In W. K. Cummings & N. F. McGinn (Eds.), *International handbook of education and development: Preparing schools, students and nations for the twenty-first century* (pp. 393–403). Oxford: Pergamon.

Gardner, H. (1984). The development of competence in culturally defined domains: A preliminary framework. In R. A. Shweder & R. A. LeVine (Eds.), *Culture theory: Essays on mind, self, and emotion* (pp. 257–75). Cambridge: Cambridge University Press.

Hofstede, G. (1997). I, we, and they. In *Cultures and organizations: Software of the mind* (pp. 49–78). London: McGraw-Hill.

Hsu, F. L. K. (1985). The self in cross-cultural perspectives. In A. J. Marsella, G. Devos, & F. L. K. Hsu (Eds.), *Culture and self: Asian and western perspectives* (pp. 24–55). New York: Tavistock.

Huang, X. (1992) *Zhongguo kaoshi fazhan shilue* [A brief history of the development of examinations in China]. Fuzhou: Fujian People's Press.

Ministry of Education, Development and Planning Department. (2003, February 27). *Education statistics bulletin, 2002.* Beijing: Ministry of Education, Development and Planning Department.

Reform of China's educational structure: Decisions of the CPC Central Committee. (1985). Beijing: Foreign Language Press.

Solomon, R. H. (1971). Confucianism and the Chinese life cycle. In *Mao's revolution and the Chinese political culture* (pp. 28–38). Berkeley: University of California Press.

World Bank. (2003a). *Country assistance strategy of the World Bank group for the People's Republic of China.* Washington, DC: World Bank.

————. (2003b). *World development report 2003.* Washington, DC: World Bank.

2

Russia: Struggling with the Aftermath

Mary Canning and Stephen T. Kerr

If you cry, "Forward," you must make plain in what direction to go.

—Anton Chekov (1860–1904)

Russia began its transition to a market economy in the 1990s with an apparently strong education system; it boasted a proud tradition in psychology and pedagogy, almost universal school enrollment, and high adult literacy rates. However, the excessively centralized Soviet education structure had operated without incentives to be efficient and with inadequate accountability. Moreover, the education system was increasingly perceived as constraining individual development and growth. Early post-Soviet efforts at reform included a rapid decentralization of responsibilities for general education to Russia's eighty-nine regions, but there was no commensurate transfer of resources, and the roles and responsibilities at each level of government were often unclear. Although decentralization created new opportunities for the system to become more responsive to individual learning needs, it also placed new burdens on administrators and assigned them roles for which they were untrained. During all of the 1990s and into the third millennium, these problems deepened greatly because of Russia's severe fiscal plight, which entailed a steadily falling gross domestic product to finance the system. Years of inadequate and unpredictable public financing for education, badly conceived decentralization policies, and poor management of education resources all combined to limit access to education and affect quality.

By 2002 these shortfalls had begun to have an adverse effect on student educational outcomes (Organization for Economic Development [OECD] Program for International Student Assessment [PISA], 2001) and had led to growing social pressures and inequalities. Today there is an acknowledged risk that many children are trapped in a cycle where access to good-quality education services and, especially, to tertiary education will be denied to all but those able to pay. This chapter considers the educational inheritance from Soviet times, examines the reform policies developed under perestroika and during the 1990s, and then reviews the outcomes of those policies, the resultant tensions, and current initiatives. It closes with some speculation on how Russia, with a fresh emphasis on the importance of investment in human capital, will address the pressing issues of ensuring access to a good quality of education for all within an emergent knowledge society.

THE HERITAGE OF SEVENTY YEARS OF SOVIET CENTRALISM

The system of education created in the Soviet Union was impressive: It was massive, crudely effective, and perfectly suited to the needs of a rapidly industrializing autocratic state. Over the forty-year period from 1914 to 1954, the USSR succeeded in transforming the human potential of the country, moving the literacy rate from 33 percent to 99 percent.

These successes, however, came at a cost to individuals, to those who worked in the system itself, and, ultimately, to the country's further potential for economic development. Essential features of Soviet education included its high degree of centralization, its deeply rooted ideological content, and the conflict existing between academic development and labor preparation.

Centralization meant that all important decisions regarding the curriculum, teaching methods, assessment, and school management came from the center, in the three ministries (the Ministry of Education, the Ministry of Higher and Specialized Secondary Education, and the State Committee on Labor Education) responsible for their various sectors. Basic decisions, made in Moscow, passed verbatim through edicts and decrees down to the level of the local school. Teachers and school directors were expected to conform: to teach what was mandated by the centrally developed texts, to teach in ways specified by pedagogical colleges and teachers' guides, and to shape students' understandings to what the state required. Although some very minor variation did exist for some schools (for example, in parts of the country with non-Russian-speaking populations), and although there were a number of "special schools" for gifted children, the limits on school practice were well understood and rarely violated. The system demonstrated a high level of bureaucratic inertia, protectionist infighting among various parts of the system, and a general absence of innovation (Dunstan, 1987; Eklof & Dneprov, 1992).

All school subjects were infused with Marxist-Leninist ideology. Ideology permeated all levels of schooling, and, while it was a major litmus test for instructors in any aspect of history, economics, or literature, it also was surprisingly powerful in such fields as biology, psychology, cybernetics, and linguistics. The expectations for conformity to established views were widely understood and acted as a very effective filter, encouraging those willing to comply to enter more strongly ideological fields and steering those with imagination into the few domains where dogma was less pervasive: mathematics, physics, and the performing arts (Sutherland, 1999; Webber & Webber, 1994).

Finally, education under the Soviet Union was strongly conflicted between academic and vocational purposes. Although students potentially encountered a curriculum designed by highly qualified academic specialists and were encouraged to grapple with complex topics (particularly in mathematics and physics) rarely addressed in American or most Western European high schools, the requirements of an industrial system predicated on the continuing availability of a large manual labor force often subverted the high intentions of the academics. As a result, the teaching of an imaginative curriculum often resulted, in practice, in requiring rote memorization and the solving of problems under fixed conditions. The powerful pedagogical and psychological traditions of early Soviet scholars were "dumbed down" so that they could be used in pursuit of proletarian educational ends, the preparation of (as one noted psychologist later put it) "un-questioning cogs for the military-industrial complex" (Davydov, 1993). The daily reality of this conflict in Soviet-era schools included authoritarian (and often frankly abusive) teaching methods, overbur-dening students with an excessive number of required subjects, and heavily restricted access to desirable opportunities for higher educa-tion. Combined with the bureaucratic inertia noted earlier, these ten-dencies contributed to an increasing disconnect among the real needs of an increasingly technological economy, what students were taught in schools, and a narrow vocational focus with little generality, for ex-ample, engineering (Davydov, 1993).

An education reform promulgated in 1984, just as Soviet leader Mikhail Gorbachev came to power, attempted to address these issues. Schools and teachers were to be encouraged to try new approaches (including the use of computers); the term of general secondary and vocational education was to be expanded from ten to eleven years; and new connections were to be made between schools and facto-ries, offices, and farms. Had Gorbachev been content to rule as his predecessors had, the education system might have responded as it typically had to prior reform proposals: Some documents would have been created at each level of the system, proclaiming that the aims of the reform had been accomplished, and things would have returned to normal. But, as it happened, Gorbachev had other ideas in mind, and his efforts to budge the static Soviet economy through perestroika (restructuring), *novomyshlenie* (new thinking), and *uskorenie* (mov-ing faster) soon percolated into the education system as well.

PERESTROIKA AND EARLY
POST-SOVIET POLICY REFORM EFFORTS

Perestroika and glasnost (openness) were, in the Soviet context, not merely neutral strategies for doing things in new ways. They were deeply contrary to fundamental ways of working and worldviews that had evolved over seventy years of Soviet power in Russia. This was no less true in education than in other parts of society. Several developments in the mid- and late 1980s had serious implications for the way that the education system developed and the way it entered the post-Soviet era.

One of the first places these contrary tensions found expression was on the pages of the official education newspaper, *Uchitel'skaya gazeta* (*Teachers' Gazette*). The editorial staff pushed for a new emphasis on the importance of education, not only for society but also for individuals. Grassroots groups of teachers gathered with the paper's encouragement to try to reform the teaching process in Soviet classrooms. A nascent movement among education innovators, dubbed the "Pedagogy of Collaboration," championed a move away from rigidity toward democracy; fostered cooperation among teachers, parents, and students; and pushed for alternative paths for children to use their creative talents (Frumin, 1988; Petrovskii, 1989; Tubel'skii, 1989).

Parallel to the semiofficial activities of the journalists were a number of initiatives cautiously supported by the state and the still-powerful Communist Party. Under the aegis of Eduard Dneprov, a historian of education with political inclinations, the USSR Academy of Pedagogical Sciences established VNIK-Shkola (the Temporary Scientific Research Group on the School). This unprecedented collection of educators, intellectuals, academicians, and social activists worked to develop a new and broadly conceived concept of general education that would be consistent with an evolving humane and democratic socialism. Two critical documents resulted: a *White Paper on General Secondary Education* and a draft *Decree on the General Secondary School,* both published in August 1988. These provided guidelines for reorienting education policies toward more humane, more psychologically grounded, and more democratic schools and teaching processes. Dneprov was convinced that radical reform would not succeed using a system that had failed to support the individuality of Soviet young people. While retaining the encyclopedic study plan, VNIK attempted to introduce problem-based learning, and more engaging activities, as the organizing basis for new study plans and syllabi. For the first time since the ill-fated "pedological" movement of the 1930s, schools were to offer differentiated opportunities to match pupils' individual abilities, provide equal opportunities and access across ethnic and social barriers that were generally ignored during most of the Soviet era, and allow for varied content and electives in the curriculum (Dneprov, 1993).

In spite of these suggested revisions, real change was slow in coming. Conservatives within the Communist Party forced the resignation of the editor of *Uchitel'sksaya gazeta* at the end of 1988, and the power structure of the various education ministries and the Academy of Pedagogical Sciences promoted only slow reforms over the next two years. The ideas of VNIK, however, survived. And, although only a few of the original propositions of VNIK were implemented during this period, the ideas were nurtured and developed further by Dneprov and his colleagues.

The year 1990 brought Boris Yeltsin to prominence as leader of the Russian Federation within the now-crumbling USSR, and that summer he appointed Dneprov to the position of minister of education for the federation. Dneprov immediately set to work to realize the vision of VNIK: democratization, decentralization, and demonopolization. He rescinded thousands of orders issued over the years by former education officials, and schools received the right to reorganize and restructure themselves with the approval of local education administrations. They could now choose "profiles" of study, propose new curricula for some subjects, plan additional group and individual lessons, and gather additional financial resources in support of the school's "material base." In a Soviet educational "first," the Central Committee of the Communist Party was restricted in its control, and final decisions were delegated to regional and municipal authorities who were to be allowed to determine a portion of the overall school curriculum.

With Dneprov in the minister's chair, VNIK underwent a transformation into a Center for Pedagogical Innovation, and the real focus of educational change moved into the schools themselves. After the final collapse of the Soviet Union at the end of 1991, Dneprov continued as minister of education for the Russian Federation, and the early 1990s saw further decentralization. According to the new Russian Law on Education passed in 1992, the system was to be organized on three levels: (1) the federation as a whole, (2) regions and territories, and

(3) local jurisdictions (cities and towns). The Russian Ministry of Education controlled such core subjects as language, literature, science, and mathematics but delegated civics, history, social sciences, humanities, and non-Russian languages to the regional and local levels. The traditional academic load was reduced to lessen the pressures on the average student. There was a pronounced shift away from the former ideal of a single uniform pattern of general education for all Russian children and toward a variety of school types and specialized profiles: gymnasiums, lyceums, and a variety of specialized colleges all appeared, many in cooperation with the tertiary education system. Experimental and innovative schools were encouraged, and plans were made to modernize and upgrade vocational and technical schools to meet world standards. Private schools emerged, and some became eligible for state financing; meanwhile, teachers worried increasingly about the effects of these new "stratifying" educational practices on society as a whole (Dneprov, Lazarev, & Sobkin, 1991).

New prominence in the pedagogical training of teachers was given to the ideas of pioneering Soviet psychologist L. S. Vygotsky, whose studies on learning in social contexts (published during the 1930s) began to percolate rapidly into both Russian and foreign educational practice. Although Vygotsky's approach is distinctly Marxist in some ways, it allows for a more nuanced and individual image of human growth and development than Soviet education bureaucrats could countenance, and it had long been discredited under the former regime. But teacher training still generally failed to instill a sense of independent professional identity among teachers or to enable them to more easily assume leadership positions in local or regional education offices (Kerr, 1995; Moll, 1990; Vygotskii, [1926]1996).

During the mid- and late 1990s the hopeful but amorphous educational trends of the early post-Soviet era gradually coalesced into firmer patterns, some still positive, but others negative. The dynamic change promised by Dneprov's team in the Ministry of Education failed to materialize, and Dneprov himself departed in late 1992. The education bureaucracy at all levels remained more a hindrance than a support for reform efforts. Under Dneprov's successors, the delegation of responsibility for providing social services to regions and municipalities, often without the fiscal resources to fulfill the task (unfunded mandates) and with poorly defined roles and responsibilities, proved to be especially difficult for education. At the regional and municipal levels, administrators experienced new burdens, requiring them to fulfill roles for which they were often untrained.

Throughout the 1990s Russia's economy experienced a series of economic shocks: rapid inflation, poorly managed currency revaluations, pyramid schemes and other blows to the confidence of citizens, growing dependence on imported goods, and regular difficulties in moving finances from one part of the system to another. These shocks culminated in the "crisis" of August 1998, when the ruble lost 80 percent of its value overnight. These events, taken together, gave rise to a series of problems for Russia's education system from which it is still struggling to recover.

Regional budgets for education during the 1990s were often allocated to municipalities and schools in a nontransparent way, and budget execution was poor; for example, school utility bills often went unpaid and threatened the availability of such basic necessities as heat and electricity. A combination of these factors caused many school buildings to fall into a catastrophic state of repair while scarce resources, intended for school heating or other education expenditures, went, for example, to heat hospitals or maintain roads.

During most of the 1990s it also became increasingly difficult to get new or relevant textbooks delivered in quantity to remote regions or rural areas, even though from the early 1990s an adequate supply of new textbooks was available on the market in most urban areas for those parents who could afford to pay. A secondary problem was that, outside Moscow and major urban areas, few educators had information about the variety of new textbooks that had become available. Finally, and most critically, the teaching profession became particularly demoralized by extreme delays in paying their low salaries; sometimes pay packets were delayed by as much as nine months or a year.

A series of reforms in 1997 and 1998 aimed to arrest and reverse what was by then seen as the dramatic decline of the education system (Ministry of Education, 1998). Proposals were advanced to grant schools more autonomy and greater financial accountability, with the right to receive and retain private funds and with responsibilities for budget management delegated to the school director. At the same time, the government stressed the necessity of ensuring that no qualified student would be unable to gain access to high-quality education because of the family's inability to pay. Proposals were also developed by the Ministries of Economy and of Education to make transparent the financial flows from the "gray" economy to the tertiary education system; not surprisingly, that goal was only partially achieved because of resistance by university management. In the face of rapidly diverging levels of educational quality among regions and localities, the Ministry of Education also began to pursue vigorously the imposition of national education standards, as a way to ensure that the "unified educational space" of the former Soviet Union could, insofar as possible, be preserved.

BASIC ISSUES AND TENSIONS TODAY

As Russian educators move forward into the twenty-first century, they find themselves facing a number of complex and interrelated problems, some remaining from the Soviet past and some emerging from the economic reorientation and chaos of the 1990s. We will start with an overview of the current policy environment in education and its relation to broader development efforts for the nation as a whole and then proceed to examine some of the particulars of the situation as it affects the daily work of students, teachers, and schools.

Since September 1998, with the support and leadership of the federal Ministry of Education, and with the involvement of numerous stakeholders in the teaching profession and throughout the regions, several large-scale national initiatives have been undertaken to redefine the direction of the Russian education system for the new century. Though these initiatives were referenced briefly earlier, we need to return to them now to consider how they might interact with the central mission of the schools.

The government program, published in May 2000, highlights the recovery of social services as a major goal of the new government's reform program and recognizes that the underfunded and deteriorating education system would affect the availability of well-educated human capital and the growth of a flexible and well-trained labor force. The government strategy acknowledges the need to undertake fiscal and managerial reforms to address problems such as the non-payment of teachers, the increasing difficulties experienced by poor families in accessing good-quality educational services, and the obsolete system of vocational education (Center for Strategic Research, 2000). The strategy is explicit about the urgent measures needed to ensure that Russia can keep up with technological change, as well as continue to access and use global knowledge resources. It also recognizes that, ultimately, the impact of these forces on the already troubled school system might pose serious threats to Russia's survival as a major world economic and scientific power.

The government approved a separate strategic statement identifying education as a state priority in 2001 (*O kontseptsii modernizatsii,* 2001). That strategy, coupled with the initiative of the State Council of the Russian Federation, *Educational Policy of Russia at the Current Stage* (2001), identifies three key objectives for reform: accessibility, quality, and merit. Measures to achieve these goals include (1) extra budget allocations, (2) the introduction of transparent financing schemes, and (3) measures to increase teachers' social status and salaries. A midterm review of these programs in February 2003 (Center for Strategic Research, 2003) continues the emphasis on the need to develop a new economy that relies in significant measure on investments in human capital, building on the relative advantages of the Russian Federation, and on the assumption that access to education upgrades the quality of the country's human capital.

The result of these several initiatives has been a change in the overall level of discussion about policy for Russian education: In place of an idiosyncratic, multiply defined, poorly linked set of policy directions, a set of more thoughtfully considered policy proposals, intended to bring the several parts of the education system together and to point them in a coordinated direction, has characterized the discussion in recent years. But there are other, equally difficult issues that are connected to the further development and reform of the education system. We will review these factors briefly later.

The Shifting Balance between the Regions and the Center

Developing education policy, setting standards, and ensuring educational quality are prime responsibilities of the federal Ministry of Education, but the ministry now must operate through stakeholders at the level of the regional and municipal governments and of the community. The involvement of those sometimes informed, sometimes untrained local agencies means that progress in education reform now varies greatly among regions; the current federal fiscal relationships and arrangements in Russia give the Ministry of Education little policy leverage to assist or encourage the regions where education reform is lagging or national priorities are ignored.

The first major constraint is the amount of financing available from public funds for the education system. Real public expenditure per school-age child in 2000 was less than two-thirds its level at the end of the 1980s. Public financing for education in 2004 continues to be inadequate to ensure long-term quality, and the lack of predictable, transparent financing at all levels of government contributes to the poor management of education resources. Schoolteachers and directors continue to receive meager salaries, and the teaching profession is now failing to attract new entrants. (The average wage in the education sector in 2001 was only 55 percent of the national average wage.) One practical effect is that many teachers are well past normal retirement age and continue to work because it is the only livelihood they have. The result, however, is that many of these older teachers lack contemporary information or perspectives on the development of the economy, current job prospects, or even contemporary culture to pass on to their young charges.

Second, compulsory education, like other functions of the regions, continues to be supported (in the case of "receiving" regions) by federal transfers from central government to the regions. In most cases, these transfers are not earmarked but instead take the form of general block grants, which regional authorities can allocate as they see fit, and there is evidence that education is not always given high priority. Indeed, even in the extraordinary circumstances in which transfers earmarked for education occur, it appears that these have not fully reached their target. This has happened during crises over wage arrears, with transfers earmarked for education-sector wages reallocated to other sectors. Most preschool education has been handed over to municipal authorities, which increases their financial burden. Fiscal difficulties have also resulted in plans to reduce federal government financing of professional education, most especially at the first level of vocational education.

Third, scarce resources are also frequently used inefficiently. Although most teachers prefer lower student–teacher ratios, and smaller classes may facilitate the educational process, these advantages come at a high cost. Student–teacher ratios are likely to fall further in the years ahead as the smaller cohorts resulting from lower birthrates pass through Russia's school system. Federal regulations, however, unnecessarily limit regional freedom to raise student–teacher ratios in compulsory education. Federal laws specify that no class should exceed twenty-five students in number and that the maximum teaching load, as written into the basic contract of a secondary school teacher, should not exceed eighteen class periods. Although classes and teaching loads sometimes exceed the legal maximum, a more serious problem arises in rural schools with very few students; lack of access to good roads and regular bus service in rural regions makes the consolidation of schools in these areas especially problematic. The proportion of nonteaching staff also tends to be high in Russian schools, which is at least partly the result of diseconomies of scale of running many small institutions, so that the fixed costs of administration are spread over too few students.

Fourth, in trying to maintain the level of educational inputs and ensure the quality of student outcomes, administrators and teachers encounter the same lack of clarity of the roles and responsibilities at different levels of government. Since 1992 much work has been done to define minimum standards, curriculum, assessment procedures, and testing systems, as well as to reform institutional accreditation processes and provide systems to review materials and textbooks so that these meet more closely the needs of the market and modern life. But standards are still most commonly defined in terms of inputs to the learning process rather than as student outcomes.

Finally, Russia's transition to a market economy has led to increasing divergence of incomes across regions. A few of Russia's regions have been able to capitalize on their resource endowments, location, and other factors to increase per capita income relative to the rest of the country and have consequently been able to spend more on education. Russia's poorest regions, however, continue to struggle to maintain even the basic requirements needed to promote student achievement in schools. Hence, at a time when Russia as a whole should be attempting to equip its citizens with the skills needed for full participation in a knowledge economy, the problems of the Russian federal system of fiscal collection and distribution, combined with the results of overhasty decentralization in the 1990s, have resulted in growing inequities and uneven quality across the education system.

Current Reform and Innovation Efforts: Building Capacity for Change

Within the context of the government and state council programs noted earlier, active discussions are also taking place on Russia's need to move rapidly toward development of a contemporary "information economy." This movement is highly visible in two ambitious federal programs, which aim to increase both domestic consumption and export of information technologies and services (Ministry of Economic Development, 2002). Their common strategy includes accelerating the introduction and integration of information and communication technologies into education. For the first time in recent education directives, higher education is not the exclusive focus of attention: Russia has recognized the need to embed information and communication technologies into its educational practices in both general and vocational education, and the government views the improvement of quality and quantity in distance education at the general education level as a means to overcome current access and equity issues.

In addition to these major federal programs, many serious initiatives are in progress in reform-minded regions, including Samara, Novgorod Velikii, the Chuvash Republic, Irkutsk, and Khabarovsk, to mention only a few. Through the efforts of committed and gifted educators and administrators, the strengths of the "old" system are being retained and reinforced through a combination of determination and innovation, and modern fiscal-management techniques, such as the introduction of per capita financing mechanisms, are being introduced. In some regions, pilot programs of rural school rationalization are under way, which include the creation of school clusters with appropriate transportation services in order to benefit from economies of scale in education. These clusters are designed to improve quality on the premise that larger schools can attract more highly qualified teachers and can also afford better equipment, more pedagogical materials, and a greater choice of subjects, all of which are expected to benefit learning achievement. Although these initiatives to improve rural schools have already been piloted in some regions of European Russia, this strategy may not be suitable for all regions, especially in the north and far east, because of climatic or geographical factors. In remote areas, distance education and other applications of new teaching technologies may be an alternative approach to reduce costs and to improve the learning environment.

Two major education newspapers—*Pervoe sentiabria* (*September First*) and *Uchitel'sksaya gazeta*—have played significant roles in fostering a climate supportive of educational innovation. *Pervoe sentiabria,* in particular, has offered penetrating analyses of school reform and education policy in a way previously unseen in Russia. Among the subjects it has repeatedly tackled are school financing, social control of schools (through boards and representative bodies), curriculum reform, standards, development of school administrators, and federal versus regional policy debates.

One factor on the educational scene that represents something genuinely new in Russian experience is the emergence of a number of nongovernmental organizations with a special focus on education, education policy, curriculum development, and continuing professional education for teachers and administrators. One of the first to emerge, the Eureka Center (2003), gained prominence together with *Pervoe sentiabria*. Eureka runs several networks of innovative schools and organizes annual competitions for the designation of schools as "Federal Experimental Sites," a title accompanied by some federal funds and other benefits. Other consultative bodies of this sort have been formed by *Uchitel'sksaya gazeta,* as well as by publishing houses, regional educational in-service training centers, and research institutes.

General curriculum reform, attempted in most schools, in many subjects, and on all levels, has produced varying results. In contrast to the late years of the Soviet era, during which all subjects were radically reimagined, the more recent efforts have been more modest but, therefore, also more likely to be achieved. Special attention has been focused on teaching social studies and history, the fields that were most ideological under the old regime. A number of new curricula on civics education and "citizen studies" (*grazhdanovedenie*) have been offered, and some regions have used these very effectively. But the problems of introducing new curricula do not lie only in the domain of printing textbooks and disseminating materials; they also necessarily involve the retraining of teachers, an especially difficult task because the older teachers recruited into the field of social studies education in Soviet times were arguably the most politically docile and most devoted to Communist ideology. Because low salaries have not attracted many young teachers into the field in recent years, and because low pensions force many teachers to continue to work well past the traditional retirement age, there has been a kind of "demographic imperative" that makes progress in social studies reform especially problematic.

In contrast to the situation in social studies, some curricula, developed under the Soviet regime but never receiving wide encouragement, have now started to be used much more broadly. A good example is the Davydov–El'konin method for early mathematics instruction, an approach that is based on the novel idea that learning mathematical principles at all levels will come more easily if the student is introduced, from the start, to the notion of mathematics as a way of thinking about the world in terms of quantities and comparisons, rather than immediately through numbers. Under this model the young student is not introduced to numbers per se until the middle of the second grade; initial experiences are all cast in terms of comparisons of "more–less," "longer–shorter," "deeper–shallower," and so on. The materials and texts for this curriculum were initially developed in the 1970s and 1980s by Vasily Davydov and Danil El'konin and recently have become increasingly popular with Russian educators. The curriculum has also attracted attention in the West, and a study to pilot its use in American schools is currently under way (Best Practices in Education, 2003).

Increasingly Visible Effects of Social Stress: Access, Quality, Child Health, and Stratification

The historical strength of Russian education was its declared commitment to equity and access, regardless of ethnic background, gender, or geographical location, although, even in Soviet times, there have always been "elite" and highly selective schools. As has been discussed, however, by the mid-1990s Russia's poorest regions were struggling to maintain even the most basic educational services. There is now a danger that although educational and fiscal decentralization has had some benefits, the net effect of years of fiscal crisis may be to increase interregional inequality among schools. In addition, the application of rigid funding formulas (if implemented) could have inequitable consequences for the distribution of funds within a region, as some *raions* (districts) might attract comparatively scarce resources, whereas isolated communities could be further penalized. Difficult choices face regional administrators, who may have to choose between heating schools during cold winter months and paying teachers' salaries on time, and *raion* administrators, who might have to choose between keeping hospitals open and paying teachers. Under these conditions, it seems inevitable that the necessity for frugal budget management in less well-off regions will undermine support for rural schools, special schools, minority pupils, and those coming from "at-risk" families, unless a practical "weighting factor" for special needs can be developed.

Although the schools generally continue to function in Russia, the strains on quality show quite clearly in some places. One of these is rural schools, where the student population has been declining. One estimate suggests that as much as one-third of the $1.5 billion currently being spent to maintain the complete network of rural schools could be saved through some relatively simple restructuring and consolidation. Of all the country's general secondary schools, over 70 percent are in rural areas; they employ 41 percent of the teachers, but they enroll only 29 percent of the students. The quality of education in rural schools in general is considered to be poor because of antiquated facilities and a lack of supplies, a lack felt especially in such fields as the sciences, where access to contemporary laboratory facilities and equipment is critical. The worry is that most schools in remote and rural regions of Russia will deteriorate further and will be unable to benefit from any new improvements in the quality of educational services. As with students and the situation of schools more generally, teachers working in rural areas suffer under special circumstances and face reduced opportunities for professional development. Rural teachers also have typically had less rigorous pedagogical training, have more often come from rural backgrounds themselves, and have included an even larger percentage of females than are present in the Russian teacher corps generally.

Other phenomena appear to be converging; this observation is based in some cases on anecdotal evidence and in others on some emerging (although unofficial) education statistics that indicate that the education system is beginning to be affected by a number of issues, including increased dropout rates because of social upheaval or migration and growing rates of substance abuse and crime among adolescents. Another cause of concern is the growing incidence of chronic illness among children: Anecdotal evidence indicates that the percentage of children unable to make regular and reasonable progress in school because of incapacitating physical, mental, or other conditions might range as high as 30–50 percent of the primary school-age cohort in some parts of the Russian Federation. Children's health, and how to improve it in the context of the schools, is a growing priority for education leaders at various levels. At the local level, teachers increasingly see health as a major curricular and practical issue for their work and express the need for better materials to deal with it ("Shola i zdorov'e," 2003).

Enrollment in private schools is still a small proportion of the total, but selective primary schools and gymnasiums/lyceés for high-ability pupils (in which poorer families are underrepresented) grew to encompass more than 10 percent of total secondary enrollment by 2001. Enrollment rates in such schools for fifteen- to twenty-two-year-olds are much higher in urban than in rural areas.

There is evidence of increasing elitism in secondary schools throughout Russia. Of course, elitism is not new in Russia, but it is especially fostered by the present fiscal climate and can lead to a situation where special linkages between particular universities and feeder schools are cultivated beginning in grade ten (or even earlier). This system leads to several problems. Early specialization and the streaming of students in the secondary system may be inefficient because "late bloomers" are often sidelined and not given the kind of education that will equip them to function in the market economy. It also has serious equity implications, for the ability to pay often influences admission to extra courses (and, in some cases, access to the school itself) and may thus narrow educational choice for students from poor families. This system is also open to potential abuse. Some faculty members at elite institutions of higher education have come to rely on income from specially tailored tutoring that assures access to a particular institution, and these practices, though officially disowned, have not been conclusively quashed by the powers that be.

Changes in Teacher and Administrator Preparation and Professional Development

Russian teachers have borne more than their share of the economic and social chaos that swept over the country in the immediate post-Soviet era. They suffered from stagnant wages that were commonly paid on an increasingly irregular basis; many lived far from urban areas and lacked training or perspectives that might have allowed them to take other places in the newly emerging market economy. In addition, the low general status of teaching as a career generated demographic pressures on education even before the collapse of the USSR: More teachers were coming from rural backgrounds, more were women (this in a country where traditionally a higher percentage of teachers had been female, as in many countries), and fewer were entering the profession than were needed to maintain the teacher corps. In mid-2002 teacher wages ranged from $15 to $68 per month, and, not surprisingly, there continued to be sporadic teachers' strikes in numerous regions.

In addition to these problems, teacher training went without fundamental revision for some time. Most studied in teacher-training institutions (*pedogogichesie instituty* or "pedagogical institutes" under the Soviet system, now increasingly renamed as *pedagogicheskie universitety* or "pedagogical universities"), where they received both the equivalent of an undergraduate degree and a teaching license. Although some of these institutions provided superb preparation for future teachers (in such cities as Moscow, St. Petersburg, and Krasnoyarsk, for example), many were still seen as providing less than excellent tertiary education and as unable to foster creative approaches to instruction.

The models of pedagogy that these institutions instilled in future teachers, in spite of the efforts of the Russian pioneers of current "constructivist" thinking, remained quite classical and focused on teachers' abilities to develop in students the necessary intellectual "knowledge, skills, and habits" (in Russian, *znaniia, umeniia, navyki* or *ZUNy*). Although Russia's teachers most often defended these traditional instructional patterns and felt that they had provided the basis on which their country's impressive successes in science had been based, international comparisons provided accumulating evidence that Russia's high school graduates were, in fact, performing less well than those in many other parts of the world, especially in those arenas most valued in the contemporary world economy: creative thinking, active problem solving in real-world settings, and the ability to work collaboratively (see specific data on PISA test results later).

Addressing these shortcomings of the education system would clearly involve more than simply working with existing teachers. The programs for preparing teachers would themselves need to be reformed, and careful attempts would need to be made with education administrators throughout the system, regional education planners and managers, representatives of business and industry, and, perhaps most important, parents so that all of them might come to see the potential value for young people of instructional practices that would prepare them to live and thrive in the contemporary world.

The Need for New Instructional Materials: Texts, Software, and Online Education

By the mid-1990s Russia's schools faced a pervasive lack of access to new teaching materials, equipment, visual aids, and information about new teaching methodologies. However, this situation has now somewhat improved overall, and shortages of modern school text-books and learning aids in certain key subject areas, such as civics, history, economics, and languages, have been addressed. However, in order to improve overall educational quality, teachers will require training in how to use the new kinds of materials in real classrooms and in how to modulate their practice with updated pedagogical methods. Many schools lack teachers' manuals and other pedagogical information. The shortage remains and is particularly acute for rural schools and for vocational education, which need new materials to reflect market needs.

Teacher-training programs need to develop more competency-based and individualized approaches to learning in a student-centered classroom environment, in contrast to the currently excessive rote learning. Core education programs need to be modernized to encourage problem solving, innovative thinking, and creativity in the classroom. New teacher training, examinations, and qualifications arrangements will reflect these developments.

Computer-based, online, and distance-learning materials offer special advantages in the Russian context but also present special challenges. The international experience demonstrates that technologically based materials, though not a panacea, do allow more students to have more engaging, and potentially more productive, learning experiences with more challenging subject matter over a shorter time than is possible using traditional materials and methods (Bransford, Brown, & Cocking, 1999). But such materials are not widely available in Russia now and so would need to be developed or at least aligned to the requirements of the local situation. Although Russia boasts a large and impressive population of highly skilled software programmers and engineers, these have not commonly turned their attention toward the design or creation of educational software, and so the problems noted earlier with teacher training and retraining also apply to software programmers. They must not merely reproduce the types of instructional experiences with which they have been familiar from their own past; they must come to grips with what it means to create new materials using a specifically "constructivist" pedagogy.

A variety of computer-based and online materials could be productively applied in the Russian context, especially in those curriculum areas (science and mathematics, for example) where federal standards are in effect. Online materials would be important for those students living in remote rural areas, where courses in these core subjects are often not adequately supported with resources or prepared teachers. Online courses could be especially valuable for advanced or gifted students, who are at a disadvantage when locally available materials and instructional support do not match their own potential levels of achievement. Though Russian educators are quite sensitive to the risks inherent in stratifying the education system according to student achievement, they do not share the U.S. hesitation to provide extra support or special curricula for gifted students, seeing these as an essential resource for their country's future development.

Linking General Education to Other Parts of the Education System

Education and training are increasingly perceived as "a fundamental key to wealth creation and competitiveness in the current global information economy" (Dryden, 1998). Russia, with its strong academic and intellectual traditions, has the potential to develop a skill-based high-technology role in the world economy through further development of its human capital. However, the *Global Competitiveness Report* (World Economic Forum, 2003) has underlined the magnitude of the task ahead: On the criterion of microeconomic competitiveness, Russia ranked fifty-eighth out of eighty countries in 2002. In the ranking by growth competitiveness (one element of which is "economic creativity," based on economically effective innovation or technology transfer), Russia ranks even lower, at sixty-fourth place, and it will take more than the education system to fix that.

Although Russian students continue to perform relatively well in the Third International Mathematics and Science Study (TIMSS) tests of academic achievement in mathematics and science, the 2000 results of the OECD PISA are a further indication that the education system is not producing students with skills that are relevant to real-life situations. Although TIMSS does not tell us a great deal about the quality of educational outcomes, PISA methodology takes a broader approach and tests fifteen-year-old students' ability to use their knowledge rather than just present it, to interpret a text, and to recognize scientific and mathematical problems. Among thirty-one countries that participated in PISA 2000 (twenty-seven OECD countries plus Brazil, Latvia, Liechtenstein, and the Russian Federation), Russia's fifteen-year-old students ranked only twenty-seventh in reading literacy, twenty-sixth in scientific literacy, and twenty-second in mathematical literacy (OECD PISA, 2001). We do not suggest placing undue emphasis on country rankings; however, the general pointers about curricular relevance, school autonomy, teacher morale and commitment, and classroom climate are important in the Russian context.

Approximately 61 percent of the age cohort graduate from secondary school, 41 percent go to some form of tertiary education, and 19.7 percent attend a university. About 50 percent of the students enrolled in higher education now pay for it (as opposed to 15 percent in 1995). Payments range from tuition fees as high as $10,000 a year to informal payments for library use or access to computer laboratories (OECD, 1999).

In the absence of a reliable, nationally standardized assessment system for school-leavers, higher education institutions have been obliged to organize their own entrance examinations, which consume scarce financial resources and raise questions about objectivity and fairness. However, the single unified state examination, administered in five regions in 2001, in sixteen regions in 2002, and in forty-seven regions in 2003, is yielding good first results, including emerging evidence that students from rural schools who take the examination have more opportunities to attend higher education institutions. The exam is subject based and conducted before graduation from secondary school. The intent is that it will replace final examinations in secondary schools and entrance examinations to universities and secondary vocational institutions for all social groups, and create a system for objective evaluation of school-leavers' knowledge. It should be noted that standardized testing, as a method of assessing student knowledge, is quite new in Russia and is met with skepticism, opposed by rectors of higher education institutions who have managed to survive the economic crisis of the 1990s and for many years controlled latent financial streams in education, including those connected to admissions.

In 2004 vocational education in Russia remains largely unreformed, a situation that is especially worrisome as it consumes a large amount of scarce resources (current student–teacher ratios average around 8:1 in the vocational education system) and has a rigid subject-bound curriculum and a teaching force that is relatively inflexible, highly specialized, and not easily retrained. With some exceptions in regions that are particularly reform minded, the system of vocational education provides little evidence that it is ready to initiate the sort of competency-based, modular approach adopted by most OECD countries. Moreover, vocational school graduates are poorly equipped with the foundation learning, attitudinal, or metacognitive skills necessary for employment in knowledge-based jobs or for access to lifelong learning opportunities. With the anticipated increase in knowledge-related employment opportunities in parallel with other developed economies, over the coming years even fewer jobs for poorly qualified blue-collar workers and those leaving schools without some formal qualification may be expected. Some regions have taken the initiative to integrate and restructure vocational institutions, and new federal guidelines reduce the number of vocational specializations. However, much remains to be done. A June 2003 decision plans to transfer property rights and financial responsibility for vocational education from the federal level to all regions of Russia. This decision is expected to become effective on January 1, 2005. Although this reform could result in improved provision of demand-driven vocational skills relevant to regional labor markets, there is a danger that the initiative will become an unfunded mandate and that poorer regions will not have the resources to cope.

System Support: Statistical Data, Educational Research and Development

Russia lacks an accurate, easily accessible database from which policy makers or education managers can assemble information about student numbers and placements, unit costs, and achievement levels. To date, there is little general understanding that the development of statistical data about education could have value for policy makers.

Educators have been faulted generally for their lack of attention to data in making key policy decisions, but the situation in Russia was exacerbated by seventy years of Soviet-era practices, which made gathering, using, and presenting data suspect, if not downright dangerous, for education practitioners. Although for many years Western education policy makers have recognized the value of accurate data as a lever to be used in fine-tuning the system, Russian educators had available only relatively crude aggregate statistics that did not cover such essential features of the system as differential student achievement, cohort survival rates at key transition points (into initial vocational education or higher education), investments in school construction, and also such essential features as teachers' professional development.

Perhaps even more critical than the lack of data was the lack of a mind-set oriented toward the use of data as an essential element in solving educational problems, managing the system, or planning. In an environment where all resources came from the state and did not need to be closely accounted for after they had been disbursed, and in which all planning and policy making were done centrally (with regional and local offices reduced to simply transmitting identical directives), these perspectives and practices made some sense. Under current conditions, they are counterproductive for achieving what the system so desperately needs, not only to survive but also to prosper. Accordingly, one of the more pressing problems for the education system is to create a mind-set among education managers that features gathering, analyzing, and using data as desirable features (Fishman, 1997).

A further characteristic of the system that has been lacking in recent years is an effective structure for studying the effectiveness of the system itself. Soviet bureaucrats did conduct some studies of educational and instructional issues—but only under the auspices of the Academy of Pedagogical Sciences, a centralized and highly static structure that was famous for work that dragged on endlessly and rarely produced a "final report" on any project. Moreover, commonly accepted Western models for data gathering and statistical analysis were largely absent until very recently. This was partly the result of mistrust and suspicion of methods (surveys, questionnaires, interviews) that had the potential to "embarrass" those in positions of power and authority. But it also partly resulted from the lack of familiarity with Western approaches and the work that had been done to advance the study of pedagogical issues during the roughly fifty years that Russian educators were cut off from the West.

Some efforts have been made to address these problems. There are more regional and local centers for educational development, some of which are developing significant capacity to conduct their own studies on education issues. Central institutions, such as the Russian Academy of Education, have become somewhat more responsive to the needs of the regions and have done more studies and established more regional affiliates and connections to universities that can help to extend the R&D structure (examples of this include the Center for Sociological Research and the Institute of Psychology within the Russian Academy of Education). Funding and lack of orientation toward the value of this sort of information, however, will continue to be problems for these efforts, at least in the near future.

TRENDS AND POSSIBLE
FUTURE DEVELOPMENTS

The Center versus the Regions

In the mid-eighteenth century, Catherine the Great, writing about legal reform in Russia, noted that the most intractable issue was getting right the relationship between the center and the regions. There is no doubt that the post-Soviet decentralization of the education system has the potential to increase efficiency and accountability by providing greater autonomy to regions, municipalities, and schools and encouraging greater participation of major stakeholders at the community level. However, the challenges remain to improve and modernize service delivery, primarily through major but attainable increases in efficiency, the reduction of the curriculum overload and improvement of its relevance to a knowledge society, and the introduction of new pedagogical methods and modern technologies. A drop in the number of school-age children caused by demographic changes creates an opportunity to accomplish this modernization and to push for necessary efficiencies without sacrificing access to high-quality services.

Today in Russia these core fiscal and policy issues (who pays for what, who owes what to whom, who is responsible to whom for seeing that certain outcomes are achieved, and how the attainment of such goals will be tracked and measured) remain unresolved and continue to impede effective collaboration between the federal and regional educational authorities. These are a source of ongoing tension and controversy, and addressing them will be critical for the further effective development of the system.

Fiscal issues are one part of this knotty set of problems; education standards are another. The latter, somewhat sidetracked in recent years as the basic financial solvency of the system was regularly called into question, may now come back into focus more as a central problem. Even though the federal government has a strong interest in maintaining what some call the "unified educational space" that existed under the USSR, many regional and local authorities chafe under a set of standards and controls that were initially imposed from the center with little or no public debate. The challenge will be to balance the clear needs of a still-centralized government (in such domains as articulation among levels in the system, higher education admission standards, testing, data gathering, etc.) with the demands of regions and municipalities to provide more diversity in curricular content and methodological approaches, in order to match their own students' needs and their local economic conditions.

One area in which these sorts of tensions have been especially strong is that of experimental and innovative school programs and curricula. Although there was considerable enthusiasm for these in the late Soviet and early post-Soviet period, they fell from favor, as more and more regions appeared to be defining their own curricula and their own approaches to instruction and evaluation. Attempts were made in the mid-1990s to curtail the spread of "illegitimate" variations (curricula or programs that were seen as too divergent from the norm or too unusual to give their students viable economic prospects). In recent years, however, a balance appears to have been struck between the forces interested in fostering innovation, on the one hand, and the center's desires to control and direct such developments.

Getting the center-versus-regions balance right in education represents a huge task for the Russian education system. It is a system that never placed much value on local control, local innovation, or the development of local capacity. To generate ideas and follow up on them at the local level, with sufficient data flowing throughout the system to evaluate the worth of emergent practices, is a large challenge for a system with little experience in these realms. If Russia can handle these questions deeply and thoughtfully, it will have gone a long way toward addressing its education problems.

A Modern ("Twenty-First Century") System versus Traditional Academic Approaches

"Lifelong learning" has become something of a mantra for Western educators in recent years. Though the jargon is thick, the basic idea can be outlined: Workers and citizens today must be given a set of mental habits and worldviews that will allow them to address their own educational needs in a proactive way as they proceed through life and careers. Although some industrialized countries handle this better than others, most seem to have concluded that it is more important for individuals to be able to solve real-world problems, rather than simply calling up predigested facts; they need to be able to identify the elements of a new problem and various ways they might approach it, rather than simply recalling a textbook solution; they need to know where to look for information and how to assess its quality, rather than simply relying on factual information they encountered in school thirty years before.

Russia has a long and distinguished history of preparing world-renowned scientists, mathematicians, and engineers. The concern today is that this illustrious history does not become a barrier to making the educational changes that the country needs in order to move forward. Academic preparation in traditional subjects, using classical curricula, is still revered by some Russian educators who hope that they can reconstruct the Soviet system that seemed to work with these established tools so successfully. Changing these assumptions about how the system should operate will be a major challenge for Russia in the coming years; doing so will be essential for the country's economic future.

One approach would be to build on the more innovative practices used under the Soviet system—practices that were limited to the most promising students, who were siphoned off early into "special schools" (*spetsshkoly*) where they were exposed not so much to a special curriculum as to one that was taught in a different way, emphasizing qualities of analysis and creative problem solving. The curriculum (largely in science and mathematics) was introduced and explained differently; it was supplemented by more diverse and interesting material; and the expectations teachers had for students were much higher. Many educators would like to recapture the original underlying intent of that educational approach—to provide serious and challenging curriculum and instruction not just for an elite but for a wider audience that includes all students.

Active Professional Orientation for Teachers and Administrators

Improved incentives for teachers, as well as training and retraining programs that are flexible and market-relevant, may be the most essential element in the reform of Russian education, for, without well-motivated and well-trained educators, the quality of the system will decline over time and new graduates will be unable to satisfy the requirements of the changing labor market. Increases in standard class sizes will have implications for how classes are taught and will necessitate the introduction of in-service training in new methodologies of teaching and learning. Additional teachers of foreign languages and teachers who can teach more than one discipline are particularly needed.

Perhaps the most intractable problem with teacher preparation for Russia is the lack of a deep understanding by teachers of what pedagogical professionalism might look like. Even though other nations have spent considerable effort in recent years to provide continuing education to teachers, in Russia teachers have continued to think of their work largely as a prescientific craft, as opposed to a rationally controlled process of gradual discovery and development. There is an almost feudal quality to some Russian discussions about what it means to be a professional teacher: a powerful and deep respect for the teacher's work but little understanding of how that work might change over time or the need to retain one's skills at a high level. Overcoming this bias will take considerable effort as Russia seeks to address the various issues noted earlier.

CONCLUSION: CHALLENGING THE STATUS QUO

The Russian education system is moving, sometimes fitfully and sometimes with surprising speed, to address the issues noted earlier. There are many committed educators who see new patterns and new ways of working, but they work within a system in which the larger set of expectations—from employers, parents, government figures, and indeed students themselves—often supports the status quo rather than needed change. Whether the system can, in fact, work itself out of this bind remains to be seen, but the patterns of the past five years suggest both a much more realistic view of the options and a much more determined stance toward the various agencies and attitudes that need to be modified if change is to occur. The chances for Russia truly to capitalize on its impressive educational heritage have never been better.

REFERENCES CITED

Best Practices in Education. (2003). *Measure up: The El'konin–Davydov approach in elementary mathematics.* Available at www.bpeducation.org/projects/MeasureUp/index.html (accessed March 31, 2004).

Bransford, J. D., Brown, A. L., & Cocking, R. R. (Eds.). (1999). *How people learn: Brain, mind, experience, and school.* Washington, DC: National Research Council, National Academy Press.

Center for Strategic Research. (2000, May). *Strategiia razvitiia Rossiskoi Federatsii do 2010 goda* [Development strategy of the Russian Federation until 2010]. Moscow: Center for Strategic Research. Available at http://oivtran.iitp.ru/~site/mat/d0008211.htm (accessed May 22, 2003).

———. (2003, February 5). *Proekt programmy sotsial'no-ekonomicheskogo razvitiia Rossiiskoi Federatsii na srednesrochnuiu perspektivu (2003–2005 gody)* [Draft socioeconomic development program of the Russian Federation over the near term (2003–2005)]. Moscow: Center for Strategic Research. Available at www.csr.ru/materials-economy/05-02-03.html (accessed May 22, 2003).

Davydov, V. V. (1993). Russian psychology and educational reform. Paper presented at the Annual Meeting of the American Educational Research Association, Atlanta, April.

Dneprov, E. D. (1993). Al'ternativa [The alternative]. In B. Eklof & E. Dneprov, *Democracy and the Russian school* (pp. 142–47). Littleton, CO: Westview.

Dneprov, E. D., Lazarev, V. S., & Sobkin, V. S. (1991). *Obrazovanie v Rossiskoi Federatsii v perekhodnyj period: Programma stabilizatsii I razvitiia* [Education in the Russian Federation in the transition period: A program of stabilization and development]. Moscow: Ministry of Education of the Russian Federation.

Dryden, J. (1998, October 7–9). *A borderless world: Realising the potential of global electronic commerce.* Ottawa: OECD Ministerial Conference. Available at www1.oecd.org/publications/observer/215/a-dryden.htm (accessed May 22, 2003).

Dunstan, J. (1987). *Soviet education under scrutiny.* Glasgow: Jordanhill College Publications.

Eklof, B., & Dneprov, E. (1992). *Democracy and the Russian school.* Littleton, CO: Westview.

Eureka Center. (2003). *Innovatsionnaia obrazovatel'naia set' Evrika* [Eureka innovative educational network]. Available at www.eurekanet.ru (accessed May 22, 2003).

Fishman, L. (1997). *Model' obrazovatel'nogo menedzhmenta v Rossii: Tsennoist i stereotipi* [The model of Russian educational management: Values and stereotypes]. Kazan-Samara: PO RAO, SamGPU, SIPKRO.

Frumin, I. D. (1988). *Pedagogika sotrudnichestva: Metodicheskie rekomendatsii* [The pedagogy of collaboration: Methodological recommendations]. Krasnoyarsk: Krasnoyarsk University.

Kerr, S. T. (1995, November). The development of Russian teachers as a professional group and the fate of Russian school reform. Paper presented at the Annual Meeting of the American Association for the Advancement of Slavic Studies, Washington, DC.

Ministry of Economic Development. (2002, January 30). *Federal'naia tselevaia programma "Elektronnaia Rossiia na 2002–2010 gody"* [Federal targeted program "Electronic Russia for 2002–2010"]. Moscow: Ministry of Economic Development. Available at www.e-russia.ru/program (accessed May 22, 2003).

Ministry of Education. (1998). *Osnovnye polozheniia kontseptsii ocherednogo etapa reformirovaniia sistemy obrazovaniia Rossiskoi Federatsii* [Basic propositions of the concept of the next stage of reform of the educational system of the Russian Federation]. Moscow: Ministry of Education of the Russian Federation.

Moll, L. C. (Ed.). (1990). *Vygotsky and education: Instructional implications and applications of sociohistorical psychology*. New York: Cambridge University Press.

O kontseptsii modernizatsii Rossiiskogo obrazovaniia na period do 2010 goda [On the concept of modernization of Russian education for the period up to 2010]. (2001, December 29). Government of the Russian Federation Decree No. 1756-r. Available at http://teacher.fio.ru/news.php?n=14393&c-78 (accessed March 31, 2004).

Organization for Economic Cooperation and Development. (1999). *Tertiary education and research in the Russian Federation*. Paris: Organization for Economic Cooperation and Development.

Organization for Economic Cooperation and Development Program for International Student Assessment. (2001, December). *Knowledge and skills for life: First result from PISA 2000*. Paris: OECD Program for International Student Assessment. Available at www.pisa.oecd.org/knowledge/home /intro.htm (accessed May 22, 2003).

Petrovskii, A. V. (Ed.). (1989). *Novoe pedagogicheskoe myshlenie v* [New pedagogical thinking]. Moscow: Pedagogika.

Shola i zdorov'e. Rossiia na grani katastofa! [The school and health. Russia on the edge of catastrophe!]. (2003, March 18). *Uchitel'skaya gazeta* [Teachers' Gazette], *11–12*, 13–26.

State Council of the Russian Federation. (2001, June 25). *Obrazovatel'naia politika Rossii na sovrtemennom etape* [Educational policy of Russia at the current stage]. Available at www.philippov.ru/news/27/138 (accessed May 22, 2003).

Sutherland, J. (1999). *Schooling in the new Russia: Innovation and change, 1984–95*. New York: St. Martin's.

Tubel'skii, A. N. (1989). *Shkola samoopredeleniia: Pervii shag* [The school of self-determination: The first step]. Moscow: Academy of Pedagogical Sciences.

Vygotskii, L. S. ([1926]1996). *Pedagogicheskaia psikhologiia* [Pedagogical psychology]. Moscow: Pedagogika-Press.

Webber, S., & Webber, T. (1994). Issues in teacher education. In A. Jones (Ed.), *Education and society in the new Russia* (pp. 231–59). Armonk, NY: M. E. Sharpe.

World Economic Forum. (2003). *Global competitiveness report 2002–2003*. Available at www.weforum.org/site/homepublic.nsf/Content/Global+Competitiveness+Programme%5CGlobal+Competitiveness+Report%5C Global+Competitiveness+Report+2002-2003 (accessed May 22, 2003).

3

South Africa:
Overcoming Past Injustice

Luis Crouch

The Struggle is my life.

—Nelson Mandela (letter from the underground, 1961)

The education reforms instituted in South Africa since the end of apartheid are some of the most profound attempted anywhere in the world in the last few decades. To give the reader an idea of the comparative scale of the attempted transformation, and to defend this statement, here is a quick description of what the system is attempting:

1. Merging and reshuffling some eighteen or nineteen apartheid, racially based administrative ministries or departments into nine geographically based, decentralized ministries or departments in nine new provinces (with a national policy-setting ministry and department), where each province is inheriting four, five, or even as many as six of the previous racial ministries or departments and where personnel, payroll, school resources, exams, procurement, accounting, information, policies, and procedures have had to be merged and unified;[1]

2. Shifting the resource and funding system from one that was pro-rich and based on race, in that whites traditionally had per-learner expenditures ten times greater than Africans, to one that is pro-poor in distribution and based on income rather than race;[2]

3. Attempting to do all this while preventing spontaneous privatization and flight of the (increasingly nonracial) middle class to
   private schools, that is, attempting to maintain public schools as
   a center of community life;[3]
4. Attempting large-scale reforms in curriculum and teaching methods (in a country that has eleven national languages), both to remove apartheid content and ideology and for the sake of pedagogical modernization; and
5. Attempting to do this across all key subsectors, including making subsectors that were previously only for the privileged accessible to all (schools that encompass grades one–twelve; Early
   Childhood Development; Further Education and Training,
   which comprises at this point mostly technical colleges not requiring a secondary leaving certificate; Adult Education and
   Training; inclusive education or education for learners with special needs; and a tertiary sector consisting of both universities
   and *technikons*—essentially degree-granting polytechnic institutes).

In short, the system is attempting a set of reforms that is much larger
in scope than what was attempted in, say, the desegregation of school
systems in the United States, in that it is starting from a much greater
level of inequality, where the poor and disadvantaged are the majority rather than the minority, where there is a simultaneous modernization and quality agenda at the same time as an equity and justice
agenda, and while attempting to prevent, for the country as a whole,
the sort of white-flight privatization of education common in American cities. South Africans themselves are frequently unconscious of
the scope of the tasks they have set out for themselves.

The African National Congress (ANC), the decades-old national lib-
eration movement, came to power in 1994 under the first universal-
suffrage democratic elections. In that sense, the reforms have been
under way some ten years. But one could argue that these reforms
had been under way for some years before, as key racial restrictions
on various segments of schooling were relaxed at least four–five years
before the ANC came to power (Department of National Education,
1992; National Education Policy Investigation, 1992). Similarly, the re-

forms were under way on paper, as the ANC (1994) had considerable time to deliberate and prepare policy papers based on progressive islands of experimentation within the country—private schools or public schools where nongovernmental organizations (NGOs) developed interesting experiments—and an enormous amount of consultation, negotiation, and deliberation with the then-government and the social groupings it represented. The accession of the ANC to power was hardly an undeliberated surprise. On the other hand, the reforms have been under way, in a serious fashion, for only ten years. The South African reforms have been extremely deliberative and have been based on legislation and regulation to a degree perhaps unusual around the world. This means that they were not rushed and took some time to design (Department of Education, 1995b). Thus, for ex ample, even though the new government came into power in April 1994, the basic schooling law, the South African Schools Act, was not signed by the president and gazetted until late 1996.[4] The permanent constitution of the new republic was not certified until late 1996. Thus, the school resource reforms, deliberated between 1996 and 1998, did not start being implemented until 2000 (Department of Education, 1998). (Improved resources for provinces, as opposed to schools within provinces, on a postapartheid model, started much earlier.) It may be possible to question the need to base policy so firmly in legislation and to deliberate and consult on the legislation for so prolonged a period, but, given that the history of struggle has created a society with a proclivity to contestation, it seems likely that such deliberativeness during the policy-making process sets a foundation less likely to be continually questioned later.

Given the depth and ambition of the reforms, and given that in reality they have been under way for some time, one would have expected more international attention to these reforms than they have received. The reasons for this relative lack of attention are not clear. Two hypotheses are suggested: First, the reforms, to a large degree, are home crafted. They have paid considerable attention to international literature and best practices, but they have not been designed with much formal, large-scale, well-structured donor assistance or fanfare. They have been led and structured largely by South Africans themselves. Second, and partly in explanation of the first reason,

South Africa was quite isolated by apartheid itself. It has not been until relatively recently that "normal" intellectual exchange between South Africa and the rest of the world has come back to a reasonable level. It could also be argued that both white and black South Africans have traditionally had, for quite different reasons, a tendency to try to deploy their own inventiveness and ingenuity to solve problems: the whites out of a distant colony's sense of isolation; the blacks out of a sense of self-sufficiency during the antiapartheid struggle, which led to a pride in originality. In any case, the reforms have not received much international attention until very recently, and what little attention has been received has often been naively critical (in my view) of government effort, in that it tends to underestimate the nature of the task facing government in 1994 (see, e.g., Weber, 2002).

This chapter attempts to bring some of these reforms to the attention of an international audience and to add some balance to the commentary. Because it is also true that the reforms have not been fully under way for very long, and because the focus is on system reforms rather than controlled experiments, it is too early and difficult to judge in what sense the reforms are a success or not. Thus, this essay attempts to describe the reforms more than it tries to test hypotheses, closely argue any particular point of view, or make technical policy prescriptions. It does attempt to make some judgment, where possible, as to success or failure, though this judgment is usually limited to whether the policies are being implemented and must hold back on how much progress there has been on learner achievement. It is important to emphasize, for the sake of full disclosure, that I was and still am involved in many of the described reforms. Whether the degree of resulting personal knowledge and historical memory is worth the possible bias and lack of academic distance this might produce is, of course, hard for even me to decide.

NATURE OF THE REFORMS

One of the few hypotheses to submit, but not really test here, is a simple characterization of the reforms. The ANC and the various progressive forces expected some of the needed reforms. These fall largely and simply into two areas: (1) equity and redistribution in resources and (2) curricular and pedagogical reform. Resource distribution during apartheid was extremely unequal. At the height of apartheid, spending on the best-resourced public schools for white children was some ten times higher than spending on the worst-resourced public schools for African children. This does not describe one or two individual school extremes but, rather, whole categories of schools. The whole homeland of the Transkei, for example, spent approximately one-tenth as much per child as the best-off white provincial subsystem (South African Institute of Race Relations, 1988). The best-resourced province had one noneducator (administrative, support, clerical staff) for every five or so educators in its white school system; in some of the poorer homelands, there was one noneducator for every fifty or so educators (Department of National Education, 1988). In terms of pedagogy, the system was largely oriented toward teaching and reproducing apartheid; it attempted to functionalize whites into privilege and Africans into servitude, not only in terms of skills imparted (or lack thereof in the case of Africans), but also in attempting to teach a historical and ethical justification for the system. Furthermore, the delivery of the curriculum was largely traditional and teacher centered, including the use of corporal punishment.

Nelson Mandela described it this way:

In 1953 the Nationalist-dominated Parliament passed the Bantu Education Act, which sought to put apartheid's stamp on African education. The act transferred control of African education from the Department of Education to the much-loathed Native Affairs Department. Under the act, African primary and secondary schools operated by church and mission bodies were given the choice of turning over their schools to the government or receiving gradually diminished subsidies; either the government took over education for Africans or there would be no education for Africans. African teachers were not permitted to criticize the government or any school authority. It was intellectual *baasskap* [bossing], a way of institutionalizing inferiority. (1994, p. 167)

The need for reforms (funding equity and curricular change) was quite evident, and it was toward these areas that much of the transition policy debates oriented themselves (Department of Education, 1995a, 1997a).

However, there were also some "surprises" or needed reforms that were not quite as anticipated. These fall into three types. First, most of the progressive opposition made the implicit assumption that the apartheid state was, if repressive, at least reasonably modern and efficient in approach. In any case, equity and injustice were glaring. Inefficiency was often hidden, except in a few obvious areas such as the duplication of administrative apparatuses needed by the existence of eighteen separate administrative departments. Thus, there was little early discussion and awareness of the need for efficiency improvements and little realization of the degree to which the apartheid state was itself a relatively inefficient bureaucracy: It was debt ridden and rule based, with tendencies either to ignore problems in the case of African schools or to solve problems by throwing money at them in the case of the whites. An assumption that the state is efficient justifies a focus on increasing spending and on redistribution by bringing up the bottom and a relative tendency to ignore the need for fiscal control and efficiency-enhancing measures. Thus it also tends to justify an assumption that educational quality and enhanced learning for the poor majority are largely a matter of redistributing resources. Second, much of the practical progressive opposition to apartheid during the 1970s and 1980s took communitarian forms, which led to an interest in schools as self-managed units, as loci of community power and decision making. This was a result of localized experiences of resistance, NGO collaboration with schools, and struggle-based heroic energies that tend to be unsustainable in "normal" functioning. The task of building a postapartheid *system,* which could implement such a vision as a matter of "normal" functioning and under bureaucratic control of a new state, perhaps was underestimated. Third, the progressive forces did not anticipate the problem of HIV/AIDS. The drain of resources this represents has only recently started to be faced. It is, of course, only an analytically useful exaggeration to say that these problem areas were unanticipated; they were simply less anticipated.

These two anticipated and three unanticipated areas of reform largely set out the reform agendas. The two anticipated ones naturally occupied most of the early attention. The three unanticipated ones came to receive more attention later. They are all equally difficult to address.

The rest of this chapter attempts to describe the nature of the reforms and problems and to discuss some measures of success as well as areas that need further work. Because of my own comparative advantage, the focus is on issues of financial equity and efficiency and the HIV/AIDS problem.

Equity Reforms

It is no secret, of course, that distribution of income and of social opportunity in South Africa is very unequal—among the most unequal in the world, along with, say, Brazil, certain Central American countries, and a few others. An assessment is made of how inequality of educational opportunity has changed over the past few years.[5] That there have been significant, maybe dramatic, improvements in equity since 1994 cannot be denied. There has been improved equity in interprovincial allocations but also, and perhaps more important, in intraprovincial allocations.

In 1991–92 there were only four traditional provinces, as well as ten "self-governing territories" or *Bantustans*. Unpublished data exist for these territories from legacy administrative information systems (SANEX) on the proportion of learners from various ex-departments that went into the new provinces at the moment of transition. The data used allow the construction of a good approximation (but an approximation only) of what per-learner public expenditure would have been in 1991–92, had the new provinces existed. The notable finding is that the reduction in inequality since the early 1990s has been a remarkable 67 percent. In 1991–92 provincial deviation from the mean was 31 percent of the mean; by 2001–2 this had been reduced to only 10 percent. The same measure of provincial inequality, if applied to either average provincial family expenditure or the average income per family in school catchment areas, is at least twice as high today, showing twice as much inequality in income distribution as in the distribution of schooling inputs. There was some reduction in inequality to 1995–96, but there has been a strong reduction since then. Thus, the story on interprovincial inequality is one of considerable achievement.

Unfortunately, it is impossible to perform a similar analysis for intraprovincial allocations, that is, allocations to schools. Accounting systems for tracking expenditure down to the school level are only now being developed. However, one can approximate the analysis by focusing on two key inputs: the distribution of the learner–educator ratio and the distribution of the learner–classroom ratio. These two factors account for some 90 percent of the total budget (recurrent and capital). This analysis, however, has to rely on two episodic censuses, not on yearly administrative records: the 1996 and 2000 School Register of Needs (SRN1996, SRN2000). These censuses measured the allocation of key inputs school by school. The years 1996 and 2000 encompass the period when most equalization was taking place both between and within provinces.

Equality in teacher allocation improved quite dramatically. The improvements in interprovincial inequality were the most notable, even though interprovincial inequality was already smaller than intraprovincial inequality. However, improvements in intraprovincial equality of teacher allocation, which are in the range of 20 percent or so (e.g., 10 percent in one case, 27 percent in the other case) in just four years, are quite notable, especially because equalization has continued after 2000 and allocations were becoming pro-poor in 2003. Inequality in classroom allocation was higher than that in teacher allocation in 1996, and the situation appears not to have improved, except, significantly, in the case of interprovincial inequality. (The numbers for classrooms have to be interpreted with some caution, as most of the differences are not statistically significant.) Thus, although teachers represent the enormous majority of the total cost of education and are arguably a more important input in the production of learning than classrooms, the point remains that the story of equalization—thus far—is not a total success on every indicator—just on the most important ones. The reasons for this will become clearer later.

Because resources were being withdrawn from affluent schools in order to create this increased equalization, one might have expected a massive flight of the higher-income groups away from public schools toward private schools. In a sense, the better off, who are increasingly of multiracial origin, were not being allowed to use their tax base to strengthen their children's schools, as the *public* allocations for these schools were being reduced. One might have then expected a flight toward the private sector, where the more affluent families could use their resources to send their children to private school. This has taken place to some degree, but the changes have hardly been massive, and higher-income privatization has been kept to much lower levels than in, say, Latin America or the inner cities of the United States. The reason is that public schools are allowed to supplement public income with private income, which schools' governing bodies can vote themselves as a means of supporting their local schools. The better off are thus given a chance to make private contributions within the public sector. There are trade-offs involved, of course, as will be noted later.

It turns out that the distribution of teacher qualifications, as measured by years of training and experience, is actually quite good, much better than one would have expected. In 1997, based on the Education Management Information System's administrative records, it seems that equity in the distribution of teacher qualifications is fairly good. One has to admit that some of this equity might exist, to a large extent, only "on paper," on the assumption that a degree or diploma from one university is as good as that from another. Nonetheless, just in terms of years of training, the degree of equality in teacher provision is quite high.

Thus, the story on the most easily measurable and costliest indicators is quite good. There are, however, inputs whose psychological importance in conveying a sense of justice and entitlement, or whose actual importance in the learning process, are both quite high. These are items such as quality of classroom space and items of equipment more directly related to learning. Unfortunately, the definitions of these variables changed between 1996 and 2000 sufficiently so that one should not make comparisons over time in their distribution. However, even as of the year 2000, the distribution in both the quality of infrastructure and the provision of per-learner equipment was much worse than the distribution of educators in 1996.[6] The distribution of infrastructure is thus obviously a serious concern.

Furthermore, particularly in the case of the quality of infrastructure, there is the issue of poverty in some absolute sense, that is, numbers of schools below a certain standard, the total poverty gap, and the geographical distribution of that gap by political units in the country. The reality is that much of the absolute poverty (as measured by the cost of bringing truly wretched schools up to some absolute standard) is highly concentrated geographically and easily traceable to particular apartheid homeland administrations. Thus, for example, though the old homeland of KwaZulu had some 22 percent of the reporting schools at the primary level, it has some 35 percent of the poverty gap in equipment.[7] Similarly, though the old homeland of Transkei had only some 4.7 percent of the schools reporting data on infrastructure, it had 21.1 percent of the infrastructure poverty gap. Clearly, these issues require work.[8]

Finally, equity in the distribution of the outputs of the education system is not nearly as high as in the distribution of inputs. This is, of course, to be expected. After all, educational results are produced to a large degree by family socioeconomic status and social capital, not just by school inputs.[9] If factors such as parental literacy and income are distributed very unequally, one would expect that educational results would also be. However, even in actual educational results there has been considerable improvement, though this improvement started way before the end of apartheid. Furthermore, given that until 1994 public allocation to schooling emphasized, rather than combated, parental income inequality (because the rich got more public resources than the poor), the distribution of basic results is, surprisingly, not much worse than the distribution of income and, in some measures, perhaps more equal. This finding suggests that the education system is playing a role in ensuring that the distribution of income of the coming generation will be more equal than that of this generation.

The generational story is reflected in trends in grade-level achievement by successive population cohorts. As measured in the 1999 October Household Survey (OHS99), the differences have been large: Every five years the average grade achievement of learners has increased by another 0.6 grade. Better yet, the inequality of achievement is narrowing dramatically.

This is good news indeed. Yet, even as late as the 1990s, only some 60 percent of each cohort was making it to grade twelve, and only some 50 percent of these were passing the all-important "matric" (secondary school–leaving) national exams, which means that only about 30 percent of each cohort was achieving twelve grades and entering life with a "pass" to offer the labor market (Crouch & Mabogoane, 1997a).[10] In addition, only some 10–15 percent were passing with "exemption" or "endorsement," which allows access to higher education.

On the other hand, the inequality of distribution in the pass rates is (1) decreasing and (2) lower than that of the distribution of income. Note that this indicates only the distribution of the pass rates among schools, not the distribution of the actual average marks or grades among students. Nonetheless, it is clear that the situation has improved. (Note that during the same period the average pass rate has improved from about 50 percent to about 60 percent.) As only some 60 percent of the learners even make it to grade twelve (taking all provinces and all racial groups into consideration), the distribution of "matric" exam pass rates might still mean a distribution of passes based on population cohorts that is worse than the distribution of income. This is because all those who never made it to grade twelve are being ignored, when in some sense they should be considered not to have passed the exam. A simulation was done to see what would happen if one added sufficient schools with zero pass rates to make up for the learners who never even make it to grade twelve, and it found that the distribution of pass rates is at worst about as unequal as income and at best maybe a bit better. But the distribution of "exemptions" (a mark high enough to allow entrance to tertiary education), even considering that those who take the exam are already a selection, is worse than that of income. If one includes those who never make it to grade twelve, then the distribution of exemptions would be worse than the distribution of income, by a lot.

Of course, it is not just schooling that determines one's income success later in life; to the degree that education does contribute, passes and exemptions are not the only measure of success in schooling, for in South Africa, as elsewhere, there is some, but only some, sheepskin effect (the tendency for graduation points in the education system to be compensated much more than participation alone, even though participation might involve only a little less human capital than graduation).[11] Nevertheless, these indicators do give cause for cautious optimism, on both total grade achievement and pass rates, though not so much on exemption rates, although they also suggest that more needs to be done to equalize quality and achievement.

All this begs the question of whether redistributing resources will lead to redistribution of achievement. Unfortunately, research on the determinants of educational achievement in South Africa is somewhat inconclusive. My own analysis suggests that, if one takes the high school–leaving exam as a measure of achievement, and one makes comparisons across the entire set of schools, then environmental and parental poverty and socioeconomic status, as well as managerial tradition (as measured by which apartheid department the school formerly was run by), together explain about as much of interschool variation as the variation in traditional resources does (Crouch & Mabogoane, 1997b). In particular, some of the variables that tend to exercise the public imagination about inequality, because they are so visible and so clearly deficient, such as the quality of physical infrastructure, appear relatively uncorrelated with achievement. However, other resources, such as equipment and inputs closely related to the pedagogical process and teacher education, do definitely appear to matter. (In any case, access to decent infrastructure is a matter of dignity and justice even if it is, relatively speaking and in terms of actual learning achievement, only a "nice to have" rather than a critical determinant of output.) Furthermore, to the degree that resources can make up for parental poverty (e.g., by allowing schools to devote more teacher attention to children whose parents are unlikely to be able to help with homework), then resources definitely would matter because poverty itself matters.

On the other hand, in evaluating the results of pilot project schools in poor areas (thus, schools in a narrow spectrum of achievement), and measuring achievement at grade three level, one finds little correlation between achievement and resources—in fact, little correlation between achievement and anything else, as if achievement were a more or less random thing or depended on the sorts of things education systems tend not to measure (Crouch & Vinjevold, 2002). This is somewhat expected, for the range of variation in both outputs and inputs would be smaller in poorer schools than in the whole range of schools. However, it cannot be the main explanation because there is still some variation in both results and inputs even in what, to "unaided observation," appear equally poor schools.

How Are These Improvements Being Achieved?

Education in South Africa is relatively decentralized. The constitution makes education a "concurrent" matter. Implementation is largely a provincial matter governed by provincial legislation. Provincial governments are, for example, the employers of teachers. National education legislation prevails over provincial legislation in certain circumstances: where it is a matter of correcting interprovince issues and where preserving uniformity and homogeneity requires national standards and policies. The national level sets policy, but implementation is up to the provinces. Furthermore, a province's own legislature and cabinet largely determine its education budget. Grants and transfers from the national government largely finance the budget. These transfers do not stipulate how much each province must spend on education: They are multisectoral block transfers driven by a formula (the "Equitable Shares Formula"). This process of revenue sharing has been relatively successful, though not without criticism. Relative to apartheid financing, equity is generated by making the formula largely population driven. Importantly, the formula does not produce absolute amounts of funding; nor is it based on an "adequacy" or "costed norms" approach to meet needs: It simply produces shares of revenue that are then divided among claimants on that revenue in what is hoped to be an equitable manner.[12] The reasons for this are complex and have been the subject of much debate, but the situation is that, at present, national government favors a simple shares approach. Education is an important nominal "driver" of the allocation, in that it carries a weight of 41 percent in the total allocation of shares. Thus, one could take 41 percent as the nominal proportion of its revenue share that a province "should" spend on education. In practice, internal provincial allocations to education come fairly close to this proportion, on average, though they vary.

Each province's share of education "need" drives each province's share of the total allocation. In turn, the average of school-age population and enrollment is the driver for education "need." Population serves as a driver, in addition to enrollment, to minimize incentives for repetition and to encourage efficient flow-through. (This is coordinated with a national education policy norming the amount of allowable grade repetition.) Thus, provincial spending per learner can vary largely, depending on (1) the gap between population and enrollment; (2) how much internal revenue each province has, in addition to what it derives as a share of national revenue (with more than 90 percent of education expenditures generally coming from the national government); and (3) how much of its total revenue it chooses to spend on education versus other social and economic needs. This approach was applied in a phased manner, starting from a historically driven baseline.

Only one of the components in the formula is related to poverty, namely, a "backlogs" component that has a weight of only 3 percent and is used to give more funding to provinces with particularly poor school (and other) infrastructure. Furthermore, the formula contains a component that returns revenue to each province in proportion to the degree of national output the province generates, and this component has a weight of 8 percent. Population drives most of the other elements. Thus, because the formula returns to each poor province a share of revenue much larger than the share of national income generated by it (e.g., though Limpopo generates only some 3 percent of national income, it receives some 14 percent of the shared revenue), this process of allocation is redistributive even though it does not have a strong, explicit poverty component. Furthermore, there have been special allocations outside the formula, for example, for school construction and improvement.

It is largely the application of this approach that has been responsible for the improvement in interprovincial variation in per-learner expenditure. However, this begs the question of what political and economic factors have allowed the application of this formula. A detailed explanation would take us too far afield. Elements of the explanation would be (1) a national government with a strong majority and mandate at the national level to carry out redistribution and (2) a modern approach to crafting fiscal formulas that are clear, simple, transparent, and well studied to avoid perverse incentives. In particular, it could be argued that focusing on shares, rather than absolute amounts, increases transparency and reduces debates, though this focus on shares, ignoring as it does issues of "adequacy," has been the target of some criticism.

As noted, intraprovincial equity has also improved. Clearly, the interprovincial allocations cannot have driven this, although the improvement in allocations to the poor provinces has permitted poorer provinces to improve local distribution by leveling up, rather than leveling to the median or mean. Instead, the national government has issued policies that regulate intraprovincial resource distribution, thus issuing provinces with a mandate that forces them to redistribute internally out of a fixed bottom line, but this does not result in an unfunded mandate affecting total expenditure on schooling.[13] The history of these policies is of interest. For example, early in the transition, national policy mandated learner–educator ratios for schools in the country as a matter of national policy and standards. The application of these ratios led to budgetary problems, however (or perhaps was a convenient excuse), because the budgetary process and the standard-setting process were divorced from each other. Some provinces had to, or had the excuse to, employ more teachers than they could afford. Accusations that the national level was imposing unfunded mandates on the provinces followed. The national government then issued purely distributional mandates, stating that each province should calculate the number of teachers it could afford but then mandating their distribution to schools according to an enrollment-driven formula. At the primary level the formula is very strongly enrollment driven. This has resulted in a speedier process of equalization at the primary level. At the secondary level the formula makes allowances for specialized subjects. To the degree that some schools offer more specialized subjects than others do, it is natural that total learners-per-educator allocations should then be unequal. If curricular policy drove these differences, and there was a fair and rational distribution of curricular options, this would not be a problem. However, the reality is that historical privilege drives, at least partially, the offering of specialized subjects. Thus, there has been some debate about these issues. Furthermore, enrollment has been driving the allocation of teachers, without any weighting toward poverty. Starting in 2003, national policy has declared that poverty weights must be considered in intraprovincial allocations of teaching posts (Department of Education, 2002). This should cause some pro-poor allocation of teacher resources.

The process followed with nonpersonnel allocations has been similar but has its own interesting peculiarities. The National Norms and Standards for School Funding allocate funding for noncapital, nonpersonnel expenditure such as books, stationery, and utilities (Department of Education, 1998). There are two key differences between these norms and the personnel norms. First, the nonpersonnel norms started out simply mandating distribution within the province, not absolute levels of spending, thus avoiding the possibility of provincial accusations that the national level was creating unfunded mandates. Second, the norms were pro-poor from the beginning. In fact, they are stated in terms of incidence of spending, mandating that, for example, 65 percent of the spending has to target the poorest 40 percent of the learners. However, implementation of these norms did not start until 2000. Furthermore, the norms are complex because they also try to implement certain aspects of school-based financial management that are consistent with the South African Schools Act of 1996. Thus, implementation has been relatively slow, and there has been little time for them to make an impact.

CURRENT EQUITY DILEMMAS AND FUTURE DIRECTIONS

At the time of this writing, the minister of education commissioned the Department of Education to review funding and cost issues in the sector. This report found many of the same problems noted earlier and others in addition (Department of Education, 2003a). For example, the report notes the existence of pockets of deep poverty, rather than simply inequality, and notes the fact that these pockets are geographically specific and often traceable to apartheid administration.[14] However, new problems are noted and assessed. One could separate these into two general areas.

First, there is the problem of school fees. Public school governing bodies in South Africa can self-assess fees on a local democratic basis. These remain at school level rather than flowing into national or provincial treasuries and do not count as part of government revenue. One has to remember that public funding is being made pro-poor; that is, the better-off schools' public funding is being gradually reduced and funds are being redistributed to the poor. One function of fees is to allow the better-off schools to make up for this withdrawal and thus induce middle-class parents to remain involved with public schooling rather than fleeing to the private school sector.

Poorer schools are now supposed to be getting more resources than ever and thus should not see a need to vote themselves fees. However, developing the accounting and financial transfer systems to target individual schools takes time; thus, it is not clear that poorer schools are getting resources as quickly as desirable. Furthermore, because of wage pressure on the system, even poor schools might find themselves with insufficient nonpersonnel funding. Finally, it is not clear to what degree fee setting is truly democratically parent driven. As a result of these various pressures, fee setting in poorer schools might not be optimal. The review discusses this issue, which is being studied further.

Second, there are inputs into schooling that either are not paid for by government at all or are paid for by government but are produced by private providers. Items such as school uniforms and textbooks are examples. These have been found to be expensive and do put a burden on families or the state. However, reducing their cost involves complex economic and sociological considerations. School-specific uniforms, for example, are used to create school identity, which some argue might be related to achievement and a sense of client satisfaction, though there is no research in South Africa that would support this assumption. On the other hand, the specificity of the uniforms tends to encourage single-source provision by monopolistic producers and might tend to encourage possible collusion between school administrators and uniform purveyors. Thus, dealing with these matters will require some care and sensitivity. Textbooks are a similar problem. So are transportation and school nutrition. All these require careful study, not just of bureaucratic provision but also of privately supplied markets and how these markets interact with public bureaucracies in a complex manner. For example, too much decentralization in textbook choice might encourage smaller print runs than optimal, as companies try to sell particular books to particular schools; it might also encourage market segmentation and collusion, again, between school administration and suppliers, to the detriment of families. This has not been sufficiently studied, so the emphasis is on "might."

Third, the level of bureaucratic skill in budgeting, budget management, and progressive school resourcing is not as high as desirable. As noted, resources are not necessarily reaching schools as quickly as possible. As of the writing of this article these issues are beginning to receive considerably more attention.

Necessary Efficiency and Quality Reforms

As noted earlier, it was logical, given the history of South Africa, that equity reforms would be tackled first. However, it did not take long to notice that there are serious efficiency and quality problems in education in South Africa, not just equity problems. Of course, the two are not necessarily unrelated. As noted in an earlier example, if one apartheid system had ten times as much administrative and support assistance per teacher as another system, which is an equity problem, it is logical to expect efficiency to differ disproportionately in the new provinces that inherited these apartheid systems, for one province will tend to have many fewer experienced administrators per teacher (and hence per student) than another. Although South Africa has tackled equity issues, the efficiency reforms have been slower to start, and there is still considerable debate about their nature. In particular there has been little research on the degree to which resource provision, poverty, and managerial effectiveness are most important in determining school outcomes.[15]

The system is attempting to come to grips with these issues. The ministerial review on resource allocation has also drawn attention to the issue of efficiency (Department of Education, 2003a). As resources come to be distributed more equally (or even on a pro-poor basis), the fact that performance does not track resources as closely as one might have hoped tends to be noticed. Pressure from central government levels, such as national and provincial treasuries, provincial premiers, and the nation's presidency, for the education system to show "impact" in return for funds spent is likely to increase in coming years. The education system will have to respond creatively, not only in terms of managing expectations (as it may not be reasonable to expect outputs to track inputs in such a short time frame, and the tracking will never be perfect in any case, as poverty and other social variables play an important role) but also in terms of tightening up management to deliver more impact for the money spent.

Various attempts also have been made in the past few years, for example, to improve the curriculum and the "culture of learning" in schools, to improve whole-school evaluation, and to strengthen district assistance to schools in improving school management. Some provinces have increased pressure on nonperforming schools or areas. These attempts have had various degrees of success, but there is no clear, overall conclusion as to how to press the matter of quality. An important issue is that most of these efforts target nonperformance by using the "matric" exam (the national high school–leaving exam) as a tracking device. However, a leaving and filtering exam applied at grade twelve is hardly the most effective diagnostic device. Also, until very recently, there was no systemic assessment applied in earlier grades. A grade three assessment was applied for the first time on a nationwide pilot basis in the year 2000 and on a nationwide nonpilot basis in 2001 (Department of Education, 2003b). However, this is on a nationwide school sample basis, rather than on a universal one, so it is difficult to track the performance of every school using this approach. Nonetheless, the evidence provided by this assessment should be of increasing use in deciding which factors to prioritize. Donor-based projects also have begun to focus on learning in the early grades, and there are starting to be some indications of success in increasing learner performance. For example, schools in the District Development Support Program, funded by the U.S. Agency for International Development, have improved learner performance by a significant degree in a few years.

At the same time, South Africa, which has eleven national languages, is implementing reforms in language policy. Not all languages are used in official affairs; a pragmatic policy generally tends to imply that in practice English and a language of local interest are used, depending on the province, with English currently predominating in most official business at the national level. In general, individuals are seen as having the right to have the government address their needs in the language of their choice, subject to practical limitations. School language policy attempts to satisfy the pedagogical needs of children to learn, if possible, in their own language, against the practical demands of parental wishes, availability of teachers and materials, and the policy of promoting ability in more than one national language. Ability in a second national language is required for

promotion in the higher grades. Thus, children would learn the curriculum in one language but receive exposure to at least another language as early as practicable. In a school where more than a minimum number of parents (thirty-five or forty, depending on the level
of schooling) request a given language of instruction, the government
must make efforts, subject to various practicality and equity concerns,
to supply instruction in that language. Finally, each school must stipulate how it will promote multilingualism, by using more than one
language of instruction and by offering languages as subjects of study
(see Department of Education, 1997b).

The Threat of HIV/AIDS

It was noted earlier that there have been three problems that the
democratic government has had to deal with and which had not received much attention in the lead-up to democracy and in the first few
years of democracy: efficiency issues, the difficulty of establishing
community-based education, and the HIV/AIDS epidemic. This last
section discusses the HIV/AIDS epidemic and the way it complicates
equity and quality reforms.

As in most other countries, the problems posed by HIV/AIDS in the
education sector show up quantitatively and financially, as well as hu-
manly, in two main areas: (1) the morbidity and mortality of teachers
and (2) the problems presented by orphans. Because the epidemic in
South Africa is relatively "new," the specific patterns of the morbidity
and mortality of teachers have not been firmly established—much of
what is assumed about infection rates for teachers, for example, is
based on simple extrapolations from the general population, correcting for age and gender. Thus, some basic numbers are presented to tell
the general story so that the points are easier to follow; the specific
numbers, however, are not known with any great certainty. South
Africa has some 350,000 teachers—an amount more or less stable as of
the mid-1990s. The "normal" rate of attrition (retirement, leaving, and
base death rates prior to the AIDS epidemic) has been variously calculated at approximately 5 percent over the past few years, before any
serious AIDS-related mortality or morbidity had set in (Arnott & Chabane, 1995). An infection rate of 25 percent, with a death-to-infection

ratio of 7 percent, can be assumed, based on extrapolations from the general population and other countries (this is higher than in Hall [2002]), but the infection rate appears to be rising (see also Actuarial Society of South Africa, 2003; Human Sciences Research Council, 2002). This means that approximately an extra 2 percent of the supply of teachers, possibly in addition to normal attrition, will die every year by the middle of the first decade of the 2000s. If one assumes that, in the face of such mortality, policies are put in place to reduce normal or underlying attrition or reemploy previously retired teachers or teachers who had abandoned teaching, one might then assume a total ("normal" attrition plus AIDS) "net" attrition rate or, rather, "net replacement need rate" of 6 percent. The 6 percent figure means a yearly loss of some 21,000 teachers, with about one-fourth of that caused by the epidemic and three-fourths caused by normal attrition. If it is not possible to reduce normal attrition or attract former teachers back into the profession, the attrition rate would be as high as 6.5 or 7 percent, and the yearly need to replace losses with newly trained teachers would be some 23,000 or a bit more (Crouch, 2001). But at current enrollment rates in teacher-training programs, that is, if nothing changes, the yearly output of newly trained (as opposed to the total output, which might include mid-career retraining or in-service training) teachers is likely to be only about 3,600 per year in the next few years (Hall, 2002). Thus, there is a gap between demand and supply of some 17,000–19,000 teachers per year. The irony in all this is that in the 1990s the teacher-training system was overtraining: Some 30,000 newly trained teachers were produced each year. From 30,000 to 3,600 is clearly an enormous drop. The knowledge that overtraining was going on in the early 1990s, in addition to restricted demand in the late 1990s because of macroeconomic adjustment and fiscal austerity, resulted in changes in policy and in the attitudes of potential teacher trainees (secondary school graduates) that tended to reduce enrollment in teacher-training programs. The result is that, in the more recent past, fewer and fewer high school graduates tended to see teaching as a logical career choice.[16] The problem is now being addressed, but it will take some work and some time to achieve a balance. It is important to note that—given how much overtraining took place in the early 1990s—there is a supply of previously trained persons who are not working in teaching and who could potentially be attracted back into the profession. That number has been estimated, perhaps optimistically, as somewhere in the range of 100,000 persons (see Crouch, 2002). Thus, the system might have a little "cushion" in this respect—but not for long.

The other critical factor is the number of orphans and the need for the education system to respond to these children's increased financial, educational, and emotional requirements. It is estimated that by 2010 somewhere between 1 and 1.5 million children will be either double- or single-parent AIDS orphans, with about one-half, or somewhere between 500,000 and 750,000, being from each category (Actuarial Society of South Africa, 2003; Department of Social Development, personal communication, 2001; UNICEF, 1998). As a comparison, in the late 1990s, R. Shell (1999, in Office on the Rights of the Child, 2002) noted that some 100,000 children had lost both parents to AIDS. Thus, the expectation is that the number of AIDS orphans will grow by some seven times in the next ten years. As a proportion of total enrollment, this is an increase from approximately 3 percent of total enrollment to about 15–20 percent.

To put very approximate financial numbers on the problem, note that it costs—in round numbers—some 100,000 rand (approximately US$12,000 at the early 2003 exchange rate) in direct costs to train a teacher. If an extra 6,000 teachers per year need to be trained because of AIDS itself (noting that many more would have to be trained anyway because of normal attrition), the bill comes to somewhere under one billion rand or around 2 percent of current education expenditures. The cost of morbidity must be added to this. If one assumes that 15 percent of teachers are ill, on average, over the coming decade, and that among the ill the absenteeism rate is one in ten days, then the labor cost is some 1.5 percent higher than it otherwise would have been. With regard to orphans, if one assumes that orphans imply direct costs to the system that are, as a plausible policy target (not as an empirical observation), one-third higher than those for nonorphans, then total costs on this account would go up by some 7 percent (one-third of 20 percent). There are other imponderables and inherently fuzzy areas, such as the cost related to the enormous emotional wear and tear on the system, with the loss of both parents and teachers.

Precise cost estimates in the end are probably more foolhardy than useful. In total, considering the need to train more teachers, the costs of morbidity, and the cost of orphan care, the financial implications of AIDS can be summarized, very approximately, by saying that the total cost for the education system will increase by some 10–12 percent over a non-AIDS scenario, an amount that could have been used for improvements in quality at the primary and secondary levels of education and in access to higher education.

CONCLUSIONS

South Africa has taken on an educational transformation of immense proportions compared with what almost any other country has tried in the last few decades. This transformation has been approached deliberatively, consultatively, and with considerable attention to a sound legal base. The transformation is beginning to produce results, first in equity and now, slowly but increasingly, in quality. Along the way, there have been some surprises and some very tough environmental changes that work against the earlier hopes. These are being faced, some better than others. The innovativeness and careful dedication with which extremely thorny problems have been tackled are perhaps a useful lesson for other countries, as is the fact that such profound reforms take years to design, more years to implement, and even more years to bear fruit. South Africa—some eight years after the transformations started—is only now beginning to reap the fruits, and more in some areas than in others, but the fruits are increasingly and measurably there.

NOTES

The comradely and technical quality of my interactions with officials in South Africa's Department of Education and various nongovernmental organizations is gratefully remembered and acknowledged, as is the funding by the U.S. Agency for International Development during the period 1995–2002. The opinions and conclusions expressed here are, of course, my own and are not to be associated with any institutions with which I have worked. The following Department of Education data sets were analyzed in the compilation of this chapter: School Register of Needs 1996, 2000; Annual School Survey 1997; and Examination Data 1997, 1998, 2001.

1. Determining how many systems or ministries of education existed in apartheid South Africa is in itself a bit of an interesting counting game. There were ten "homelands," and each one had its own education system. These were "independent" states, which the worldwide community generally did not recognize, but they had some operational independence in education matters. Then there were four racially based systems that operated in the apartheid republic itself: one for Africans, one for the so-called coloured group, one for "Indians," and one for whites. (The new government still uses this racial terminology because it is sociologically useful in understanding the ongoing dynamics of social change.) If one notes that the white system operated with some decentralized independence in the four old provinces, that makes another four. Overseeing everything was a general policy ministry without much administrative implementation mandate. That would make nineteen "ministries," probably the maximum count that can be produced.

2. The racial terminology that came to be used during apartheid has continued to be used, for example, by Statistics South Africa (see 2001), because of its importance for statistical and analytical purposes. However, whereas during apartheid each person received a nonvoluntary assignment to a racial category, today one is generally asked to self-classify (e.g., in census returns) and one can generally opt not to self-classify at all. The chapter adopts the practice of Statistics South Africa of using *white* for those of European ancestry, *African* for those of African descent, *coloured* for those of mixed ancestry but often associated with "Malay" ancestry, and *Indian* for those whose ancestry is in South Asia. *Black,* in the common parlance of the anti-apartheid movement, generally refers to all but whites.

3. In common with South African practice, this chapter generally uses the term *nonracial* rather than *multiracial*. There is much written on the meaning of this term, and the debate continues, for the term has no official definition, even within the African National Congress. For an international audience, a former U.S. ambassador to South Africa has put it this way: "South Africa's new politics is a novel practice of non-racialism. Having ended legal apartheid, the ANC government is committed to nation building that goes beyond racial to national claims. This vision of nonracialism is uniquely South African and should not be confused with what is often called multi-racialism in the American context. For black South Africans, apartheid was multi-racial. It brought racial distinctiveness to new heights. Even the term multi-cultural was a euphemism for apartheid's notion of separate development" (Joseph, 1998). The political and ideological uses of the term,

and the implications of various definitions for practical policies, are ongoing debates in South Africa; it is by no means a term with a universally accepted definition. What is clear, though, is that the terms of these debates are quite different from those common for dealing with race and ethnic relations in Europe or the United States. See also Kotzé (2000).

4. The *Government Gazette* publishes official government laws, regulations, and so on. The act of publishing a law, regulation, or norm often is called "gazetting."

5. In order to fix ideas, it is good to have some sense of the magnitude of the most important indicators of overall inequality, namely, the distribution of personal or family income or expenditure. The Gini coefficient is the most widely used measure of inequality of distribution of income or any other indicator. The measure of inequality ranges from zero, for total equality where everyone has the same income or wealth, to one, for total inequality where one person controls a nation's entire income or wealth. For example, very unequal countries (such as Brazil or South Africa) have Gini coefficients for their income distributions around 0.55–0.65, whereas, say, Nordic countries typically have Gini coefficients around 0.25. This coefficient is applicable to just about any wealth-like concept such as educational inputs or outputs. For example, the Gini coefficient for the distribution of educational attainment in Korea improved from about 0.55 to 0.30 from the 1960s to the 1990s. This coefficient for income or expenditure distribution in South Africa has been variously measured. But a good, round-number benchmark for the recent past and the present is approximately 0.60. Two other useful indicators of inequality are the zero-order entropy coefficient, also known as the Theil mean logarithmic deviation, and the simple ratio of the average deviation to the mean. The former, in stylized terms, is also 0.60. The latter is about 0.80. These provide a basis of comparison for educational inequality.

6. Calculated from SRN2000.

7. Percentage is based on reporting schools, not necessarily on all schools, as the census was not 100 percent complete for every item.

8. The standards were defined as one-half of the median of simple multifactor indexes of the quality of school infrastructure and the provision of equipment per learner. I developed the indexes.

9. In South Africa this appears to explain some 30 percent of variation in school results.

10. Officially, the school-leaving test is the Senior Certificate Examination, popularly and almost universally known as the "matric" exams, the twelfth (last) year of secondary school also being called the "matric" grade. The "matric" pass rate thus measures the proportion of twelfth graders who are successful in the secondary school-leaving exam.

11. For example, having completed twelve grades as opposed to eleven confers much more extra income than having completed eleven grades as

opposed to ten, which would not make sense if income is accruing truly in proportion to learning and years of education.

12. An "adequacy" or "costed norms" approach would attempt to provide each school with the inputs "adequate" to provide a given standard of education. These concepts generally originate in developed countries, where the poor are a minority. The appropriateness of such an approach to the South African context is debatable. The tendency might arise to define adequacy in a manner that would be fiscally unsustainable, leading to promises that cannot be fulfilled. The current approach simply takes the total budget available, which is fairly high as a proportion of gross domestic product, and divides it up in a pro-poor manner. It is very much a "shares" approach rather than an "absolute amounts" approach.

13. An "unfunded mandate" occurs when a higher level of government imposes some functions or service standards (e.g., a pupil–teacher ratio) but does not fund the lower-level government to pay for the needed inputs and (even worse but not necessary for the definition of an "unfunded mandate") does not allow the lower-level government the local tax-raising capacity to pay for it.

14. The pockets of poverty refer to poverty of school infrastructure or equipment in this case.

15. My analyses imply that if one takes into account only poverty and resources, there is still a considerable variation in performance; that is, equally poor and resourced schools vary in performance by at least 100 percent. The findings suggest that socioeconomic and environmental factors, taken by themselves, have about the same effect as resources. It seems a futile exercise to attempt to allocate *precisely* how much explanatory power is related to which variables. Controversies around this issue seem capable of infinite statistical analysis and deliberation, as is known from ongoing debates around these issues in developed countries, which often show more significance attached to socioeconomic background than we find in South Africa. If one assumes that some of the unexplained variation is caused by still-unmeasured resource and social variables, then an agnostic but probably wise conclusion would suggest that about one-third of performance is probably related to resources; one third, to quality of management and efficiency; and one-third, to environmental and socioeconomic variables, largely but not perfectly translatable to the general and human capital wealth of parents and the social capital of communities (see Crouch & Mabogoane, 1997a, 1997b). This is probably a sufficient basis for focusing on the quality of management and efficiency and on resource improvement, as well as a basis for being reasonable about expectations, given family and community poverty. The results are strong enough, and suggestive enough, to imply that the limited quality of management and the lack of incentives to increase efficiency are quite important constraints for the education system but hardly all that mat-

ters. Thus, a dual focus on efficiency and managing for quality, as well as equity of resource distribution, is justified. I would like to express my gratitude to Helen Perry, who provided the data and performance index for these analyses; the data were drawn from official sources, in particular the Education Management Information System and exams areas at the National Department of Education. However, I take responsibility for the analysis and any resulting errors.

16. Other analysis suggests that pay itself probably is not a significant factor, as teachers appear approximately as well paid as other professionals with similar levels of training (see Crouch, 2001). During apartheid, teaching and nursing were two of the formal sector professions easily open to Africans. As the labor market restrictions eased, and as the private sector began to open up to educated Africans, the range of choices opened up for young Africans—a range of choices that was always there for young whites. In that sense, teaching might now be relatively less attractive to Africans as a career choice.

REFERENCES CITED

Actuarial Society of South Africa. (2003). *ASSA2000: AIDS and demographic model of the Actuarial Society of South Africa.* Available at www.assa.org.za/default.asp?id=1000000050 (accessed June 14, 2003).

African National Congress. (1994). *A policy framework for education and training.* Johannesburg: African National Congress.

Arnott, A., & Chabane, S. (1995). *Teacher demand, supply, utilisation and costs.* Johannesburg: EduSource.

Buckland, P., & Fielden, J. (1994). *Public expenditure on education in South Africa, 1987/8 to 1991/2: An analysis of the data.* Johannesburg: CEPD.

Crouch, L. (2001). *Turbulence or orderly change? Teacher supply and demand in the age of AIDS.* Pretoria: Department of Education.

———. (2002). *A note on estimating the stock of potential teachers.* Research Triangle Park, NC: Research Triangle Institute.

Crouch, L., & Mabogoane, T. (1997a). Aspects of internal efficiency indicators in South African schools: Analysis of historical and current data. *EduSource Data News, 19,* 4–28.

———. (1997b). *No magic bullets, just tracer bullets: The role of learning resources, social advantage, and education management in improving the performance of South African schools.* Unpublished MS.

Crouch, L., & Vinjevold, P. (2002). *Grade 3 learner assessment: A baseline study in four districts.* Research Triangle Park, NC: Joint Education Trust/Research Triangle Institute.

Department of Education. (1995a). *Report of the committee to review the organisation, governance and funding of schools.* Pretoria: Department of Education.

———. (1995b, March 15). The white paper on education and training in a democratic South Africa: First steps to develop a new system. Notice 196. *Government Gazette,* 16312.

———. (1997a). *Curriculum 2005: Learning for the 21st century.* Pretoria: Department of Education.

———. (1997b). *Language in education policy.* Pretoria: Department of Education.

———. (1998, October 12). National norms and standards for school funding. General Notice 2362. *Government Gazette,* 19347.

———. (2002, November 15). Amendment of regulations for the distribution of educator posts to schools in a provincial department of education. Government Notice 1451. *Government Gazette,* 24077.

———. (2003a). *A review of the financing, resourcing and costs of education in public schools: Report to the minister.* Pretoria: Department of Education.

———. (2003b). *Systemic evaluation, foundation phase, mainstream, national report.* Pretoria: Department of Education.

Department of National Education. (1988). A formula for the subsidisation of an education department in respect of ordinary school education. *NATED 03-136* (88/05). Pretoria: Department of National Education.

———. (1992). *Education renewal strategy.* Pretoria: Department of National Education.

Hall, G. (2002). The impact of the AIDS pandemic on teacher supply and demand in South Africa 2001–2010. In *Conference on HIV/AIDS and the education sector: Report and sector plan of action.* Pretoria: Department of Education.

Human Sciences Research Council. (2002). *Nelson Mandela/HSRC study of HIV/AIDS: South African national HIV prevalence, behavioral risks and mass media: Household survey 2002.* Pretoria: Human Sciences Research Council.

Joseph, J. (1998). Reconstruction and reconciliation in South Africa: The role of race. Hart Leadership Lecture, Duke University.

Kotzé, D. (2000). The political economic of development in South Africa. *African Security Review,* 9 (3). Available at www.iss.co.za/pubs/ASR/9No3/PolEconom.html.

Mandela, N. (1994). *Long walk to freedom: The autobiography of Nelson Mandela.* Randburg, South Africa: Macdonald Purnell (PTY) Ltd.

National Education Policy Investigation. (1992). *Education planning systems and structures.* Cape Town: Oxford University Press/NECC.

National Treasury. (2001). *Intergovernmental fiscal review 2001.* Pretoria: National Treasury.

———. (2002). *Provincial budgets: 2001 outcome and 2002 MTEF budgets.* Pretoria: National Treasury.

Office on the Rights of the Child. (2002). *Children in 2001: Report on the state of the nation's children.* Pretoria: Office on the Rights of the Child—the Presidency, Republic of South Africa.

South African Institute of Race Relations. (1988). *Race relations survey 1986.* Johannesburg: South African Institute of Race Relations.

Statistics South Africa. (2001). *South Africa in transition: Selected findings from the October household survey of 1999 and changes that have occurred between 1995 and 1999.* Pretoria: Statistics South Africa.

United Nations International Children's Emergency Fund. (1998). Orphan assistance in South Africa: Developing partnerships and leadership in a new paradigm for community care. Draft report of an assessment of UNICEF programming in South Africa for families and children affected by HIV/AIDS.

Weber, E. (2002). An ambiguous, contested terrain: Governance models for the new South African education system. *International Journal of Educational Development, 22,* 617–35.

4

Chile: Vouchers and Beyond

Robert W. McMeekin

> The Reform of educational quality and equity doesn't take place in
> some privileged part of the system, it is carried out in the thousands
> of schools; the Reform of learning processes isn't accomplished by
> some omnipotent actor; it is done by tens of thousands of teachers;
> the Reform of the 90s doesn't take place at some moment in his-
> tory, but rather every day, in "class hours" and "homework assign-
> ments;" the Reform of learning doesn't depend on some decree but
> rather on the conviction, commitment and responsibility of all
> those who have something to say or do so that children may learn;
> the Reform of quality has no end date or "expected outcome;" it is
> put on trial every day with every boy or girl.
>
> —Cristian Belleï (2001)

Programs of education "reform"—usually large-scale, top-down
activities—tend to encounter difficulties of implementation. Often,
they are based on some new body of ideas or theory that offers a "sil-
ver bullet" solution to what are perceived to be the problems of education. Although their designers always hope that these reforms will
have a positive effect on educational performance, they rarely give
serious attention to the effects of the proposed changes on the learning environment in the classroom or the quality of teachers' professional lives.

In addition to efforts to improve instruction, many of the recent
education reform programs that have swept both developed and

developing countries include interventions designed to influence teacher behavior. They attempt to do this by establishing external standards, accountability, market-like competition, and a variety of incentives based on rewards and sanctions. These impose a special kind of stress on teachers, who not only feel subject to pressure but may also feel that external factors, such as testing, distract time and energy from what they perceive as their most important tasks. Or the teachers may feel that the interventions are not designed to recognize and reward activities that are truly important. Though the reform measures seek to influence behavior in desirable ways, their combined effects on working conditions may verge on the traumatic. This is especially true when one reform follows another; it is a problem in Latin American countries where leadership changes frequently and each new minister wants to bring in his or her new ideas.

Chile has experienced two major waves of education reform that are still having a strong influence on the way the education system is organized and on the education process at the level of individual schools. The first of these brought a wave of neoliberal, market-oriented changes in Chile's education system, beginning around 1980. The most important of these changes included (1) decentralizing the management of public schools from the central Ministry of Education to municipal levels of government, (2) opening the way for private operators to create schools to compete with public schools, (3) creating a nationwide voucher system that pays equal amounts per child to both public and private schools, and (4) creating a testing system to provide information on school performance that will enable parents to choose where to send their children (Delannoy, 2000; Gauri, 1998; Parry, 1997). These changes, instituted during the period of military government, were not subject to political debate, objections, or opposition from teachers' unions or any other group. The changes caused teachers to feel stress, without question, but they took place in a broader context of such profound sociopolitical turmoil and anxiety that developments in the education sector were of secondary concern.

The second wave of reform, begun since the return of democracy in 1990, has been implemented during three successive political administrations. Under a series of presidents and ministers of education drawn from a center–Left coalition of political parties called the Concertación (coming together), there has been relative continuity of education policies. In addition to increases in teachers' salaries and measures to improve the equity and quality of education begun in 1990, a series of measures begun around 1995 has come to be called Chile's education reform. There are four main "pillars" of the reform (Belleï, 2001; Delannoy, 2000; García-Huidobro, 2001; Molina, 2001). The central element is provision of a "Full School Day," extending the hours of the school week from thirty to thirty-eight hours. This means that schools will no longer be able to operate on a two-shift basis as in the past (and also means that teachers will tend to work full-time in a single school rather than in two or more schools). A second, related pillar provides the additional infrastructure required to eliminate double-shift schools. This involves a large capital investment and a great deal of construction and is being implemented over a period of several years. The third element is curricular reform, beginning with a curriculum framework called "Fundamental Objectives and Minimum Content," developed for both primary and secondary levels. This has been implemented progressively, beginning with the first years of primary and secondary education. The new curriculum is now fully operational in all grades and in all subject areas. Associated with this is a change in the standardized "system for measuring the quality of education" (SIMCE in its Spanish acronym) tests to align them with the curricula (and also a change in the test that regulates university admission). The fourth pillar is a combination of measures designed to improve teaching and includes better preservice and inservice training (including study tours for selected teachers within Chile and outside the country) as well as related efforts to improve the quality of professional life and teaching performance. The most important of these has been an increase of over 100 percent in the real value of teacher salaries since 1990. Also included is an incentive system that provides merit awards to schools (not to individual teachers) in the form of bonuses for all teachers in the school.

These two waves of reform designed to strengthen the system—the series of radical changes involving decentralization, partial privatization, and vouchers and instituted under the military government beginning in 1980, and the subsequent set of reform efforts that followed the return of democratic government in 1990—continue to shape and have strong effects on virtually every aspect of education in Chile. What have been the results of the reforms? Chile has a relatively high standard of living, and its education system is one of the best in Latin America, yet education still suffers from serious problems of low quality and inequity. The results of an international comparative assessment of third and fourth grade achievement, conducted by UNESCO in thirteen Latin American countries in 1997, showed Chile in second or third place in Spanish language achievement and in a closely packed group of the best countries in mathematics (Laboratorio Latinoamericano de Evaluación de la Calidad de la Educación [Latin American Laboratory for the Evaluation of the Quality of Education], 1998, 2001). On the other hand, Chile ranks low in international comparative studies in comparison with First World countries. Chile was one of the few countries of the developing world to participate, along with countries of the Organization for Economic Cooperation and Development (OECD), in the Third International Mathematics and Sciences Study in 1999. On these standardized tests, Chile's average score in mathematics was 392, compared with the average score of 487 for thirty-eight countries. In sciences Chile's average was 420, in comparison with the international average of 488 ("Chile evaluado," 2000). In both tests, it outperformed only a few non-OECD countries, such as the Philippines, South Africa, and Morocco.

Chile also participated in an OECD test of literacy among adults fifteen to sixty-five years old, called the Program for International Student Assessment (PISA). Of the twenty countries participating, only Chile and Slovenia were not OECD members. This international comparative test of reading, described in the OECD's study *Reading Levels in the Age of Information* (2000), showed reading levels in Chile to be among the poorest. Only 2 percent of the adult population sampled attained the top two levels (4 and 5) of reading ability, whereas 60 percent read at level 1, the lowest level. According to the PISA criteria, readers at level 1 are not fully equipped to participate in the modern world. As an example, level 1 readers "would have difficulty understanding the formula for preparing a baby bottle" ("Los Chilenos no entendemos," 2002, p. E8). Even though 13 percent of the sample tested had completed university and many were in senior executive positions, their comprehension of prose was average or below, and their understanding of text involving quantities was poor. So although there have been improvements in Chile's education system, which ranks well among systems in the countries of Latin America, test performance is still far from excellent by First World standards.

THE EFFECTS OF TWO SETS OF REFORMS ON TEACHING

How have these two quite different waves of reform influenced what goes on in classrooms in Chile? What have been their effects on the quality of teachers' working lives and on their performances? The following sections consider ways in which the reforms have influenced teaching, looking first at the military government's reforms and then at the more recent reform activities since 1990.

The Education Reforms of the Military Government

The profound changes in education made by the military government, which held power from 1973 until 1990, were driven by a combination of neoliberal ideology and political motives (Delannoy, 2000; Gauri, 1998). The University of Chicago–trained advisers to the government sought to implement Milton Friedman's concept of privatizing education by giving parents vouchers to pay for their children's education in any school they chose. Children may attend public or private subsidized schools, either within or outside their neighborhoods (although there are no transportation subsidies to facilitate choice on the part of poor families). This was, and continues to be, one of the purest tests of Friedman's ideas in the world. Vouchers do not affect the 10 percent of the student population that attends elite, paid private schools (with much higher per-pupil costs and strong selection and self-selection). Except for this 10 percent of enrollment, the entire education system is based on voucher payments. Both private subsidized schools, established as part of this reform, and the schools decentralized to the municipalities receive equal per-student payments based on attendance as measured monthly (Partnership for Educational Revitalization in Latin America [PREAL],

2002). The payments go directly to the schools from the treasury, without passing through the Ministry of Education. This differs from Friedman's idea of literally giving parents vouchers that they could carry to the school of their choice, but this difference is not highly significant.

Public schools were not abolished and have continued to operate, and private operators have opened schools to provide for an increasing share of total student demand. Public school enrollment decreased but never fell below about 77 percent of its 1981 level, when the voucher system was implemented. Absolute enrollment in public schools dropped from 2.2 million in 1981 to a low of 1.7 million in 1991 but still accounted for 60 percent of voucher-paid enrollment and 54 percent of total enrollment in 2000. Since the 1991 low, absolute enrollment in public schools has increased. Enrollment in voucher-paid private schools has increased dramatically since 1981 (when relatively few preexisting private schools were in operation), especially as a share of total enrollment, but most of this increase and the most rapid rate of increase took place between 1981 and 1989 (Ministry of Education, 2000a). In other words, even though private voucher-paid education provides 40 percent of voucher-supported primary and secondary education in Chile, municipally provided public education still accommodates over one-half of total enrollment.

Why have vouchers not led to a wholesale transfer of enrollment from municipal schools to private voucher-paid schools? For one reason, much of the municipal enrollment occurs in very poor urban neighborhoods, in slums that have grown up around major cities, and in rural areas with sparse population. These are areas where most private operators choose not to establish schools because the student populations come from families with low socioeconomic status. (For many years, however, there have been some private operators, both religious and secular, who intentionally locate their schools in these areas with the aim of combating poverty and disadvantage.) Another reason is that the proximity of a school to the home (or to a parent's workplace) is a factor that weighs heavily in school choice. While location may facilitate transporting children, parents may also choose to enroll their children where their friends from the neighborhood attend and where their children will share the same social class as their fellow students. Finally, although private subsidized schools are not supposed to exercise any form of screening (unless they are over-subscribed), there are subtle forms of dissuading parents from en-rolling their children in these schools.

The decentralization and privatization of schools that had been un-der the Ministry of Education undoubtedly had a powerful, deeply disturbing effect on teachers. As noted, however, these changes took place during the military government, when no expression of dissent was permitted and when tremendous social turmoil (including hu-man rights violations) tended to distract attention from the changes in education. Some teachers lost their jobs, in many cases for political reasons. The teaching force as a whole was strongly opposed to the de facto government. Because the control of education was frag-mented into roughly 300 communities (plus private operators), teach-ers had to negotiate salaries and working conditions with not one but many employers. Teacher salaries declined during the 1980s to roughly one-half their real levels before the military coup. At least in part, the decline occurred because the country experienced a serious economic recession during this period.

All this is in the past, however, and after fourteen years of demo-cratic government during which teachers have received highly favor-able treatment, the teaching force is relatively content with its situa-tion. A study by Mizala and Romaguera (2000b, pp. 28–31) found that a majority of teachers accept the "Chilean model of education," in-cluding decentralization, vouchers, competition between public and private schools, and the provision of test-based information on school performance to parents, although there are differences of opinion about some aspects of the system. The level of acceptance is higher among teachers in private subsidized schools than among those in public schools.

Along with opening the "market" for education to private providers and establishing a voucher system, the military government instituted a testing system designed to provide information so that parents could make informed choices about which schools provide the best education. Chile's "system for measuring the quality of education" was established in the late 1980s. It tests students at the fourth, eighth, and (in recent years) tenth grade levels in Spanish and mathematics.

(The natural sciences, history, and geography have been added in recent versions of the tests.) Data are published on schools' average scores on Spanish and mathematics tests (not individual student scores or class averages). It is, therefore, a low-stakes test that supports voucher-based competition by providing information so that parents can choose schools on the basis of performance, without constituting a direct or serious threat to either students or teachers (PREAL, 2002). In theory, the pressure of competition will have an effect on performance: If parents move their children from poorly performing to better-performing schools (and subsidy payments follow the child), schools with less-than-adequate performance will be forced to improve (or will be forced out of business). In fact, few schools in Chile have closed during the more than twenty years the system has been in operation, not even those public schools with very poor showings on the SIMCE tests.

The SIMCE tests have an influence on the Ministry of Education, for they provide a basis for evaluating how the ministry and its education reforms are influencing educational performance ("Estancada educación municipal," 2000). There have been harsh criticisms, especially during the period from 1997 to the present, because the SIMCE scores have not risen as rapidly as they did in earlier years and because the gap between public and private subsidized schools has widened. Direct comparisons of SIMCE scores between years are complicated, however, because the tests and grading system were changed in 1997 and scores are reported according to a different scale. Some questions have been raised about whether the SIMCE tests, which are managed by a division of the ministry, are reported objectively and about their comparability between years. The publication of SIMCE data that are unfavorable to the ministry tends to indicate that the tests have been objective and that the information provided has been transparent.

In general, Chilean society has accepted the education system instituted in the 1980s, including decentralization, vouchers, partial privatization, and testing. The main criticisms come from liberal observers concerned about equity, who object that the system will inevitably lead to greater stratification or "segmentation" of education. In other words, children of families with higher education and income levels will tend to go to the private subsidized schools, but children of the poorest families are channeled, for various reasons (an inevitable degree of selection, lack of subsidies for transportation costs, and other factors), into attending the municipal subsidized schools. This segmentation has the effect of withdrawing from the public subsector the more educated and concerned parents who could exercise "voice" in favor of improving the public schools. One can speculate that there is also an inevitable tendency for the better teachers to seek work in schools that have students from families with a higher socioeconomic status, although there have been no studies on this.

Some who are concerned about equity single out for criticism a policy that allows private subsidized schools to implement a system of "shared financing" (*financiamiento compartido*). This policy, established in 1993, allows parents to make payments in addition to the voucher payments. Parents in a school must vote in favor of the system before the school can implement it. Fifteen percent of the private subsidized schools have adopted shared financing. Private payments, opponents argue, have the dual effect of providing more resources for the children of more affluent parents (who can afford to participate in the shared financing system) while effectively screening out the children of poor families, who cannot afford the extra fees and therefore continue to enroll their children in the municipal schools. But many municipalities also provide financing in addition to the voucher payments by supplementing the voucher payments with funds from other budgets. This makes it possible to cover salary costs when these exceed the amounts provided by the vouchers. The debate on shared financing still rages, and an extensive study of the system has failed to produce a definitive answer to the question (Corvalán & Gayner, 2002).

The first thing that must be said about Chile's twenty-year experiment with vouchers, competition between private and public providers of education, and the provision of test-based information to facilitate competition is that it has not had the impact on performance that Milton Friedman and his followers would have predicted. Comparing average scores between the private and municipal subsectors of education shows that the private subsidized schools have somewhat higher average scores than the municipal schools. (Both have scores considerably below those of the elite, fee-charging private schools.) Studies by Mizala and Romaguera (2000a, pp. 400–5) and McEwan and Carnoy (2000) indicate that, with appropriate controls for students' socioeconomic background and selection factors, there are essentially no differences between the two categories of subsidized schools. The relative positions of schools in each category remained roughly the same for a decade beginning in the late 1980s, indicating that there is no substantial change in relative performance over time. Mizala and Romaguera (2000a) emphasize the high dispersion of scores within both categories of schools, indicating that being private does not guarantee high quality and that some public schools are capable of high levels of performance.

With regard to the effect of the SIMCE tests on teachers, these low-stakes tests do not appear to have a strong impact on what happens in classrooms. The teachers' union fought to keep the results from being published in the form of rankings or "league tables," but such publication began in 1995. In their study of Chile's system of merit awards to schools, Mizala and Romaguera (2000b) found that teachers do not give much importance to the SIMCE tests and that they share a prevailing doubt about whether the SIMCE gives a legitimate picture of student learning or of their own performance: "Teachers' evaluations of the quality of teaching in their own schools tend to reflect complacency. A large proportion of teachers characterize the level of quality in their own school as 'good' or 'superior,' even in schools with low indicators of results" (p. 33). In interviews with school directors, Mizala and Romaguera heard comments about a "teachers' culture" that resists the use of standardized tests as a basis for evaluating their work. There is also a feeling of egalitarianism among teachers and opposition to competition or distinctions between the performances of peers.

In recent research, my colleagues and I asked focus groups of teachers in a small sample of public and private primary schools in greater Santiago how the SIMCE tests influenced their work in the classroom (McMeekin, Latorre, & Celedón, 2001). The responses indicated that, although the teachers are aware of the tests, they do not alter their teaching significantly in order to assure good performance on the part of their students. Our field notes include teacher comments on the SIMCE tests such as these:

"We don't make special efforts to prepare for the SIMCE. If a child is doing poorly, we work with them, whether there's a SIMCE test that year or not."

"It [SIMCE] is just one more evaluation."

"We think of good SIMCE scores as kind of a by-product of what we're doing."

"The SIMCE is not very important for the parents. The kids want to do well, but it's because they want to make a good showing for the school."

"We think of the SIMCE as a test of whether the kids have covered the minimum content."

"We want the students to do well, but for their own sake, not for the sake of the SIMCE score."

Teachers did not indicate that the tests caused them, or their students, anxiety. Some said that because the SIMCE tests do not have any direct consequences for students, the students do not make great efforts to do well.

School directors in the same schools said that they (and their teachers) consider the tests important but do not think that parents give great importance to a school's average scores in deciding where to enroll their children. One director commented that parents do not ask about the school's SIMCE scores when interviewing about enrolling their children. In the directors' opinions, parents give greater weight to factors such as the role of the school in developing strong values than to average scores on the SIMCE. There were no indications that the directors took special measures to improve their schools' SIMCE averages. They specifically said that they do not practice student selection (except to admit siblings of children already in the school) and do not urge their teachers to prepare children especially for the SIMCE tests. One commented that at her school there were no absences on the days of the SIMCE tests (meaning that the school did not urge low-performing students to stay at home on test day). In one school that had notably low SIMCE scores the previous year, the director indicated that she was concerned. She said that the municipal authority had sent mathematics and Spanish specialists to help teachers prepare the children for the tests.

The fairly low importance given to the SIMCE indicates that this test, now in use for almost twenty years, has come to be accepted as part of the system but is not a source of stress or anxiety. The low-stakes standardized tests may produce some pressure to perform well, especially in the case of schools that have low average scores, but they neither cause undesirable distortions in behavior, such as teaching to the test, nor lead teachers to leave the profession because of stress.

Thirteen Years of Reform under the Concertación

With the return of democratic government in 1990, there were strong pressures to reverse many of the education policies instituted under the military regime. These initiatives came especially from the teachers' union, which takes a strong position that the teachers suffered greatly during the military regime and that the country owes a "debt" to the teachers. Belleï (2001) says that the teachers' union adheres to a policy of *reivindicación,* meaning "reclaiming the right to be repaid," referring to the treatment of teachers during the military regime. Teachers approve of this posture on the part of their union (and are pleased with improvements in their salary levels), although most teachers do not share the union's position of intransigence and tend to be more content personally with the reform. The union, permitted to operate freely from 1990 on, has been one of the strongest political supporters of the Concertación.

For a number of reasons, it was decided to leave the decentralization measures and accompanying voucher system in place (see Delannoy, 2000, pp. 12–14). One of the first actions of the center–Left government was to establish a new "Teachers Law" (Estatuto Docente) that provided for increases in salaries over a period of years, as well as programs of in-service training (and strengthening preservice training). The Estatuto Docente had the effect of partially recentralizing the control of education by overriding the autonomy of municipalities and private operators in terms of teacher pay and conditions of service. The statute has been criticized for introducing rigidities into the system (especially limiting schools' ability to change or dismiss teachers). Subsequent modifications of the law have revised some of the original provisions that tended to recentralize education, but the law's main thrust, of improving salaries and working conditions, remains unchanged.

During the second democratic presidential administration under the Concertación, activities tending toward reform began to gain momentum. In 1994 the Ministry of Education established a commission of national and international experts, chaired by noted Chilean education expert José Joaquin Brunner, to advise on policy directions for improving education in Chile. The National Commission on the Modernization of Education, as the Brunner Commission was officially called, made a number of recommendations, including giving quality improvement top priority, strengthening the teaching profession, increasing the amount of time students spend in school, increasing school autonomy, instituting a reform of secondary education on an urgent basis, and increasing total spending on education from 4.8 to 8.0 percent of gross domestic product. The findings of the commission won the support of the major political parties on both the Left and the Right in a "Framework Agreement for Modernization of Education" signed in 1995 (Delannoy, 2000, pp. 23–37; Molina, 2001).

From the Brunner Commission's work and the astutely managed political agreement that followed, there emerged what would become the main pillars of the current education reform. The reform ideas were not new or revolutionary; and they had political support from both the Left and the Right; knowledgeable educators had been advocating these or very similar measures for some time. But the commission report provided a coalescing point from which to launch the reforms, which have affected the professional lives of teachers and the way education is delivered in the classroom. The next sections consider each of the pillars of the reform and their impact on teachers.

Full School Day

Adjustments in teacher salaries, which more than compensated for the increased number of hours worked, meant that full-day school could be implemented without objections from the union or feelings of being exploited on the part of teachers. The measure's effects on teachers came in other ways.

One initial effect was to create crowding and confusion as the schools that had operated on a double-shift basis struggled to provide places for virtually double the number of students that previously had been enrolled one shift at a time. The measure is being implemented on a phased basis, giving some schools more time to make preparations. Full implementation is now projected for 2006, although various completion dates have already been set and slipped. Schools that have now made the changeover to full-day school, and their teachers and students, have had to suffer through crowding, scheduling changes, makeshift arrangements to accommodate more classes at the same time, and ongoing construction during class hours. That period of adaptation, though painful, only lasts for a limited time, usually about one full year, although the lingering effects of crowding continue to be felt in some schools.

Educators in Chile generally favor lengthening the school day and increasing the time available for covering the curriculum. Some teachers who were working two shifts under the previous system will suffer some decrease in total income, but they will also experience much less stress. In terms of the quality of professional life, teachers in single-shift, full-day schools are unanimous in their approval of this mode of working versus having to shuttle from one school to another. Working a full day in a single school not only increases the time available for teaching. It also greatly strengthens the feeling of community in the school and the personal and professional contacts between teachers as peers and between teachers and the students and their families.

Curricular Change

Creating the space to make single-shift, full-day schooling feasible is one challenge. Perhaps a more important and difficult one is determining how to use the additional time to improve student learning. The Fundamental Objectives and Minimum Content reform plan for the primary and secondary curricula was already under way. The curriculum changes had two important implications for classroom teachers: First, the teachers had to make adjustments in the content of their classes to conform to the curriculum requirements; second, the SIMCE tests that evaluate student and school performance had to be changed to align them with the new curricular content, and children had to be prepared for a test based on different content. Although teachers do not give great importance to the SIMCE tests or distort their teaching practice in reaction to it, they still need to make sure that students have been taught the same material that will be covered on the test, and this means that teachers have to make some changes in their established teaching patterns.

Knowledgeable observers who are in direct contact with teachers and classrooms say that teachers have reacted to the barrage of changes brought by the reforms by remaining as close as possible to their previous activities, behavior, and routines. Curricular changes in response to the reforms may have led teachers to change the content covered in their classes but not their methods of teaching. Because these methods have tended to be highly traditional, lecture-based, or "frontal" approaches to instruction, many of the weaknesses that existed earlier continue to be found in the classes. One knowledgeable informant said that when fourth grade students take reading tests, as many as one-quarter—or in the worst cases more than one-half—are unable to read with comprehension.

Difficulties of implementation, noted at the beginning of this chapter, are particularly apparent here. On the whole, the post-1990 reforms have been designed with care, and there have been sincere efforts to communicate clearly and completely about the reforms and to follow up with attempts to ensure that the various measures are implemented as intended. These efforts have not been entirely adequate, however. Belleï (2001) is especially critical of the ministry's failure to communicate clearly to the teachers about the reform and its inability to overcome a "teachers' culture" that views aspects of the reform as contrary to teachers' professional self-image. (Teachers tend to view themselves as unselfish, noncompetitive workers with high aims and intrinsic motivation.) It is, of course, true that many of the changes resulting from the reform have not been assimilated fully, and there has not been sufficient time to implement improved methods completely. Critics of the reform say that it has not resulted in notable improvements in performance, as measured by the SIMCE tests. Results in public (municipal) and private subsidized schools improved overall from 1990 through 1997, but they appear to have remained largely unchanged in more recent years. Moreover, the gaps have widened between the performance of the municipal schools and that of both the private subsidized schools and the elite, paid private schools.

Strengthening the Teaching Profession

The most important measure to improve the conditions of teachers is the series of increases in pay that successive administrations have given to teachers, both before and after the change to the full school day. The teachers' union has called for repaying a "debt" to teachers to compensate for the difficult years the profession suffered during the military government, when the real value of teachers' salaries did indeed fall by approximately 40 percent. Salary increases that have restored and, to some extent, gone beyond the real value of salaries at their earlier peak have contributed to relative peace between the union and the ministry.

The set of measures designed to "strengthen the teaching profession" under the reform of the 1990s includes extensive in-service training; programs to improve the quality of preservice teacher education in university faculties of education; professional enrichment activities; study tours to observe and learn about improved methods, both in Chile and in other countries; and a program of merit awards to whole schools. The last is an innovative incentive system, Sistema de Evaluación del Desempeño de los Establecimientos Educacionales Subvencionados (System for Evaluating the Performance of Subsidized Educational Establishments [SNED]), which avoids most of the shortcomings of traditional merit pay to individual teachers. The SNED system makes awards to the top 25 percent of schools in each of five "strata," or groups, of schools. The strata are established on the basis of criteria related to parent and community background and other factors that assure that the competition is among schools serving populations with comparable socioeconomic status. The competition is based on an index in which absolute scores on the SIMCE tests count for 37 percent of the total and *changes* in test scores since the last application of the SIMCE count for 28 percent. Other factors relate to efforts to improve quality and equity, parental involvement, and the working conditions of teachers, and these count for the remaining 35 percent (McMeekin, 2000; Ministry of Education, 1998a,

1998b, 2000b; Mizala & Romaguera, 2000b). Teachers approve of the SNED system because this index is based not only on cross-sectional comparisons of examination scores but also on longitudinal changes in test performance, as well as other factors.

Not surprisingly, these positive measures have been well received by teachers. There has been some concern on the part of teachers about the incentive system, especially about the fairly heavy weight given to scores on the SIMCE tests (measured on both a cross-sectional and a longitudinal basis, taking account of something approximating "value added"). As the sources cited explain, however, the ministry has taken action to modify the SNED system in response to these concerns (reducing slightly the weight of test scores in the index used to identify award winners). Interviews with teachers indicate that, just as they do not give great importance to the outcomes of the SIMCE tests, they largely accept the incentive system that is based, in part, on those tests. A majority of teachers, in both schools that won awards and those that did not, indicate that they accept the idea of rewarding teachers in schools that perform well. The teachers' union has not objected to the incentive system, in part because it is perceived as reasonably fair and valid and because the awards result in temporary increases in the income of all teachers in the selected schools.

A Change in the Tests for University Admission

One change that has produced great controversy and turmoil relates only indirectly to the education reform. In 2002 the ministry announced that there would be a change in the Academic Aptitude Test (Prueba de Aptitud Académica), the single examination that governs admission to all the "traditional" universities in Chile. The twenty-five traditional universities existed before 1980, when the military government permitted private universities to open and to charge fees. The private universities compete with the traditional ones, which continue to be partially publicly supported. Among the traditional group are Chile's two best universities, the Pontifical Catholic University of Chile and the University of Chile. At least in part, the rationale for the present change in the admissions examination was to make it conform to the changes in the secondary curriculum resulting from the education reform. Another reason was to orient the test more toward academic achievement rather than "aptitude," a change that follows, to some degree, changes in U.S. college admissions testing.

Students with the highest 25 percent of the scores on the university admissions examination receive scholarships to the traditional universities (in the order of their three highest preferences). Chile has a system of university fees that cover a substantial portion of actual costs, which is most unusual in Latin America. Because the fees are quite high, even for public universities, the entrance examination can be considered a high-stakes test. The examination, first instituted in 1963, has evolved in various ways in the intervening years, including the way test scores are used to allocate scholarship resources. Winning one of the top places on this single ranking—especially a place at either the Catholic University or the University of Chile—is thus of great importance to students and their parents.

A proposed change in the university admissions test has caused great turmoil. The Ministry of Education first put forward a Higher Education Admissions System (Sistema de Ingreso a la Educación Superior) to be implemented in 2002, but this produced strong opposition from various quarters and for various reasons. The University of Chile, which has designed and administered the test (and derives very substantial income from this function), had a number of objections. These include criticisms of the test on both technical (psychometric) and procedural grounds. Secondary schools whose graduating seniors will have to sit for the test complain that the proposed change would be too rapid to enable them to understand what the new test will cover and do a reasonable job of preparing their students for it. Indeed, final decisions on the design of the new testing system were long delayed, making it impossible either for experts to evaluate it or for secondary schools to understand what their students should know. There were actions taken on the part of both the Council of Rectors and the University of Chile to block the change. The ministry then announced, late in 2002, that there would be no change that year but that an interim system—the Transitional Admissions Test (Prueba de Admisión Transitoria [PAT])—would be in operation for the admissions process at the end of 2003. The PAT was to incorporate some aspects of both the traditional test and the proposed new version. Still another change made in 2003, to a University Selection Test (Prueba de Selección Universitaria), appears to be final. The ministry, the rectors, and the secondary schools appear to have reached a truce on the subject (and the minister of education was replaced). Students are receiving sample questions and other information about the new form of the test, but there is still a high degree of uncertainty and anxiety on the part of the senior class students who will take the test, their parents, the secondary school teachers, and school directors.

In this context, the emergence of published information on the rankings of all secondary schools in the country on the university admissions test has further exacerbated an atmosphere of uncertainty and dissatisfaction on the part of parents and others concerned with education in Chile. The newspaper *La Tercera,* published in Santiago, began some years ago to publish "league tables" of test scores of every secondary school in the country. These were grouped by category: municipal subsidized, private subsidized, and paid private schools. Although the information had been public and theoretically available to all for some years, this publication in a regularly accessible source brought the matter of the relative performance of secondary schools to the immediate attention of the public, including many critics of the system. An affiliated publication of *La Tercera*—the weekly news magazine *¿Qué Pasa?*—has also published the rankings in recent years. In 2002 *¿Qué Pasa?* added a special report on how schools compared in terms of the quality of their teachers, their students' academic excellence (measured by average scores on the university admissions test), the variety of their curricular and extracurricular offerings, and their infrastructure ("Exclusive ranking de colegios," 2002; "Reportajes especiales," 2002).

Parents became disturbed (or incensed) that their children's schools were not performing better (especially in the case of some of the very costly private schools). Educators expressed concerns that quality continues to be low in many schools (which was obvious from the gaps between the highest-performing schools and others) and that the reforms have not produced greater improvement. Indeed, there continue to be serious inequities, especially between the performance of the municipal schools and both the private subsidized schools and paid private schools. Teachers felt criticized. Some school directors were specifically criticized and in some cases were forced to resign.

To say that the publication of these data caused stress on the part of teachers and others with interests in the education system would be an understatement. Added to uncertainty about the admissions testing situation, this has created a great deal of turbulence throughout the secondary education system (but very little in terms of productive results). As noted, concerns about the outcomes of secondary education and changes in the university admissions system are not specifically the result of the education reform. They are indirectly related, however, and the effects of this combination of factors make it clear that Chile's education system is not immune to high levels of stress caused by policy changes, high-stakes testing, and the provision of readily accessible information.

CONCLUSION

Chile's education reforms have had significant implications for both teachers and students. The neoliberal reforms of the 1980s have now become fully institutionalized within the education system and have not, for the most part, been overturned by the three democratic presidential administrations since 1990. They provide one of the world's most thoroughgoing examples of a nationwide system of voucher-based finance of elementary and secondary education, including the decentralization of control to approximately 300 municipalities, permission for private operators to open schools to compete with the public ones, the provision of equal voucher payments directly to the public and private subsidized schools, and a testing system that provides information to help parents choose where to enroll their children.

Competition between public and private schools might provide some pressure to encourage low-performing schools to make extra efforts to raise their scores, but the available evidence suggests that teachers in poorly performing schools tend to be fairly complacent and to blame poor outcomes on students and their families (Ministry of Education, 1997). Enrollment in private subsidized schools has increased greatly as a share of total enrollment, but in absolute terms enrollment in municipal schools has not declined much since the early years of the voucher and privatization program. Thus, public schools appear to be shielded, at least partly, against competitive pressure. Although there have been some improvements in scores on the SIMCE tests, the establishment of competition has not produced the dramatic improvements that advocates of vouchers predicted. Schools in the private subsidized subsector have somewhat higher scores than municipal schools, but after controlling for differences in the socioeconomic backgrounds of students and some degree of selection on the part of the private schools, the differences are minimal, and some research indicates that there are no significant differences (McEwan & Carnoy, 2000; Mizala & Romaguera, 2000a).

The multiple components of Chile's more recent reform have had different impacts on teachers, ranging from benign (in the case of measures to improve the quality of teachers' professional lives), to challenging (implementing curricular reform), to inconvenient (turbulence caused by implementing the full school day). There have been no dramatic effects as a result of the external examination system and the publication of data on SIMCE results. Many teachers appear to have a feeling of indifference (and even of complacency) about their performance, even when their schools achieve only relatively low scores.

One example of the strong effects of an external examination on all members of school communities is provided by the change in the test that determines university admission (and the confusion associated with implementing the change). This is essentially a by-product of the reform, necessitated in part by the need to align the test to the revised secondary curriculum. The university entrance test is not designed as an external examination to hold schools accountable. But when the stakes are high, as they are when a test determines who gains admission and who wins important scholarship aid, the impact on students, parents, teachers, and school directors can be very powerful.

Chile offers an interesting case, for it has put into operation forms of all three categories of incentives to improve education. These include (1) competition (permitting private voucher-paid schools to compete with public schools), (2) standards (both the tests designed to facilitate competition among schools and the test designed to replace the traditional university admissions test), and (3) the incentive system that provides monetary rewards to all teachers in the best-performing 25 percent of schools (McMeekin, 2003). All these interventions seem to be reasonably well accepted in the educational culture of the country, although there are some critics who object that they tend to produce stratification between rich and poor.

Contrary to the situation in many countries, there has been a fairly high degree of continuity of leadership in Chile's education reforms. The Concertación, a center–Left coalition, has remained in power through three presidential administrations. Although there have been seven ministers of education in the thirteen years since the return of democracy, many of the key people involved in designing the reforms have either remained in positions in the ministry or continue to be influential advisers and opinion leaders in the education community. Because of this continuity, Chile has avoided the tendency of new administrations to overthrow the policies and programs of their predecessors and launch new initiatives. Although teachers have had to assimilate numerous dimensions of reform over the last thirteen years, these have all stemmed from the same general policy framework and have been designed to support, rather than override, earlier reform measures. This consistency has ameliorated the kind of overload of new policies that teachers in some countries feel.

After substantial efforts—in two major waves of reform—to promote improvements in educational quality, what have been the effects on school performance? Although few would argue that there have been no positive changes, the reform programs have not led to radical improvements as would have been hoped. Although Chile's education system is one of the best in Latin America, international standardized tests show that the performance of its students falls far below that of students in OECD countries. In part, this is because a number of years must pass before the impact of the reform can be fully felt and the reform itself can be subject to a valid evaluation. Generally, the reforms also have not resulted in changes in the teaching methods used in the classroom. Moreover, until there are basic changes in the societal context and the home situations of students from poorer families, the effects of the reform programs are dampened by the poverty and low education levels of parents.

Academic improvement is not the only objective of Chile's reform, however, and some critics argue that it has failed to achieve its equity objectives. In particular, critics decry the tendency of the education system to become more segmented and stratified as a result of competition between public and private schools. Critics are especially concerned about programs such as the "shared financing" provision that makes it more difficult for families with limited means to enroll their children in the highest-performing private subsidized schools. Although gaps between the municipal and private subsidized subsectors narrowed for some years, they now appear to be widening again, though this may be a short-run phenomenon. On the whole, however, in spite of some inevitable problems and shortcomings, Chile's education reform measures generally respond well to the needs of the system, have not caused a great deal of stress on teachers, and have the potential to improve student learning once they are fully implemented.

REFERENCES CITED

Belleï, C. (2001). El talón de Aquiles de la reforma: Análisis sociológico de la política de los 90 hacia los docentes en Chile [The Achilles heel of the reform: Sociological analysis of the policy of the 1990s toward teachers in Chile]. In S. Martinic & M. Pardo (Eds.), *Economía política de las reformas educativas en América Latina* [Political economy of education reforms in Latin America] (pp. 227–57). Santiago: Centro de Investigación y Desarrollo de la Educación/Partnership for Educational Revitalization in Latin America.

Chile evaluado, ¿Chile reprobado? [Chile evaluated, Chile failed?]. (2000, December 10). *El Mercurio* (Santiago), E12.

Corvalán, J., & Gayner, M. (2002). *Efectos de la modalidad de financimiento compartido en la educación media subvencionada en la Región Metropolitana en Chile* [Effects of the policy of shared financing in subsidized secondary schools in the Metropolitan Region of Chile]. Santiago: Centro de Investigación y Desarrollo de la Educación.

Delannoy, F. (2000). *Education reforms in Chile: 1980–1998: A lesson in pragmatism.* Education Reform and Management Series, 1 (1). Washington, DC: World Bank.

Estancada educación municipal [Stagnant municipal education]. (2000, July 6). *El Mercurio* (Santiago), A1, A8, C6.

Exclusive ranking de colegios según los resultados de la PAA 2001 [Exclusive ranking of secondary schools according to the results of the 2001 PAA]. (2002, April 19). *¿Qué Pasa?* (Santiago), 1–98.

García-Huidobro, J. E. (2001). Conflictos y alianzas en las reformas educativas: Siete tesis basadas en la experiencia Chilena [Conflicts and alliances in the education reforms: Seven theses based on the Chilean experience]. In S. Martinic & M. Pardo (Eds.), *Economía política de las reformas educativas en América Latina* [Political economy of education reforms in Latin America] (pp. 205–18). Santiago: Centro de Investigación y Desarrollo de la Educación/Partnership for Educational Revitalization in Latin America.

Gauri, V. (1998). *School choice in Chile: Two decades of educational reform.* Pittsburgh: University of Pittsburgh Press.

Laboratorio Latinoamericano de Evaluación de la Calidad de la Educación [Latin American Laboratory of Evaluation of the Quality of Education]. (1998). *Primer estudio internacional comparativo* [First international comparative study]. Santiago: UNESCO-Santiago.

———. (2001). *Primer estudio internacional comparativo, segundo informe* [First international comparative study, second report]. Santiago: UNESCO-Santiago.

Los Chilenos no entendemos lo que leemos [We Chileans don't understand what we read]. (2002, July 2). *El Mercurio* (Santiago), E8.

McEwan, P., & Carnoy, M. (2000). The effectiveness and efficiency of private schools in Chile's voucher system. *Education Policy Analysis Archives, 22* (3), 213–39.

McMeekin, R. (2000). *Implementing school-based merit awards: Chile's experience.* Education Reform and Management Series, Technical Notes, 3 (1). Washington, DC: World Bank.

———. (2003). *Incentives to improve education: A new perspective.* Cheltenham, England: Edward Elgar Publishing.

McMeekin, R., Latorre, M., & Celedón, F. (2001). *Institutions within school organizations: Looking inside the black box.* ERIC Document Reproduction Service No. ED453571. Portland, OR: ERIC Clearinghouse on Educational Management.

Ministry of Education. (1997). Evaluación de la implementación y resultados del SNED, 1996–97 [Evaluation of the implementation and results of SNED 1996–97]. Study commissioned by the Ministry of Education, performed by Alejandra Mizala and Pilar Romaguera. Santiago: Centro de Economía Aplicada, Facultad de Ingeniería Industrial, Universidad de Chile (typescript).

———. (1998a). Evaluación del desempeño, SNED [Evaluation of performance, SNED]. Santiago: Ministry of Education, Republic of Chile (typescript).

———. (1998b). *Reconocimiento al compromiso docente* [Recognition of teacher commitment]. Santiago: Ministry of Education, Republic of Chile.

———. (2000a). *Compendio de información estadística educacional, año 2000* [Compendium of educational statistics information, 2000]. Santiago: Ministry of Education, Republic of Chile.

———. (2000b). *Performance evaluation of subsidized schools: SNED 2000-2001*. Santiago: Ministry of Education, Republic of Chile.

Mizala, A., & Romaguera, P. (2000a). School performance and school choice: The Chilean experience. *Journal of Human Resources, 35* (2), 400–5.

———. (2000b). *Sistemas de incentivos en educación y la experiencia del SNED en Chile* [Incentive systems in education and the SNED experience in Chile]. Serie Economía No. 82. Santiago: Centro de Economía Aplicada, Facultad de Ingeniería Industrial, Universidad de Chile.

Molina, S. (2001). Acuerdos y conflictos en la reforma educacional en Chile [Agreements and conflicts in educational reform in Chile]. In S. Martinic & M. Pardo (Eds.), *Economía política de las reformas educativas en América Latina* [Political economy of educational reforms in Latin America] (pp. 175–81). Santiago: Centro de Investigación y Desarrollo de la Educación/Partnership for Educational Revitalization in Latin America.

Organization for Economic Cooperation and Development. (2000). *Reading levels in the age of information*. Paris: Organization for Economic Cooperation and Development.

Parry, T. R. (1997). Theory meets reality in the education voucher debate: Some evidence from Chile. *Education Economics, 5* (3), 307–31.

Partnership for Educational Revitalization in Latin America. (2002). *Sistemas probados: Evaluación de los aprendizajes en Chile y en Brasil* [Proven systems: Evaluation of student learning in Chile and Brazil]. Formas y Reformas de la Educación. Washington, DC: Partnership for Educational Revitalization in Latin America.

Reportajes especiales: Los mejores colegios de Chile [Special report: The best secondary schools in Chile]. (2002). *La Tercera* (Santiago).

5

Germany: After Reunification

Barbara M. Kehm

Because things are the way they are, things will not stay the way they are.

—Bertolt Brecht (1898–1956)

EDUCATION POLICY IN THE
FEDERAL REPUBLIC OF GERMANY

Following the end of World War II, the German education system underwent restructuring in each of the three German zones occupied by Western allied forces (American, British, French). The new system was derived from the federalist traditions of the late nineteenth century and the Weimar Republic. Under this system, the federal government had no responsibility for education, science, or culture, which again became the prime responsibility of the individual German states. The reintroduction of the federal structure was considered appropriate to traditional German regionalism and to diversity in a democratic federal republic.

There were eleven states in West Germany, including the three city-states of Berlin, Hamburg, and Bremen. It soon became clear that some form of coordination was needed to guarantee equality of opportunity and to ensure cross-state recognition of school-leaving certificates. This coordination function became the responsibility of the Standing Conference of the Ministers of Culture and Education of the German States (Ständige Konferenz der Kultusminister der Länder in der Bundesrepublik Deutschland [KMK]), established in 1948 and still in existence today.

Because the West German states had different education policies, it was not feasible to implement structural reforms in the 1950s; any reforms that were attempted were limited to individual pilot projects. The first nationwide education reform took place in the mid-1960s, which had a more favorable climate for reform: Germany was experiencing an "economic miracle," along with an increased birthrate, and, at the same time, was reacting to "Sputnik shock" and to an essay by a German philosopher, *The German Educational Catastrophe* (Picht, 1964), which received wide coverage by the media.[1]

Beginning in 1970, education planning became more systematic and was based on priorities set by the German Council of Education (Deutscher Bildungsrat, 1970), a policy body with representatives from the federal government, the German states, and relevant societal groups. These priorities included, for example, unifying the school systems of the German states, implementing compensatory measures to ensure equal opportunities, strengthening "individual rights" through greater differentiation, broadening the curriculum, increasing participation in higher education, and linking education to economic competitiveness. The West German education system expanded rapidly until the 1980s and then began to face gradual declines in funding.

EDUCATION POLICY IN THE
GERMAN DEMOCRATIC REPUBLIC

In the German Democratic Republic, the Soviet military forces established a centralized system of education guided by Marxist-Leninist principles. The Socialist Party was responsible for all education and science policies and linked them to central economic planning.

The system of education was highly unified and homogeneous; after primary school, students attended one comprehensive type of school, the "polytechnic secondary school," which lasted through tenth grade. A strictly limited number of young people then continued for two additional years of upper secondary education, designed to prepare them for higher education. The other students started vocational education after tenth grade.

After the signing of the Unification Treaty between the Federal Republic of Germany and the German Democratic Republic in 1990 (increasing the total number of states to sixteen), the West German system, with all its positive and negative characteristics, was transferred to East Germany. Any positive characteristics of the East German system were disregarded, as well as the opportunity to make badly needed reforms in West Germany: The comprehensive East German school system was replaced by West Germany's differentiated system.

In the process of unifying the two education systems, many East German teachers lost their jobs for reasons of ideology or for lack of integrity. In addition, a high proportion of those who continued teaching had to participate in additional studies to upgrade their qualifications or to change fields, for example, from teaching Russian as a foreign language to teaching English or French.

THE GERMAN SCHOOL SYSTEM TODAY

Administration and Funding

The German school system is basically a public one, with only a relatively small number of private schools that have state recognition of their curricula and certificates and which may charge tuition. Although officially there is separation between church and state, some of these private schools have a religious affiliation, and public schools offer religious instruction (Roman Catholic and Protestant) on a voluntary basis. East Germany, which had a strictly atheistic system before 1989, subsequently developed a new subject called "ethical instruction" that was designed to substitute for religious instruction.

The states cover about 80 percent of the overall costs of education, and the local authorities cover the remaining 20 percent. State and local authorities jointly administer the public schools; the state pays teacher salaries and makes hiring decisions, and local authorities cover material costs. Generally, individual schools do not control their own budgets, although there is some trend in that direction under management plans described later in the chapter. The school system's structure is very hierarchical, from the state ministry, through the regional and local authorities, to the head of the school. There are, however, procedures in place to ensure opportunities for participation by teachers, parents, and students. For example, though the states establish general curriculum guidelines, teachers also have a role in determining the content and teaching methods that are most appropriate for their students' individual needs.

The KMK coordinates "logistics" across states to ensure that there is sufficient interstate consistency to enable students to move across systems. Agreements between states cover such areas as school organization, vacations and holidays, recognition of school reports and certificates, recognition of teacher examinations, and sequencing of foreign language instruction.

School Organization and Student Selection

The primary school is the only part of the German school system that is "integrated," where all children study together regardless of achievement level. In most German states, primary school covers grades one–four; some states (e.g., Berlin and Brandenburg) wait another two years before students face tracking. Secondary schools are highly differentiated, with the school system divided into three distinct types of schools at both the lower secondary level (grades five to ten) and the upper secondary level (grades eleven to thirteen).

After primary school (in most states, around the age of ten), student selection into secondary school begins. The parents must then decide, based on the teacher's recommendation, which type of secondary school their child should attend. If the teacher's recommendation conflicts with the parents' wishes, sometimes the parents, and sometimes the school, decide the child's assignment. If a child enrolls in a school that turns out to be too demanding (that is, failure two years in a row), the child usually reenrolls in a lower-level school.

There are three main types of schools: *Hauptschule, Realschule,* and *Gymnasium.*[2] Each of these schools leads to the attainment of a specific school-leaving certificate. Compulsory full-time education generally ends after grade ten or, for students in the *Hauptschule,* after grade nine.

The *Hauptschule* typically provides students with a standard level of general education and prepares them for vocational training. It is generally attended by students whose performance in primary school was lower than average; it is also the school with the highest proportion of migrant children. Pupils with a school-leaving certificate from the *Hauptschule* may go into vocational training or decide to continue in upper secondary school. However, the *Hauptschule* also produces the highest proportion of students without any school-leaving certificate at all, as well as the highest proportion of young people unable to find either vocational training or employment.

The *Realschule* provides a more extensive general education. It offers a larger range of subjects as well as some electives beginning in grade seven or eight. *Realschule* students typically performed at an average level in primary school. A school leaving certificate from the *Realschule* qualifies students for vocational training or higher-level vocational schools but also—for those with grades that are somewhat above average—for transfer to a *Gymnasium.*

The *Gymnasium* provides the academic track and covers grades five–thirteen. Students have choices within a wider, and more demanding, range of subjects than in the other types of schools, and they learn at least two foreign languages. It is possible to leave the *Gymnasium* after grade ten with a school-leaving certificate equal to a *Realschule* certificate.

General upper secondary education can be completed with a certificate after either twelve or thirteen years. A school-leaving certificate can be obtained from a *Gymnasium* or *Fachoberschule* after grade twelve and provides access to higher education studies at *Fachhochschulen* (universities of applied sciences offering a range of short and applied degree programs); a school-leaving certificate after grade thirteen, called the *Abitur,* provides access to universities. Students are required to pass a final examination to obtain this certificate.

Comprehensive Schools

During the West German reform period from the mid-1960s to the mid-1970s, a number of integrated comprehensive schools were established in those states governed by the Social Democratic Party. Their purpose was to teach children of mixed achievement levels together during lower secondary school and differentiate within (rather than between) schools through basic and advanced courses. In contrast to the traditional schools, most integrated comprehensive schools were "day" schools; instruction did not end around 1:00 or 2:00 p.m. as it did in most schools but, rather, continued well into the afternoon and included supervision of homework by teachers. Although some comprehensive schools of this type have continued, in general the model has had difficulty surviving.

Vocational Education and Training

Finally, there are a number of schools providing full-time vocational education at the upper secondary level. Entrance requirements and the duration of schooling vary according to the intended career specialization, which includes a wide range of options—for example, technology, business and administration, nutrition and domestic science, agriculture, social work, design, and seafaring. The programs typically offer both general and specialized courses. Students completing full-time vocational schools receive a state certificate.

Part-time vocational education takes place at the *Berufsschule*. Students who choose this type of vocational training are required to attend school, along with in-company training, until age eighteen. This "dual system," of vocational education at the *Berufsschule* and vocational training in a company, covers about 350 recognized occupations. Generally, students attend school one day a week, or in blocks of several weeks, and receive in-company practical training four days a week, or in blocks of several weeks alternating with schooling. About two-thirds of all young people in Germany receive their training in this system. In 2000 there were almost 2.7 million trainees in the dual training system.

Although states are generally responsible for education, the federal government does play a direct role in vocational education through the Federal Institute for Vocational Training, which brings together representatives of employers, trade unions, the federal government, and the state governments to determine training regulations for in-company training and coordinate these with the curriculum taught at vocational schools (EURYBASE, 2001; Sekretariat, Ständige Konferenz der Kultusminister der Länder in der Bundesrepublik Deutschland, 1997). As a percentage of all young people leaving school in 2000, 7.4 percent left without any certificate; 23.2 percent, with a certificate from the *Hauptschule*; 39.3 percent, with a certificate from the *Realschule*; 7.7 percent, with a certificate for access into *Fachhochschule* (successful completion of twelve years of schooling); and 22.4 percent, with a certificate for access to a university (completion of grade thirteen in a *Gymnasium*).

KEY POLICY ISSUES

A Second Educational Catastrophe?

The performance of German students on three international comparative studies—Program for International Student Assessment (PISA), Third International Mathematics and Science Study (TIMSS), and Progress in Reading Literacy (PIRLS)—has created the perception of a "second educational catastrophe," reminiscent of the reaction to the concerns about education after the launch of Sputnik in the 1950s.[3] With the exception of reading literacy in primary schools, the test results for German pupils were considerably lower than expected: In most cases, Germany was ranked in the middle or lower end of the scale. One of PISA's most dramatic results was that German students' test-score rankings were more strongly influenced by the family's socioeconomic status (SES) than were those in almost any of the other participating countries (Deutsches PISA-Konsortium, 2001). It appears, therefore, that German schools are not successful in counterbalancing the effects of low SES and might even increase the achievement gap between low and high SES students.

The results of the international comparisons, which were highly publicized, have influenced the German public's perception of its schools. In 2002 the federal government's minister of education and research published "The Future of Education," which states that Germany's goal is to score high on the PISA comparisons within ten years. Proposed initiatives include creating 10,000 new full-day schools by the year 2007; establishing national standards, a national evaluation agency, and a national reporting system; and starting a program administered jointly by the federal government and by states to eliminate the most serious weaknesses of German students in reading and writing, to support students with learning problems, and, in general, to increase the individualization of instruction (Bundesministerium für Bildung und Forschung, 2002).

The states responded by rejecting any interference by the federal government in their internal affairs, with the exception of the funding promised to build new schools, which—not surprisingly—they welcomed. The states, however, through the KMK (2002), issued their own action statement (on the same day as the release of the federal plan), which generally was quite consistent with that plan. In addition, most relevant societal groups (e.g., trade unions, parents' associations, employers, and political parties) also issued reform proposals recommending how to respond to the international test-score rankings. Most of the proposals were reminiscent of those made forty years earlier after the launch of Sputnik.

National Standards and Evaluation

The German education system does not have a highly developed culture of evaluation, although there are procedures for state supervision of classroom teaching, curricula, textbooks, and examinations. The PISA results have led to attempts to introduce national standards and performance indicators. Although there is little chance that national standardization will occur in the context of Germany's decentralized education system, the KMK has supported state initiatives to develop comparative measures for assessing the quality of the system as a whole and the quality of individual schools. The procedures developed so far vary from state to state but generally include standardized school performance tests at the state level and comparisons of test results across states in specific subjects.

Teacher Training and Status

Teacher training consists of two phases. Students first take a three- or four-year program in a higher education institution or teacher-training college, which leads to a state examination rather than to an academic degree. On passing the examination, students spend a one-and-a-half-year period primarily in practical training at a school, with an experienced teacher as a mentor, and then take a second state examination. Teaching degrees are differentiated according to the level of schooling: primary, lower secondary, and upper secondary, with primary school teachers having somewhat lower academic qualifications than teachers in secondary schools. Newly qualified teachers are then eligible to apply for permanent employment in public schools; not all of these teachers are able to obtain teaching positions because of the declining student population in the past ten years.

In the former West Germany, about 80 percent of all teachers in public schools are civil servants who are tenured for life and can be dismissed only under extraordinary circumstances. In the former East Germany, most teachers are not civil servants; rather, they are salaried employees in the public service. With the collapse of the former regime in East Germany, the economy and public administration also collapsed and the states were almost bankrupt. Although West Germany provided large amounts of funding for restructuring and renewal, productivity continues to be lower in East Germany. In an attempt to compensate for low productivity, the working week in East Germany remains at forty hours (in comparison to 38.5 hours in West Germany), and salaries are about 90–93 percent of those in West Germany. Following a 1993 agreement with the KMK, however, most East German states established regulations under which teachers can obtain civil service status and be integrated into West Germany's salary structure.

Teachers traditionally have enjoyed a relatively high level of social prestige in Germany, with incomes and pensions well above average. That advantage still exists for income and pensions, although public service positions have received lower salary increases during the past ten years than have other professions. Social prestige, however, has declined: Teachers recently have endured criticism as a class for being lazy, overprivileged, and excessively eager for early retirement. Teachers, on the other hand, complain about what they perceive as a lack of parental care that results in behavioral problems among students. They also are concerned about responding to the needs of the high proportion of immigrant children who have limited knowledge of German and attend schools that do not have the funding, time, or expertise needed to integrate them into the school program or to offer remedial instruction.

Because of budget reductions, teachers have also experienced an increase in workload—more class periods and higher student–teacher ratios. At the same time as resources for support services have declined, more demands are being placed on schools to provide supervision and services that previously were not their responsibility; these include, for example, extra hours for supervision during opening hours, language instruction for immigrant children, counseling, and extracurricular activities. Because of the additional requirements, the declining prestige of the teaching profession, and the restricted access to public school employment, teaching has become a less attractive choice for young people entering higher education.

Applying Business Models to School Management

As resources decline and responsibilities increase, the perception also increases that schools need professional management in order to function efficiently. In recent years, a number of pilot projects have been designed to strengthen school management by giving schools a budget and more autonomy. Former school heads have become school "managers," and their "competencies" are defined. In addition, schools face expectations to develop individual profiles, to formulate "vision" and "mission" statements, and to be accountable for them to the authorities and to parents. The emphasis on management, also introduced into higher education, is expected to remedy a wide variety of problems. It is uncertain, however, whether "professional" management practices, based on business models, are effective when generalized to educational settings.

Retention in Grade

Debates have focused on whether to "weed out" low-achieving students by retaining them in grade or to support and promote them. The PISA results show that, among all Organization for Economic Cooperation and Development countries, Germany has the highest proportion of students taught at a grade level too low for their age. The concern is that retention in grade does not lead to better performance. Indeed, it is difficult for students to integrate into a class of students younger than they are because the instructional content is inappropriate for their age and they tend to become bored. The result is that these students have high absentee rates and fall further behind academically.

Future policy decisions about how to address the problem of grade retention can be expected to differ among states. The traditional German solution would be for the more conservatively governed states in the south of Germany to opt for greater selection and weeding out of low-achieving students as early as possible while at the same time providing these students with special schools or special tracks and additional support—thereby creating more homogeneous learning groups. The more liberally governed German states will opt for integration and attempt to keep low-achieving students in regular classes and give them special support in these classes.

Equal Opportunity

Apart from attempts to integrate students of diverse nationalities into the German school system, equal opportunity has not been high on the agenda of German school policy for quite some time. Although equal opportunity was an issue in the 1960s and 1970s, political decision makers generally consider it no longer a problem because of the increasing participation of girls in higher levels of education, the availability of student financial assistance, and the existence of legislation designed to remedy injustices.

There has been increased participation of the second-generation children of Turkish migrant workers in upper secondary schools and higher education, but there are more recent groups of migrant workers and refugees from various war zones whose children need additional educational and social support. Typically, these children enroll in the *Hauptschule* for their lower secondary education; in certain sections of large cities, it is not unusual for primary schools and *Hauptschulen* to have between twenty and thirty nationalities represented in their student population.

Policies vary from state to state about the appropriate level of support. The main policy issue is whether children of migrant workers and refugees need additional German language instruction to make integration easier or whether they should also receive instruction in their national language in order to prevent them from losing their cultural identity. The general concern, however, is that these students clearly will be at a disadvantage in the German school system if they are not able to speak German fluently.

In recent years, the problem of xenophobia and violence among students has become a major policy issue. To address this problem, schools use specialists—psychologists, mediators, and actors—to work with students to make them aware of unacceptable behavior, discuss prejudices, or act out conflicts in order to learn how to resolve them peacefully.

Internationalization

Many German schools are quite "international," in terms of both the composition of their student population and their cooperative programs with other countries. In some schools, a significant proportion of the students are children of immigrants, refugees, or migrant workers. In addition, there are a number of programs designed to encourage international cooperation by introducing a European dimension into the education program and encouraging the exchange of teachers and students.

Most German schools have one or more international programs: city partnerships, a wide variety of state-level programs, bilingual teaching in regions close to a border, national exchange programs with partner schools all over the world, and the COMENIUS Program to support European cooperation and exchange among schools. Foreign language learning is compulsory in all schools, beginning at the lower secondary level. English is typically the first foreign language students learn, followed by French and often Spanish and Italian. Increasingly, Eastern European languages (mainly Polish and Czech) are part of the curriculum, and the traditionally humanist *Gymnasium* often requires Latin. The general European policy to which Germany has agreed is that all students should learn at least two foreign languages. In addition, the support programs of the European Union in the field of education also promote the learning of languages (in Germany, mainly Danish and Dutch) that are less widely taught.

Two policy issues with respect to internationalization have recently become quite visible. First, there is greater attention to foreign language teaching in primary schools. Second, the international comparative studies have contributed to an increased awareness of the performance of German schools. These comparisons have reduced the public's traditional complacency about the rather bureaucratic German school system and have served as a reminder of the potential benefits of reassessing the status quo; they can be expected to continue to influence education reform.

Educational Technology

The use of technology as a teaching aid, as well as a subject of teaching, is an important policy issue in Germany. In 1995 the federal minister responsible for education, science, and research initiated a program to get "schools online" in cooperation with German Telekom. Additional German companies, including textbook-publishing companies, were also encouraged to join the initiative and contribute to a pilot program that invited schools to apply for computers, software, and online access.

Up to 10,000 schools had the opportunity to access the German Science and Research Net, and teachers received in-service training in the use of instructional software and databases. Indeed, it often turned out that teachers required more training in the use of computers than did their students. Funding for the technology initiative was based on the submission of proposals, which were invited in four areas: school access to computers and the World Wide Web; pilot projects for the development of instructional materials; teacher training; and infrastructure projects to improve regional, state, and interstate communication capabilities.

The initiative continues to make a significant contribution to the modernization of the German school system, and almost every German state now has developed its own initiatives in this area. It is also the first time in many years that companies have become involved in the school system, which generally enjoys strict protection from outside influence ("Schools Online," 1996).[4]

CONCLUSION

The German public school system is decentralized yet, at the same time, rather bureaucratic and hierarchical. Each of the sixteen German states is responsible for its own school system, and that responsibility is closely guarded against interference by the federal government. Although there are coordinating bodies (in particular the KMK) that make recommendations, each state's education minister determines whether the recommendations will be implemented.

Thus, modernizing the school system and implementing general reforms have always been rather difficult. Typically, reforms are implemented by launching pilot projects in certain schools, providing additional funding, and analyzing the results. Even when a new practice appears to be effective, however, it will not be widely applied without each state's commitment to implement the practice and to provide the necessary funding.

The disappointing results of the international comparative studies have led to a gradual opening up of the German school system and an increased acceptance of reform on the part of political decision makers—although the early selection and differentiation of students by achievement, while often criticized, continues to be a central feature of the school system. It is important, however, that Germany was willing to permit international comparisons, which, in turn, triggered interstate comparisons. As the German public school system has not yet developed a culture of external quality review and evaluation, international comparisons are often considered risky and potentially embarrassing. The increasing willingness to evaluate the education system, however, might prove to be an important step in reforming and modernizing what has become a chronically underfunded system.

Germany has always been quite proud of its public school system, which has had a reputation of functioning well and providing a good education for many students. Over the years, however, problems accumulated, resources declined, and schools were blamed for broader societal problems at the same time that they were expected to take on additional responsibilities. Moreover, as German states continue to restrict the number of new teachers entering the system, the average age of teachers has increased. Because it is unlikely that funding levels will increase, the hope is that the new emphasis on management and on school autonomy will help alleviate inertia and introduce more competition among schools and, therefore, more willingness to implement changes. It remains to be seen, however, whether the introduction of management concepts is the appropriate remedial measure to address the problems of the education system.

NOTES

1. "Sputnik shock" describes the perceived technological gap after the Soviet Union launched Sputnik in 1957. "The German Economic Miracle" (1958–61) refers to the rise of the West German economy during the administration of Chancellor Konrad Adenauer, after Germany became a member of the World Trade Organization. "The German educational catastrophe" is the term used by Picht in his book to describe what he concluded was a rather backward education system, which did not provide equal opportunities to children from lower socioeconomic status groups.

2. A fourth type of school, the *Fachoberschule,* is a vocationally oriented school between *Realschule* and *Gymnasium*; it ends after grade twelve.

3. PISA tested fifteen-year-old students in several subject matter areas; TIMSS tested secondary school students in mathematics and science; and PIRLS tested nine-year-olds.

4. The information contained in this section is based on a written examination thesis accessed through the Internet (www.chrischi.de/examen.htm).

REFERENCES CITED

Bundesministerium für Bildung und Forschung [Federal Ministry for Education and Research]. (2002, June 25). Press communication. Berlin: Federal Ministry for Education and Research.

Deutscher Bildungsrat [German Council of Education]. (1970). *Strukturplan für das Bildungswesen. Empfehlungen der Bildungskommission* [Structural plan for the system of education. Recommendations of the Education Commission]. Bonn: Bundesdruckerei.

Deutsches PISA-Konsortium [German PISA Consortium] (Ed.). (2001). *PISA 2000: Basiskompetenzen von Schülerinnen und Schülern im internationalen Vergleich* [International comparison of basic competencies of students]. Opladen: Leske und Budrich.

EURYBASE. (2001). *The education system in Germany (2000/01)*. Available at www.eurydice.org/Eurybase/application/frameset.asp?country=DE& language=EN (accessed March 29, 2002).

Picht, G. (1964). *Die deutsche Bildungskatastrophe* [*The German educational catastrophe*]. Freiburg: Olten.

Schulen ans Netz? [Schools online?]. (1996). Available at www.chrischi.de/ examen.htm (accessed October 26, 2003). English version available at http://en.schulen-ans-netz.de.

Sekretariat, Ständige Konferenz der Kultusminister der Länder in der Bundesrepublik Deutschland (KMK) [Secretariat of the Standing Conference of the Ministers of Culture and Education of the German States]. (1997). *Das Bildungswesen in der Bundesrepublik Deutschland. Darstellung der Kompetenzen, Strukturen, und Bildungspolitischen Entwicklungen für den Informationsaustausch in der Europäischen Union* [The system of education in the Federal Republic of Germany. Account of competencies, structures, and developments in education policy for the exchange of information in the European Union]. Bonn: KMK Sekretariat.

Ständige Konferenz der Kultusminister der Länder in der Bundesrepublik Deutschland (KMK) [Standing Conference of the Ministers of Culture and Education of the German States]. (2002, June 25). Press communication. Bonn: KMK Sekretariat.

II

LETTING GO

6

France: Diverse Populations, Centralized Administration

Gérard Bonnet

> Usually those who rule over children forgive them nothing while they forgive themselves everything.
>
> —François Fénelon (1651–1715)

In France the issue of whether or not to decentralize the education system affects its administration, staffing, and pedagogy. The centralized system, prevalent since the nineteenth century, is no longer able to regulate the fundamental educational changes that France, like most industrialized countries, has had to face over the past few decades. The massive expansion of the number and diversity of pupils attending school from ages five to sixteen, and in fact of many from ages three to eighteen and over, has had untold consequences for the way the system works. The style of teaching, and consequently of teacher training, which was satisfactory when applied to relatively limited numbers of children from essentially middle-class backgrounds, is clearly no longer in keeping with the demands of the large, heterogeneous population currently being educated. Centralized teaching of a subject can be organized easily; it is more difficult to organize the teaching of individual pupils with very different needs. This requires a flexible set of pedagogical and management rules that can easily adapt to local specificity. The central government has started to make the necessary statutory changes in earnest, but this process will be successful only if local stakeholders are prepared to use this newfound freedom to change their professional practices. This will require new intellectual approaches to education, which not everyone has been trained to develop.

BACKGROUND

In France the state is responsible for providing education, and it establishes most of the rules and regulations.[1] The public sector is by far the largest education provider, but there is also a semiprivate sector, mostly denomination (Roman Catholic), which is practically all state funded. It has to follow the national curriculum, and most of its teachers are paid by the central government (many are, in fact, public sector teachers). For all intents and purposes, this semiprivate sector works very much like the public sector except that schools charge fees (but very affordable) and can select their pupils. There is also a very small private sector in the truest sense of the word (mostly nondenominational), where registration fees are high but where teaching is free from national regulations and no funding comes from the state.

In 2000 the French state provided 60.7 percent of all resources for education (at all levels). This represented 21.6 percent of the national budget. Overall education spending, excluding overseas territories, was 98.2 billion euros and represented 7.1 percent of the gross domestic product. The average cost of a primary school pupil is 4,200 euros per annum, and a lower secondary school pupil costs 6,700 euros; an upper secondary school pupil (general stream) costs 8,000 euros, and a university student costs 6,500 euros.

The school system consists of three levels: primary schools (ages five/six to ten/eleven), lower secondary schools or *collèges* (ages eleven to fifteen/sixteen), and upper secondary schools or *lycées* (ages fifteen/sixteen to seventeen/eighteen+). Schooling is compulsory from age six to sixteen. The end of compulsory education at sixteen is difficult for some pupils because it does not correspond with the end of *collège* and they have to attend a *lycée* at least until they are sixteen. However, more pupils attend school beyond the compulsory age than they did thirty years ago. A distinguishing feature of the French school system is that early education (i.e., preprimary) is highly developed, with practically all children starting preschool at age three, before moving on to primary education at age six.

To understand better the considerations shaping primary and secondary education, it is useful to have some idea of what exists beyond. Higher education consists of two separate systems: the usual public sector university stream, which is accessible by right to anyone in possession of the upper secondary school graduation certificate (*baccalauréat*), and the typically French parallel stream of *grandes écoles* or specific higher education institutions. Some of the higher education institutions belong to the public sector, whereas others belong to the private sector and are highly selective and usually fee based. They take on only students who have passed a competitive examination (with a limited number of places each year, which students prepare for by taking special one- to two-year courses, available in selected *lycées*).

The French elite regards the selective system of the *grandes écoles* as preferable to a university education, with the exception of legal and medical education, which is available only in universities. Although the number of students from less-privileged backgrounds in the *grandes écoles* has increased over the years, it is nonetheless true that most of the students are members of the French elite. Thus, the French establishment (military, administrative, and political for the public sector; banking and business administration for the private sector) comprises the alumni of the *grandes écoles,* rather than those of the universities. A particularly shocking and dangerous situation exists regarding the "inbreeding" of national politicians and senior civil servants, most of whom studied at the École Nationale d'Administration and who, in the course of their careers, move freely between political and civil service jobs. Similarly, senior managers trained at the same *grande école* run whole sectors of the French economy or administration. This is not conducive to daring changes and reforms.

ORGANIZATION: TOWARD
A MORE DECENTRALIZED SYSTEM

Because the French education system has been organized centrally for over a century, the institutional role of regions and schools has been, and still is, less fundamental than in some other countries. This explains why the devolution of power to regional and local levels is one of the main organizational concerns of administrative reform in education. School development is largely dominated by national decisions; one of the most important ones has been to try to devolve administrative (as opposed to political) responsibility from the national ministry to regional and school administration. Additional changes will have to be made to make schools more autonomous and responsive to a changing environment. Real power remains with central government, with local political bodies enjoying only partial responsibilities. For example, the central government retains overall responsibility for teaching staff and all pedagogical aspects of education, even if some of it is devolved to the lower administrative units. The exception is vocational training, as this is shared with regional government. Public sector higher education (universities and public sector *grandes écoles*), on the other hand, is the responsibility of central government.

Within this context, one of the main objectives of administrative reform in recent years has been the devolution of more responsibility from the ministry to the regions (*académies*). There are thirty *académies* in all, including overseas territories. Although it is clearly understood that education in France will remain "national," it has also become apparent that more initiative has to be entrusted to the *académies*. The education minister appoints the head of each *académie,* usually a senior academic, to serve as the ministerial representative in each region. In order to achieve more responsibility at the regional level, a recent policy initiative has been the implementation of a contract between each *académie* and the ministry, whereby the regional level is responsible for the priorities and specificity of its own education policy, within the national education framework laid down by the ministry. In return, the ministry provides additional resources (either staff or funds) to allow the *académie* to implement the mutually agreed-on priorities. Schools should benefit from wider devolution as well, but this has proved more difficult to achieve because schools in France are traditionally very weak from an institutional point of view, compared with those in the Anglo-American model.

First, there is a fundamental legal difference between primary schools, which are not independent entities from a legal point of view, and secondary schools, which are proper legal entities in their own right. Primary schools do not have a governing board; nor do they have a regular head. Instead, one of the teachers acts as coordinator for the day-to-day running of the school, and the person legally responsible for the school is the local primary inspector, who is the head of all primary schools in a given area.

All lower secondary schools and upper secondary schools have a governing board and a head. Head teachers are recruited among teachers through an examination. They undergo a specific training period. Although they are in administrative and pedagogical charge of the school, they have no control over the appointment of teachers, little control over teachers' work other than setting timetables, and little control over resources. Attempts are being made to give head teachers more autonomy in teacher appointments under specific circumstances, as well as more freedom in the use of resources (Joutard & Thélot, 1999).

From a pedagogical point of view, France is also moving toward more local autonomy. Although one of the main features of instruction is the predominance of a national curriculum for all school levels, some amount of local adaptation is encouraged. The curriculum is couched in terms of objectives rather than in terms of content, which makes it possible to entrust more freedom to teachers in what they teach. Head teachers are increasingly encouraged to exercise some flexibility with respect to time allocation for certain subjects and to emphasize some areas of the curriculum to suit their school development plan, all within national guidelines. The provisions made in the 1989 Education Reform Act for the compulsory introduction of such school development plans are a clear move to integrate local circumstances and initiatives into the national framework. However, questions arise about the real impact of such plans on schools, for in actuality they are often no more than empty shells drawn up by schools to comply with the rules, rather than a real instrument of school policy.

Teachers, for their part, retain the enormous freedom they have always enjoyed in the way they implement the curriculum. It is obvious, however, that the national curriculum and, beyond, the national examinations are of paramount importance for what happens in the classroom: Teachers teach to the examinations.

By and large, the devolution of power from the ministry toward regional and school administration remains imperfect. It exists on paper; all the rules and regulations to implement it have been published. Yet in practice less has happened than was aimed for. This is partly related to political difficulties: French trade unions are very suspicious of such moves, which they see as a threat to the unity of the education system and its national character; they also realize that they will not be so influential at the local level. And this is largely because of the attitude of most teachers and local administrators, whose professional practices were molded by and for a different system.

THE EVALUATION AND MONITORING OF EDUCATION

Educational evaluation comes under many guises. The more traditional ones, such as pupil assessment for the purpose of selection or examinations, naturally are present in the French system. In addition, policy makers at the ministerial level have evolved a theoretical framework for evaluation that takes into account the need for teachers and administrators to make changes in the way they work. Yet this approach, intellectually promising in theory, has limits when the educators do not respond to, or ignore, the tools that they possess to promote change. The sensitive question, therefore, is to what extent—given the specific context of the French education system, where teachers and administrators tend to work for the system rather than for the pupils—sophisticated evaluation procedures can be relied on to bring about the voluntary changes needed to make instruction more relevant to the needs of pupils (Bonnet, 1996a).

It is worrisome, for instance, that teachers do not always feel that they are responsible for pupils' results or that they are not held responsible for them. It is a major flaw of the system that a proportion of teachers, particularly among the older ones, do not see evaluation as a way to improve their teaching. Instead, they intuitively develop their own idea of a "norm" that must be attained by pupils rather than seeing evaluation as a tool to promote change.

Assessment by Teachers in the Classroom

As in many countries, French teachers assess their own pupils informally on a regular basis through oral and written exercises in the classroom or through homework. Individual teachers determine the content and frequency of assessments. Pupil performance is assessed with reference to a norm, and pupils are then given a score. Although explicit criteria sometimes determine the scores, in most cases pupils must complete a complex exercise that combines a large number of skills, none of which is considered separately. As in the case of any assessment, a portion of the variance in student scores is associated with socioeconomic status and teachers' expectations. The design of the assessments, especially the use of norms, tends to increase the dispersion of scores, which raises an important equity issue because the assessments are used for selection purposes to decide on promotion to higher grades and to advise on the most suitable courses of studies for students to take. Marking, which is generally used at all levels, is also a personal affair, even though the tendency in France (where the marking scheme is normally 0 to 20 in secondary schools) is to award marks in the medium region rather than to use extremes; for example, a very good piece of work will rarely be rated 18 or 20 but, instead, will receive 14 or 15. This reflects practice in examination marking. The cutoff point in class work and examinations is 10 out of 20 because educators feel—and this is purely conventional and traditional—that scoring less than 50 percent shows that the expected standard has not been reached.

Examinations

Examinations are another important aspect of curriculum evaluation. The *brevet des collèges* is the first examination that pupils take during their school career. It marks the end of lower secondary school (age fifteen/sixteen). Until recently, however, it was not compulsory to pass to move on to higher secondary education. The examination itself is composed of specific questions in mathematics, French, history, and geography, and other subjects are evaluated through continuous assessment. Although its actual value on the job market as a graduation qualification has become rather slim, the examination has recently been given a new lease on life by strengthening its role in the syllabus and making it compulsory. A standardized test might also become part of the examination in order to monitor standards. In addition, specific examinations exist for pupils of comparable ages in the vocational stream. Two of the more common are *certificat d'aptitude professionnelle* and *brevet d'études professionnelles.*

The *baccalauréat,* or rather one of three types of *baccalauréat—général* (academic), *technologique* (technological), and *professionnel* (vocational)—remains the aim for all pupils because it is both the ultimate graduation certificate and the compulsory passport to higher education, as all *baccalauréat* holders have a right to a place in a university. In 2001 the average success rate for all three types of *baccalauréat* combined was 78.6 percent. Nationally, the proportion of *baccalauréat* holders is 61.9 percent of the age group. It is interesting to note that this relatively high proportion of *baccalauréat* holders is in part caused by the introduction of the vocational *baccalauréat* in 1987. It is clear that this new type of *baccalauréat,* meant for less academically gifted pupils, has opened up access to this level of qualification and therefore to university education for increased numbers of young people who would otherwise have left school earlier. Needless to say, these pupils are mostly from less-privileged backgrounds.

In the late 1980s the education minister announced that it was official government policy to reach, by the year 2000, the target that 80 percent of a generation would attain *baccalauréat* level. This target is often misunderstood both at home and abroad to mean 80 percent of a generation would be *baccalauréat* graduates. This is clearly not so. In broad terms, the policy means that 80 percent of a generation should be enrolled in the last form of secondary education. Over the past twenty years, this rate has risen from 34 percent in 1980 to 55.5 percent in 1990 and to just below 70 percent for the past few years. There are no indications that the 80 percent target will be achieved in the near future. Educators generally believe that 70 percent is as high as one can get, given the present educational and social context.

The question of reforming the *baccalauréat* crops up periodically. The preparation for the *baccalauréat* is nerve-racking and time-consuming for both the candidates and the administration. For the former, it means spending the whole last year in upper secondary school learning the topics included in the examination curriculum in upward of six or seven subjects, mastering the formal and rhetorical tools that must be used in the papers, and more generally making sure they will deliver what is expected of them in the way that it is expected of them. For the latter, it means conducting a quasi-military campaign to ensure that everything is ready on time: for example, printing the examination questions and sending the right number to each school where the examination is held, having enough teachers on hand to mark the papers externally, and arranging for examiners. Most experts agree that organizing this examination each year is both incredibly costly and extremely tedious. Yet both educators and parents are extremely keen on retaining the examination as it stands. One of the suggestions for reforming the examination is to inject a fair dose of continuous assessment. Some already exists, but teachers could resist any more (Bonnet, 1999).

All these examinations are national, in contrast to the case in many other countries where they are set and sometimes marked in each school. However, although the framework applies nationally, each region or group of regions sets the actual questions, and marking is conducted externally by teachers from other schools. For the *baccalauréat*, dates and times for the various examinations are also national, so that all candidates are working at the same time on the same exams but not necessarily on the same questions. National examinations generally contain a series of exercises in each subject that involve the application of numerous skills. The mark given reflects global success in the paper. Doubts persist as to the consistency of the marking, however, despite efforts to guarantee the reliability of results.

National Testing

Since the 1989 Education Reform Act, evaluation, and particularly pupil assessment through standardized testing, has become a priority for the education system. Pupil evaluation currently has two purposes. Various countries are familiar with the first: using assessment as a monitoring device and measuring performance over time. The second is specific to France: using diagnostic assessment as a teaching tool for quality development.

First, measuring pupils' achievements provides data for policy makers and informs the public debate on education. Basically, representative samples of pupils are tested at key stages in some or all subjects taught. So far, the most elaborate of such sample testing is conducted on a regular basis every few years at the end of lower secondary school for all the subjects taught there. Following recent policy decisions, assessments of this type will be extended to other levels from primary to lower secondary schools, and additional assessments will deal specifically with foreign languages at various levels. This sample-based pupil-assessment procedure is devised both to provide snapshot information on achievement at a specific time and to make comparisons over time.

Second, the French assessment system encourages educational change and promotes the dissemination of a culture of evaluation among stakeholders throughout the system. This objective is based on the belief that such stakeholders, among whom teachers are prominent, will improve their professional practices only if they are shown the consequences of their actions (Thélot, 1993). Standardized tests enable teachers to assess the strengths and weaknesses of their pupils. Since 1989 these have taken place at the beginning of each academic year for all pupils, ages seven/eight to ten/eleven, in French and mathematics. A similar survey for pupils, age sixteen, had been given since 1992 in all subjects taught in upper secondary schools, but it was recently discontinued because it proved not to be sufficiently used by teachers. Testing is intended primarily for diagnostic use by teachers and parents within the school. However, a representative sample of the test for each level is analyzed centrally by the Education Ministry to obtain a statistically valid national picture of pupil achievement for that year. It must be emphasized that this does not allow for time comparisons between years to be made because the tests might vary from year to year in keeping with changes in the curriculum (Bonnet, 1997).

France participates in the main international surveys of pupil achievement: the Program for International Student Assessment (PISA), run by the Organization for Economic Cooperation and Development (OECD); the Progress in International Reading Literacy Study (PIRLS), organized by the International Association for Educational Achievement (IEA); and the IEA's original Third International Mathematics and Science Survey (TIMSS)—although France is not involved in TIMSS Repeat. When the TIMSS results were reported, it appeared that French pupils were doing well, especially in mathematics, but fared rather poorly in science. The recently published PISA results broadly confirm previous findings: Though France has average results in reading and science literacy, mathematics scores are above average. A broadly similar picture for reading at primary school has emerged from PIRLS. It is too early to say what impact the present international studies will have on the French education system. However, judging by experience, it might be very little.

School Monitoring

Over the past decade, the Education Ministry has set up a national scheme of indicators for schools. Head teachers use this scheme of indicators for management and monitoring purposes and to facilitate discussions among the different levels of educational responsibility (ministry, regions, schools) using shared data. The scheme first covered secondary schools and later encompassed primary education.

Twenty-one standard indicators are available to all secondary schools. Their values, calculated for the regional and national levels, allow the schools to have an accurate description of their mode of functioning and to compare themselves with similar schools. They are meant to be used by schools to revise their policies where appropriate to improve results. The scheme also enables schools to construct specific indicators to suit their own needs and, in particular, to devise and monitor their school development plan.

As part of this scheme, three performance indicators are calculated nationally each year, based on *baccalauréat* results, to estimate the value of upper secondary schools. This is done by comparing the result for each with that which could be expected, taking into account the school's characteristics and the pupils' socioeconomic background. That value, in turn, can be compared with the values obtained by similar schools at regional and national levels. This comparison provides useful information on key issues of school policy, such as student selection, while giving an idea of the value added, a

measure that is less crude than that derived from raw examination results. These indicators are available each year in print and on the Internet. A similar system of indicators exists for primary education. The
objective is to facilitate a working relationship between primary
schools and lower secondary schools within the same district, to foster smoother continuity between the two educational levels.

Unfortunately, with the exception of the three performance indicators based on *baccalauréat* results, there has been limited success
with the monitoring indicators, despite the fact that they could be useful tools for school policy. Head teachers are not trained to use them
and are overburdened by other duties, and the vast majority of teachers find them totally alien to their professional culture and consequently view them with deep suspicion. Moreover, as two separate national reports pointed out recently, French policy makers at all levels
of the system also make only limited use of the evaluation findings.

TEACHERS: STATUS, TRAINING, AND RECRUITMENT

In France, the legal status of teachers, their recruitment, and their initial training are closely interwoven. This is not the ideal situation, particularly as far as the secondary school sector is concerned. There is a
contradiction between recruitment, which is based on the ability to
teach a subject, and training, which places more emphasis on teaching methods. The dissonance between the two creates confusion in
the perception that teachers have of their profession. The conception
of teaching, and its necessary evolution, is at the core of the 1989
teacher training reform, which took place in the context of an educational environment that is growing increasingly heterogeneous and
which needs to remain as equitable as possible.

Teacher Status

Because the state oversees everything involved with education,
both teaching and nonteaching education personnel are normally
part of the civil service. The concept of civil service in France is very
different from and a lot more all-encompassing than, say, that in En-

gland or the United States. Education personnel belong to the civil service in the same way that, for instance, staff of the Armed Forces or of government departments at home or abroad belong. Its main characteristic is life employment. The very idea that a public servant, however low or high ranking, could be made redundant and given the "golden handshake" is both alien and abhorrent to French society. Qualified teachers enjoy total job security because they have full tenure. This security applies also to most of the teachers working for the state-funded private sector. However, not everyone who works in the public service enjoys full civil service status, for the system also employs part-time or full-time auxiliary staff. In 1999–2000, 774,268 teaching staff and 234,369 nonteaching staff on the state payroll were full civil servants; 35,293 and 60,375, respectively, were not (including higher education).

It may happen, whether for financial reasons or because of the lack of candidates, that not enough teachers are recruited at the national level using the official procedure. Therefore, regional administrators might have to hire people outside of the civil service as temporary teachers. In order to qualify for such a job, applicants must hold at least a first university degree in the subject they will teach. They are on a contract for as long as they are needed, and in some cases, they stay on for years. When it is felt nationally that there are too many temporary teachers on contract who have been employed for too long in this capacity, steps are taken to incorporate them into the civil service. This transfer either is accomplished through specific recruitment examinations or might be based simply on the number of years the temporary teachers have been employed. Thus, several thousand teachers are working in French schools without ever being trained properly.

Teachers' Pay and Promotion

Most primary and secondary teachers are on the same pay scale. The two ends of the scale are represented by primary teachers recruited before 1990 who, without a university degree, earn less and the 11.5 percent of secondary school teachers (*agrégés*) who hold higher academic qualifications and earn more. On average, a junior primary or secondary school teacher earns about 22,800 euros; after fifteen years, the salary increases to 30,300 euros. An older teacher earns 44,000 euros, whereas *agrégés* might make as much as 53,000 euros.

Seniority generally determines promotion, even though the system provides for some amount of promotion by merit. Typically, beginning teachers receive a mark, or designation, based mostly on national calculations and on their rank in the competitive examination. They then move automatically to the next increment on the national scale every few years. Normally, the time they spend on each point of the scale is calculated nationally and applies to all teachers. However, following a successful visit by an inspector, a teacher's mark might increase by more than the national norm, resulting in more rapid promotion to the next point on the scale. In practice, most teachers move along the scale at the slow rate, while fewer, "better" teachers progress at a faster pace. In addition, there is the possibility for 10–15 percent of the workforce to move to a higher pay scale, which will take them beyond the salary normally given to the most senior teachers. This opportunity is given to the "best" teachers, as selected by inspectors, to give an extra financial benefit to a career otherwise bound by civil service pay scales.

Teachers' Terms of Employment

Primary and secondary school teachers experience different working conditions. Depending on the level at which they were recruited, secondary school teachers teach either fifteen or eighteen hours a week. Normally, they teach only one subject (two in vocational schools). When not teaching, they are not required to be present on school premises except to attend statutory staff meetings and for meetings with parents. They may perform whatever other work is necessary to their teaching (preparation, research, marking, etc.) away from school. They are under no statutory obligation to get involved in out-of-school activities, such as sports, or even in nonteaching activities within the school, such as supervising school meals or even enforcing discipline outside the classroom (specific nonteaching staff exist for this purpose).

According to a recent study, secondary school teachers work on average almost forty hours per week. That average includes teaching, class preparation, grading, work with other teachers, meeting with parents, and research; 65 percent of secondary school teachers' weekly working time takes place at home (Ministère de la jeunesse, de l'éducation nationale et de la recherche, 2002).

Preprimary and primary school teachers, on the other hand, are fully responsible for the education and well-being of a whole class of pupils twenty-six hours a week. They teach all the subjects on the syllabus, including sports, although outside specialists sometimes help with subjects such as art, music, and foreign languages. Qualified primary school teachers can teach in either preprimary or primary classes.

At least in secondary schools, the fact that teachers' duties do not extend beyond actual teaching limits school life in France, especially because teachers do not have to remain on the school premises when they are not teaching. The limited amount of parental participation in school activities and school management beyond the statutory requirements—particularly for parents from lower socioeconomic backgrounds—also inhibits the social potential of schools and poses serious equity problems because more affluent parents typically do not hesitate to make their voices heard when they think that their children are not being well served. Furthermore, teachers in a limited, but far from negligible, number of schools must currently deal with acts of violence directed toward school property, pupils, or even themselves.

In some cases, all these features combine to create an impression of schools with obsolete rules and regulations (although they have been updated) where staff members find it difficult to work successfully in situations for which they have not been trained. With over half the current educational staff due to retire by 2015, it may be possible to make the necessary changes with the next generation of teachers. A lot depends on how quickly and successfully proper devolution and decentralization of education take place in practice and in the minds of educational stakeholders. This is as much a question of changing the way of thinking as one of drawing up new rules. As policy makers in Paris are fond of saying, education will only remain national (which is what citizens want) if the regional and local levels efficiently use the freedom they are asked to exercise. This is not part of the cultural heritage of the present generation of teachers.

Teacher Recruitment

The teacher recruitment and training processes described later apply only to those who follow the official pathway to teaching. As noted earlier, temporary teachers are also employed, sometimes for years, without having followed this procedure.

Qualified teachers are recruited into the profession—and into the civil service at the same time—by the state in the same way as all other types of civil servants: by passing specific competitive examinations after completing their training. In any given year, the number of new posts agreed to by the Treasury determines the number of places available for each category of teacher and in each subject. Therefore, all other things being equal, competitive examinations vary in difficulty from year to year according to the number of places available and the number of candidates competing for them.

The competitive examinations are the key to becoming a teacher. There is a basic difference between the competitive examinations for the primary sector and those for the secondary sector. The latter are national competitive examinations, and all candidates in a given subject throughout the country compete on the same examinations for the same places. The former are regional, meaning that each of the education regions is responsible for devising its own examinations according to overall national specifications. They are taken by the candidates in that region who compete among themselves. A candidate may take the examination in several regions. Even though the actual examinations may be of comparable standards, the competition is more difficult in some regions than in others because the number of candidates competing for available positions varies from region to region. In response to this variation, a national examination for primary school teachers has recently been proposed.

Competitive examinations consist of two parts: the first is a set of written questions, and the second is an oral examination with several tests. Only those candidates who achieve a certain, nationally set score in the written examinations are allowed to proceed to the oral examination—hence, the overwhelming importance of performing well on the exclusively academic written examinations.

For the primary sector, the competitive examination includes questions in several subjects taught in primary schools and in the theory and practice of teaching. French language and mathematics are the only compulsory subjects tested in the written part of the examination, along with physical education. Other subjects, such as science, music, art, history, geography, and foreign languages, are optional, and candidates have to choose several of them for the oral. It has recently been decided that foreign languages will become a compulsory component.

At the secondary level, there is a specific competitive examination for each subject. The written part is purely subject based, but one part of the oral examination assesses the communication skills of the candidates, their understanding of the development of their subject, and their knowledge of schools. Successful candidates must then follow a year's training before they are recruited for teaching positions (Bonnet, 1996b).

Teacher Appointment

Once they have obtained their state qualification and been recruited, new teachers are assigned to a specific school. The process is different for primary and secondary school teachers. Because each region organizes its own competitive examination, new primary school teachers are appointed to a school in the region where they took their competitive examination. New secondary school teachers previously were appointed to a school anywhere in the country directly by the Ministry of Education in Paris, for their competitive examination is national rather than regional. In 2000 this process was partly decentralized so that newly recruited secondary school teachers are now allocated to one of the regions by the ministry; the representative of the education minister in the region makes the actual appointment to a specific school. The trade unions, which feared that their bargaining power over appointments would be weaker in the regions than at the national level, opposed this measure at first, but the opposition did not continue after it was observed that the new system helped to facilitate the placement of new teachers across the country.

Decisions about the transfer of teachers to different schools within a region are entirely the responsibility of the representative of the education minister in the region. For teachers wishing to move to another region, the application procedure is dealt with nationally. Significantly, in all but a handful of cases (for example, special education and subjects taught in a foreign language), head teachers are never consulted on appointments and have no power to choose or refuse teachers.

Possible Shortages and Geographic Distribution

France, like most developed countries, has started to face the challenge of recruiting new teachers to cope with the retirement of large numbers of teachers born after World War II. In 2001 nearly 35 percent of secondary school teachers were over fifty. This trend is ongoing: 42 percent of the secondary teaching force will have to be renewed by 2010. The latest official estimates give some idea of the numbers: On average, around 34,000 new teachers are needed each year for the next ten years to make up for retiring staff and changes in education policy (Ministère de l'éducation nationale, 2002).

Unlike some countries, France has little problem with retention. Because they enjoy civil service status, teachers are content to stay within a system that guarantees them a job for life. Although there is generally no real shortage of applicants at the moment, particularly when the world economy is flagging and other jobs are difficult to find, there is no guarantee that this situation will continue. Already, dwindling numbers of degree holders in some subjects, including science, are an indication that serious recruitment problems might be around the corner.

Another source of disquiet for the national authorities is the question of the geographic distribution of teachers, mainly for the secondary school sector. Broadly speaking, everybody wants an appointment to a good school in Paris or on the French Riviera. No one wants to go to a difficult school in the north or the less attractive rural or suburban areas. In theory, teaching resources are meant to be distributed equitably throughout the country, based primarily on pupil numbers. In practice, the organization of recruitment and teachers' individual strategies make this very difficult to manage and contributes in part to the need to employ temporary teachers.

Before going into the profession, primary school applicants choose the region in which they want to compete. If they are successful, they are assured of staying in that region. Thus, there is a shortage of candidates in some areas, including the huge suburbia around Paris, but there are many applications for positions in the capital and the sunshine regions. Where there are fewer candidates for a specific number of places, the competitive examination is easier than where the ratio is high. In practice, although competition is fierce in the south of France, practically everyone has a good chance of succeeding in the north. The implications in terms of teacher quality are obvious.

The mechanism is different for secondary school teachers. The successful candidates are dispatched anywhere in the country by the national ministry, whose job it is to make sure that teaching resources are equitably distributed across France. Clearly, very few are happy to be sent to a remote and bleak northern town. Yet that is what happens because the comfortable posts are already held by older teachers. Having been sent by administrative directive to a region with which the teachers have no empathy, their morale and teaching will not be optimal, and their objective is to get transferred to a better posting as soon as possible. The transfer, based largely on seniority, typically takes at least five or six years. Thus, over the years teachers will get posted closer and closer to their ideal choice, so that by the time they are fifty they end up where they always wanted to be. Inevitably, the turnover in some schools is high; even within regions, teachers will often keep changing schools to avoid the more difficult ones. As the more experienced teachers are finally assigned to a school in a middle- or upper-middle-class area where teaching is not particularly demanding, absolute beginners have to teach at difficult schools in depressed areas.

To combat this vicious cycle, ministry officials have provided incentives to encourage teachers to stay for a minimum number of years in the same difficult school by promising a faster transfer to a better region. Some financial incentives, which challenge the teaching unions' insistence that all teachers should be paid the same wherever they are, have also been introduced with limited success.

Teacher Training Reform

In the early 1990s, a new system for initial teacher training was introduced. Previously, teacher training had been institutionally and pedagogically distinct for the different categories of teachers.

Primary school teachers (*instituteurs*) had trained for two years *after* passing a competitive examination in several subjects at local teacher-training centers (*écoles normales primaires*). They could take this examination only if they had successfully completed a two-year university course and obtained the *diplôme d'études universitaires générales*. They were not, however, holders of a full university degree, which requires three years of study.

Secondary school teachers, on the other hand, had generally been university graduates. After completing their first degree they would usually stay on at university to prepare for the mostly academic competitive examination in their subject. If they succeeded, they went through a one-year probationary period during which they were in charge of one or two classes and received advice from a mentor. There had also been a separate system for training vocational school teachers.

This dual system was thought, accurately, to be confusing, and a more unified system was devised; the expectation was that a simple and more easily understood system would help attract students to the profession. Thus, since the early 1990s, primary and secondary school teachers have been expected to be university graduates. In a system where teachers, like all civil servants, are paid according to incremental scales based on their educational degrees, for the first time primary and secondary school teachers would be on the same pay scale.

The teacher training reform also provided for the creation of regional institutes for primary and secondary school teacher training, distinct from the universities but with higher education status: the Instituts Universitaires de Formation des Maîtres. The main purpose was to bring together primary and secondary training in a single regional structure to provide some common training in the theory of education, as well as some mutual understanding of the specificity of teaching at each level, while at the same time improving the quality of the training. This objective implies providing equal standards of quality for both academic and professional training for primary and secondary school teachers: Primary school teachers should receive more academic training in keeping with the overall increase in the education standards of the general population, and secondary school teachers should receive more "professional" (as opposed to purely subject-based or academic) training (Bancel, 1989).

Although it is true that the institutes are responsible for the training of teachers through a two-year course, it is also true that the first year is not compulsory. Access to state employment is a constitutional right for all citizens, so that everybody with the required qualifications is entitled to take the various competitive examinations leading to a post in the civil service. This right naturally applies to teaching positions; although the teacher-training institutes are the officially recognized pathways to the profession, they are by no means the only road to the qualifying examinations. In other words, people might choose to take the examinations by preparing for them elsewhere, by themselves, or not at all; it is the result that matters—passing the examination. Thus, there is no obligation to enroll in the institutes for the first year of training. For the second year, the situation is quite different because those who were successful in the competitive examination must undergo a probationary period and complete the second year in one of the institutes before being recruited as fully qualified teachers. The first year of training in the institutes is essentially directed toward preparing for the teacher recruitment competition, whereas the second year is characterized by a greater emphasis on teaching practice, much of it school based. The failure rate at the end of the second year (including those who are asked to repeat the year) is about two to five percentage points. The low failure rate shows the weight of the competitive examination in the combined training/recruitment process (Bonnet, 1998).

The new training system was described as an imaginative and promising innovation by the three independent international experts commissioned in 1994 by the OECD to carry out a study of the French education system. Over the past decade the system has been successful in producing the numbers of new teachers needed, despite periodic criticism of the way it works (Gallouin, 1995). One of the enduring concerns, however, is the limited amount of "professional" training (as opposed to academic education) provided by the two-year course in the training institutes. A proposed solution is to increase the amount of time spent in the second year on teaching practice in the classroom, but there are limits to what can be done in that respect. The only real solution would be to change the competitive examinations, in particular for the secondary school level, but academics, inspectors, and the main teaching unions continue to oppose this alternative. Another unresolved challenge is the training of primary school teachers in foreign language teaching, as this is one of the priorities for the years to come.

Efforts are being made to organize teacher training as a continuum ranging from university, through the two years in the institutes, to induction at the time of starting to teach. Various provisions allow new teachers to receive in-service training from an early stage. The continuing challenge is to make the competitive examinations more relevant to teaching and to reinforce teaching practice during training, in order to ensure that a more professional approach to teacher training prevails while also preserving academic standards.

CONCLUSION: CURRENT POLICY ISSUES

Curriculum reform is a national pastime in France; education ministers want to leave their mark on the system. Over the past few years, reforms have tended to lighten the content of each curriculum area while bringing it up to date and rehabilitating the humanities and art.

The emphasis in the primary school curriculum is on reading, writing, and arithmetic, which are regarded as the basic skills that must be attained quickly by pupils. Curriculum reform in secondary education is a very emotional issue for teachers, and a major national dispute erupted recently on the reform of the philosophy curriculum, even though this subject is taught only in the last year of *lycée*. Another controversial reform has been the introduction at both the *collège* and *lycée* levels of specific timetable slots for small groups of pupils to work with one or several teachers on cross-subject projects. Teachers have mixed feelings about this interdisciplinary approach because the time allocated must be taken away from regular subjects—many teachers believe that the time allocated to certain subjects should be increased.

Two major issues currently head the education policy agenda. The most prominent one comes from the concern that about 8 percent of ten/eleven-year-olds leave primary education without sufficient reading skills. Various innovations, including small-group instruction, are being tried to improve teaching and thereby increase pupils' success rate.

The second major issue concerns vocational training, which, despite various initiatives implemented by past education ministers, is still very much felt to be "second-best" education. A recent decision will introduce some vocational education at the lower secondary school level in order to provide as early as possible for pupils who are not academically oriented. There is clearly an equity issue here, because it is pupils from lower income backgrounds and children of immigrants who are in danger of being relegated to the vocational stream from a relatively early age. The standards by which French parents and society gauge a proper education are those of the classical *lycées*. Yet a large part of vocational education is the responsibility of the education system, so that efforts are made periodically to demonstrate that it is as important and as respectable as academic education.

Other issues are currently under discussion. The first pertains to language policy. Compared with most other major countries, the strong emphasis of the French education system is the modern language policy, whereby, over the next few years, all students will learn a foreign language beginning in the last year of preprimary school. Almost everywhere in the country, students already begin a foreign language in the last two years of primary school. At the *collège* level, a second foreign language will be taught beginning in the first year. In addition, specific measures have been taken to promote the teaching of regional languages. This policy, however, is running into difficulty because of the lack of properly trained staff at the primary level, and its implementation will be slowed down for reevaluation. Foreign language teaching is well developed in terms of numbers of languages taught and numbers of pupils taking language classes throughout primary and secondary school, in keeping with the official objectives of the European Union and the intention to promote linguistic diversity in Europe. However, it is debatable whether the major effort and resources deployed in France for this purpose are being rewarded with adequate results in terms of students' ability to understand, speak, read, and write foreign languages. This is particularly true of English, which is taken by over 90 percent of the secondary school population. A recent survey of fifteen-year-old students' achievement in English, repeating a test taken by a similar sample in 1997, shows that overall performance has declined.

The introduction of information and communication technology (ICT) in education has naturally been one of the priorities in recent years. The vast majority of schools have the relevant equipment and an Internet connection, sometimes through a series of arrangements with local elected assemblies and industrial partners. At the same time, little is known about the large-scale use of the technology and even less about its impact on teaching and learning. This situation is not unique to France, and extensive work lies ahead in order to assess the consequences of ICT in the school context.

Another question that periodically arises and is currently gaining importance is the debate about the organization of the school year and the school week. The school year debate focuses on the length of the school holidays, notably that of the summer holidays, which are particularly long in France (approximately nine weeks) and of the "short" holidays given every seven weeks throughout the year (a total of seven to eight weeks). Some educators insist that this generous amount of leave results in a daily and weekly workload that is much too heavy. This issue has not been resolved so far because the dates of holidays (fixed at a national level) constitute major social events and have important consequences for different sectors of the economy, such as tourism and transport.

The other debate is particularly controversial and conflict ridden: It is the question of how to organize the school week and in particular whether there should be classes on Saturday morning. Changes in society and the reduction in adults' working times have increased pressure for the Saturday classes to be eliminated, at the expense of heavier loads the rest of the time—an outcome criticized by some scientists as being against the interest of children. However, the organizational changes are expected to continue.

Finally, the question of decentralization discussed earlier is fast becoming a critical issue that might determine the fate of governments, present and future. Spring 2003 was particularly tense from the point of view of social relations because of the pension law reform, about which teachers are deeply unhappy. In addition, the government announced its strategic plan for the decentralization of education, which includes more autonomy to schools and the transfer of all nonteaching school staff from central government to the regions.

This plan resulted in major school strikes to oppose the move. Teachers themselves reacted very strongly, as they saw this change (unrealistically) as the first step toward privatizing education. The government was finally compelled to water down these plans for the time being, following the very real possibility that teachers would disrupt the *baccalauréat* examination, often with the support of parents who are also in favor of retaining the national character of education. The cancellation or postponement of the examination was unthinkable and might have led to the fall of the government. This episode is a good example of the difficulty of reforming the French education system in the face of militant trade unions and conservative public opinion. Making regional and local governance a reality for education will be a very slow process as long as teachers' attitudes do not change and will probably require years of careful management from Paris.

NOTE

1. Whenever the word *state* is used in this chapter, it refers to national government as opposed to regional or local government. It is equivalent to the federal level in the United States.

REFERENCES CITED

Bancel, D. (1989). *Créer une nouvelle dynamique de la formation des maîtres* [Promoting a new dynamic approach to teacher training]. Report to Ministre d'Etat, Ministre de l'éducation nationale, de la jeunesse et des sports. Paris: Ministère de l'éducation nationale, de la jeunesse et des sports.

Bonnet, G. (1996a). Effects of evaluation procedures on educational policy decisions in France. *International Journal of Educational Research, 25* (3), 249–56.

———. (1996b). La formation initiale des enseignants du premier et du second degré dans les instituts universitaires de formation des maîtres [Initial primary and secondary teacher training in the teacher-training institutes]. *Education et Formations, 46,* 25–38.

————. (1997). Profiles of educational assessment systems worldwide: Country profile from France. *Assessment in Education: Principles, Policy and Practice, 4* (2), 295–306.

————. (1998). La formation au métier d'enseignant [Training to become a teacher]. *Cahiers français, 285,* 62–68.

————. (1999). French without tears: On the concept that underlies education in France. *Parliamentary Brief, 5* (9), 36–37.

Gallouin, F. (1995). Les IUFM après quatre ans de fonctionnement [The teacher-training institutes four years after their creation]. In *Rapport d'expertise de la mission scientifique et technique sur les projets d'établissement des IUFM pour 1995–1999* [Report of the scientific experts regarding the teacher-training institutes' strategic plans for 1995–1999]. Paris: Ministère de l'éducation nationale, de l'enseignement supérieur et de la recherche.

Joutard, P., & Thélot, C. (1999). *Réussir l'école: Pour une politique éducative* [Making education a success: For an education policy]. Paris: Seuil.

Ministère de la jeunesse, de l'éducation nationale et de la recherche [The ministry for youth, national education and research]. (2002). Temps de travail des enseignants du second degré en 2000 [Actual working time of secondary school teachers in 2000]. *Note d'information, 2* (43).

Ministère de l'éducation nationale [The ministry for national education]. (2002). Projection du système éducatif à dix ans [Ten-year forecast for the education system]. *Education et Formations, 63.*

Thélot, C. (1993). *L'évaluation du système éducatif* [Evaluating the education system]. Paris: Nathan.

7

Turkey: Innovation and Tradition

Hasan Simsek and Ali Yildirim

Teachers! The new generation will be your creation.

—Mustafa Kemal (Ataturk, 1880–1938)

Changes in economic and social conditions worldwide have had a major influence on education reform. Economists describe several periods in the evolution of these changes during the past 200 years, called "Long Waves" or "Kondratieff cycles," after the Russian economist Nicolai Kondratieff, who first conducted the analyses in the early twentieth century. Kondratieff cycles define each period both by its scientific and engineering breakthroughs and by its "worldview" or economic and social characteristics (Simsek, 2002).

In the first cycle (1789–1849) inventions such as the steam engine and machine tools contributed to the Industrial Revolution and capitalist economic systems. The railroads and iron and steel industries dominated the second cycle (1849–94), which saw the emergence of Social Darwinism, monopoly, and laissez-faire capitalism. The third cycle (1894–1945) featured major breakthroughs in electricity, chemicals, automotive engineering, and communications, along with the development of humanist progressive movements. The fourth cycle included unprecedented acceleration of scientific and technological progress, as exemplified by major advances in communications, information technology, aeronautics, materials, genetics, and medicine; the modern welfare state also developed during this period.

Economists describe a fifth cycle, beginning in 1995, as defined by the information revolution, which made instant access to information available worldwide, and by the growth of a free market global economy built primarily on the classic principles of liberal capitalism. Precursors to these trends are still fresh in the memories of many adults: the Vietnam War; the Organization of Petroleum Exporting Countries oil crisis that led to a worldwide economic recession; political instability in many parts of the world; the ascendance of the East Asian economies; the birth of the European Union; the emergence of other economic blocks, such as the North American Free Trade Agreement; and the collapse of Communism.

Large-scale education reforms tend to cluster around the downswings (or crises) in Kondratieff cycles and the early phases of the upswings. As nations have responded to crises in the transition to global competition, they increasingly view human resources and education as central priorities. It is not surprising, therefore, that educational growth, from preschool through adult education, has become part of the political agenda, accompanied by the belief that education requires fundamental reform to address changing world conditions. In many countries, it is common now to hear discussions of privatization, decentralization, site-based management, curriculum standards, accountability, multiple intelligences, constructive curriculum, community schools, home schooling, and other reform proposals. For example, both conservative and liberal governments restructured the British school system during the past twenty years. The system, a classic Anglo-Saxon education model emphasizing local control of education, became centralized with respect to standards, curriculum, and testing, although some emphasis on local control continues, particularly with respect to school choice and the management and organization of individual schools.

A similar mix of increased centralization and local control is also occurring in the United States, where states, and now the federal government, have mandated standardized tests to hold schools and teachers accountable for student achievement and, in some cases, to determine students' promotion to higher grades and their graduation from high school (although, unlike Great Britain, the United States has neither a national curriculum nor a national test). The United States continues its tradition of local control in most other respects, with an increasing emphasis on school choice.

In contrast to Great Britain and the United States, the French system historically has been highly centralized and serves as the model for many European education systems, including that of Turkey. However, as Great Britain and the United States moved to greater central control, at least for certain purposes, France began a process of decentralization to bring greater diversity and more flexible organization to what was believed to be an education system that was too uniform—even monolithic—in the context of changing societal conditions (Discoverfrance, 2003). Although the French education system, in many ways, remains more centralized than the British and American systems, the trend clearly has been in opposite directions.

The French education model has been the most influential model in Turkey since the founding of the Turkish Republic in 1923. The Turkish system currently is "more French than the French system" because the French model has experienced significant changes during the past twenty years. Signs of educational crisis in Turkey, along with proposals for resolving the crisis, revolve around issues related to France's Napoleonic educational ideals.

The foundation of the Republic of Turkey, on October 29, 1923, followed a bloody war for independence under the leadership of Mustafa Kemal, later renamed Ataturk (Father of Turks) by the early Turkish Parliament. It was the first successful war of independence waged against the Western imperial powers of Britain, France, and Italy, which were committed to breaking apart the crumbling Ottoman Empire. Ataturk's primary goal was to create an independent, modern, secular Turkish state with a parliamentary democracy; he emphasized the critical importance of education in nation building and the creation of a modern society. In one instance, he proclaimed that the Turkish nation won the war on the battleground but that the job would not be complete unless the army of teachers and educators would win another victory over ignorance and the enslavement of minds.

Indeed, Turkey's success in education from 1923 to 2002 was quite impressive, at least with respect to participation: The number of schools increased from 5,000 to 49,000; the number of students, from 362,000 to 16 million; and the number of teachers, from 13,000 to 579,000. However, these numerical trends, spanning over eighty years, do not tell us much about the structure, content, delivery mechanisms, teaching/learning processes, equity, and other important indicators of educational quality and distribution. The Turkish education system requires reform in most of these areas, especially in the context of societal change both within the country and internationally. It is widely accepted by scholars, journalists, and politicians that the need for reform is particularly important in areas of resource distribution, access to higher and vocational education, pedagogy, bureaucratic structure, curriculum, student assessment and evaluation, and equity as it relates to urban–rural disparities and to the education of girls, especially in rural areas. The remainder of this chapter gives a brief history of the Turkish education system, describes societal conditions from the 1980s to the present that contributed to the current crisis, analyzes the key areas requiring reform, and suggests factors that both accelerate and inhibit reform initiatives.

THE TURKISH EDUCATION SYSTEM:
A HISTORICAL OVERVIEW

Four major periods describe the history of Turkish education: the Ottoman period (prior to 1923), the modernization era (1923–1950), the quest for democracy (1950–1980), and the crises created by dichotomies (1980–present).[1]

The Ottoman Period (before 1923)

Before the formation of the Turkish Republic in 1923, religious teachings dominated the education system of the Ottoman Empire. For example, a typical elementary (*sibyan*) school curriculum included subjects such as the Holy Koran, religious rules, religious readings, Ottoman history, and arithmetic and ethics (Akyuz, 1994). Schools at the secondary level (*medrese* schools) continued with advanced levels of religious instruction. Education foundations financed and governed schools with a religious orientation. Other schools (*iptidai* and *idadi* schools), typically managed by government, reflected the influence of Western education and emphasized sciences and humanities more than religious subjects. In addition, foundations or organizations in other countries (such as France and the United States) established and provided the primary financing for private schools. Girls and boys studied separately at all levels of education. Education generally was not given high priority in the country; only 10 percent of men and less than 1 percent of women were estimated to be literate (Guvenc, 1998).

The Modernization Era (1923-1950)

After the formation of the Turkish Republic in 1923, a full-scale restructuring of educational institutions began, for education was perceived as the vehicle for the social, cultural, and economic revolution in the country. The Ottoman period had created a political and religious system that was essentially hostile to change and Westernization (Yildirim & Ok, 2002). Therefore, the transformation of the society from an illiterate, agrarian, and Islamic state to an educated, urbanized, and republican state was not easy. Ataturk attached such significance to educating the public that one of the first measures he promoted was the Unification of Education Law. This law brought all educational institutions under the control of the Ministry of National Education (MONE). Schools with a religious orientation were closed. All public schools were free for all students, and primary education became compulsory. Coeducation began in elementary schools in 1924, in middle schools in 1927, and in high schools in 1934.

Ataturk gave speeches throughout the country to accelerate the adoption of these measures. At a teachers' convention in 1924, he said: "Teachers! The new generation will be your creation. The Republic needs and wants guardians who are strong physically, intellectually and spiritually" (Guvenc, 1998, p. 50). On another occasion he declared, "Science is the most reliable guide in life" (Guvenc, 1998, p. 50), a direct reference to the secular education he promoted.

As part of the educational renewal, in 1924 Turkey invited John Dewey, the American philosopher and educator, to study the school system and make recommendations. His suggestions included turning workplaces into schools and schools into workplaces (Guvenc, 1998), so that students would receive on-the-job training and as a short-term solution to the problem of insufficient schools.

In 1927 Ataturk declared "laicism" (secularism) as one of the fundamental principles of the republic, to find expression in all aspects of social life, government affairs, and education. This declaration led to a number of measures that transformed fundamental components of the society, including the schools. In 1928 a constitutional amendment deleted the article stating that Islam is the state religion.

Increasing the literacy rate became an essential component in national development and industrialization. The Arabic script, then used as the official alphabet, was seen as an obstacle to teaching reading and writing to the larger population because it is so difficult to learn. It was replaced, therefore, with the Latin alphabet through Ataturk's direct intervention, a step to distance the republic from its Ottoman past and to bring it closer to Westernized ideals. Following this move, a full-scale literacy movement (the "Illiteracy Eradication Project") began in 1928, in order to increase the country's literacy rate, a priority that required the allocation of a significant portion of the nation's scarce financial resources to education (Guvenc, 1998).

During the republican period, a structure for the education system was established that lasted until the mid-1990s: five years of primary school, three years of middle school, and three years of high school. The curriculum was secular at both primary and secondary education levels, with no emphasis on the Holy Koran. Primary schools concentrated on the three Rs, life studies, history, geography, science, and civics, plus handiwork, drawing, and music. The middle and high schools covered the sciences, social sciences, and humanities in more depth in discipline-oriented courses (Guvenc, 1998).

These dramatic changes in the focus of education required comparable changes in teacher education, which had previously emphasized religious subjects but now concentrated on sciences and the humanities. Teachers were viewed as change agents for the society. Because the majority of the population lived in villages, village institutes were established in 1938 to train teachers specifically to serve in village schools. Their task was not only to educate the children who attended the schools but also to educate the men and women in many areas of life (ranging from agriculture to birth control) so that they could contribute to social change. The village institutes seemed to fulfill John Dewey's idea of combining work and education, and the teachers, by and large, became quite successful both in raising the educational level of the children and in acting as community leaders where they served (Turan, 2000).

The 1940s were years of discontent and upheaval, resulting in changes in the government. Although Turkey did not take part in World War II, the country was greatly affected by the war economically; food shortages, high prices, and high taxes contributed to a reaction against the government. The Peoples' Republican Party, which had governed the nation since the founding of the republic, lost much of its public support. The opposition Democratic Party, established as the second political party in 1945 as part of the democratization of the elections, therefore gained the opportunity to consolidate public support and win the parliamentary elections in 1950 (Guvenc, 1998).

The Quest for Democracy and Turmoil (1950–1980)

Education between 1923 and 1950 emphasized gender equality, scientific positivism, and republican ideals, such as secularism and modernity in schools. The adoption of Latin script, the restructuring of the school system along the lines of Western models (i.e., primary, middle, and high school), the adoption of coeducation in schools, and the deemphasis on religious education were all signs of this effort. This educational philosophy began to change in the 1950s. The emerging power of the Democratic Party, along with the threat of Communism, found reflection in both societal and educational changes. The village institutes, labeled "leftist" and criticized by the village landlords who gained more political power through the Democratic Party, were closed in 1954. Religious teaching returned to schools, first as elective, then as compulsory, courses; and religious middle and high schools reopened, and their numbers increased steadily. The threat of Communism led to increased nationalism in school curricula and textbooks.

The Democratic Party emphasized economic growth and the democratization of society in its policies but ignored education's central role in transforming society, which had been a priority before 1950. The previous increases in rates of schooling came to a halt as investments in education declined (Basaran, 1999). At the same time, the education system had to respond to another crisis: the increase in migration from villages to cities, which promised a better life. The magnitude of the social and economic problem can be demonstrated by the fact that the 70/30 rural/urban ratio in 1950 was essentially reversed to 30/70 by the end of the 1990s (Guvenc, 1998). In economic terms, the share of agriculture declined from about 70 percent of gross domestic product in the 1950s and 1960s to 16 percent in 2000, a decline that is expected to continue (State Institute of Statistics, 2003).

The primary schools in urban areas, therefore, could not absorb the sudden increase in student population and initiated first a two-shift, and then a three-shift, system to accommodate the children. Despite shortened school hours and the hiring of substitute teachers, class size increased dramatically; not surprisingly, the quality of education suffered enormously. Schools faced multiple expectations: to provide education for the children who had migrated to the cities, to acclimate them to urban life and to their urban peer group, and, at the same time, to provide quality education for all children. However, the schools were not well equipped to meet the demands arising from the rapid "demographic transition" from rural to urban areas.

In 1960 the military took over the government in a secular reaction to the Democratic Party, now described as a threat to Ataturk's republican ideas. An education convention recommended closing religious schools and improving school curricula (Basaran, 1999). The recommendations were partially achieved: Religion courses again became optional, and curriculum reforms in some areas incorporated new developments; on the other hand, religious schools remained open, and their numbers increased during the latter part of the 1960s.

The deterioration of education continued in the 1960s. The high inflation rate decreased teachers' salaries in real terms, resulting in lower professional status and morale. Moreover, new schools could not be built because of financial constraints: Classrooms originally designed for thirty students now held seventy-eighty students.

In the beginning of the 1970s efforts were made to increase five-year compulsory schooling to eight years and curtail the growth of religious schools. Immediately after the second military intervention in 1971, the MONE closed down religious middle schools. In 1973 Parliament passed the Basic Education Law, which required the government to provide all children with an uninterrupted eight-year compulsory education. However, the Basic Education Law was labeled "an effort to block religious education," and in 1974 the coalition government formed by the social democratic Republican People's Party and the religious Welfare Party reinstated earlier models of religious schools (Kaplan, 1999). As a result, the extension of basic education to eight years for all children was not achieved until 1997—twenty-four years later.

Educational institutions suffered greatly from the violent conflict between extremists on the "Right" and "Left" in the 1970s. Teachers also wound up divided into political camps, and politically motivated students exercised power in secondary schools. The turmoil in the streets and in the schools, throughout the 1970s, prevented policy makers from giving attention to the inherent problems of schools, such as overcrowded classrooms, poor-quality educational materials, and unmotivated teachers and students.

Dichotomies in Education (1980–Present)

The Turkish military intervened to end the turmoil for the third time in 1980, an intervention largely supported by the public, who considered it a last resort to prevent anarchy. Toward the end of the 1970s, five to ten people died in street shootings almost daily. The intervention led to increased centralization in the education system, and, at the same time, curricula and textbooks became more nationalistic. Under this policy, courses like history and geography were relabeled national history and national geography (Kaplan, 1999). Biology curriculum went through a "Turkish–Islamic revision" that eliminated the study of evolution because it was considered inconsistent with Islamic thought.

The quality of education was once again a major issue in the 1980s. The MONE was strongly criticized for giving in to political pressures and not taking the necessary measures to improve the quality of school infrastructure, curriculum, textbooks, teachers, and other aspects of education. Students felt pressure from the university entrance exam; fewer than 11 percent of the 1.5 million high school graduates who took the exam in 2003 passed. Students and parents blamed schools both for not preparing students for the entrance exam and for not responding to their individual interests and needs. These complaints encouraged the growth of private schools that claimed to provide better-quality education and of private courses (*dershane,* the equivalent of *jukus* in Japan) that promised students better preparation for the entrance exam.

In the 1991–92 academic year, in response to growing criticism of schools, high school students received more freedom to choose courses in an attempt to transform the philosophy and structure of high school education. However, the MONE abolished the reform four years later; the ministry declared that it had failed because of serious problems in implementation: (1) insufficient classroom space to offer a variety of courses; (2) inadequate counseling to guide students in course selection; (3) confusion on the part of teachers, administrators, and parents about how the system worked, how to offer new courses, where to get materials, and how to collaborate with other schools; and (4) rigidities in the centralized education system, with its large bureaucracy, which did not allow effective communication and coordination between schools and local and central administrative bodies (Caner, 1999). In general, the MONE had not recognized the difficulty of transforming a traditional system to a progressive one and assumed that the change in structure would "automatically" change other aspects of education—a problem in implementing partial education reforms that exists in countries throughout the world. The result in this case was to damage public confidence in the government's ability to implement educational change.

In 1997, with pressure from the National Security Council, the Turkish Parliament passed laws enforcing the Basic Education Reform, first outlined in 1973, to increase the educational level of the population to bring it closer to European Union norms.[2] A nationwide campaign began to open more schools and classrooms and to decrease class size to thirty, a reform that required faculties of education to train more teachers. As a result, new departments opened in the areas of classroom teaching, preschool education, upper primary Turkish, mathematics, the sciences, and social studies (Simsek & Yildirim, 2001).

With the Basic Education Reform of 1997, the middle school sections of religious schools closed once more. The remaining high school sections of these schools shared the status of vocational high schools. When the Higher Education Council later revised the calculation of university entrance exam scores, so that vocational high school graduates had less chance to enter university departments that were not directly related to their high school specialization, the number of students seeking religious education at the high school level decreased.

Along with the secular–religious dichotomy, public–private school and school–private course dichotomies continue today. The number of private schools is increasing as a result of the continuing deterioration of public school education. As can be expected, private schools, which attract students from middle and high socioeconomic backgrounds, achieve higher rankings in university entrance exams than do public schools. The private courses, which prepare students for the university entrance exam, pose another problem for public schools, for both students and parents believe that the private courses (not the schools) are the important factor in university entrance.

Increasing basic education from eight to twelve years is currently being discussed as another step in improving education. This change would result in the elimination of all religious and vocational education at the high school level, an issue that creates sharp divisions among political parties. This disagreement over the role of public education in teaching religion once again appears to be a major obstacle in increasing basic education to twelve years.

THE NEED FOR REFORM

The current opposition party in the Turkish Parliament, the Republican People's Party, has stated a need for fundamental reform in all areas of education. The party program argues that the basic principles and methods of education must be rethought in order to raise a generation of young people who are self-confident and who can think critically and creatively. Similarly, the current ruling party, the Justice and Development Party, also states a need for fundamental education reform: "Turkey experiences a real chaos in the field of education . . . for this, our party will engage in a fundamental reform movement in education" (Adalet ve Kalkinma Partisi, 2003). Indeed, almost all of the political parties have expressed similar concerns about education. The Turkish public shares these concerns, an awareness furthered through the efforts of the news media and nonprofit organizations, which have encouraged the general public to increase the pressure on politicians to restructure education. The sections below describe potential areas for reform.

The Social Context: High Birthrates

In 2000 the population of Turkey was 67,803,000. Estimates are that the population will be 83,400,000 in 2015 and 90,488,000 in 2023. The annual rate of population increase in Turkey has been no less than 2 percent (excluding 1945, at 1 percent) since the founding of the republic in 1923. The annual rate of increase peaked to 2.8 percent in 1960 and has declined slightly since 1980. The 2000 census indicates that the annual rate of increase has now declined to 1.8 percent, below the 2 percent threshold level for the first time in the republic's history (State Institute of Statistics, 2003).

However, Turkey continues to have one of the highest birthrates in the world and the highest in the world when compared with other countries with a similar level of industrialization and economic development. Annual rates of population increase above 2 percent typically occur in the world's lowest-income countries, such as Kenya (2.4 percent), Pakistan (2.4 percent), Zambia (2.6 percent), and Tanzania (2.7 percent). Turkey's rate of increase is far above the Organization for Economic Cooperation and Development average: For example, it is 0.3 percent in Belgium, 0.3 percent in Germany, 0.4 percent in Denmark and Great Britain, 0.5 percent in Austria, 1.1 percent in Canada, and 1.2 percent in Australia and the United States (State Institute of Statistics, 2003).

Turkey's rapid increase in population presents a major challenge for the education system, which must serve increasing numbers of students while also strengthening quality. If we assume the lowest, 1.8 percent, rate of increase for the current population of approximately 68 million, we can expect 1.2 million additional children to enter the education system each year. These children will stay in the system until the end of compulsory school (from ages six to fourteen). The high rate of increase creates a continual need for opening new classrooms. For example, between 6,282 and 21,620 new classrooms opened each year between 1994 and 1998 (TUBITAK, 2003, pp. 8–11).

If the system cannot meet the changing exit ratios, the flow of students will create blocks at various stages, leading to a waste of national resources and bottlenecks within the system. Two examples highlight the problem: First, because migration from rural to urban areas was ignored, the government built school buildings for each village during the 1960s and 1970s. As a result, 72 percent of total school buildings are located in villages, although only 27 percent of the students currently live in villages; therefore, many of these buildings remain unused today. Second, because of underutilization of the vocational and technical systems, as well as the fact that Turkish industry cannot absorb the large numbers of high school graduates, Turkey faces an increasing demand for higher education—a demand far beyond the available openings in universities, a situation leading to some of the world's worst "exam anxiety" for young people applying to university. This discrepancy between supply and demand, which makes a major contribution to Turkey's serious educational problems, will be discussed later in the chapter.

Prospects for Reform

Population dynamics involve a combination of social, economic, and cultural factors. It might not be proper, therefore, to call this issue an area for education reform. However, high birthrates, especially in the case of Turkey, have major implications for education. A positive sign is that the population increase might be declining, with the rate of increase estimated at around 1.4 percent by the year 2023 (State Institute of Statistics, 2003). A major reason is increased urbanization, which tends to be associated with lower birthrates.

Turkish policy makers face the critical issue of how to accelerate this natural tendency for decline. No matter what strategy is used, a long-term investment will be needed. Both public and nonprofit organizations have waged successful birth control campaigns, especially in the rural areas. For the past five to six years, there has been a debate about whether to include sex education as part of the formal school curriculum—a proposal that religious groups oppose. Because of intense lobbying by several nonprofit organizations, the MONE initiated two projects on sex education for adolescents. The first project, between 1993 and 1998, included two million girls in a sample of 10,224 schools. The second project, completed in 2000, targeted boys and girls in grades six to eight (MONE, 2003). This type of project could be incorporated into the regular school curriculum and also into adult education.

One of the Root Problems: Memorization-Based Pedagogy

Ryan and Cooper write, "Everyone, at some level, has a philosophy of life . . . a general theory of how the world is put together, what laws regulate the universe and underlie all knowledge and reality. . . . Philosophy provides us a lens through which we observe and interpret reality" (2000, p. 331). It is an individual endeavor that also has social and communal aspects. A widely shared worldview among community members creates the basis for common interpretations, communication, and behavior (Simsek & Louis, 1994). Shared educational philosophies provide a certain degree of regularity and predictability in teacher, student, and administrator behaviors, which become based on common educational values, priorities, curriculum content, and even teaching methods.

The basic philosophical conflict is between "traditional" and "progressive" approaches to education. The traditional approach emphasizes conventional subject matter and teaching methods: "The role of the student is simply that of learner. The individual child's interests, motivations, and psychological states are not given much attention. . . . [Students are viewed] as deficient and needing discipline and pressure to keep learning. School is viewed as a place where children come to learn what they need to know.

Teachers are not guides but authorities. The student's job is to listen and learn" (Ryan & Cooper, 2000, pp. 340–41). The "progressive" approach focuses on children's problem-solving ability and individual interests and needs. Teaching methods are of primary importance: "Progressive teachers often use traditional subject matter, but they use it differently from the way it is used in a traditional classroom. . . . The focus is on *how* to think rather than on *what* to think. . . . Rather than being a presenter of knowledge or a taskmaster, the teacher is an intellectual guide, a *facilitator* in the problem-solving process" (Ryan & Cooper, 2000, pp. 335–36). Progressive education, which is relatively young, is genuinely American in the sense that it came to prominence in the 1920s through the work of the American educator John Dewey.

Progressive education had a brief impact on Turkish education during the republic's early years, when several Western thinkers, including Dewey, were invited to Turkey and advised on how to build the new system. For example, village institutes—a genuinely Turkish educational innovation—had Dewey's philosophical imprint, but they had minimal impact on the system because of their abolition after a short time.

With the exception of the village institutes, classroom practices at all levels of education were highly traditional, even though a progressive education philosophy dominated the written principles of Turkish education, as well as political discourse and party programs throughout the history of the republic (Sonmez, 1996). As Sonmez describes it: "Not student but teacher and subject-matter have become the central focus; instead of raising persons who can use scientific methods, who are able to think freely and flexibly, who are democratic and secular, the system has raised individuals who memorize what the teacher says and what the books write" (1996, p. 155). Other scholars generally support Sonmez's analysis (Erturk, 1971; Yedikardesler, 1984). In a recent study, Balcı asked a sample of elementary school teachers to use metaphors to describe their students (Balcı & Yildirim, 1999); the majority used metaphors such as dough and clay (to be shaped and formed). In the same study, a majority of students described their school administrators as strict disciplinarians.

Prospects for Reform

Worldviews are the intangible component of all education systems; they are the socially constructed realities that we are born into and "take for granted." Their construction takes many years, decades, and, in some instances, even centuries. They are very resistant to change; indeed, "to switch from one paradigm to another is as hard as to convert from one religion to another" (Simsek, 1992, p. 58).

Change will require long-term strategies, which can be accomplished best by changing specific components of the education system: organization and governance, curriculum, teaching and learning methods, preservice and in-service teacher training, and textbooks. That is, by changing the tangible components of the system, we might modify, indirectly, the underlying assumptions on which Turkish education currently is based.

The reforms described in the remainder of the chapter are based on progressive education: individualized instruction, an understanding of child psychology, and flexible curriculum content that is responsive to the professional knowledge of teachers and the interests and expectations of students—all designed to enable students to solve problems and to think analytically and creatively, skills demanded by the Turkish economy in a global environment. The discussion of educational philosophies raises an issue mentioned previously: The Turkish prospects, along with reforms in other traditionally centralized systems, such as the French system, show a tendency toward decentralization and more progressive pedagogy; the reform movements in Britain and the United States, however, have tended to move in the other direction (although in many ways they remain more "child centered" in their education philosophy and provide more options for school autonomy and parental choice). If the current trend continues, we might witness less variation in the world's education systems (Ramirez & Boli, 1987) in the coming years as the two competing models (Napoleonic and Anglo-Saxon) regress toward each other.

Centralized Governance and Hierarchical Structure

A centralized bureaucracy has controlled all public enterprise in Turkey since the founding of the Turkish Republic in 1923. Although there have been periodic adjustments over the past eighty years, the underlying administrative principle remained intact. Moreover, to keep pace with one of the world's fastest-growing populations, the Education Ministry also has shown a phenomenal growth in structure and functions over the years. Next to the Turkish Army, it is the largest single public organization in the country. The result of this growth is a huge bureaucracy, whose major activities revolve around maintaining the bureaucratic procedures that severely limit the capacity for change and innovation and for addressing the country's educational problems.

A major contributing factor to the ministry's limited flexibility is its size, combined with a centralized and hierarchical structure, which has not changed over the years in response to the changes that have occurred in Turkey since the 1920s (except to grow as Turkey's population has grown). Thus, the Turkish MONE has grown progressively since the formation of the republic and retains its centralized hierarchical structure, although Turkey has changed in many ways since the 1920s.

The highly centralized education bureaucracy has severely limited the ability of local educators to formulate policies to address local needs. Local school administrators have no say in personnel decisions, nor do they have control over local budgets. Without the ability to participate in selecting staff or allocating funds, they do not have the human or financial resources to implement the types of reforms they believe would be most relevant to the needs of the community (Güncer, Simsek, & Yildirim, 1995).

Moreover, the centralized bureaucracy, which controls decisions about all areas of education policy, from curriculum to personnel, is a target for political influence. Political groups vie for power over education because they perceive it as a powerful resource, which can be influential, for example, in shaping the political orientation of the participating students. Therefore, the government, through the curriculum, can potentially have a major impact on the political and social direction of the country in future years. Political groups that wish to influence the direction of the country might attempt to do so by gaining control of the curriculum. Local administrators, in turn, who wish to adjust the curriculum to the needs of their communities, are limited to a curriculum that might be more representative of a political group's interests than the interests of the students and families they serve.

Education also is highly political because many employment opportunities are available only to those with educational credentials. It is not surprising, therefore, that education can be a powerful bargaining chip in political struggles. Its highly centralized nature makes the ministry especially vulnerable to political intervention by various groups whose interests might not be consistent with the interests of the majority of the population. Another reason why the government might wish to continue a highly centralized ministry is to retain control of the organization that employs 570,000 teachers or approximately two-thirds of all the public servants in Turkey.

Prospects for Reform

From an organizational perspective, the Turkish national education system shows many of the characteristics of a "mechanistic-stagnant bureaucracy" (Morgan, 1986, p. 22). Morgan further describes the chain of command that characterizes this type of bureaucracy:

> From any place at the bottom of the hierarchy there is only one route to the top, a reflection of the principle that each subordinate should have no more than one superior. That is, commands come from the top and travel throughout the organization in a predetermined way. In such a structure, subordination of the individual for the general interest is common. As a result, mechanistic organizations encourage employees to comply with the rules rather than encouraging them to take initiative. (1986, p. 28)

Bolman and Deal (1991) put it this way:

> These are usually *older organizations* controlled by past traditions and turning out obsolete product lines. A predictable and placid environment has lulled the organizations to sleep, and top management is heavily committed to the old ways. Information systems are not sophisticated enough to detect the need for change. Lower-level managers feel ignored and *alienated*. Many old-line corporations and *public bureaucracies* have these characteristics. (p. 80, emphasis added)

According to Morgan (1986), a mechanistic approach could work well if the task were straightforward and the environment were stable. However, this type of organization has great difficulty in adapting to changing circumstances. Because organizations based on a mechanistic paradigm are designed to achieve predetermined goals, some set many years in the past, it is difficult for them to adapt to new demands that naturally occur in the field of education as a result of changing economic, social, and international events. In a field like education, the tasks are never straightforward and the environment is hardly stable. Because the mechanistic organization is designed for efficiency based on predetermined rules and regulations, it can easily turn into an unquestioning bureaucracy in which employees—in this case, school administrators and teachers—might feel dehumanized.

We suggest that decentralization would provide an effective basis for education reform by shifting power from the centralized bureaucracy in Ankara to provinces and localities and even to the school building level. Though it is not a panacea (political influence can occur at local as well as national levels), we believe that decentralization would facilitate the innovations in curriculum and teaching practices that Turkey needs to strengthen its education system. Education systems in many parts of the world have begun to decentralize, especially in countries that have used Continental European models of centralized governance, such as France, Italy, Spain, Brazil, and China. Educators and politicians generally support these reforms, although policies are needed to ensure that decentralization does not lead to increased inequities across different regions and population groups. The current education minister in Turkey (as others did before him) has recently announced that the Turkish education system, along with the overall structure of the Turkish governance model, should be decentralized.

Curriculum: The Outdated Software of the Education System

All public and private schools use a uniform curriculum, closely monitored by inspectors from the MONE. The State Board of Education (BOE), a department of the MONE, has the main responsibility for curriculum development, which takes place directly through its own commissions or through other institutions. In either case, the BOE must approve all curricula for use in schools.

Textbooks can be written either by commissions formed by the BOE or by independent authors. Again, the BOE must approve all textbooks before they can be used in schools. The most important criterion in the approval process is the conformity of the textbooks with the subject matter curriculum guidelines produced by the BOE. Because of this strict approval process, the textbooks are quite similar to each other in terms of the selection and organization of the content and the treatment of topics (Yildirim, 1999).

The standardized curriculum has a major influence on teaching practices because it controls what is taught and when it is taught and allows little flexibility to the teacher. All teachers are required to cover the same content within a standard school year. Teachers act mostly as technicians, for the curriculum does not leave much room for creativity or flexibility. Students feel that their individual needs are not taken into consideration; as a result, their motivation decreases as they move to upper grade levels (Yildirim, 1994).

Teachers' instructional plans, which the school principals and the provincial inspectors monitor, are largely influenced by the curriculum guides. Within this framework, teachers must plan their lessons in considerable detail through yearly and even daily plans. Teachers often complain about the gap between the curriculum requirements and the realities of their own classrooms. They feel that their plans must meet the requirements of administrators and inspectors, rather than reflecting the needs of their students (Yildirim, in press).

Prospects for Reform

The MONE is changing both the design and the implementation of the centralized curriculum. One of the purposes of the National Education Development Project, which took place between 1991 and 1999, was to introduce new approaches to curriculum development and teaching designed to give teachers more flexibility in content coverage, teaching strategies, and student assessment. Curriculum guides were introduced in the nation's schools to achieve this purpose and generally to improve the quality of teaching (Demirel, 2000). The guides emphasize the critical role teachers have in shaping the teaching and learning environment and encourage teachers to consider the needs of individual students and the community in making their decisions. Teachers are encouraged to plan their own instruction around the broad objectives of the course, to assess the curriculum content critically, and to view textbooks as instructional materials rather than as fixed content to be followed verbatim. The curriculum guides highlight student thinking and understanding and provide examples of "active learning." These new approaches, therefore, are a hopeful start at the central level in transforming memorization-based instruction into meaningful learning. Their objective is to continue providing an overall plan for courses while delegating to teachers the preparation of detailed curricula based on local needs. Teachers would have more power and would be more accountable for creating a meaningful teaching and learning environment (Yildirim, 1994).

In addition, the MONE is piloting the decentralization of curriculum development in five provinces through the direct initiatives of provincial education boards. The purpose is to develop curriculum based on regional needs and contexts. The BOE will still have to approve the final curriculum. Nevertheless, this initiative might be the beginning of relaxing tight control and standardization and giving more responsibility to local jurisdictions.

Teacher-Centered Teaching and Learning Process

Despite the changes described in the previous section, research on teaching practices in Turkey shows that most classrooms continue to be dominated by teacher-centered activity, generally through lectures and recitation. Teachers typically transmit knowledge to students and expect that they will reproduce more or less the same knowledge in the exams. Students rarely ask questions, and student-to-student interactions through small group activities or group projects are atypical (Balcı & Yildirim, 1999; Engin & Yildirim, 1999; Yildirim, 1997).

There are several reasons for the teacher-oriented teaching and learning process in schools (Yildirim, 2000). First, the practice of teaching focuses on testing, which takes place both at the end of basic education and at the end of high school. Entrance exams for the Anatolian high school and science high school (the "prestigious" schools) and for universities influence what is taught and how it is taught. Long before they are close to graduation, students begin seeing everything they learn in school in terms of its relevance to the entrance exams they will take. Teachers also feel that it is necessary to cover the content that might be included in the test questions and therefore align instruction for that purpose. The result is memorization without understanding; what students have learned is how to take the test.

Second, the centralized education system and the strict control of textbooks and curriculum create uniformity among teachers in terms of what they teach and how they teach it. This uniformity means that teachers in effect act as technicians, who apply decisions made elsewhere and whose behavior is closely controlled.

Third, textbooks, which adhere to curriculum guidelines, heavily influence class content and instructional methods. Moreover, the typical practice in Turkish schools of using only one textbook for each subject sends a message to students that there is only one reality, as validated through the material in the textbooks. Even teachers might not question the textbooks, assuming that the highest levels of the ministry have validated their accuracy and relevance. Alternative interpretations of events rarely find room for discussion in class (Yildirim, 1999).

Fourth, developing thinking skills is a low priority in many schools; both teaching and assessment strategies are focused on the "right" answer. Students assume that there is a universally accepted right answer to any question; teachers feel more comfortable in classrooms where they enjoy the authority of knowledge and where all students learn the same thing and in the same way. Questions that do not have easy answers are ignored because they carry a risk for highly structured learning. For example, the didactic approach makes it difficult to enter into a class discussion about multiple, and sometimes conflicting, interpretations of historical events or about the benefits and disadvantages of alternative policy options in the fields of economics and political science.

Thus, success at school becomes associated with learning (or memorizing) the curriculum content; for many students, constructing meaning has nothing to do with success in school. So knowledge is perceived as "absolute," something to maintain at least until the entrance exams are passed. Many teachers also tend to see knowledge in this way. Constructing meaning, therefore, is neither a priority among teachers nor an objective of the education system. Although there is growing interest in active learning, at least in theory, most classrooms discourage this approach in practice.

Finally, individual differences are ignored in organizing the teaching and learning activities. Curricula and teaching practices assume that all students have the same interests, learning needs, and learning styles. Contextual differences rarely lead to variation in the content or strategies used in the classroom. Only those students categorized as learning disabled or slow learners typically qualify for curriculum alterations; all others can expect to follow the curriculum designer's prescriptions. The slogan of official curricula might be active learning, but active learning rarely occurs in practice. The didactic approach appears to be holding strong.

The traditional view in Turkey is that teaching is a simple matter. "Good" students will learn regardless of the teaching strategy; the other students will never learn, no matter who teaches them. Another traditional view is that effective teaching is defined by students' test results. This definition of effectiveness gained popularity since the introduction of the high school and university entrance exams in the 1970s. Finally, the perception of effective teaching is based partially on teachers' personality characteristics, especially characteristics such as patience, altruism, fairness, responsibility, a pleasant personal appearance, and positive relationships with students, teachers, and administrators.

These traditional and vague perceptions of effective teaching still play an important role in the way Turkish schools function today. The views apply interchangeably, sometimes inconsistently, in supervisory practices, in teacher hiring and promotion practices, and even in teacher training and professional development. The vagueness in the criteria of effective teaching, certainly not unique to Turkey, makes it difficult to improve teaching practices.

Prospects for Reform

There are hopeful signs of reform efforts to define effective teaching in Turkish education and to take steps toward training more qualified teachers. Opposition to memorization and test-based instruction is increasing in education circles, with more emphasis on new theories of learning and student involvement. The "buzzwords" in these efforts are student-centered instruction, active learning, and information technology. The MONE (2001) has increased its efforts to define effective teaching and to use these criteria to reform teacher education, hire better-prepared teachers, and improve professional development for current teachers.

It is not surprising, however, that the implementation of these initiatives has not progressed smoothly. Although the message might have changed, the "top-down" approach has not been effective in encouraging either teachers or students to change. In order for the reforms to appear in classrooms, teachers would have to change their teaching ideologies and then pass on those new ideologies to their students, who also would have to change their classroom practices. This "double demand puts teachers under strain where the changes represent a major shift in beliefs and practices, and can threaten successful implementation unless necessary logistical and professional conditions are met" (Kennedy, 1995, p. 13).

A similar situation is apparently the case in MONE's efforts to influence teaching practices through more flexible curriculum guides, described previously. Teachers find it difficult to change the methods they have long used. Their traditional dependence on prescribed curricula, with an external definition of what is required, tends to feel comfortable and safe. When they are asked, instead, to make decisions based on alternatives and the realities of their own teaching context, and to be accountable for these decisions, many teachers feel that they are taking a great risk and continue to look to an authority to tell them what to do and how to do it. Although these circumstances pose serious obstacles to redefining the role of teachers, the ministry's initiatives are positive steps toward more effective teaching.

Measurement and Evaluation Practices

Teachers largely assess student performance in individual courses, generally by administering two exams—one in the middle of the semester and one at the end. The individual teacher prepares the exam questions, whether they are multiple choice, short answer, or essay. There is no formal collaboration among teachers in preparing tests and assessing their results, and the results are not used to inform the teaching and learning process.

Standardized tests typically are not used in Turkish schools to measure student performance in courses. However, in recent years there have been attempts to conduct national standardized testing in math and science. One of these initiatives originated with the Third Mathematics and Science Study, sponsored in 1999 by the International Association for the Evaluation of Educational Achievement. Eight thousand students in the eighth grade (the last year of compulsory elementary school in Turkey—roughly equivalent to the last year of middle school in the United States), in forty provinces from seven geographical regions, took the mathematics and science achievement tests prepared under this project. The results showed that Turkey ranked thirty-first in mathematics and thirty-third in science among the thirty-eight countries participating in the study (National Center for Education Statistics, 2003). Because Turkish schools were involved in this wide-scale project for the first time, the results should be interpreted with caution.

Although schools generally do not use standardized testing to assess student achievement, it is what awaits every student who wishes to attend a prestigious secondary school and then enter university. Students who graduate from elementary schools and apply for "high-status" secondary schools (e.g., Anatolian high schools and science high schools) must compete in a nationwide examination. In 2002 these schools accepted only 24 percent of 550,000 students who took the examination (MONE, 2003). Those students wishing to pursue university education after they graduate from secondary school must again take a nationwide examination; this time the acceptance rate is only about 11 percent for four-year colleges, plus another 8 percent for two-year colleges (Ogrenci Secme ve Yerlestirme Merkezi, 2003). This highly competitive context forces students to take private courses that focus on developing their test-taking skills, a practice that tends to increase "the gap" between affluent and low-income populations or those in remote rural areas, who have less access to the private courses.

Prospects for Reform

In some respects, Turkish schools are fortunate because they do not have to respond to frequent standardized tests. Teachers, therefore, can align their assessments with the curriculum. However, schools do not have procedures for measuring the accuracy of teachers' assessments or for providing them training in assessment practices.

Although students do not take standardized tests as part of their school program, the high school and university entrance exams they take have adverse effects on the teaching and learning process in schools. Moreover, students do not take the teachers' assessments seriously because they know that these assessments will not prepare them for the entrance exams. This problem could be alleviated partially by replacing the selection system based on standardized testing with a system that assesses students more holistically, using such measures as previous school achievement, teacher recommendations, and service to the community along with the entrance exams.

A Major Equity Problem: Urban–Rural Disparities and Girls' Education

According to the 2000 census, 59 percent of Turkey's total population of 67.8 million resides in urban areas, up from 51 percent in 1990 (State Institute of Statistics, 2003). Turkey is one of Europe's largest countries, and size brings with it population and socioeconomic diversity. For example, the Marmara region (including Istanbul, with about 12 million residents) is Turkey's most economically developed region. Generally speaking, the west and southwest parts of the country (comprising the Marmara, Aegean, and Mediterranean regions), with about half of Turkey's total population, are more developed economically than the rest of the country. The most economically disadvantaged regions are the northeast, east, and southeast. Overall, these east–west disparities are the source of major social and cultural differences. Those living in the western regions generally have a more modern and Western lifestyle and more liberal views, whereas those in the eastern and southeastern regions tend to be more conservative and religious. Disparities in educational opportunities accompany these variations in economic, cultural, and value orientations. Most domestic migration from rural to urban areas is from east to west, and a main motivation for migrating is the better educational opportunities available in the western parts of the country.

Within this context, girls' education is a more serious problem in rural areas of the country, especially in eastern and southeastern areas. Girls have fewer educational opportunities than boys. Girls' access to basic education opportunities increased, however, with the extension of basic compulsory education from five to eight years in 1997. In the 2000–1 academic year, the percentage of boys at the age of compulsory education in school was 94 percent, and the comparable percentage for girls was 88 percent (Kavak, 2003, p. 34). However, the gap has been declining since 1997, suggesting that the basic education extension bill has been particularly advantageous to girls (Kavak, 2003, p. 35).

Prospects for Reform

The compulsory basic education policies appear to have the greatest impact on girls' access to education in rural areas. About two million children (mostly girls) did not participate in basic compulsory education before 1997; however, this number declined to 900,000 in the 2000–1 academic year. The extension of basic education in 1997 from five to eight years alone contributed to this positive development (Kavak, 2003, p. 35). The 2001–5 plan states as a priority the extension of compulsory education to twelve years, until the end of secondary education, a requirement that would further increase girls' educational opportunities. Although not much was done to realize this target by 2003, it still is a key priority because educational indicators will play an important role in gaining European Union membership.

The educational and political elite, and nongovernmental national and international organizations, are well aware of the problem in girls' education, and periodic campaigns attempt to eradicate illiteracy among rural women and increase girls' access to basic education. The MONE and UNICEF launched the latest campaign on June 5, 2003. The campaign, which targets parents of girls, will initially be launched in ten provinces located in the eastern and southeastern parts of the country, with twenty additional provinces added in each of the next two years. The campaign's strategy is to involve local and national news media and governmental and nongovernmental organizations in order to raise parents' awareness of the importance of girls' education (*Hurriyet,* 2003).

EDUCATION REFORM IN RETROSPECT:
IT DOESN'T COME EASILY

Education systems and school organizations are resistant to change and reform. Along with the technical difficulties, education systems are social domains with deeply held beliefs, myths, and symbols that increase resistance (Weick, 1976). For example, Covaleskie (1994) argues that, within the U.S. context, systemic education reform is difficult to achieve because some practices are taken for granted. One example is students' progression through grade levels, with the corresponding sequencing of curriculum, which provides an enormous degree of transferability across the country: "Curricula are standard enough so that a child at [grade] L in New York can move to California and still be in grade L. . . . In short, there are 15,000 independent school districts supervised by 50 independent state governments doing essentially the same thing" (Covaleskie, 1994, p. 3). In addition, the author describes the impact of the textbook industry and standardized achievement tests, which help unify the education systems. He concludes:

> Thus, one of the fundamental features of the system also makes it resistant to change. Note that an individual school could dramatically change the nature of the education it provides, but that change would hamper transfer. As long as we use nationally normed tests and nationally distributed texts to manage education, and as long as teachers are evaluated by the performance of their students on these tests, and as long as students are expected to be in grade L at X years of age, there will be a tendency for education to be based in scope and sequence charts rather than on interaction between children and their teachers. On the other hand, without some force leading toward such standardi-

zation, the system would dissolve into individual units, disconnected from each other. (1994, p. 4)

Covaleskie's point is, in a sense, strikingly similar to what Adam Smith, in the nineteenth century, called the "invisible hand of market." In the educational context, the "invisible hand" is represented by national practices that are generally assumed to be a "given" and, therefore, impede reform. Covaleskie's assessment of resistance to change in a traditionally decentralized education system, as in the United States, is quite different from Turkey's case, where there is the "visible hand of state monopoly."

With a state monopoly, reform must come from above; however, education also is a target for political power struggles. In the November 2002 elections—for the first time in the recent republic's history—a single party, the Justice and Prosperity Party, won two-thirds of the vote and therefore formed a single-party majority government in the Turkish Parliament. The Islamist background of the party founders, along with some extremist Islamist factions within the party, has created considerable discomfort among the secular Turkish population. Although the party leadership declared long before the elections, and continues to state, that its ideological stance is center/moderate Right, questions continue to be raised by the more educated groups in the country, as well as by the business establishment and the state and military bureaucracies. Amid this confusion, one of the current government's education reform priorities is the decentralization of the state-regulated school system. Even apart from the government's ideological stance, the idea of decentralization has always created a backlash from the state and military bureaucracy and from some of the strong secular-modern population groups. The concern is that decentralization might weaken national control so that local religious and separatist factions would have a "golden opportunity" to gain control of schools—an outcome, it is feared, that would eventually lead to the disintegration of Turkey's national identity and the unity of the country.

Another obstacle to education reform is the scarcity of resources required for successful change. For example, education's share of Turkey's gross national product in 2002 was 2.9 percent, compared, for example, with 7.3 percent for Canada and 5.3 percent for the United States. Almost 85 percent of resources for education go for the salaries of teachers, administrators, and other staff; another 10–12 percent is for capital investments. Therefore, "extra" resources for major reforms are not available.

Finally, Turkey, like all countries, faces the inherent difficulties in moving from a reform idea to implementing it in practice. Akarsu (1990) labels Turkey's reforms as "patchwork" (p. 17). Many valuable reform ideas have been attempted without giving careful consideration to the potential impact of these individual initiatives on other parts of the system, without conducting small-scale pilots before full implementation, and without paying much attention to the large, inherently inert, bureaucracy.

In spite of these obstacles, there currently are positive signs. There is a consensus among a large proportion of the business, intellectual, and political elites that Turkey's education system must be fundamentally restructured if Turkey is to become competitive in the world market. The hopeful sign is the fact that Turkey is a candidate for full membership in the European Union. The European Union's standards in all domains of society are currently paving the way for radical changes in economic, political, and social policies. Education is at the top of the list.

NOTES

1. The word *dichotomies* is used to mean divisions in educational ideals, activities, and institutions created as a result of inconsistent government policies or the diverse goals of the public for children's education.

2. The National Security Council is composed of the president, the army chiefs of staff, the prime minister, the interior minister, and the foreign relations minister. It meets on a monthly basis and makes policy recommendations to the government. The army chiefs of staff have been quite influential in decisions the council makes.

REFERENCES CITED

Adalet ve Kalkinma Partisi. (2003). *Başbakan RECEP TAYYİP ERDOĞAN Tarafından TBMM'ne Sunulan 59'uncu Hükümet programı* [The program of the 59th Turkish government presented by Prime Minister Recep Tayyip Erdogan to the Turkish Grand National Assembly]. Available at www.akparti.org.tr/hukumetprg.doc (accessed June 23, 2003).

Akarsu, F. (1990). The Turkish educational system. Unpublished report, Middle East Technical University, Ankara.

Akyuz, Y. (1994). *Türk eğitim tarihi* [History of Turkish education]. Ankara: Kultur Koleji.

Balcı, A., & Yildirim, A. (1999). Liselerde sosyoloji dersinin oğretimi uzerine bir calışma [An assessment of sociology teaching at the high school level]. *Çukurova Üniversitesi Eğitim Fakültesi Dergisi, 2* (17), 102–17.

Basaran, I. E. (1999). Türkiye'de eğitim sisteminin evrimi [Evolution of the educational system in Turkey]. In F. Gok (Ed.), *75 yılda eğitim* (pp. 91–110). Istanbul: Tarih Vakfi.

Bolman, L., & Deal, T. (1991). *Reframing organizations: Artistry, choice and leadership.* Newbury Park, CA: Sage.

Caner, A. (1999). Sisteme radikal müdahale ve fiyasko: Ders geçme ve kredi sistemi uygulaması [A radical intervention to the system and fiasco: Credit system implementation]. In F. Gok (Ed.), *75 yılda eğitim* (pp. 210–11). Istanbul: Tarih Vakfi.

Covaleskie, J. F. (1994). The educational systems and resistance to reform: The limits of policy. *Educational Policy Analysis Archives, 2* (4). Available at http://epaa.asu.edu/epaa/v2n4.html (accessed October 6, 2003).

Demirel, O. (2000, September). Türk eğitim sisteminde öğretim programlarının geliştirilmesinde bilimsel yaklaşım ve 2000'li yıllar için öneriler [Scientific approach in curriculum development in the Turkish educational system: Recommendations for the year 2000 and beyond]. Paper presented at the Conference on the Turkish Education System Entering 21st Century, Ankara.

Discoverfrance. (2003). *Education in France,* part 2. Available at www .discoverfrance.net/France/Education/DF_education2.shtml (accessed June 23, 2003).

Engin, C., & Yildirim, A. (1999). Liselerdeki felsefe dersi oğretiminin değerlendirilmesi [An assessment of teaching philosophy at the high school level]. *Çukurova Üniversitesi Eğitim Fakültesi Dergisi, 2* (17), 80–94.

Erturk, S. (1971). *On yıl öncesine kıyasla öğretmen davranışları* [Teacher behaviors today and ten years ago]. Ankara: Hacettepe University.

Güncer, B., Simsek, H., & Yildirim, A. (1995). *A case study of the Basic Education Project for the children of seasonal agricultural workers in the Cukurova region in Turkey: Mid-decade review of Progress towards Education for All.* Paris: UNESCO Education for All Forum Secretariat.

Guvenc, B. (1998). *History of Turkish education.* Ankara: Turkish Education Association.

Hurriyet. (2003, June 6). Available at www.hurriyet.com.tr.

Kaplan, I. (1999). *Türkiye'de milli eğitim ideolojisi* [National education ideology in Turkey]. Istanbul: Iletisim.

Kavak, Y. (2003, May). Türk eğitim sisteminin genel görünümü [General outlook of the Turkish educational system]. Paper presented at the Conference on Teacher Training in Modern Educational Systems, Sivas, Turkey.

Kennedy, C. (1995, February). Teachers as agents of change. Paper presented at the First International Bilkent University School of English Language Conference, Bilkent University, Ankara.

Ministry of National Education (2001). *Öğretmen yeterlikleri* [Teacher competencies]. Ankara: Ministry of National Education.

———. (2003). Available at www.meb.gov.tr (accessed June 23, 2003).

Morgan, G. (1986). *Images of organizations.* Newbury Park, CA: Sage.

National Center for Education Statistics. (2003). Third Mathematics and Science Study. Available at http://nces.ed.gov/timss/results.asp#mathscience1999 (accessed June 23, 2003).

Ogrenci Secme ve Yerlestirme Merkezi. (2003). *Sayisal bilgiler* [Quantitative data]. Available at www.osym.gov.tr/BelgeGoster.aspxz?DIL=1& BELGEBAGLANTIANAH=153 (accessed June 23, 2003).

Ramirez, F. O., & Boli, J. (1987). Global patterns of educational institutionalization. In G. W. Thomas, J. W. Meyer, F. O. Ramirez, & J. Boli (Eds.), *Institutional structure: Constituting the state, society and the individual* (pp. 132–55). Newbury Park, CA: Sage.

Ryan, K., & Cooper, J. M. (2000). *Those who can, teach* (9th ed.). New York: Houghton Mifflin.

Simsek, H. (1992). Organizational change as paradigm shift: Analysis of change process at a large, public university by using a Kuhnian change model. Unpublished Ph.D. dissertation, University of Minnesota, Minneapolis.

———. (2002, November). Kondratieff cycles and long waves of educational reform: Educational policy and practice from 1789 to 2045. Paper presented at the Annual Meeting of the International Society for Educational Planning, Istanbul.

Simsek, H., & Louis, K. S. (1994). Organizational change as paradigm shift: Analysis of the change process in a large, public university. *Journal of Higher Education, 65* (6), 670–95.

Simsek, H., & Yildirim, A. (2001). The reform of pre-service teacher education in Turkey. In R. Sultana (Ed.), *Challenge and change in the Euro-Mediterranean region: Case studies in educational innovation* (pp. 411–32). New York: Peter Lang Inc.

Sonmez, V. (1996). *Eğitim felsefesi* [Educational philosophy] (4th ed.). Ankara: PEGEM.

State Institute of Statistics. (2003). *Nüfus ve kalkınma göstergeleri* [Population and development indicators]. Available at www.die.gov.tr (accessed June 23, 2003).

TUBITAK [the Scientific and Technical Research Council for Turkey]. (2003). Eğitim ve İnsan Kaynakları Paneli Ara Rapor, *Bilim ve Teknoloji Strateji-*

leri: Vizyon 2023 [Interim report of Panel on Education and Human Resources, *Science and Technology Strategies: Vision 2023*]. Ankara: TUBITAK.

Turan, S. (2000). John Dewey's report of 1924 and his recommendations on the Turkish educational system revisited. *History of Education, 29* (6), 543–56.

Weick, K. E. (1976). Educational organizations as loosely coupled systems. *Administrative Science Quarterly, 21,* 1–19.

Yedikardesler, M. (1984). Ankara ili ilçelerinde görev yapan ilkokul, ortaokul ve klasik devlet lisesi öğretmenlerinin meslek deneyimi, cinsiyetleri, bitirdikleri okul ve görev yaptıkları okul türü ile eğitim felsefesi görüşlerini belirleyen bir araştırma [A study on educational philosophies of teachers who work in elementary, secondary and high schools in counties of Ankara Province, based on their years of experience, gender, the type of school from which they graduated and the type of school in which they currently work]. Unpublished M.A. thesis, Hacettepe University, Ankara.

Yildirim, A. (1994, April). Temel program geliştirme modelleri ve ülkemizdeki program geliştirme çalışmalarına etkileri [Curriculum development models and implications for curriculum development in Turkey]. Paper presented at the First National Educational Sciences Conference, Adana, Turkey.

———. (1997). Teaching and learning of middle school social studies in Turkey: An analysis of curriculum implementation. *Mediterranean Journal of Educational Studies, 2* (2), 63–84.

———. (1999, April). An assessment of high school history textbooks in Turkey: Teachers' and students' perceptions. Paper presented at the Annual Conference of the American Educational Research Association, Montreal.

———. (2000, February). Teachers as constructors of meaning: Changing roles of teachers and the case in Turkey. Plenary speech at the Fifth International Bilkent University School of English Language Conference on Excellence in Teaching, Bilkent University, Ankara.

———. (In press). Instructional planning in a centralized school system: An assessment of teachers' planning at primary school level in Turkey. *International Review of Education, 49* (5), 525–43.

Yildirim, A., & Ok, A. (2002). Alternative teacher certification in Turkey: Problems and issues. In R. Sultana (Ed.), *Teacher education in the Mediterranean region: Responding to the challenges of society in transition* (pp. 259–76). New York: Peter Lang Inc.

8

Sweden:
A Welfare State in Transition

Eva Forsberg and Ulf P. Lundgren

> Only he who keeps his eye fixed on the far horizon will find his right road.
>
> —Dag Hammarskjöld (1905–1961)

During the 1990s Sweden implemented a series of education reforms. Taken together, these reforms are probably the most basic and extensive in the history of Swedish education. They affect the structure, distribution, and content of education and, above all, the governance and control of education. Thus, the reforms have changed education policy, administration, and teaching. The restructuring of the education system, in turn, reflects ongoing societal changes that require adjustments of the welfare state (Klette et al., 2000; Lindblad & Wallin, 1993). This chapter presents major reforms of the 1990s, describes the background and motives for restructuring, and concludes with general comments about restructuring in Sweden.

BACKGROUND AND MOTIVES FOR
RESTRUCTURING SWEDISH EDUCATION

Compulsory elementary education was formally established in Sweden in 1842, and a century later, a process of reform began aimed at expanding compulsory elementary education and making it a basis for upper secondary school. In 1962, nine years of compulsory schooling was established for all children ages seven to sixteen, followed in 1970 by a voluntary comprehensive secondary school. With these reforms, a long period of political discussion about when and how to "track" children temporarily ended. The system's goal was to ensure all children and young people access to equivalent education, regardless of gender or social, economic, and geographical background. Curricula and timetables for primary and secondary education became uniform nationwide, and government grants depended on adherence to detailed state regulations on school buildings, organization, and staff. The system, originally intended for local governance, became highly centralized, partly because of the reforms (Lundgren, 1996; cf. Paulston, 1968). Implementation assumed that a comprehensive system, equal for all, requires uniformity and centralized planning and control. The National Board of Education became the central administrative body, with related regional boards of education. Any changes were determined centrally, and implementation followed a top-down model in which politicians, administrators, and, to some extent, education researchers were considered especially important (Carlgren & Hörnqvist, 1999; Lindblad & Lundahl, 1999).

Public education came to be both a part of the Swedish welfare state and a prominent example of it. During the post–World War II expansion of the modern welfare systems in the 1950s, the implementation of reforms appeared relatively straightforward. Decision makers would set the goals, provide the necessary resources, and thereby guarantee that the goals would be achieved. The various sectors and the society would be the "instruments" for achieving the political goals. If the goals were not met, the blame was often ascribed to shortcomings in the original plan. The problems, it was argued, could be solved at the next stage. There was confidence that with educational planning, social engineering, and a rational paradigm that drew on educational research, failure could be prevented (Marklund, 1986; cf. Hirdman, 1990; Wildavsky, 1976).

Entering the 1970s—New Conditions for Education Policy

By the 1970s it became clear that the education system had not delivered what it promised. The goal of social equality through equal educational opportunity was unfulfilled; differences among students of different backgrounds remained and, in some cases, increased (Karabel & Halsey, 1978). In addition, students seemed to learn subordination rather than democratic citizenship (Jackson, 1968; Official Investigations for the State [SOU], 1985, p. 30). Education, as an instrument for social change, seemed to be a fairly blunt instrument and difficult to control from the center. Although the reforms did succeed in increasing access to education, socially and geographically, social background remained the best predictor of educational attainment (Härnqvist, 1992).

In the mid-1980s and the early 1990s, two national commissions recommended major changes in the governance of the welfare system (Englund, 1995; Lindblad, 1994; SOU, 1990, p. 44; 1993, p. 16). As a result, in the 1980s, Swedish education policy underwent a shift from central control, uniformity, social engineering, and consensus to decentralization and diversity (Lindblad & Wallin, 1993), as well as school choice (Lindensjö & Lundgren, 2000). This trend was consistent with those of many other countries at the time and incorporated elements of local development, school improvement, and school based management. These educational innovations, in turn, were adapted to a more conservative ideology that emphasized local control and freedom of choice (Telhaug, 1994). Both Social Democrats and nonsocialist parties contributed to these changes, which the Social Democrats introduced and nonsocialist parties developed. There were, however, different motives for the changes. Although the Social Democrats, at least initially, considered the new form of governance as a way to reach equality and inform local school development through evaluation, the nonsocialist parties wished to introduce both new goals and new instruments that would promote individual choice (Englund, 1995). Because the prior stability in political leadership had been replaced with a less stable political context, the reforms of the 1990s came to include elements of both motives. Indeed, the Social Democrats moved partly toward the Right by adopting, for example, the freedom of choice strategy (National Agency for Education, 2003; Schüllerqvist, 1995).

The Challenged Modern Welfare State

It is important to point out that policies aimed at decentralization and freedom of choice were not limited to education alone (Weiler, 1988,

1990). Rather, the crisis was a sign of problems affecting the entire public sector and the modern welfare state (Lindblad & Wallin, 1993; Olsen, 1990, 1991). The criticism of the welfare state focused on difficulties in governance, inefficiencies, and an overload of administrative tasks (Held, 1997). Government bureaucracies appeared large, costly, and inflexible, giving civil society few opportunities for participation. In addition, better-educated citizens called for more influence over their own lives and in social affairs. The Swedish model, with its strong public sector, was now under attack and considered more a problem than an effective instrument for the distribution of benefits or for social change.

The problems also were related to external changes: greater dependence on the global economy and international cooperation and agreements; the development of new communication technologies, with consequences for the labor market; and the transition from an industrial to a service and knowledge society (SOU, 1990, p. 44). Increasing taxes to finance reforms, a feasible strategy during the earlier period of expansion, became a limited option in a more global economy; reforms now had to be financed by economic growth in an international context (Organization for Economic Cooperation and Development [OECD], 2001). At the same time, the transformation from an industrial to a service and knowledge marketplace, which required new information technologies, put new and increased demands on education to respond to the adult population's need to obtain the skills required to compete in the changing job market (Kim, 2002a; OECD, 2000). The dilemma, then, is how best to finance reforms and educational expansion in a more global economy, where new resources cannot be easily raised by increasing taxation. Expansion now had to be financed by higher productivity, which required reforms that were quite different from those of earlier years.

Education in Sweden is increasingly discussed in the context of international competition and international test-score comparisons. The government that came into power in 1991 placed on the agenda a goal for Swedish schools to become the best in Europe. The current minister of education, in turn, has announced a goal for Swedish students to achieve the top test scores in the Program for International Student Assessment (PISA), the international comparative study sponsored by the OECD.

The political context also changed. During the 1970s and 1980s the central government became increasingly fragmented. The long-standing Social Democratic governance struggled within fragile coalitions, sometimes under conservative, but mostly under Social Democratic, administrations. Several new political parties entered the Parliament, and there was, at the same time, a trend toward less coherence in the administrative organization, with increasing specialization and division of labor. As a result, by the 1970s it had become more difficult to reject conflicting demands (Crozier, 1977). These political and administrative changes were exacerbated by the fact that limited resources also led to increased competition among various sectors in the society, with increases in lobbying and conflicting political pressures. It is not surprising, therefore, that the earlier planning models became ineffective and it was more difficult for the central government to implement reform policies to manage complex interrelated problems and to set priorities (Lindensjö & Lundgren, 1986; Wildavsky, 1976). The educational "restructuring" that occurred in the 1990s represented an attempt to respond to problems in the welfare state and thereby restore the legitimacy of the state in addressing social issues (Klette et al., 2000; Lindensjö & Lundgren, 2000).

Finally, Sweden has experienced demographic changes resulting from major increases in immigration. Currently, 12.7 percent of students have at least one or both parents born outside of Sweden, and as many as fifty different languages might be spoken in some schools. These trends create new challenges for the education system. Until the past fifty years, most immigration to Sweden was from Finland (which was part of Sweden until 1809), with some immigration from other Western European countries. Most of the immigrants in the second half of the twentieth century, however, were political refugees—from Chile, Ethiopia, Hungary, Iran, Iraq, Libya, Poland, Somalia, Turkey, Turkistan, and the former Yugoslavia. The ethnic, racial, and cultural diversity of Sweden, therefore, has increased enormously in the past two generations.

In general, the education policy has been to integrate immigrant students into regular classes. The exception is the "home language" policy, established in the 1970s, which guaranteed these students instruction in their home language. In the 1990s the policy changed,

and municipalities now are required to provide home language instruction only if five or more students request it; the number of re-
quests for this type of instruction decreased during the 1990s. The issue of language policy reflects broader questions of education goals:
whether to design education programs to maintain students' home
language and culture or to place the emphasis instead on students' integration into mainstream society. The current trend toward decentralization and school choice means that these decisions increasingly
will be made by educators and parents at the local level.

Democracy, Efficiency, and Professionalism

Educational restructuring focused on three main goals: increased
democracy, greater efficiency, and enhanced professionalism. The
goal of democracy inspired strategies of increasing participatory governance and freedom of choice. Decentralization and deregulation
would move the political decisions closer to where education was
taking place, in turn strengthening ties between central administration and local politicians, civil servants, school staff, parents, and students (SOU, 1992, p. 94). As a result, previously marginalized groups
in the society would have greater power (Kreisberg, 1992). The related freedom of choice strategy would both increase families' rights
to make choices within and among schools and reduce the power of
what many perceived as a dysfunctional bureaucratic, monopolistic
state (Lindblad, Lundahl, & Zachari, 2001). Thus, democracy would
increase efficiency; indeed, the argument for efficiency assumes the
need for more outcome-based measures of student and school performance and better adjustment of resources in relation to these outcomes (Klette et al., 2000). The demands inherent in these reforms
would enhance professionalism by encouraging more professional
autonomy and control over educational content and methods of
learning (Weiler, 1988, 1990).

Decentralization and market competition change the relative influence of the governance "instruments" available to ministries of education. The ability to influence through regulations and resources declines, while ideology and evaluation play a more significant role
(Lundgren, 1981, 1991, 2001). The remaining work for the ministry in

a decentralized system is to strengthen the ideological rationale (referred to in the United States, for example, as the "bully pulpit") and the evaluation and accountability system, that is, to govern by goals and control of results. These changes, described in the next section, apply to the entire education system, from early childhood education to higher education.

REFORMS OF THE 1990s

The Swedish public school system is organized into compulsory schooling for children ages seven to sixteen, a noncompulsory preschool class for six year olds, and noncompulsory upper secondary school.[1] Also included are Sami schools for Sami children, special schools for deaf children, programs for children with learning disabilities, and adult education.[2] In addition, children ages one to five have the right to attend preschool or family day care, and schoolchildren through age twelve are entitled to child care, in either leisure-time centers or family day care. There are national curricula for all these forms of education. The state also provides free higher education in universities and university colleges. The overall responsibility for education in Sweden is borne by the central government, with almost all education under the jurisdiction of the Ministry of Education and Science. The main changes of the 1990s involve early childhood education, compulsory school, and upper secondary school, but reforms of adult, as well as higher, education, including teacher education, have also been undertaken. The Swedish school system was restructured in several ways: (1) increased decentralization and deregulation; (2) increased access to child care and to higher education; (3) revised curriculum content and grading systems; and (4) increased consistency of the evaluation systems to respond to the other changes.

Decentralization and Deregulation

In the mid-1980s Parliament initiated a process designed to increase decentralization, reduce regulations, and focus instead on goals and results. The central government retained the responsibility for curriculum and national evaluation, in order to facilitate equality of opportunity, but delegated to local school systems the responsibility for deciding on school organization and staff policies (including salary negotiations) that would best meet the goals. National subsidies, now given to municipalities as block grants rather than as categorical aid, were designed to facilitate this transfer of responsibilities and reduce regulation. (Recently, however, direct federal grants have been reintroduced, e.g., to increase teachers' skills in certain areas and to reduce student–teacher ratios.) Along with increased flexibility, municipalities also had increased responsibility for meeting the curriculum goals, conducting local evaluations, and preparing reports and data analysis for the national government.

The shift from a centralized to a more decentralized education system meant that local politicians and civil servants now had responsibilities for financing, organizing, and monitoring the local education systems. Education, therefore, became a local as well as a national political issue in Sweden. According to the minister of education and science at that time, the present prime minister, Göran Persson, the central government had not abolished its responsibility for education but, rather, continued to be very much involved and to exercise influence and control by establishing the framework for the value system that would guide education, for the main goals of education, and for the outcome measures by which schools would be evaluated. Currently, there are two main central agencies for education: the National Agency for Education, which is responsible primarily for education inspections, surveys, and evaluations and also for curriculum development and grading criteria; and the National Agency for School Development, which supports municipal and local school development in preschool, compulsory school, and adult education.

At about the same time, several decisions were made to increase the participation of teachers, parents, and students in school governance. Teacher involvement reflected interest primarily in increased professionalism, whereas parent and student involvement found expression in a desire to strengthen influence on school policies and the freedom to choose among schools, programs, and courses (Forsberg, 2000, 2002). Because restructuring increased demands on teachers, particularly in areas of curriculum design and evaluation, and parental and community involvement (Klette et al., 2000), teacher associations, in turn, were able to make agreements with local employers that connected those demands to an individualized salary system (*A Drive to Two Thousand,* 2000; Översyn Läraravtalet, 2000). In addition, an experimental period, beginning in 1997, gave parents the majority on local school boards for compulsory school and students the majority for upper secondary school.

As part of the freedom of choice policy, parents during the past decade have been able to choose between municipal and independent schools and among different municipal schools. Independent schools received municipal funding if they followed the national curriculum—a significant change in the Swedish policy toward independent schools, which had traditionally operated outside the public school system. There is, however, a restriction on freedom of choice because children have the right to attend the nearest school, which means that other children can choose the school only if spaces are available. In addition, independent schools still represent a small portion of the system, although student enrollment in these schools has increased significantly. The independent schools, like the municipal schools, are free, with the exception of transportation fees for the independent schools. In practice, freedom of choice is much more likely to operate in large cities than in small towns and rural areas.

Child Care and Higher Education

During the 1990s, preschool, compulsory school, and school child care gradually became more closely associated. By 1995 municipalities became obligated to provide child care for all children ages one to twelve. As of today, this applies to all children with special needs or with parents who are working, studying, or on parental leave; in addition, a free preschool class has been established. With the transfer of preschool and school child care from the Ministry for Social Affairs to the Ministry of Education and Science, early childhood education and care became part of the education system, with national curriculum guidelines. Child care has increased rapidly: In 2002 more than 70 percent of children ages one to five were enrolled in preschool, with about the same percentage of six- to nine-year-olds in leisure centers.

All youths, up to the age of twenty, have the right to attend upper secondary school and, at least in principle, to select their program. The former difference between theoretical and vocational programs has ended, although in practice universities often add eligibility requirements that continue the distinction. Most young people go directly from compulsory school to upper secondary school. Students age twenty or older may attend adult education programs. These include basic and upper secondary adult education programs corresponding with the content of compulsory and upper secondary school, along with Swedish for immigrants. A new form of postsecondary school vocational education also is in place, which complements institutions of higher education. The vocational courses normally last for two years and are characterized by their close contact with the workplace. A new adult education initiative seeks to reduce unemployment and the growing gap in levels of education. In addition, Sweden has a long tradition of folk high schools and study circles organized by adult education associations, designed for a wide range of the population and covering a wide variety of subjects.

Additional financial incentives encourage students to attend upper secondary school and then university. For example, all students sixteen to twenty years old attending upper secondary school receive state study assistance. Moreover, in addition to free university education, the students' nonrepayable portion of study assistance is higher than before. A new state study assistance program also facilitates attendance for unemployed persons, twenty-five to fifty-five years old, in higher or adult education.

During the 1990s there was a major expansion in higher education, involving institutions, programs, types of examinations, and students. The number of students in higher education has increased by more than 60 percent since 1990. In 2002, 42 percent of the student age group entered higher education before twenty-five years of age, with noticeably more women (48 percent) than men (37 percent) and a larger proportion of children from highly educated families (69 percent) than from families with low educational attainment (23 percent). Even though policies have been introduced to reduce differences among students of different backgrounds, the gap between children of high and low economic status has been relatively stable over a long period. In addition, very few doctoral students (10 percent) have a working-class background.

In 2001 Sweden spent 8 percent of its gross national product, or 174 billion Swedish crowns (SEK), on education.[3] The costs increased by 18 percent in the five-year period between 1996 and 2001. Almost 40 percent of the Swedish population is enrolled in either educational programs or working schools. In this context, the Swedish population is a prime example of the *Homo pedagogicus* (Lundgren, 2002). This description is further supported by the large increases in education levels during the 1990s.

Curriculum Content and Grading Systems

The national curriculum states fundamental values, basic objectives, and guidelines. Although there are nationally approved syllabi for separate subjects, individual schools determine the organization, content, and teaching methods within the framework of national and municipal goals. A general timetable recommends the minimum number of instructional hours for each subject, but the guidelines apply to the entire nine years of compulsory school and, in addition, give schools the option of reducing the recommended time by up to 20 percent. At present, a comprehensive five-year trial permits schools to dispense with the timetable in order to investigate whether the amount of time spent on a subject makes a significant difference in student achievement. At least in theory, these provisions give teachers and students considerable flexibility.

The grading system also has changed. Before the reforms of the 1990s, students were assessed in relation to each other and not in relation to established knowledge objectives. The new system awards grades to students in years eight and nine on a three-point scale: pass, pass with distinction, and pass with special distinction. Students not passing have the right to receive a written report on their accomplishments. At the end of grade nine, nationally approved examinations in the subjects of Swedish (or Swedish as a second language), English, and mathematics are used as part of the assessment.

(A national, optional test is available for grade five, as well as diagnostic materials for earlier years.) Currently, student assessment is based on achievement goals stated in the syllabi and nationally approved criteria for different grades. New requirements for attending upper secondary school were established in connection with the grading system. Students now must receive at least a pass in Swedish, English, and mathematics in order to attend these schools, a standard reached by 90 percent of the students. Students who do not reach that standard can attend "individual programs," which are designed to help them gain entry into upper secondary school and vary in content and length, depending on each student's needs. However, these programs are at risk of being abolished because of a concern that too many students are attending them.

The grading structure in upper secondary school is generally similar to that in compulsory school. Completion rates pose a major problem: Although 98 percent of the age group attends upper secondary school, only about 70 percent of the students receive a "leaving certificate" within four years.

Educational Evaluation

Educational quality is a central theme in discussions about education reform in Sweden and in assessments of the specific reforms that are implemented (Nytell, 2003). The concern about quality has been translated (as it has in many other countries) to a focus on outcome measures, program monitoring, and program evaluation. Not surprisingly, the generation of statistics has increased in recent years because of a rising interest on the part of politicians, the media, and the public, as well as participation in international studies. Municipalities and schools now are required to review their activities and present the results in "quality" reports. Based on these reports, the national government provides support to municipalities to help them achieve national goals. Rankings for lower and upper schools, and for universities, have become a more frequent phenomenon in recent years, and during 2001 the national government constructed an extensive database, containing quantitative and qualitative data, which is now available on the Internet. In addition, national school inspectors monitor the quality of education for a range of special topics. Although at least some of the Swedish education reforms have been designed to decentralize and increase flexibility, central control also has been strengthened by the focus on outcome measures as a way to improve educational quality.

CONCLUSION

This section highlights the following issues, which have been promi nent in public discussion, agency reports, and education research: (1) whether restructuring promotes a narrow curriculum at the expense of broader education designed to encompass societal values, (2) the impact of restructuring on social inclusion or exclusion, and (3) the consequences of "participatory governance."

Cultivating Instrumental Knowledge Transmission or Broader Societal Values?

A key issue is whether educational restructuring narrows the curriculum, especially in comprehensive and upper secondary schools but also in early childhood and preschool classes. The new grading system, combined with the eligibility criteria for entrance to national programs in upper secondary school, has contributed to a focus on Swedish, English, and mathematics in compulsory school and has reduced attention to broader education goals. The quality indicator system, the quality reports, and the ranking lists, all of which contribute to increased competition among schools, have exacerbated this trend. A related issue is whether the transfer of early childhood programs and school child care to the school sector also has contributed to a narrowing of education (Kim, 2002b; National Agency for Education, 1999).

Social Inclusion or Exclusion?

After the reforms of the 1960s, the compulsory and upper secondary schools became more integrated. The expansion of school child care and early education, as well as higher education, has made it possible for new groups to enter the education system earlier and leave it later. In addition, adult education has been expanded both to new groups and to a greater number of persons. Moreover, the system is highly integrated. Children and students of different cultures, religions, and genders are generally taught together. In the upper secondary school, the border between theoretical and vocational programs has become less distinct; both now permit formal eligibility to higher education. Higher education has expanded so that there are more programs and openings and more opportunities to attend school closer to home.

Sweden, however, is a more divided and polarized country today than it was ten to fifteen years ago, with respect to income, wealth, living conditions, and housing segregation, in part because of increased immigration. Categories traditionally associated with exclusion, in Sweden as in other countries, are unemployment, low education, low income, and ethnic background; less frequently mentioned, but equally important, are persons with disabilities and single mothers. Even though education has expanded significantly, societal divisions continue to be reflected in education and, in some respects, are enhanced. A rather large number of students cannot enter a national program at the upper secondary school level, and many of those who enter do not complete their studies in upper secondary school or higher education. Also noticeable is the more frequent use of ability grouping in schools, as well as the decrease in special education within classes and the increased number of children attending special schools. Children from "marginalized" families are less likely to succeed in school; the new grading system makes this division between those who succeed and those who fail more visible than before. Moreover, a larger proportion attend special programs in upper secondary school, and dropout rates are high; a relatively small proportion attends higher education at all, and few of them can be found in high-status programs. The differences between the educational choices of men and women are also increasing. During the last decade women have tended to use education as a means to a career more frequently than men, doctoral studies excepted. Social inclusion and exclusion, in today's public discourse, are more frequently perceived as an individual responsibility, rather than the effect of structural phenomena (Beijer & Bolin, 2001; Lindblad, Lundahl, & Zackari, 2001).

In 2003 the National Agency for Education reported on the consequences of the freedom of choice strategy. In general, the information available to parents has improved, but the system understandably continues to demand knowledge and time to be used effectively. Most parents and students, especially better-educated parents, are in favor of the right to choose schools, even though most parents continue to select the closest school. In addition, both parents and students think that freedom of choice has facilitated their participation in school policies. School choice also has given some schools the opportunity to expand, though others have lost competent teachers and students. Choice does not appear to promote more efficient use of resources. In general, the report of the National Agency for Education views freedom of choice primarily as a "social project" for better-educated parents living in big cities, where choice is an option. With respect to equity, the report describes a trend to segregate students by ethnicity and achievement. Overall, the school system has become more segregated, and, in a way, a parallel school system is being established that increases the status differences among schools.

Participation in School Governance

As mentioned earlier, participation in school governance was one of the prominent features of the rhetoric of Swedish reforms in the 1990s. For students, participation implies the right to have an impact on the content and working methods in courses, as well as the right to choose among programs and, to some extent, courses. Although students report some increased influence, a majority of students continue to consider their potential contribution, particularly on curriculum content, too restricted (Forsberg, 2002; SOU, 2000, p. 1).

The participation of teachers in school governance has been discussed primarily in terms of professionalization. The new curricula are intended to leave room for professional judgment in the choice of content and working methods. Thus, Swedish teachers are expected to design curricula. The curricula also emphasize student outcomes rather than simply the transmission of information. Apparently,

Swedish teachers have accepted the new curricula or at least have adjusted to them rhetorically. At the same time, however, they point out the time limitations resulting from other pressures: budget problems, individualized salaries, heavy work demands, and accountability for learning results in combination with the grading system. The changes have been described as "shock professionalization" because teachers are expected to fulfill a wide range of responsibilities for which they are not prepared. In addition, the signals teachers receive are conflicting: increased professionalization and autonomy, on the one hand, but greater external control resulting from restructuring and accountability, on the other (Klette et al., 2002; cf. Kallós & Lundahl, 1994).

The restructuring of Swedish education provides a case study of policy change implemented by a welfare state in transition, with scarce finances, governance problems, and (at least in the perception of some of the population) a lack of legitimacy. The hope was that decentralization, deregulation, and freedom of choice would increase democratic participation, efficiency, and professionalism. At the same time, however, greater control in the form of accountability for results occurred at every level of the education system and, in fact, contributed to renewed centralization. To complicate matters, the restructuring began during the economic recession of the 1990s. In short, the consequences of the changes for students and teachers, as well as for Swedish society as a whole, remain to be seen.

NOTES

We would like to thank the members of the Research Unit for Studies in Educational Policy and Educational Philosophy for their valuable comments and contributions to the chapter.

1. If not otherwise cited, this section draws on data produced by the Ministry of Education and Science, the National Agency for Education, the National Agency for Higher Education, and official statistics.
2. The Sami population is an ethnic and linguistic minority living in northern Scandinavia and the Kola Peninsula. Of a total population of approximately 60,000, 17,000 live in Sweden. The Sami language is an official language in Sweden.
3. Nine SEK equal approximately one euro (June 2004).

REFERENCES CITED

Beijer, M., & Bolin, S. (2001). Curriculum development for social inclusion. Paper presented at the Regional Seminar for the Baltic and Scandinavian Countries, Vilnius, Lithuania.

Carlgren, I., & Hörnqvist, B. (1999). *När inget facit finns . . . om skolutveckling i en decentraliserad skola* [When there are no key answers . . . about school development in a decentralized school]. Stockholm: Skolverket.

Crozier, M. (1977). *The governability of West European society*. Essex: University of Essex.

A drive to two thousand. (2000). Stockholm: Kommunförbundet.

Englund, T. (Ed.). (1995). *Utbildningspolitiskt systemskifte?* [A paradigm shift in educational policy?]. Stockholm: HLS förlag.

Forsberg, E. (2000). *Elevinflytandets många ansikten* [The many faces of student influence]. Uppsala Studies in Education, 93. Acta Universitatis Upsaliensis. Uppsala: Uppsala Universitet.

———. (2002). Governing by participation. Paper presented at the 26th Association for Teacher Educators in Europe Annual Conference, Stockholm.

Härnqvist, K. (1992). Utbildningsreformer och social selection [Educational reforms and social selection]. In R. Åberg (Ed.), *Social bakgrund, utbildning, livschanser* [Social background, education, and life chances]. Stockholm: Carlssons.

Held, D. (1997). *Demokratimodeller. Från klassisk demokrati till demokratisk autonomi* [Models of democracy: From classical democracy to democratic autonomy]. Göteborg: Daidalos.

Hirdman, Y. (1990). *Att lägga livet till rätta—Studier i svensk folkhemspolitik* [To make life right—Studies in Swedish welfare policy]. Stockholm: Carlsson Bokförlag.

Jackson, P. W. (1968). *Life in classrooms.* New York: Holt, Reinhart and Winston.

Kallós, D., & Lundahl, L. (1994). Recent changes in teachers' work in Sweden: Professionalization or what? In D. Kallós & S. Lindblad (Eds.), *New policy contexts for education: Sweden and the United Kingdom.* Pedagogiska Rapporter, 42. Uppsala: Pedagogiska institutionen, Uppsala Universitet.

Karabel, J., & Halsey, A. H. (1978). *Power and ideology in education.* London: Oxford University Press.

Kim, L. (2002a). *Lika olika: En jämförande studie av högre utbildning och forskning i de nordiska länderna* [Same difference: A comparative study of tertiary education and research in the Nordic countries]. Stockholm: Högskoleverket.

———. (2002b). *Masshögskolans paradoxer—Fem inlägg i den svenska högskoledebatte* [The paradoxes of mass universities—Five contributions in the debate about tertiary education in Sweden]. Stockholm: SISTER.

Klette, K., Carlgren, I., Rasmussen, J., & Simola, H. (2002). *Restructuring Nordic teachers: Analyses of interviews with Danish, Finnish, Swedish and Norwegian teachers.* Oslo: University of Oslo.

Klette, K., Carlgren, I., Rasmussen, J., Simola, H., & Sundkvist, M. (2000). *Restructuring Nordic teachers: An analysis of policy texts from Finland, Denmark, Sweden and Norway.* Oslo: University of Oslo.

Kreisberg, Seth. (1992). *Transforming power: Domination, empowerment, and education.* Albany: State University of New York Press.

Lindblad, S. (1994). Notes on post-welfare education: Towards a new-liberal education reform in Sweden? In D. Kallós & S. Lindblad (Eds.), *New policy contexts for education: Sweden and the United Kingdom.* Pedagogiska Rapporter, 42. Uppsala: Pedagogiska institutionen, Uppsala Universitet.

Lindblad, S., & Lundahl, L. (1999). Education for a re- or de-construction of "the strong society"? In S. Lindblad & T. S. Popkewitz (Eds.), *Education governance and social integration and exclusion: National cases of the educational system and recent reforms.* EGSI Project. Uppsala Reports on Education, 34. Uppsala: Uppsala University.

Lindblad, S., Lundahl, L., & Zachari, G. (2001). Sweden: Increased inequalities—Increased stress on individual agency. In S. Lindblad & T. S. Popkewitz (Eds.), *Education governance and social integration and exclusion: Studies in the powers of reason and the reason of power.* EGSI Project. Uppsala Reports on Education, 39. Uppsala: Uppsala University.

Lindblad, S., & Wallin, E. (1993). On transition of power, democracy and education in Sweden. *Journal of Curriculum Studies, 25* (1).

Lindensjö, B., & Lundgren, U. P. (1986). *Politisk styrning och utbildningsreformer* [Political governance and educational reforms]. Stockholm: Liber.

———. (2000). *Utbildningsreformer och politisk styrning* [Educational reforms and political governance]. Stockholm: HLS förlag.

Lundgren, U. P. (1981). *Model analysis of pedagogical processes,* (2d ed.) Lund: Liber Läromedel/CWK Gleerup.

———. (1991). *Between education and schooling.* Geelong, Australia: Deakin University Press.

———. (1996). Utbildningspolitik och utbildningsplanering. Personliga reflektioner [Educational policy and educational planning. Personal reflections]. In C. Gustafsson (Ed.), *Pedagogikforskarens roll i utbildningsplanering* [The role of the educational researcher in educational planning] (pp. 97–124). Uppsala: Pedagogiska institutionen, Uppsala Universitet.

———. (2001). Governing the education sector: International trends, main themes and approaches. In *Governance for quality of education* (pp. 25–37). Budapest: Institute for Education Policy/Open Society Institute.

———. (2002). "*Homo pedagogicus?*" *Framtider, 3,* 4–10.

Marklund, I. (1986). Pedagogisk forskning i skolans tjänst [Educational research in the service of the school]. In J. Gustafsson & F. Marton (Eds.),

Pedagogikens gränser och möjligheter [The limits and possibilities of pedagogy]. Lund: Studentlitteratur.

National Agency for Education. (1999). *Skolverkets underlag till välfärdsbokslut över 1990-talet* [The national agency on welfare in the 1990s]. Stockholm: Skolverket.

———. (2003). *Valfrihet och dess effekter inom skolområdet* [Free choice and its effects on schools]. Stockholm: Skolverket.

Nytell, H. (2003). Kvalitetsvågen—Några utsnitt i en dokumentstudie [The quality wave—Some parts of a document study]. In E. Forsberg (Ed.), *Skolan och tusenårsskiftet: En vänbok till Ulf P. Lundgren* [The school and the millennium shift: A book in honor of Ulf P. Lundgren] (pp. 135–44). Studies in Educational Policy and Educational Philosophy: Research Reports. Uppsala: Uppsala Universitet.

Olsen, J. P. (1990). *Demokrati på svenska* [Democracy in Sweden]. Stockholm: Carlsson Bokförlag.

Olsen, J. P. (Ed.). (1991). *Svensk demokrati i förändring* [Swedish democracy in transition]. Stockholm: Carlsson Bokförlag.

Organization for Economic Cooperation and Development. (2000). *The management of knowledge*. Paris: Organization for Economic Cooperation and Development.

———. (2001). *The well-being of nations: The role of human and social capital*. Paris: Organization for Economic Cooperation and Development.

Översyn Läraravtalet. (2000). *Evaluation of the labor market for teachers*. Stockholm: Kommunförbundet.

Paulston, R. G. (1968). *Educational change in Sweden*. New York: Teachers College Press, Columbia University.

Schüllerqvist, U. (1995). Förskjutningen av svensk skolpolitisk debatt under det senaste decenniet [Changes in Swedish debates on school policy during the last decade]. In T. Englund (Ed.), *Utbildningspolitiskt systemskifte?* [A paradigm shift in educational policy?]. Stockholm: HLS förlag.

State Official Investigations. (1985). *Skola för delaktighet: Betänkande från en arbetsgrupp inom 1983 års demokratiberedning* [Schools for participation: Suggestions from a working group within the 1983 democracy committee]. Stockholm: Allmänna förlaget.

———. (1990). *Demokrati och makt i Sverige: Maktutredningens huvudrapport* [Democracy and power: The main report]. Stockholm: Allmänna förlaget.

———. (1992). *Skola för bildning: Betänkande av läroplanskommittén* [Schools for the future: Report from the curriculum committee]. Stockholm: Allmänna förlaget.

———. (1993). *Nya villkor för ekonomi och politik: Ekonomikommisionens förslag* [New conditions for the economy and politics: Suggestions from the economy commission]. Stockholm: Allmänna förlaget.

————. (2000). *En uthållig demokrati: Demokratiutredningens betänkande* [A sustainable democracy: Report from the committee on democracy]. Stockholm: Allmänna förlaget.

Telhaug, A. O. (1994). *Den nye utdanningspolitiske retorikken: Bilder av internasjonal skoleutvikling* [The new rhetoric of educational policy: Pictures from the international development of education]. Oslo: Universitetsforlaget.

Weiler, H. (1988). *Education and power: The politics of educational decentralization in a comparative perspective*. Palo Alto: Stanford University Press.

————. (1990). Decentralisation in educational governance: An exercise in contradiction? In M. Granheim, M. Kogan, & U. P. Lundgren (Eds.), *Evaluation as policymaking*. London: Jessica Kingsley Publishers.

Wildavsky, A. (1976). *Speaking truth to power: The art and craft of policy analysis*. Boston: Little, Brown and Co.

9

Israel: From Egalitarianism to Competition

Adam Nir and Dan Inbar

> Whatever was accomplished in this country was accomplished collectively.
>
> Golda Meir (1898–1978)

This chapter analyzes the development of the strongly egalitarian and centralized Israeli public school system and the changes it has gone through in recent years. It focuses on the link between the social missions that faced the newly created state and the challenges to the education system. The chapter argues that the strong and rigid central structure—highly valued during the first decades after independence as a means for coping with social gaps, inequality, and the absorption of the large numbers of immigrants from different social and cultural backgrounds—has recently become dysfunctional, as it fails to adjust to the changing circumstances in Israel and in education systems around the world. Specifically, our main line of argument is that centralization led the education system to favor first-order (Watzlawick, Weakland, & Fisch, 1979) types of restructuring initiatives and policies, which in reality produced "more of the same" rather than "different" types of changes. Reforms during the past decade have attempted to increase the system's flexibility by decreasing central power and strengthening local control.

This chapter focuses on the issues and trends related to the education of Jewish children in Israel. From the inception of the State of Israel, the school system has been viewed as the main public institution responsible for integrating into Israeli society Jewish immigrants from a wide range of countries, cultures, and socioeconomic groups. The Israeli government also is responsible for funding the education of Arab children (Muslim, Christians, Druse, and Circassians) who are Israeli citizens. The Arab school system is a separate system, with Arabic rather than Hebrew used as the medium of instruction and a distinct curriculum. For these reasons and the obvious political ones—and in sharp contrast to policies for the education of Jewish children—integration between the two sectors has not been a goal.

The gap in average socioeconomic status between Arab and Jewish students is reflected in a gap in educational participation and achievement, although this gap is narrowing. For example, in 1980 the chances that an Arab child would attend high school were only about two-thirds of those of a Jewish child. By 2002 the proportion had increased to 84 percent (Cop, 2002). The improvement is also evident in the rate of children who pass the matriculation examinations. In 1991, 45.4 percent Arab and 67.3 percent Jewish children earned a matriculation diploma, and in 2001 the percentage had increased to 59.1 percent and 69.7 percent, respectively (Statistical Abstract of Israel, 2002), showing that the gap between the sectors is declining but not fully obliterated. However, the most important questions raised by the structure of Arab education in Israel—for example, the impact of separatism on equality of educational opportunity—are distinct from those addressed by the current chapter and deserve a far more detailed analysis than is feasible here.

THE BEGINNING:
GREAT EXPECTATIONS, MAJOR CHALLENGES

In May 1948 Israel became an independent state and the homeland for Jews from all over the world. The large influx of immigrants created serious difficulties for linguistic and cultural absorption. In the early years, the newcomers from Europe, America, and African/Asian countries brought with them seventy-odd dialects, and for some time Hebrew, so recently revived as a living tongue and the dominant language in Israel, was engulfed by the babel of tongues prevailing in the country (Avidor, 1958).

The Israeli society and education system experienced rapid and tremendous growth in a relatively short period, presenting an extremely complicated task for policy makers. The number of students in kindergarten through twelfth grade increased from 141,000 in 1948 to 1.3 million in 2000. Therefore, right from the beginning, the state's leaders expected the education system to serve as the main mechanism for ensuring the absorption of the immigrants and the actualization of the values for the emerging nation (Elboim-Dror, 1985, p. 57) and the evolving society (Ackerman, Carmon, & Zucker, 1985). This has not been an easy task in the context of the continuing threat to Israel's security, which places a heavy burden on the country's economy. Yet, in spite of the lack of stability in the region and the financial constraints, 9.5 percent of the national budget (approximately 9.8 percent of the country's gross national product) is allotted to the education system—a percentage comparable to that in most European countries (Israel Central Bureau of Statistics, 2002; Shprinzak et al., 2000).

The Absorption Stage

Although Israel crystallized into a unified nation, its cultural and political pluralist nature has always been one of its basic characteristics (Inbar, 1986). Therefore, an initial challenge that faced the education system in the first five years following independence was to absorb all children in spite of the mixed Jewish communities and the political, economic, and educational gaps among different social sectors in the Israeli society. These gaps were most apparent between immigrants who came from the African/Asian countries (Sephardim) and those whose origin was in the Western countries of Europe and North America (Ashkenazim).

Therefore, the education system was expected to reduce the gaps and promote cohesion among the different sectors and, at the same time, to respond to the pluralistic tendencies that characterized the different social groups. The education system was expected to achieve these goals and to provide equal educational services to the large flood of Jewish immigrants in spite of the lack of a solid structural, judicial, and pedagogical foundation and the shortage of adequate school buildings and qualified teachers. One major initiative was the establishment of a large number of teacher-training institutions in universities. As a result, teachers' level of education has gradually increased over the years; in 2000 more than 40 percent of the teachers in elementary school and 70 percent of the teachers in junior high school held academic degrees (Israel Central Bureau of Statistics, 1997; Shprinzak et al., 2001). Currently, it is compulsory for teachers to earn an academic degree before being certified to teach in the public school system.

In an attempt to ensure equality, and thereby to try to satisfy a large variety of needs and encourage better control, centralization became a main structural administrative feature of the evolving education system. After independence, a Ministry of Education and Culture was set up, which was in reality a continuation of the Education Department of the National Executive, which had been responsible for education services during the prestate (Yishuv) period. In fact, a minister of education was appointed only ten months after the establishment of the state. From that time on, the central office, located in Jerusalem and run by a political minister and a director general, set the education policies. The assumption was that centralization would provide an efficient mechanism for ensuring the equal distribution of educational services according to unified standards.

The first education law, the Compulsory Education Law enacted in 1949, was intended to ensure that all children attended elementary school. This law set the relationship among the government, which was responsible for providing educational services; the local authorities, which were responsible for maintaining these services; and the parents, who were required to ensure their children's continued attendance in school. The law served to increase school attendance by granting all children free education from kindergarten until the eighth grade (in 1968 the law was broadened to the tenth grade and, in 1979, to the twelfth grade). Indirectly, however, this law also legitimized centralization (Gaziel, 1996, p. 36).

The Consolidation Stage

Following the large influx of immigrants, the education system maintained its efforts to absorb and socialize the newcomers. At the beginning of the 1950s it faced another challenge: to play an active role in consolidating the evolving Israeli society. This task involved ensuring the political socialization of the new immigrants, from both the East and the West, to an egalitarian perspective rooted in the socialist ideology of the founders and generated mostly by Western values (Inbar, 1989). Socializing immigrants to a uniform political ideology and agenda was guided by the "melting pot" ideology considered favorable at that time. The Zionist movement adopted this ideology, which preached a new and shared culture for all, emphasizing ethnic integration and a single dominating political canon.

The need for national socialization, however, was not the only challenge that the Israeli education system faced while attempting to consolidate Israeli society. Another challenge was to ensure that the State of Israel, with its foundation in secular Zionist ideology, would serve as a homeland for both Orthodox and secular Jews. This challenge implied the need to provide national education services that would meet the values and social agendas of both religious and non-religious citizens.

A primary step in creating a national education system was the integration of a structure that had previously been divided into three value systems during the British mandate (the Yishuv period), each providing educational services based on a different political agenda. These value systems were affiliated with different political parties: The "general" value system was connected to the General Zionist parties; the "labor" system was run by the General Federation of the Labor Party (later known as MAPAI); and the "Mizrahi" system was affiliated with the religious-Zionist parties (Elboim-Dror, 1962). Therefore, in 1953 a law was enacted to ensure that education provided by the state would not be influenced by or linked only to one political, religious, or private body. This law allowed parents to choose among three types of schools: general state schools, religious state schools, and "unofficial recognized" schools, serving mainly the ultra-Orthodox sector. Although the unofficial recognized schools are financed by the state, the state has in fact very limited control over these schools or their curriculum, which is dedicated primarily to the study of religion.

The Assertive Social Integration Stage

During the 1960s the education system increasingly faced the challenge of ensuring equal opportunity for social mobility to all children regardless of their ethnic origin and socioeconomic background and developing a new social orientation for Israeli culture. These efforts to consolidate Israeli society and bring under the same national roof immigrants of various cultural and social backgrounds reached a peak during the 1970s, although they did not decrease the social gaps that have characterized Israeli society since its inception. Ethnic integration was an extension of the national desire of the Jewish subgroups to reconstitute the social and political unity of the Jewish people and to strive to achieve common goals. It was believed that social integration could contribute to the cohesiveness of a multiethnic society by demonstrating society's interest in providing all groups equal access to resources and in accepting all groups on an equal basis in public institutions (Amir, Sharan, & Ben-Ari, 1984). These attempts to increase social integration followed research evidence showing that the social gap in Israel and children's socioeconomic backgrounds were significant factors in determining their academic performance and achievements (Dar & Resh, 1995; Ortar, 1967).

Unexpectedly, in spite of its declared mission statement and the heterogeneity of Israeli society following the large influx of immigrants from North Africa and the Middle East (Sephardim), the education system did not apply differentiated teaching methods or policies designed for children of different backgrounds. Rather, a tracking system, which resulted in segregation among pupils based on their academic proficiency, was adopted. This policy was chosen mainly because the minister of education at that time opposed the initiation of diverse programs for children based on their ethnic backgrounds (Zameret, 1998).

One step toward improving the academic achievement of children who did not reach the anticipated levels was the initiation in 1956 of a national achievement test (the SEKER). The test, administered to all eighth grade pupils, was designed to identify those with potential ability for further education at the secondary level (Kashti, Arieli, & Shapira, 1992, p. 309) and then to provide scholarships to children from low socioeconomic backgrounds (Ortar, 1959). This was accompanied by a new policy intended to promote affirmative action, that is, deliberate preference for children of Asian/African origin, by employing a different and more lenient norm for children coming from groups with lower academic achievement. In summer 1955, a "Norm B" was applied to the high school admission exams, requiring lower scores from immigrant children coming from the Middle East and North Africa.

Nevertheless, evidence showed that lowering exam thresholds did not lead to significant changes in the proportion of students of Asian/African origin in high school or in higher education. These findings boosted the initiation of new measures, all directed toward promoting the "Teunei Tipuach," the Hebrew phrase used to describe "disadvantaged" children. These included the creation of new teaching materials, the introduction of better and more innovative teaching methods, supplementary study frameworks, the preparation of special textbooks, the introduction of an extended school day, and the extension of the school year. The common denominator among these measures, though, was their emphasis on providing "more of the same" rather than initiating "different" pedagogical strategies.

These intensive efforts to reduce social gaps and increase equality became highly visible in the 1960s. During this period the state education system made continuous efforts to initiate education programs that would promote equal educational outcomes. Although these increased efforts expanded existing policies and pedagogical processes, they left the main education agenda and methods unchanged. Despite significant resource investment to increase achievement, the gap remained.

In 1965 a professional committee reevaluated the entire education system and submitted a report (Prawer Report, 1965), later approved and adopted by the Israeli Parliament (the Knesset), which introduced what was then considered a radical reform in the entire structure of education. The main change was to transform the education system from an 8 + 4 to a 6 + 3 + 3 system. Other recommendations involved easing the transition from elementary to secondary education; admitting all children without tests to junior high schools; raising free compulsory education to age fifteen (which was raised again in 1979 to age sixteen for compulsory education and to age eighteen for free education); opening new secondary options of a less academic nature and establishing comprehensive schools with vocational training; promoting social integration by bringing children of different social and ethnic backgrounds to the same educational institutions; and, finally, establishing a new curriculum division in the Ministry of Education and Culture responsible for the development of a basic mandatory and uniform elementary school curriculum to replace the old curriculum (Inbar, 1986).

Implementation of the education reform began in 1968. Though one of its main purposes was to avoid selection processes and decrease the dropout rate, it did not take long before policy makers realized the difficulty of meeting the first goal. Although children did enter schools without any preliminary selection, they were soon subjected to internal school selection processes, which directed pupils, based on their previous achievement levels, to homogeneous groups or tracks developed within schools. Moreover, it was evident that most of the pupils who were selected in the comprehensive schools for vocational classes and who received a diploma after twelfth grade, rather than a matriculation certificate, were of African/Asian origin. This finding led policy makers to expand their efforts in the spirit of the reform policy and to initiate a "second chance" program, which enabled pupils who failed the matriculation examinations (and therefore graduated from school with a vocational diploma) or who dropped out of school to study for an additional thirteenth year at the expense of the state. This program led to a significant increase in the number of students who succeeded in passing at least some of the matriculation examinations.

In general, the enormous efforts invested in education did lead to impressive achievements: the ninefold increase in students over a period of fifty years, the massive construction of school buildings in a short time, the significant decrease in dropout rates, and the improvement in the training and academic level of the teaching force are only a few prominent examples. Nevertheless, despite the education system's high expectations and extensive efforts, the challenge of decreasing social gaps was not met. In 1995 only 16.9 percent of the population with more than thirteen years of education was of Asian/African origin, although, based on their share in the population (approximately 50 percent), the percentage should have been much higher (Zameret, 1998). The findings are similar for higher education: In the year 2000 the proportion of Asian/African students was only 24.9 percent of the total number of students in bachelor's degree programs, 24.7 percent of the students in master's programs, and approximately 16 percent of the students in Ph.D. programs (Israel Central Bureau of Statistics, 2002). These findings led the minister of education and culture to announce a policy in 1995 that focused on five priorities: more students completing twelfth grade, more students eligible for matriculation, more students in higher education, more students achieving their "potential," and more equality of opportunity. Following the guidelines set by this new policy, and in an attempt to increase the number of children heading for a matriculation diploma, the minister introduced a change in the matriculation exams by decreasing the number of exams and holding a lottery each year to determine which exams would be given. This move led to various accusations that the policy was a populist one that would reduce the value of the matriculation certificate. The policy was subsequently abolished; however, in reality, the policy change did not decrease the social gaps significantly, and educators today continue to confront similar problems following the large influx of immigrants during the 1990s from Ethiopia and Eastern Europe.

In short, the major strategy that was employed in the first decades of the Israeli education system, in spite of various legal and structural changes, can be termed as a "more of the same" strategy. The major policies included the following:

1. More investments: reduced class size, more instructional time, more individualized learning, and more second chance programs (Shprinzak et al., 2001; Yonai, 1990)
2. More years for teacher preparation and upgrading teacher preparation to at least the level of a bachelor of education degree, plus one year of internship (Volansky, 1996; Yogev, 1992)

3. More parental participation in school affairs and more "community schools" (Poster & Kruger, 1990)
4. More central control, by strengthening control over teaching content and methods, and over student behavior, by developing national standards and national evaluation and testing (Ministry of Education, 1995)

A CALL FOR DECENTRALIZATION

Since the 1980s the policy discussion in Israel has focused on potential ways to reshape the education system—consistent with international trends in school reform.

The Disappointment Stage

Although the Israeli education system has stood up to its major tasks and, in practice, has generally fulfilled many of its declared goals, parents, as well as many education researchers and politicians, feel a growing sense of disappointment in the educational, social, and academic outcomes. Disappointment in the results of education systems, which is essentially an international phenomenon, arises from the increasing gap between expectations and outcomes. In Israel, like most other countries, education results show improvements—but at a very slow pace. Academic gains are always slow; there are no shortcuts in education. Similarly, expectations, which can be a function of perceived realities or of comparisons with a sometimes mythical past or with other systems and social groups, are also changing. Because expectations are directed toward improving current situations and fulfilling hopes, it is natural that they will grow faster than outcomes: We hope for an exponential pace of improvement but obtain, at best, only an "arithmetic" pace. That gap, in turn, leads to public disappointment in the education system and casts a shadow on its credibility. In Israel, as in many other countries, the widespread feeling of disappointment has been a powerful catalyst for educational change, even if it means major changes in educational goals and the structure of the education system.

The Lost Credibility Stage

The reports from the United States during the early 1980s and the demands there for radical changes in education apparently have had a delayed but strong influence on the Israeli education system. *A Nation at Risk* (National Commission on Excellence in Education, 1983) argues that there was a "rising tide of mediocrity." Though subsequent reports were not quite so melodramatic, they remained highly critical of the education system (Adler, 1982; Boyer, 1983; Carnegie Forum, 1986; College Entrance Examination Board, 1983; Goodland, 1983; National Science Board, 1983; Sizer, 1984; Twentieth Century Fund, 1983). These reports emphasized not only the disappointment in educational results but also the fear that the chance for real change was limited under contemporary conditions, which indeed is one of Chubb and Moe's (1990) arguments in their support of vouchers.

In discussing the impact of school reforms, Kaestle (1985), for instance, uses the metaphor of a huge tanker going down the middle of a channel, "rocking a bit side to side as it attends to one slight current and then to the other" (p. 423), implying that reforms are like currents, moving the tanker from side to side when actually little is changed. Purpel (1989) argues that the outcomes of the education reform movement "reflect modest differences in emphasis and cannot be said to be fundamental" (p. 14). We are dealing here, at most, only with "first-order" changes and not with the "second-order" kind, which address basic goals and structures (Cuban, 1988). If Cuban (1990) is accurate in his argument that the education system is doomed to be reformed "again, again, and again," serious questions will be raised about the inherent limits of the contemporary system to adopt effective changes.

This brings us to the lost credibility stage, which reflects not only the accumulation of disappointments but also the lost confidence in the relations between investment and outcomes and the concern that no real improvements will occur under contemporary conditions. Lost credibility leads to the conclusion that progress will occur only if "different" reforms replace traditional reforms. In operational terms, it means seeking new ways to govern the education system and questioning basic assumptions about the link between investments and outcomes.

The basic argument, therefore, is that Israel is in a transition period where the "rules" that have controlled education for the past fifty years are changing dramatically. Some indicators of this phenomenon are as follows:

1. The increasing public awareness of education issues: more public debate, more media reports, more education interest groups—all of which reflect the development of civic society (Rosen, 2001)
2. The increasing role of local education authorities, which now have control over educational matters (Inbar & Choshen, 1997)
3. Increases in school autonomy and "school-based management" (Minister of Education, 1993; Nir, 2001, 2002)
4. A stronger role for the legal system in education policy, through court decisions as a powerful regulating process (Gibton & Goldring, 2002)
5. The development of market and competitive regulations (Inbar, 1994a, 1994b; Nir, 2003)

Clearly, these five trends are not mutually exclusive but, rather, mutually dependent and in some cases overlapping.

FROM "MORE" TO "DIFFERENT"

Our analysis is focused on two major strategies that are assumed to have an increasing influence on the development of a "different" approach: (1) decentralization and the development of school autonomy and school-based management and (2) quasi-market competition and "privatization."

Turning to School-Based Management

Although, traditionally, the Israeli education system has featured a high degree of central control in an attempt to ensure equality, since the early 1990s the education system has begun to decentralize its governance patterns. The Ministry of Education initiated this trend, even though it is relatively easy to control the education system because Israel is a small country (Inbar, 1986). The move toward decentralization was initiated for two main reasons. First, central officials turned to decentralization as a last resort after concluding that all the other control mechanisms had failed (Gaziel & Romm, 1988). Second, educators in Israel have long recognized the negative pedagogical effects of strong centralization and curriculum uniformity (Volansky & Bar-Elli, 1995). Hence, in 1992 the minister of education commissioned a steering committee to explore the possibility of extending the scope of school autonomy and local-level accountability and introducing school-based management. The implementation of this policy began after a number of initiatives to decentralize the education system, carried out during the 1970s and the 1980s, ended with no significant change in school autonomy and authority.

The committee recommended introducing school-based management in elementary schools, based on a set of guidelines: (1) schools would develop a clear definition of goals; (2) schools would prepare a work plan that corresponded with these goals and present the plan each year to the district superintendent and to community members; (3) schools would use extensive monitoring and assessment methods; (4) schools would be granted full independence in allocating their budgets; (5) school authority with respect to personnel matters would be broadened; and (6) each school would have a governing body. The first four recommendations were implemented, although with some constraints. The authority delegated to schools is connected to a set of binding regulations requiring all schools to operate in accordance with the education laws and regulations of the director general of the Ministry of Education and with the national curriculum. They have to maintain labor agreements; they may not decrease weekly class hours; and they must comply with the financial guidelines determined by the local authority based on the guidelines defined by the Ministry of Education (Minister of Education, 1993).

Although school-based management is intended to increase school autonomy, it is also interesting to note that schools cannot introduce it unless a contract has been signed between the municipality within which they operate and the Ministry of Education. In some instances, the municipality has forced schools to introduce school-based management after a contract has been signed in order to create unity and facilitate city-level administration. Schools have a strong incentive to participate in this initiative because they receive an immediate, and significant, increase in their financial resources. In addition, principals must participate in a one-year training program initiated and carried out by Ministry of Education officials before implementing school-based management (Nir, 2002). One immediate outcome of this training process, and of the top-down restructuring process generally, is the uniform pattern that characterizes the implementation of school-based management in Israeli elementary schools. Hence, in reality, many "autonomous" schools remain shaped, to a large degree, by the centralized education system.

Quasi-Market Competition and "Privatization"

The role of the state in controlling public schooling and the conflict between centralized and local control have been at the center of the debate in Israel as well as in other countries. Policy makers face the difficult challenge of creating a balance and reconciling these two conflicting objectives (Weiler, 1990).

A "quasi-market" policy is one of the main initiatives intended to increase local control in public schooling. This policy grants parents the opportunity to select their children's school, while, at the same time, increased pedagogical and administrative autonomy has been delegated to the schools themselves (Guthrie, 1986; Watkins & Lusi, 1989). Commentators define the combination of these two initiatives as quasi-markets in education (Whitty, 1997). Although both the client and the service provider have the option to choose, the term *quasi-market* (Glennerster, 1991; Le Grand, 1991; Le Grand & Bartlett, 1993) is used because education is not a "commodity" (Halstead, 1994, p. 11) and clients have only a single education system from which to choose; therefore, public schools do not represent what is typically defined as a free market situation (Sallis, 1988). Quasi-markets, nevertheless, introduce a more competitive environment for schools (Woods, Bagley & Glatter, 1996) and increase school dependence on client expectations and needs, although the schools have limited capacity to take into account consumer demands, even when their autonomy is increased. Despite this limitation, however, schools must present their education program in an appealing manner to increase their attractiveness to the local community and ensure enrollment. Thus, some schools will be oversubscribed, and others will remain empty if they fail to attract potential clients and promote their reputation (Carroll & Walford, 1997). It is important, nonetheless, to recognize that under quasi-market circumstances, the pedagogical ethos that was previously guided by a state bureaucracy is replaced by an ethos guided by market forces emphasizing competition (Nir, 2003). Public schools, therefore, cannot adjust to these newly created circumstances unless they, too, revise the assumptions underlying their programs and take steps that are consistent with the ideology and values inherent in a school choice policy (Nir, 2003).

In Israel, school choice, described as "a backdoor process of school privatization" (Inbar, 1989), has become a major policy issue, and the pressure for "partially privatized schooling" has become a matter of public debate. A school choice policy, which previously was almost inconceivable in a small country with a strong, egalitarian, and centralized public school system (Inbar, 1989, p. 269), has become a policy for which parents openly lobby, a demand that can be perceived as a mini revolution in Israel.

The phrase "partially privatized schooling" refers to schools that are state recognized but not official state schools—schools that resemble "charter schools" in the United States. In other words, schools are leaving the official state system and becoming "unofficial recognized" schools, which gives them more freedom than traditional schools. However, the education ministry still supports these "recognized" schools and imposes some basic obligations they must fulfill.

Educational "privatization," as defined here, describes a process in which parents are intensifying their influence on schools by increasing their direct involvement in school affairs, by exercising more parental choice, and by making direct payments for school programs; at the same time, there is a decline in centralized control and regulation. Hence, we do not refer here to schools that are totally privately owned but, rather, to a process of weakening the previously highly centralized control of schools; the "privatized" schools have multiplied by almost four over a period of approximately twenty years.

However, in Israel, as in most Western countries, privatization is not only an educational phenomenon. It is also a trend in the provision of many of the social services that formerly were a government monopoly; these include, for example, health, welfare, manpower placement, television, and telephone. Privatization, which began with these social services, was then applied to the education system, both in the form of school choice and in outsourcing some of the educational services that had previously been the responsibility of the Ministry of Education.

THE PROTECTIVE BUREAUCRACY

The trend toward privatization and school choice accompanies an increasing concern about the politicization of education. Indeed, increased politicization is evident both in the case of ministers of education and in the role of Parliament.

For many years, ministers of education came from the major leading party of the coalition, and, although they reflected a specific ideology, they maintained responsibility for implementing the National Educational Act of 1953, which was designed to maintain a national education system that was apolitical. Beginning in the early 1980s, ministers were chosen from the small parties in the government coalition; in general, the ministers have been more likely to impose direct political influence—in some cases from a religious perspective and in others from a leftist orientation. These ministers essentially paved the way for the current situation, in which the minister of education, this time from the main party of the government coalition, imposes direct ideological pressure on education through, for example, learning materials and curriculum.

At the same time, Parliament also increased political pressure on education. For example, parliamentary committees that deal with educational matters have proposed an unprecedented number of new laws, many of which Parliament has passed, although they have not always been implemented. In addition, a new religious education stream, El-Hamayan, now exists, with direct links to a political party and a specific ideology.

In general, the number of schools representing political positions and ideological perspectives has increased—a result of "privatization," school autonomy, a decline in the power of the central ministry, and the increased politicization of education. However, the centralized bureaucracy has been concerned about these changes and is attempting to maintain control over the education system.

The Paradox

One way the bureaucracy might react to the changes is to attempt to strengthen its role, both as a defensive and protective mechanism against politicization and as a means of supporting equality. In a highly centralized system with an egalitarian ideology, the processes of privatization and politicization in Israel are evident and can be monitored. The current trends are exposing the education system to multiple pressures, arising in part from the fact that these trends often complement each other, for example, when politicization reinforces privatization and sectarian education and then privatization leads to more political influence.

The Ministry of Education, therefore, is concerned that political pressures endanger the national perception of a common public school system and that the pressure for privatization or sectarian education endangers the goals of equality and desegregation, which are deeply embedded in the public consciousness. In response, the ministry attempts to protect the education system from the perceived negative effects of the trends by initiating procedures designed to prevent the moves to political influence, sectarian schools, and privatization and balance the perceived consequences of inequality. These actions include the reinforcement of the supervisory system, long and complicated procedures required for private sector involvement, the development of national standards and tests, and an attempt to develop and enforce a national core curriculum for all sectors of the education system. All of these policies reinforce the process of bureaucratization and the emphasis on administrative procedures rather than on pedagogical considerations. Thus, in a transition period when the regulations that have controlled the education system are changing dramatically, the ministry is developing a "protective bureaucracy." Paradoxically, protective bureaucracy might balance and even reverse to some degree the centralized education system's apparent decline in power resulting from the recent trends.

Protective bureaucracy appears to serve a double function. It might indeed be a protective mechanism against inequality and political influence. The irony, however, is that the ministry might become even more powerful, with all the disadvantages of a highly centralized education system. As a bureaucracy, it will return to the familiar and attempt to prevent any real structural change or the use of new teaching methods. The result might be that we end up with the worst of both worlds: the disadvantages of the privatization process combined with the disadvantages of a rigid bureaucracy, an education system that is both highly politicized and highly centralized. Thus, instead of moving from a strategy emphasizing uniformity to a strategy encouraging "different" approaches, the bureaucracy is likely to opt for conformity.

The education bureaucracy currently faces a conflict between being a "missionary" for principles of equality and political neutrality and becoming a "mandarin" in the service of politics. It is too soon to tell whether the bureaucracy can stand up to political pressure or, instead, be transformed into a political "servant," thereby moving away from its traditional civil service orientation. It will be no surprise, though, if the latter option prevails, in light of the general sociopolitical radicalization in Israel.

REFERENCES CITED

Ackerman, W., Carmon, A., & Zucker, D. (Eds.). (1985). *Education in an evolving society: The Israeli system.* Jerusalem: Van Leer; and Tel Aviv: Hakibutz Hameuchad (Hebrew).

Adler, M. (1982). *The Paideia proposal.* New York: Macmillan.

Amir, Y., Sharan, S., & Ben-Ari, R. (1984). Why integration? In Y. Amir & S. Sharan (Eds.), *School desegregation* (pp. 1–19). Hillsdale, NJ: Lawrence Erlbaum.

Avidor, M. (1958). Ten years of education in Israel. *Jewish Education, 28* (3), 3–9.

Boyer, E. (1983). *High school*. New York: Harper & Row.

Carnegie Forum. (1986). *A nation prepared: Teachers for the 21st century*. New York: Carnegie Forum.

Carroll, S., & Walford, G. (1997). Parents' responses to the school quasi market. *Research Papers in Education, 12* (1), 3–26.

Chubb, J., & Moe, T. (1990). *Politics, markets and America's schools*. Washington, DC: Brookings Institution.

College Entrance Examination Board. (1983). *Academic preparation for college*. New York: College Board.

Cop, Y. (2002). *The distribution of resources to social services*. Jerusalem: Center for Research of Social Policy in Israel.

Cuban, L. (1988). *The managerial imperative and practice of leadership in school*. Albany: State University of New York Press.

———. (1990). Reforming again, again, and again. *Educational Researcher, 19* (1), 3–14.

Dar, Y., & Resh, N. (1995). Social differentials in academic achievement and in resource returns in the Israeli junior high school. In R. Kahane (Ed.), *Educational advancement and distributive justice: Between equality and equity*. Jerusalem: Magnes Press, Hebrew University.

Elboim-Dror, R. (1962). Problems of educational administration in Israel. *Public Administration in Israel and Abroad, 3,* 69–76.

———. (1985). The formation of educational policy in Israel. In W. Ackerman, A. Carmon, & D. Zucker (Eds.), *Education in an evolving society: The Israeli system* (pp. 35–116). Jerusalem: Van Leer; and Tel Aviv: Hakibutz Hameuchad (Hebrew).

Gaziel, H. (1996). *Politics and policy-making in Israel's education system*. Brighton: Sussex Academic Press.

Gaziel, H., & Romm, T. (1988). From centralization to decentralization: The case of Israel as a unique pattern of control in education. *European Journal of Education, 23* (4), 345–52.

Gibton, D., & Goldring, E. (2002). The role of legislation in educational decentralization: The case of Israel and the United Kingdom. *Peabody Journal of Education, 76* (3–4), 81–101.

Glennerster, H. (1991). Quasi-markets and education. *Economic Journal, 101,* 1268–71.

Goodland, J. I. (1983). *A place called school: Prospects for the future*. New York: McGraw-Hill.

Guthrie, J. W. (1986). School based management: The next needed education reform. *Phi Delta Kappan, 68* (4), 305–9.

Halstead, J. M. (1994). Parental choice: An overview. In J. M. Halstead (Ed.), *Parental choice and education* (pp. 11–18). London: Kogan Page.

Inbar, D. (1986). Educational policy making and planning in a small centralized democracy. *Comparative Education, 22,* 271–80.

————. (1989). A backdoor process of school privatization. In W. L. Boyd & J. G. Cibulka (Eds.), *Private schools and public policy* (pp. 269–83). London: Falmer Press.

————. (1994a). Educational choice: From compulsory to dialogue. *Megamot, Behavioral Science Quarterly, 36* (23), 159–72 (Hebrew).

————. (1994b). *The parental choice report*. Submitted to the Ministry of Education, Jerusalem (Hebrew).

Inbar, D., & Choshen, M. (1997). *Decentralization of education authority in local government*. Jerusalem: Milken Institute for the Study of Educational Systems.

Israel Central Bureau of Statistics. (1997). *Israel statistical yearbook, 48.* Jerusalem: Israel Central Bureau of Statistics (Hebrew).

————. (2002). *Israel statistical yearbook, 53.* Jerusalem: Israel Central Bureau of Statistics (Hebrew).

Kaestle, C. F. (1985). Education reform and the swinging pendulum. *Phi Delta Kappan, 66,* 423.

Kashti, Y., Arieli, M., & Shapira, R. (1992). Israel. In P. W. Cookson, A. R. Sadovnic, & S. F. Semel (Eds.), *International handbook of educational reform* (pp. 305–19). New York: Greenwood Press.

Le Grand, J. (1991). Quasi-markets and social policy. *Economic Journal, 101,* 1256–67.

Le Grand, J., & Bartlett, W. (1993). *Quasi-markets and social policy.* London: Macmillan.

Minister of Education. (1993). *The introduction of school-based management to schools: Recommendations of the steering committee.* Jerusalem: State of Israel, Ministry of Education (Hebrew).

————. (1995, November). *Tests and evaluation in elementary schools.* General Director Special Memorandum 4. Jerusalem: State of Israel, Ministry of Education (Hebrew).

National Commission on Excellence in Education. (1983). *A nation at risk.* Washington, DC: U.S. Government Printing Office.

National Science Board. (1983). *Educating America for the 21st century.* Washington, DC: National Science Foundation.

Nir, A. E. (2001). Planning for school-based management: The teachers' point of view. *Educational Planning, 13* (1), 19–32.

————. (2002). The impact of school-based management on school health. *Journal of School Leadership, 12* (4), 368–96.

————. (2003). Quasi-market: The changing context of schooling. *International Journal of Educational Reform, 12* (1), 26–39.

Ortar, G. (1959). The SEKER test in elementary schools' 8th grade. In *General problems in Israeli education and the SEKER test elementary schools in 8th grade—Lectures and discussions in the Superintendents' Conference* (p. 84). Tel Aviv: Ministry of Education (Hebrew).

———. (1967). Educational achievements of primary school graduates in Israel as related to their sociocultural background. *Comparative Education, 4,* 23–34.

Poster, C., & Kruger, A. (1990). *Community education in the western world.* London: Routledge.

Prawer Report. (1965). *State of Israel, the Ministry of Education and Culture: Report of the public commission examining the need and possibilities of extending the Law of Free and Compulsory Education.* Jerusalem: Ministry of Education Publications (Hebrew).

Purpel, D. (1989). *The moral and spiritual crisis in education: A curriculum for justice and compassion in education.* Granby, MA: Bergin and Garvey.

Rosen, L. (2001). On the concept of civic society. In Y. Peled & A. Offir (Eds.), *Israel: From recruited to civic society* (pp. 27–34). Jerusalem: Van Leer (Hebrew).

Sallis, J. (1988). *Schools, parents and governors.* London: Routledge.

Shprinzak, D., Bar, E., Levi-Mazlum, D., & Peterman, D. (Eds.). (2000). *The Ministry of Education: Facts and figures.* Jerusalem: Ministry of Education (Hebrew).

Shprinzak, D., Bar, E., Segev, Y., Peterman, D., & Levi-Mazlum, D. (Eds.). (2001). *The Ministry of Education: Facts and figures.* Jerusalem: Ministry of Education (Hebrew).

Sizer, T. (1984). *Horace's compromise: The dilemma of the American high school.* Boston: Houghton Mifflin.

Statistical Abstract of Israel No. 53. (2002). Jerusalem: State of Israel, Central Bureau of Statistics (Hebrew).

Twentieth Century Fund Task Force on Federal Elementary and Secondary Education. (1983). *Making the grade.* New York: The Twentieth Century Fund.

Volansky, A. (1996). Opening the gates: The democratization of higher education. In O. Brandis (Ed.), *The third jump: Changes and reforms in the educational system during the nineties* (pp. 70–82). Jerusalem: Ministry of Education and Culture.

Volansky, A., & Bar-Elli, D. (1995). Moving toward equitable school-based management. *Educational Leadership, 53* (4), 60–62.

Watkins, J. M., & Lusi, S. F. (1989, March). Facing the essential tensions: Restructuring from where you are. Paper presented at the Annual Meeting of the American Educational Research Association, San Francisco.

Watzlawick, P., Weakland, J. H., & Fisch, R. (1979). *Principles of problem formation and problem resolution.* Palo Alto, CA: Mental Research Institute.

Weiler, H. N. (1990). Comparative perspectives on educational decentralization: An exercise in contradiction? *Educational Evaluation and Policy Analysis, 12* (4), 433–48.

Whitty, G. (1997). Creating quasi-markets in education: A review of recent research on parental choice and school autonomy in three countries. In

M. W. Apple (Ed.), *Review of research in education, 22* (pp. 3–48). Washington, DC: American Educational Research Association.

Woods, P. A., Bagley, C., & Glatter, R. (1996). Dynamics of competition—The effects of local competitive arena on schools. In J. C. Pole & R. Chawla-Duggan (Eds.), *Shaping education in the 1990s: Perspectives on secondary education* (pp. 11–25). London: Falmer Press.

Yogev, A. (1992). *The spreading of higher education in Israel.* Tel Aviv: Masada (Hebrew).

Yonai, Y. (1990). *The educational system of the State of Israel.* Jerusalem: Ministry of Education (Hebrew).

Zameret, Z. (1998). *Fifty years of education in the State of Israel.* Jerusalem: Israel Information Center.

10

Japan: Encouraging Individualism, Maintaining Community Values

Ryo Watanabe

You can't see the whole sky through a bamboo tube.

—Japanese proverb

The Japanese education system has long been a source of pride for the country because of the high participation rate and the nationwide homogeneity of compulsory education. However, people's confidence in the education system is now showing signs of severe strain. In recent years, reports of educational problems have increased.[1]

Since the mid-1970s observers have noted several problems. They include violent behavior, juvenile crime, bullying, a decline in students' academic motivation, and, in some cases, a refusal to attend school. Based on recommendations from advisory bodies, the Ministry of Education, Culture, Sports, Science and Technology (MEXT) has adopted a range of policies and launched a series of education reforms to address the problems. This chapter presents an overview of education in Japan, some of the issues and problems garnering attention, and recent reforms.

AN OVERVIEW OF THE EDUCATION SYSTEM

Japan has a three-tiered structure for governing and administering education with national, prefectural, and municipal components, all under the general supervision of MEXT, the national ministry.

The Organization of Schools

In 1947 Japan enacted the Fundamental Law of Education and the
School Education Law, with the goal of providing equal opportunities
for education. Six years of elementary school and three years of lower
secondary school are compulsory, with almost 100 percent of children enrolled in these schools. The three years of upper secondary
school are not compulsory, but 97 percent of graduates of lower secondary school advance to upper secondary school.

Students of the same age form a grade during the entire period of
formal education from kindergarten to university. Classmates in elementary and secondary schools proceed automatically to the next
grade every year, almost irrespective of their educational achievement, and then receive a graduation certificate after the prescribed
period. Students are not assigned to schools by achievement in elementary and lower secondary schools; in other words, students in
each school are quite heterogeneous. Though some schools have introduced ability grouping, the practice is not common in Japan.

Entrance Examinations

Those students who wish to enroll in upper secondary school
must take entrance examinations administered by the local boards
of education, in the case of public schools, or by each school, in the
case of private schools. At this stage, schools differ in terms of students' achievement level, and therefore some schools have particularly strong records in sending their graduates to prestigious universities.

Thus, entrance examinations for admission to individual schools
perform the function of sorting applicants. As a result, these schools
are ranked hierarchically in terms of the academic ability of their suc-

cessful applicants. Although educational standards vary among upper secondary schools, their curricula are almost the same throughout the country. Upper secondary schools have places for all applicants, though it is natural for schools at the middle or bottom of the hierarchy to have a considerable number of students whose educational achievement is below the norm; these students, however, rarely must repeat a grade because of their poor marks.

Japanese elementary schools and lower secondary schools use only school-based assessment. There is no external or national assessment to screen or stream students in these schools. Only students applying to upper secondary schools or universities take entrance examinations. The exception is application to private schools, where schools at all levels can require examinations. Most students in elementary and lower secondary schools are in public school; only 0.6 percent of elementary schools and 6.6 percent of lower secondary schools are private, compared with 24 percent at the upper secondary level. The more affluent and educated families do not necessarily use private schools, nor are these schools always "good" schools or schools with high-achieving students.

In addition to regular schools, Japanese students often attend private, out-of-school, supplementary educational institutions (*juku*) to boost their achievement in entrance examinations. *Juku* give instruction after school hours in such subjects as Japanese, mathematics, science, social studies, and English. About 35 percent of grade six and 62 percent of grade nine students attend *juku*. However, this figure drops at the upper secondary school level, for example, to 13 percent at grade eleven.

All students are eligible to take university entrance examinations regardless of their academic records. There is no shortage of opportunities for higher education in Japan. Indeed, because of a declining student population, junior colleges and even some universities have begun to close because they do not have enough applicants. The competitive pressures occur in applying to prestigious universities, which, like elite institutions in other countries, are extremely selective. The pressure to gain entrance to these institutions is particularly severe because they have, by far, the best record in sending their graduates to top jobs in government and industry.

Curriculum and Textbooks

The ministry establishes the subjects offered, as well as the standard number of yearly school hours for each subject, in elementary and secondary school. The ministry also specifies the objectives and standard content of each subject, or each area of school activity, in the "course of study," which presents national guidelines for the curriculum for each school level. Each school organizes its own curriculum in accordance with the provisions of the relevant statutes and courses of study, considering the actual circumstances of the school and the region in which it is located, the characteristics of the children enrolled, and the stage of their mental and physical development.

The ministry issues revised courses of study about every ten years, in order to enrich and select educational content in response to social needs and changing trends. The revisions of the late 1950s and 1960s, in particular, attempted to enrich the educational content in order to respond to developments in the economy and society.

Courses of study are developed based on recommendations from the Central Council for Education, which is an advisory body to the minister. The members of the council are experienced teachers, researchers, and others with expertise in the field. Within the terms of reference established by the ministry, the council develops courses after years of research, consultation, and deliberation. After the ministry receives the council's recommendations, it prepares a revised version, again in consultation with outside experts who work with ministry staff. Finally, the minister issues the new courses of study about three years before their implementation, to allow the time needed to reorient teachers and prepare textbooks.

All elementary and secondary schools are required to use textbooks for each subject. The ministry must either authorize or directly compile textbooks. Most of the textbooks currently used in schools are those published by commercial publishers and authorized by the ministry.

Teachers

Elementary and secondary school teachers train in universities or junior colleges. Most elementary school teachers take four-year elementary school teacher–training courses at universities. Lower secondary school teachers study at universities or junior colleges, and upper secondary school teachers receive their undergraduate training at universities and are more likely to have a graduate degree than are the other two groups. The prefectural board of education is responsible for awarding teaching certificates.

Unlike many other countries, Japan does not have a problem of teacher shortages. Instead, there is an oversupply of teachers: The number of university graduates who hold teacher certificates and want to become teachers currently exceeds the number of teaching positions. As a result, the proportion of older teachers has increased because relatively few new teachers are entering the profession, although class size reductions have created some additional demand.

Teacher surpluses have occurred for several reasons: (1) a declining student population; (2) the fact that public school teachers are civil servants with job security and relatively high salaries; (3) public respect for the teaching profession, which enjoys high social status; and (4) limited opportunities for women in many other professions. Although the education system provides equal opportunities for boys and girls, subsequent decisions by workplaces contribute to fewer professional opportunities for women.

The declining student population, resulting from a very low birthrate, is a serious problem in Japan. The fertility rate is about 1.3, compared with the 2.08 that would maintain the current population level. Thus, enrollment in elementary schools dropped from a high of 11.9 million in 1981 to 7.2 million in 2002. Similarly, enrollment in lower secondary schools declined from 6.1 million in 1986 to 3.9 million in 2002.

Resources

Japan distributes educational resources equally throughout the country. Maintaining a desired level of education nationwide requires meeting certain standards in terms of basic personnel and materials. Thus, the School Education Law established in 1947 requires the government to set standards for school facilities and equipment.

MEXT also establishes standards to ensure a high-quality teaching environment. For example, the law prescribes that the maximum number of students per class in elementary and secondary schools should be forty; the actual class sizes, however, vary among schools. In addition, Japan has instituted policies to promote the equitable distribution of teachers. Teachers and principals are required to transfer from one school to another on a regular basis and to serve in remote areas for a certain period.

The standards for floor space in public school buildings, which the government sets, are used to determine the national subsidies for the construction of new school buildings. Similarly, the government sets the amount of educational equipment, such as the minimum number of computers, televisions, and overhead projectors, based on the sizes of schools.

CHILDREN'S CURRENT LIVES

Japan, which has achieved phenomenal economic growth, occupies an important position in the world, and its citizens enjoy material wealth. However, amid major changes, such as increasing global competition and a prolonged recession following the collapse of the "bubble" economy, Japanese society now faces a turning point. As a result, some Japanese are losing their confidence and previous sense of values, creating what can be called a vicious cycle of decline in social and moral consciousness. Unable to find a clear purpose or objective, or to know which path to follow, Japanese people are unable to eliminate a pervasive sense of powerlessness.

Under such social circumstances, children face a serious situation. Unable to have a dream or a clear purpose for the future, they have lost their sense of direction and willingness to study. Because of urbanization, declining family size, and the trend away from extended families, children do not have the same type of socialization that previous generations enjoyed. These changes in demographics and lifestyle, in turn, have raised concerns that children might not be able to establish desirable interpersonal relationships. Some consider Japanese young people slow to gain social independence, compared with young people in other countries. This difference might be related, in part, to the differences in national characters regarding individualism and collectivism, but it also has something to do with Japanese youths' lack of a sense of purpose and social skills. Moreover, the problem of children's deteriorating sense of ethics and group consciousness has become obvious, reflecting a declining sense of ethics in the society as a whole. Finally, although Japanese youths have made steady growth in terms of physique, such as height and weight, their physical strength and athletic ability have declined on the whole, partly because they have fewer opportunities to engage in physical exercise in their everyday lives.

On the other hand, children of today are familiar with information and communication technology and have a strong interest in international exchange. They are also interested in social participation and contribution, such as volunteer activities.

EDUCATION REFORM

Like many other countries, Japan is experiencing rapid social changes, including internationalization, advances in science and technology, the shift to an information-oriented society, modifications in the industrial and employment structure, a decline in the number of children, and the transition to an aging society. Along with these trends, various social and economic distortions have occurred, and fundamental reforms have been attempted throughout the society, in the areas of politics, administration, finance, economics, and industry. Major education reforms are required to respond to these trends.

Japan's education system has achieved a high standard on the principle that all people should have the right to equal educational opportunity according to their abilities. Citizens perceive this system as the driving force behind economic and social development. However, various problems have arisen. They include a social climate in which emphasis is placed on academic credentials; the negative effects of uniformity and rigidity in schools; and various kinds of problem behavior by children and young people, such as child bullying, violent acts by even very young children, and the refusal of some children to go to school. The role of education is extremely important for the vitality of the country and for building a nation based on creativity in science and technology while retaining Japan's cultural heritage. The continuation of education reform will be essential to this endeavor.

The question of how to ease the excessive competition in university entrance examinations became a major educational issue beginning in the 1970s, when problems of school violence, bullying, and juvenile delinquency became major social concerns. For this reason, the National Council on Educational Reform (NCER) was established under the prime minister in 1984 to discuss education as a whole. NCER submitted a report on education reform calling for the principle of respect for the individual, a shift to lifelong learning, and a response to the new demands and changes in society. Based on the report, various reforms were implemented.

In order to promote diversified education that would satisfy individual student needs, new types of upper secondary schools were established. In response to internationalization, and in order to "cultivate" Japanese people who could live successfully in an international society, measures were taken to improve English and other foreign language education, along with education to cultivate an appreciation for the culture and tradition of Japan. In response to advances in information technology, computers began to be used in schools.

"The Model for Japanese Education in the Perspective of the Twenty-first Century," a report submitted by the Central Council for Education in 1996, proposed that future education should nurture "competencies required for real life" (*ikiru chikara* [Chuou Kyouiku Shingikai, 1996]). The purpose is to foster a "rich humanity" by encouraging students to identify problems and learn to act independently—key requirements in a rapidly changing society.

CURRENT ISSUES IN EDUCATION

At a time when Japanese society is facing a turning point, the role of education is increasingly important in order for every child to study and "grow healthy" and for the country to achieve sustainable growth. Japanese citizens still have a strong belief in education; it is the basis on which the society exists. However, despite the various efforts made so far, schools continue to have problems, such as bullying and violence, a weakening in children's willingness to learn, and an increase in nonattendance. As the problems relate in intricate ways to family and societal factors, as well as to the schools themselves, a dramatic improvement is not yet evident.

In order to cope with these social and educational conditions, the National Commission on Educational Reform was established under the prime minister in March 2000. The commission's report, issued in December of the same year, discusses the future of education in Japan. The report makes specific proposals on cultivating Japanese people with "rich humanity" and "rich creativity by letting individual abilities grow," as well as on building new schools suitable for the new era (Kyouiku Kaikaku Kokuminkaigi, 2000). Specific measures, including small-group instruction, ability grouping of students, the promotion of hands-on activities, and teacher training, are being implemented. Several principles form the foundation for these school reforms.

First, there is a need to confirm the basic purposes of education: to promote the sound academic development of each child and the cultivation of a "healthy mind," which allows children to use their capabilities to the maximum, while at the same time nurturing the qualities required to build a nation and a society. In order to realize this, it is essential for each teacher to bring to daily educational activities a sense of mission, expertise, and passion. We also should continue to realize the traditional objectives of Japanese education: to maintain and enhance the achievement levels that have been highly esteemed abroad and to cultivate a sense of self-discipline, caring for others, public duty, and the importance of tradition and culture.

Second, there is a need to respond appropriately to changes in the times and in society. Changes, such as the advancement of globalization and the advent of a knowledge society, are taking place at an accelerated pace. Science and technology undoubtedly will continue to make major contributions to the development of society in the twenty-first century. However, new problems, such as the preservation of the global environment, have come to the surface. In addition, the rapidly aging society, with falling birthrates, is affecting education. It is important, therefore, to review and improve educational content and methods in response to social changes and emerging problems.

Third, there is a need to provide education that focuses on diversity and creativity rather than conformity and allows children to use their individuality and capability to the maximum. Because Japanese society is strongly oriented to homogeneity and a lockstep mentality, schools also tend to place too much emphasis on conformity. As described earlier, one of the main pillars of education reform proposed by the National Commission on Educational Reform is the "principle of respect for individuality," and, in response, schools are implementing reforms to promote individualization and diversification so that children can learn to think, judge, and act independently and to respond proactively and flexibly to social changes. However, we also should continue to recognize the importance of providing children with the strong foundation they will need to use their individuality responsibly. Thus, it is important to promote individualization in a way that enhances abilities by offering diversified education tailored to each child, to the extent possible, while ensuring that children have acquired the qualifications needed to be contributing members of society.

Fourth, there is a need for schools to be more accountable to parents and communities and for local boards of education to play a key role in education policy and administration. In order for schools to meet the expectations of parents and communities and to gain their trust, they are expected to conduct "self-evaluations," disclose the results, and make needed improvements. These self-evaluations can address a range of topics: educational objectives, courses, teaching methods, school guidance, teacher responsibilities and the division of responsibilities, clerical work, and facilities and equipment—but not student achievement. Local boards of education also have a responsibility to support each school's distinctive educational activities and to promote locally based education administration in line with the diverse wishes of local residents, who are now encouraged to participate in formulating school policies—a practice that is new in Japan.

Curriculum Reform

At the beginning of the 1990s, implementation of curriculum revisions began on the principle that academic ability is not simply the superficial acquisition of knowledge and skills but, rather, should include thinking ability, a sense of judgment, and expressive capabilities, as well as the desire and interest to learn independently. In formulating the latest courses of study, implemented beginning in April 2002, these ideas were developed further. The goal is to have children acquire a broad range of abilities to survive independently and creatively in the twenty-first century. These abilities are to learn and think on one's own, to make judgments and take action independently, and to identify problems and solve them. These competencies also include an ability to maintain good health and physical strength and an enriched sense of humanity, for example, to feel moved by something beautiful and to be kind toward weaker beings.

The first objective of the revisions of the courses of study, aimed at fostering these "competencies required for real life," was to keep "basic skills" content to the necessary minimum and to have students acquire it by providing appropriate guidance tailored to individual needs. As part of the revised course of study, children have a choice among diverse electives in accordance with their abilities, interests, and concerns.

"Integrated studies," which emphasize experiential and problem-solving learning in cross-curricular topics, are a new offering. These studies are a response to changes in children's lives: increasing urbanization, a declining birthrate, and an increasing tendency toward nuclear rather than extended families. As a result, children have fewer chances to experience nature and a range of human relationships. Ideally, children would have the opportunities needed to integrate knowledge gained in school with "real-life" situations and thereby realize the value of that knowledge. As these opportunities diminish, the schools try to fill the gap through a period for integrated studies.

Integrated studies also attempt to cultivate independence by having children learn content created at each school based on the children's interests and concerns, instead of using only educational content from the national course of study. Problem solving and expression receive greater emphasis, by encouraging children to become actively engaged in collecting and synthesizing information and then reporting and discussing it.

Along with the implementation of new courses of study, the system has implemented a five-day school week. Over the last ten years Japan has gradually shifted from a six- to a five-day school week. The aim of the five-day school week is to allow children to spend more time at home and in the community, so that they are free to engage in activities that will make a social contribution and to have time to experience nature. Successful implementation of the objective depends on cooperation among schools, families, and communities. However, many parents worry that their children's achievement, and therefore their chance of gaining entrance to prestigious universities, will fall if they lose a school day each week. Therefore, several matters must be resolved if the new system is to achieve effective implementation: the nature of the curriculum, attitudes toward learning, and the use of extra time gained from the new system.

Some also doubt the wisdom of abandoning the content and methods of elementary and secondary education that served as the driving force behind the rapid development of the Japanese economy after World War II. Nevertheless, as Japan increasingly becomes a postindustrial, knowledge-based society, we believe that the role of education is not so much to transmit large bodies of knowledge in a uniform way but, instead, to encourage students to learn carefully selected basics while emphasizing the importance of learning independently in response to new situations—a skill that will contribute to Japan's future development.

Improving the Quality of Teaching

As a result of systematically increasing the number of teachers, there were attempts to reduce class size to fewer than forty-five students in 1968 and to forty students in 1980–1991. Although the number of teachers rapidly increased during this period, teachers' salaries also increased as a result of the Educational Personnel Securing Law, which sought to attract highly qualified teachers by offering better remuneration for them than for most other public service employees. In addition to reductions in class size, student–teacher ratios were decreased under a 2001 plan for the purpose of facilitating team teaching and small-group instruction (typically groups of about twenty students depending on the subject). Increased staffing in upper secondary schools is designed to encourage diversification of education, such as unified lower and upper secondary schools, schools with integrated courses, and more opportunities for students to select courses. Under current plans, by 2005 the number of students per teacher will be 18.6 for elementary school and 14.6 for lower secondary school.

Various measures are in place to improve teachers' skills throughout their entire careers. In 1998 universities improved their preservice teacher-training programs by increasing their emphasis on new teaching methods and the significance of establishing meaningful contacts with children, which in turn directly affect the implementation of educational activities in schools. The personality and versatility of teacher candidates are more important qualifications than before, and there are improved screening tests for teachers. Teachers are also expected to improve their competencies continuously through daily education and voluntary study. Various in-service training programs, including induction training for newly employed teachers, have been systematically arranged so that teachers receive the necessary training according to their experiences, specialties, and responsibilities. The new courses of study have contributed to the need for improved teaching skills: Teachers are required to lead students to acquire basic knowledge and skills, to cultivate students' ability to learn and think on their own, to improve academic rigor, and, at the same time, to address the needs of individual students. In order to meet these demands, there is an attempt to match in-service training to the ability of each teacher, as assessed by past records.

CONCLUSION

In general, these reforms have been favorably received. However, they are still in the early stages, and further improvements lie ahead, particularly in practices that have not traditionally been common in Japan, such as the grouping of students based on their achievement levels.

Empirical data are indispensable for future decisions about the reforms. The effect of the new curriculum is not yet clear, and many people are concerned about its consequences. The Ministry of Education has responded by conducting a national comprehensive assessment of student achievement in 2002, involving about 500,000 students at ages ten, fourteen, and seventeen. The plan is to continue this assessment on a regular basis and to use the results to inform decisions about school reform.

The challenge for education is to balance the positive characteristics of Japan's current system with the society's need for new knowledge and skills. Success in meeting this challenge ultimately will depend on the sincerity and enthusiasm of policy makers and educators.

NOTE

1. Information in this essay has been drawn from Ministry of Education, Culture, Sports, Science and Technology (2001, 2002).

REFERENCES CITED

Chuou Kyouiku Shingikai [Central Council for Education]. (1996). *21 Seikiwo tenboushita wagakuninokKyouikuno arikatanituite* [The model for Japanese education in the perspective of the twenty-first century]. Tokyo: Chuou Kyouiku Shingikai.

Kyouiku Kaikaku Kokuminkaigi [National Commission on Educational Reform]. (2000). *Kyouikuwokaeru 17no teian* [17 proposals for changing education]. Tokyo: Kyouiku Kaikaku Kokuminkaigi.

Ministry of Education, Culture, Sports, Science and Technology. (2001). *Japanese government policies in education, culture, sports, science and technology.* Tokyo: MEXT.

———. (2002). *Monbukagakuhakusho* [White paper on education, culture, sports, science, and technology]. Tokyo: MEXT.

III

TRANSITIONS

11

Singapore: Schools in the Service of Society

Batia P. Horsky and Phyllis Ghim-Lian Chew

The wealth of a nation lies in its people.

—Prime Minister Goh Chok Thong (1997)

Singapore is a compact city-state in Southeast Asia. It is highly urbanized with an overall population density of just over 7,000 persons per square kilometer. Its population of about 4.5 million is ethnically diverse, multilingual, and multireligious. About 76 percent of the population is Chinese, 15 percent Malay, 7 percent Indian and European, and 2 percent from other backgrounds. The country's four official languages are Chinese, English, Malay, and Tamil (an Indian language). The dominant language is English, the language of administration and business and, since 1978, the first language in schools.

After the British colonized Singapore in 1819, it became a major port of call for the British Empire as British ships found it expedient to stop there on their way from India to China. This strategic geographical location contributed to its fast economic growth, which attracted many immigrants, mainly Chinese from southern China, to work in the colony.

In 1959 Singapore achieved independence from Britain and, as a former British colony, became part of the British Commonwealth. It then joined the Federation of Malaysia in 1963 but resigned from it in 1965. Since then it has existed as an independent republic. The same political party has ruled Singapore since its independence, and Lee Kuan Yew, the chief architect of the nation, still serves as senior minister in the cabinet. Power is overwhelmingly in the hands of the People's Action Party, which is freely elected. Although opposition parties are legal, they are inconsequential, and nongovernmental organizations, such as trade unions, free churches, professional organizations, and autonomous universities, are weak. Therefore, education policies, established by the government, are implemented single-mindedly and efficiently, with little opposition or public debate.

Singapore's policies are influenced by a perception of political and economic vulnerability. The main island of Singapore is only 42 × 23 kilometers: It has no natural resources (except its strategic location); it imports half of its water, most of its food, and all of its energy. Thus, its survival is entirely dependent on its human resources, and, as a result, the education of its people has become its top priority— a commitment to invest in education and vocational training was made in the early days of independence (Bercuson, 1995, p. 4). The nation's education policies are tailored to support its economic plans. Education is viewed as the indispensable ingredient of the nation, and the Singaporean education system is the vehicle for social engineering. In short, the education system has always been the handmaiden to the nation's goals: first, to sustain economic development and, second, to establish a sense of national identity and commitment that is essential to national survival and to economic success.

In the past few decades, this close economics–education bond has driven many education policies and pedagogical practices. As a result, Singapore's policies are guided by pragmatism, not dogma. Few Singaporeans question the policy that education should focus on technical and business fields to respond to economic growth and manpower requirements, at the expense of disciplines such as the visual and performing arts (Teo, 2003).[1] The island republic has a centralized system of education for all levels of education, with a Ministry of Education that spearheads policy implementation and curriculum development designed to provide the human resources required to meet the country's economic growth. All children receive a minimum of ten years of education in one of Singapore's 360 schools.

The results of the government's economic policies and strategies can be seen in its economic accomplishments over a relatively short period. Since independence in 1965 and through the late 1990s, the country has experienced extremely rapid economic development, with an eightfold increase in wealth. Singapore, therefore, went from being a relatively poor country to one of the world's richest, with a per capita annual income of about US$22,000. The country's infrastructure, openness to foreign trade and capital, and market opportunities contribute to a favorable business environment. The fact that it is so small enables the government to respond to rapid change in an efficient and versatile way. Smallness, however, can also lead to vulnerability because of fragile and limited markets and increasing global competition. Thus, Singapore's economy needs to become even more diversified, efficient, and innovative.

In addition to a concern about the changing global environment, the government is concerned about the slow population growth rate: Fewer working people to support an increasing elderly population means that available resources must be redirected to health care and other social services, with the risk that economic development will suffer. Dr. Ng Eng Hen, the minister of state for education and manpower, has highlighted the challenges facing the education system: "The need to develop the full potential of every Singaporean . . . can be done through the introduction of educational and training reforms so that uniformity can be transformed to diversity, rigidity to flexibility, and conformity to resilience" (2003). Today, as in the past, the government views education as the major route for the country to maintain a competitive advantage and invests large amounts to implement and monitor new education policies. Education, training, and continuing education for adults are considered essential to meet the challenges of economic restructuring. Prime Minister Goh Chok Thong explained the government's investment in reform initiatives this way: "A nation's wealth in the 21st century will depend on the capacity of its people to learn" (1997). The remainder of this chapter describes the historical foundation of the education system, its structure and priorities, and the recent reform initiatives.

PRAGMATISM

"Pragmatism" describes the spirit of Singapore. In a republic built by an immigrant community without the burden of centuries of history, the population seems impatient to achieve economic growth efficiently, without recourse to too much soul-searching or long debates in Parliament. The ability to be well fed and comfortably housed, therefore, became a priority in the 1960s, the first decade of independence. The government began the process by establishing a stable political system and a disciplined labor force to attract multinational companies that would provide jobs for the growing population, most of whom were illiterate and unskilled. The education system was used to provide workers who would be hardworking and able to follow instructions in the workplace. Thus, the 1960s saw a major expansion of Singapore's educational facilities. Student enrollment increased rapidly at both primary and secondary levels, and in 1965 Singapore achieved universal primary education.

In the 1970s, as wages increased, it was no longer practical to retain the low-value, labor-intensive industries that Singapore had attracted in the 1960s. The emphasis shifted from manufacturing goods primarily for domestic consumption to producing goods and services for export. Once again, the education system was harnessed to facilitate the nation's economic transformation. The keyword in education policy was no longer *quantitative* but, rather, *qualitative*. Subjects such as science, mathematics, and technical education, which had originally been introduced in the 1960s, were given greater emphasis by expanding the curriculum, offering scholarships to students who chose these fields, and establishing technical colleges and training institutes. In short, the 1970s saw a massive shift in emphasis from academic to technical education as a means to facilitate economic development.

The decades of the 1960s and 1970s became known as the period of "efficiency-driven education." The keywords for these two decades were *centralized, standardized, hierarchical, competitive,* and *efficient*. Along with an emphasis on subjects such as science, mathematics, and technical education came an emphasis on tracking based on a series of competitive assessments that determined clear lines of progression from primary schools to polytechnics and universities. The Ministry of Education's Research and Testing Division regulated these assessments.

A recession in the mid-1980s provided a catalyst for the modern phase of education reform in Singapore, which was built on the recognition that restructuring would be necessary in order for Singapore to flourish in a global economy. *Singapore Economy: New Directions* (Economic Committee, 1986) suggested ways in which Singapore could carve a place for itself in the international economic system and grow to a position as developed as the West and even more competitive.

This change in economic perspective signaled further reforms in education. Not surprisingly, *Towards Excellence in Schools* (Principal's Report, 1987) was published the following year. The report recommended giving administrative autonomy to secondary education as a way to encourage student motivation and creativity. The first of eight independent schools was introduced in 1988; these schools were followed in 1994 by a number of "autonomous" secondary schools that were created mainly to provide competition for the independent secondary schools.[2] Principals in both types of schools were given increased freedom to raise funds and to make staffing and programmatic decisions.

The government also encouraged school autonomy by forming an endowment fund in which it deposited part of its annual budget surplus. The funds could be used in different ways—for example, to provide enrichment courses in speech training or stress management for students. In addition, each Singaporean student between six and sixteen receives an annual grant that can be used for enrichment programs and extracurricular activities organized by schools.[3]

The education system was further deregulated to allow for the establishment of privately owned schools.[4] These schools were encouraged in order to simulate marketplace competition. During the 1990s, for the first time, schools used promotional strategies to attract parents and students. To further simulate private industry, principals increasingly were called "chief executive officers" of the schools, and, like corporate executives, they were rewarded when their schools did well.

To encourage competition among secondary schools and junior colleges, annual school rankings based on examination results were introduced in 1992. The purpose was to permit schools and parents to compare performance on the O- and A-level examinations.[5] In 1995 the Ministry of Education began giving cash awards to the forty secondary schools that were most highly ranked in the annual league tables. Secondary schools were ranked on three criteria: (1) students' overall results in national examinations; (2) the school's "value-added," computed by comparing average student scores on terminal examinations with their average scores when they entered the school; and (3) a weighted index that measures a school's performance in a national physical fitness test, as well as the percentage of overweight students in the schools.

Early selection continues to be emphasized.[6] Since 1978, streaming has been an important instrument to ensure efficiency in the economy by enabling students of varying achievement levels to learn at different paces. Thus, in an average span of ten years of schooling, Singaporean students are streamed three times—at primary 4, the Primary School Leaving Examination, and secondary 2. Within the span of their primary and secondary education, they can find themselves in any one of the following streams: gifted, English and Mother Tongue Levels 1–3 (EM1–EM3), special/express/normal, normal academic/normal technical, express, pure science/semiscience/arts/commerce, junior college/pre-university/Institute of Technical Education.[7] Such a system has served to keep students on their toes!

Higher education opportunities expanded to catapult Singapore's academic status. The Ministry of Education has often stressed both the inevitability and the importance of competition as a means of achieving excellence. The two universities in Singapore, Singapore National University and Nanyang Technological University, increased their student enrollment, and a third university was established—the Singapore Management University. Foreign universities also received licenses to set up branches in Singapore in order to encourage more competition and high standards. The Vocational and Industrial Training Board was renamed the Institute of Technical Education in 1992 to indicate an even higher level of skills training. The government also understands the value of competition in positioning Singapore as a world-class player, and national leaders cite, for example, Singapore's high rankings on international comparative tests.

Clearly, the last decade has witnessed an increasing use of the language of market economics in the Singaporean education system, after more than two decades of centralized control. Terms such as *choice, creativity,* and *diversity* (rather than *centralization, standardization,* and *efficiency*) are now commonplace. Schools are given greater autonomy and encouraged to become entrepreneurial so that their programs and students can become increasingly effective in meeting the government's economic goals (Tan, 1998, p. 59).

MULTICULTURALISM AND MULTILINGUALISM

Singapore's policies are based on the premise that a strong national identity is essential to maintaining peace and unity. Education, therefore, has always been the chief vehicle for nation building in Singapore. In the words of Prime Minister Lee Kuan Yew (1966): "Our community lacks in-built reflexes—loyalty, patriotism, history or tradition. . . . Our society and its education system was never designed to produce a people capable of cohesive action, identifying their collective interests and then acting in furtherance of them." Thus, along with the scientific and technological subjects designed to complement economic growth, students' educational experience also includes courses and activities to promote national cohesion and identity: for example, the deeply symbolic flag-raising and pledge-taking ceremony, the compulsory study of civics, the integration of teaching in different languages within the national schools, and the promotion of extracurricular cultural activities through clubs, societies, and uniformed groups. One such group is the National Cadet Corps, introduced in 1969 to strengthen pupils' preparation for future service in the armed forces.

There was one reform introduced in the 1960s that became especially prominent in the 1970s: The policy of bilingualism, which became compulsory for all students in 1966, has since become a cornerstone of the Singaporean education system. Language has always been a key factor in building national unity. Singapore's official languages—Malay, Mandarin, Tamil, and English—can be used in all aspects of public life. Malay, the national language, is used for the national anthem as well as for giving commands in military parades. English is the language of administration. Mandarin increasingly serves as a lingua franca among the Chinese population, although the Chinese speak several different dialects, including Hokkien, Teochew, Cantonese, Hakka, Hainanese, and Foochow, depending on the regional origin of their Chinese ancestors.[8] In addition to Tamil, the Indians also speak Telegu, Malayalam, Punjabi, Hindi, and Bengali, also depending on their regional origins in India.

Singapore is therefore a pluralistic state that is both multilingual and multicultural. Multiculturalism offers many advantages to a developing economy, but it can also be a threat to social cohesion, especially in a newly independent nation. Realizing the potential problems, Singapore's leaders adopted multiculturalism as an official creed; the government recognizes rituals attached to the Chinese, Malay, Indian, and other traditions and officially sanctions them through legal and administrative measures. It also supports a policy of meritocracy—that is, that anyone can succeed regardless of race, creed, or color.

When ethnic groups do not start at the same point, however, meritocracy can accentuate original differences. To address this problem, the government has placed considerable emphasis on the role of ethnically based self-help groups to provide tuition, financial assistance, and guidance to lower-income students and their families, for example, the Chinese Development Assistance Council, the Association to Uplift the Malay/Muslim Community, and the Singapore Indian Development Association.[9]

Singapore's official policy of multiculturalism is implemented in schools through a bilingual policy, with English as the "common" language and the ethnic languages—Malay, Tamil, and Mandarin—as second languages. As in all countries, language and culture policies are politicized, and even before independence from Britain in 1959, language policy was often a response to political pressures, to demands for more resources and curriculum time, and to demands for equality. These political pressures continue. To ensure that schools would comply with official policies, second language instruction became compulsory at both primary and secondary levels and was closely tied to the assessment system.[10]

The policy of bilingualism is based on the government's belief that increased proficiency in English and the mother tongue would help both to increase employment opportunities and to reduce communication and racial barriers, thus contributing to a more harmonious and better-integrated society. The policy is also based on the belief that teaching moral values and cultural traditions is most effective when instruction is carried out in the student's mother tongue.

The bilingual policy is not without its problems, however. The vast majority of Singapore's schoolchildren find mother tongue learning burdensome, and few use the language after leaving school. There has been public dissent on this issue, with some people advocating a more flexible approach to language learning in the future. The fact is, however, that English and the native languages are not given equal time in the school system. All subjects are taught in English, except language courses. The government considers English a crucial tool for participation in the international economy and, therefore, aggressively promotes its use in schools. The government also conducts its affairs predominantly in English, even though all four languages are acceptable for use in public offices. Thus, Singapore is largely an English-speaking country, a situation that has occurred without provoking communal discord.

One policy issue, however, is the English dialect used. The majority of Singaporeans speak a highly colloquial dialect called "Singlish," which differs substantially from the varieties of English spoken in the United States, Britain, and Australia (Ho & Platt, 1996). The emergence of Singlish represents a linguistic phenomenon that is likely to become more prevalent in the twenty-first century, as English strengthens its hold and fragments into an increasing number of local dialects around the world (Chew, 1999). The government has attacked Singlish as a threat to Singapore's economic viability and competitiveness, although the common dialect might also be viewed as contributing to the country's identity and cohesion.

In addition to language policy, Singapore has attempted to promote national solidarity through specific education programs. Thus, in the 1960s moral education and civics courses were introduced into the schools, followed about a decade later with stronger courses designed to teach Singaporean students a common set of moral values encompassing personal behavior, social responsibility, and loyalty to the country. In the early 1980s "religious knowledge" was introduced into upper secondary schools as a compulsory subject. Because the religious affiliations of Singaporean students are quite diverse, this initiative required a variety of religion courses: Bible knowledge, Islamic religious knowledge, Buddhist studies, Hindu studies, and Confucian ethics. The purpose of the courses was to reinforce the moral values taught in each religious tradition. By the end of 1989, however, religion courses were no longer compulsory (although they remained an elective in upper secondary school). The concern was that the requirement, instead of socializing students to accept the state's sociopolitical agenda, was in fact contributing to a religious resurgence— a concern that intensified when evangelical groups appeared to pose a threat to the government's political legitimacy and authority (Tan, 1997).

In 1997 the prime minister launched the Singapore 21 Committee to clarify Singapore's goals for the nation's future. The five new goals emphasized

- the importance of every Singaporean,
- strong families,
- opportunities for all,
- passionate feelings about Singapore, and
- active citizenship.

The "Thinking Schools, Learning Nation" project was the educational counterpart of this political initiative. The project advocated "national education" (citizen education), in addition to its emphasis on critical and creative thinking, administrative excellence, and the use of information technology in schools. The national education project is, in some ways, a continuation of efforts begun in the mid-1960s to socialize the younger generation of Singaporeans. What makes this version different, however, is the recognition that globalization, and the economic opportunities it provides, will strain the loyalties and attachment of young Singaporeans. The government realizes that it needs younger Singaporeans to stay in the country. Thus, the national education project is designed to introduce curricular and noncurricular activities to sensitize young people to Singapore's national needs, concerns, and possibilities and to convince them that Singapore is their "best home."

These ideals are to be reflected in all educational materials; indeed, the Ministry of Education has always vetted all textbooks before their use in schools. The "ideal" product of the Singaporean education system, therefore, is a person who contributes economically to the country and, at the same time, is culturally rooted and compassionate— with a strong belief in multiculturalism and meritocracy.

THE "NEW ECONOMIC ORDER"

During the period from the mid-1980s to the present, Singapore experienced two major recessions, which served as a catalyst for its recent economic and education initiatives. The first recession, in the mid-1980s, changed Singapore's economy; the gross domestic product (GDP) per capita growth rate dropped from about 8.2 percent in 1984 to −1.8 percent in 1985. However, the recession was relatively short, and the economy rebounded after only two years. In 1997, for example, Singapore's per capita GDP was close to $28,000, compared with $29,000 in the United States. In the beginning of 1997, however, Singapore experienced another recession, which once again served as a stimulus for economic and educational change: The government encouraged more open markets in the banking and telecommunications sectors and, at the same time, encouraged schools to teach students to be innovative, flexible, entrepreneurial, creative, and committed to lifelong learning. To accomplish these goals, the entire education system, from preschool to university, underwent review; teachers, principals, and university academics participated in planning a new system. Prime Minister Goh Chok Thong emphasized, "The wealth of a nation lies in its people" (1997), and in 1997 the education initiative, "Thinking Schools, Learning Nation," was launched.[11]

The initiative's message is clear: It is important to develop the whole child and to recognize the range of abilities, talents, and skills that students possess. Schools should encourage "new worker" attributes—that is, the ability to work both independently and on teams; to be risk takers; to be capable of learning, relearning, and unlearning; and to be creative and flexible. Students would acquire skills in critical thinking and problem solving, along with mastery of information technology. Singaporean schools, for example, have introduced interdisciplinary projects as a way to encourage critical thinking and creativity. To ensure that these projects are taken seriously, the time allotted to traditional curricula has been reduced by 30 percent, and the government is requiring that participation in interdisciplinary work become a criterion for university admissions beginning in 2004.

Teacher training is also part of the "Thinking Schools, Learning Nation" initiative. It is understood that the initiative can be only as effective as the teachers implementing it; teachers, therefore, are entitled to 100 hours of in-service training per year, paid for by the government, along with work and promotion opportunities.

"Thinking Schools, Learning Nation" also includes information technology and citizen education.[12] The government strongly believes that skills in information technology are essential for lifelong learning in the twenty-first century. Thus, since 1998, the government has committed US$1.2 billion to create a technology-based teaching and learning environment in every school in Singapore. The objective, to have one computer per teacher and one computer per student in 2002, has been realized. In addition, all classrooms in all schools, starting in primary school, are well equipped with the latest instructional technology; students use computers for up to 30 percent of their instructional time. The hope is that with fully networked schools, teachers and students can extend their learning horizons beyond the classroom and have access to educational resources almost anywhere in the world.

The initiative also attempted to strengthen school administration. A new school appraisal system was introduced for the schools that had not yet become "autonomous" or independent, with the goal of gradually increasing the number of these schools. The purpose was to strengthen school management and improve the use of resources—a process that began in 1987 with the establishment of the independent schools. Thus, schools are assessed on management effectiveness as well as on student performance. One purpose of the assessment is to motivate schools to specialize in certain fields that would be "customized" to meet the needs of students with different talents.

In 2002 the Ministry of Education announced a review of junior college education (pre-university schools) to broaden the offerings and to introduce greater structural flexibility by combining various components of secondary and pre-university levels, including the option not to offer Cambridge O levels (a staple since British colonial administration) for some students. The formation of an autonomous examination authority has also been discussed. If it is established, American-style examinations like the Scholastic Aptitude Test and the Graduate Record Exam, as well as the European baccalaureate, are likely to become more prominent in the education system.

CONCLUSION

As a relatively young nation, Singapore has always used education to support its hopes for a future society. Educational planning is directly related to economic policy and, therefore, an essential part of nation building. The People's Action Party, which has been in power since independence, emphasizes the importance of pragmatic policies that respond to Singapore's small size and lack of natural resources. In the past two decades, however, Singapore has undergone two recessions and has had to face the uncertainties of the global economy. Education reforms have attempted to respond to these challenges by encouraging independent learning, problem solving, and creativity and by reducing the time spent on traditional curricula. The Singaporean government has a reputation for being strong, able, and free from corruption, and for implementing many successful public policies. Singapore's public housing, health care, and transportation are closely studied in many parts of the developing world. The country's effort to integrate information technology into the society and create an "intelligent island" is one of the most comprehensive any nation has attempted; the level of technology available to its educational institutions is high. Many graduates of Singapore's schools achieve at a very high level. All of these accomplishments facilitate the introduction of major education reforms.

The unpredictability of the global economy, however, remains a concern. Moreover—despite recent policy initiatives—forty years of traditional education have left Singapore with a standardized, content-heavy curriculum reinforced by frequent assessment and high-stakes examinations. Drilling and coaching have been the dominant teaching approaches, and that is hard to change. For real change to occur, teachers would have to change their traditional beliefs and assumptions.

Class sizes remain very large, and teachers seem to lack the time to engage in activities that would develop an innovative school culture. If large class sizes continue, innovative practices like interdisciplinary project work are likely to be stripped to their bare essentials and become a routine and superficial activity. Although these projects might continue, they would fail to meet their original objectives.

Contradictions remain: The school system still rewards traditional academic achievement, which requires students to spend a large amount of time studying for examinations. In addition, many students spend their after-school hours reviewing and mastering content in tuition centers, which are not under the Ministry of Education's supervision. It is ironic that while there is an emphasis on standardized curricula, examinations, and school rankings, the government policy has also promoted the value of distinctive schools.

Singapore's economic and educational restructuring has been innovative and highly goal-directed, but the restructuring takes place in a society that exerts a level of political and social control unique among wealthy nations. That control might be inconsistent with an education environment that encourages critical thinking and flexibility. Nonetheless, Singapore has taken a unique approach in tying education so closely to economic goals, and the leadership is resolved to give its next generation the skills needed to meet those goals.

NOTES

1. A higher premium is placed on science and engineering. In 2003 Minister of Education Teo Chee Hean said that although the schools offer a

broad range of subjects, "we do encourage our students to do science and engineering; that's because we feel that it's important both for them to find a good job, as well as for the overall competitiveness of the economy."

2. Independent schools are more independent of the Ministry of Education than autonomous schools; for example, independent schools can hire or fire their own teachers, but autonomous schools depend on the Ministry of Education to do that for them. Independent schools also charge higher fees than autonomous schools in order to fund extracurricular activities. Nevertheless, both of them still depend on funding from the Ministry of Education and do adhere largely to the curriculum set by the ministry.

3. The provision of extra funds means that schools are increasingly turning to private individuals and agencies to conduct enrichment programs and sports training for their students. Some schools even hire coaches from other countries, such as China.

4. Privately owned schools, which can establish their own goals and curricula, are usually established by foreigners, for example, the American School, the Australian School, and the United World College.

5. "O" stands for "Ordinary"; and "A," for "Advanced." O- and A-level examinations are taken by students in government schools, autonomous schools, and independent schools by students at the ages of sixteen and eighteen, respectively. One needs an O level to be admitted to the polytechnic and an A level to be admitted to the university.

6. The Goh Report (Goh, 1979) acknowledged that many schoolchildren could not pass the examination and that this has led to wastage. Therefore, Goh suggested the introduction of ability-based streaming at the end of primary 3 and the introduction of ability-differentiated curriculum, as well as the extension of the length of schooling for the weaker students.

7. Of the language levels, EM1 is the most challenging level and EM3, the least.

8. The lingua franca among Singapore's many races was Bazaar Malay (market Malay) and Hokkien (a Chinese dialect). However, with the reemergence of China onto the world stage in the 1980s and a "Speak Mandarin" campaign instituted by the Singapore government, for practical purposes, the lingua franca among Chinese Singaporeans is now Mandarin.

9. Although some countries have increased local participation because of financial constraints, Singapore's policies have taken place at a time of healthy budget surpluses and increased government expenditures for education. It remains to be seen whether decentralization will lead, as it has in other countries, to increased disparities among schools, as well as to social inequalities.

10. Under this system, about 20–30 percent of students were unable to meet the bilingual requirement, but because the policy was sensitive, few spoke up.

11. The initiative is a vision for a total learning environment, including students, teachers, parents, workers, companies, community organizations, and government: "Their ability to seek out new technologies and ideas . . . and to apply them . . . will be the key source of economic growth" (Goh, 1997).

12. "Citizenship education" has been discussed in the section on multilingualism.

REFERENCES CITED

Bercuson, K. (Ed.). (1995). *Singapore: A case study in rapid development.* Washington, DC: International Monetary Fund.

Chew, G. L. P. (1999). Linguistic imperialism, globalism, and the English language. *The Aila Review, 131,* 37–48.

Economic Committee. (1986). *Singapore economy: New directions.* Singapore: Ministry of Information and the Arts.

Goh, C. T. (1997, June). Shaping our future: Thinking schools, learning nation. Speech at the Seventh International Conference on Thinking, Singapore.

Goh, Keng Swee. (1979). *Report of the Ministry on Education 1978.* Singapore: Singapore National Printers.

Ho, M. L., & Platt, J. (1996). *Dynamics of a contact continuum: Singapore English.* Oxford: Clarendon Press.

Lee, K. Y. (1966). *New bearings in our education system: An address by the prime minister to principals of schools in Singapore on Aug 29, 1966.* Singapore: Ministry of Culture.

Ng, E. H. (2003, March 6). Speech, Minister of State for Education and Manpower, Singapore.

Principal's Report. (1987). *Towards excellence in schools: A report submitted to the minister for education.* Singapore: Ministry of Education.

Tan, J. (1997). The rise and fall of religious knowledge in Singapore secondary schools. *Journal of Curriculum Studies, 29* (5), 603–24.

———. (1998). The marketization of education in Singapore: Policies and implications. *International Review of Education, 44* (1), 47–63.

Teo, C. H. (2003, July). Getting the fundamentals right. Speech at the NIE Teachers Investiture Ceremony, Ministry of Information, Communication and the Arts, Singapore.

12

Canada: A Multicultural Policy

Ratna Ghosh

> It is part of the fabric of Canada, a brave federation of differences: multiculturalism, official bilingualism, minority rights, cultural and geographic diversity, and ancient grievances. Managing these differences is a constant juggling act, a high stakes poker game, an act of faith.
>
> —Martin O'Malley (Canadian Broadcasting Corporation, 2003)

For several years the United Nations has ranked Canada as one of the best countries in which to live. Canada is a wealthy nation, and as a liberal democracy it attempts to ensure its people equality of access to social benefits such as education, health care, and pension plans. All citizens are guaranteed important rights and freedoms through such legislation as the Constitution Act (1867), the Bill of Rights (1960), the Human Rights Act (1978), the Charter of Rights and Freedoms (1982), and numerous provincial codes.[1] Efforts to confirm Canada as a multicultural society have been further legislated through the Multiculturalism Policy (1971), the Multicultural Act (1988), and the Employment Equity Act (1986).

At the beginning of the twenty-first century, Canada is doing very well; however, a report issued in 2000 by the Conference Board of Canada describes the nation as average in social and economic performance compared with six of the largest and most internationally competitive industrialized countries.[2] Debate now centers on Canada's social policy agenda and the values underpinning it as they relate to the public versus private balance in education, health, and social services. Canadians have not been immune to cuts in social programs and the trends toward privatization that have taken place globally over the last decade. However, there is strong public support in Canada for maintaining and even increasing taxes to strengthen social welfare programs (Livingstone & Hart, 1995).

THE CANADIAN EDUCATION SYSTEM

Overview

By international standards, Canada has an excellent record in education. From the inception of mass schooling, Canadians have supported a popular democratic educational ideology. The patterns of education set by the British and French settlers in the mid-nineteenth century were formalized in 1867 by the British North America Act (also known as the Constitutional Act), which made education a provincial responsibility. This basic approach was reiterated in the Constitution Act of 1982. Policies, programs, and structures vary from province to province because of regional differences. In many respects, Canada's school systems are highly centralized at the provincial level and, therefore, are more comparable to the systems of continental Europe than to the decentralized traditions of the United States.

Elementary school is from grades one to six, and, in most provinces, high school is from grades seven to twelve, with students entering higher education after grade twelve. In Quebec, high school is from grades seven to eleven, and, for the next two years, students attend junior colleges (French or English, public or private), which are called *collège d'enseignement général et professionel*. At this level, students can choose academic programs, which prepare them for university entrance, or vocational training, which completes their schooling. About 28.7 percent of students obtain postsecondary diplomas, with 16.3 percent attending universities (Statistics Canada, 2002).

Canada has no federal office of education and no national education policy. For common educational concerns, the provinces cooperate through the Council of Ministers of Education in Canada. Federal influence in education is mostly indirect (through equalization subsidies), and policy formulation is largely at the provincial level. However, national forces are generated and expressed through political, bureaucratic, scholarly, and citizen groups that filter through to the provincial decision makers. The federal government facilitates programs such as bilingualism and multiculturalism and also plays a significant role in constitutional reforms that affect education. Provincial responses to federal legislation vary, as in the case of the Multicultural Policy and Bill. Although the federal government still controls the education of First Nations students, this responsibility is gradually being devolved to the band councils.[3]

Private and Religious Schools

Educational opportunity for all is provided through the federal charter, various provincial policies, and formal protections against discrimination. The British North America Act of 1867 confirmed the educational divisions into Catholic and Protestant school boards, which were based on the belief that religion is important for character development and, therefore, for education. In most provinces, schools run by both Roman Catholic and Protestant churches were publicly funded. This practice continues up to the present in English Canada. Religious schools of other denominations, such as Jewish, Islamic, and Sikh, are generally given some financial aid by the provinces. In June 1993 the Supreme Court of Canada ruled that Quebec would be allowed to proceed with the creation of new French and English linguistic school boards, which have since been superimposed on the denominational split and, in most cases, will replace the religious boards. The private sector in Canadian education, at the level of schools and of universities, is relatively small but increasing (4.6 percent of the total elementary/secondary school population in 1995). Only five provinces (Quebec, Manitoba, Saskatchewan, Alberta, and British Columbia) give direct public aid to private schools, and their levels of funding vary considerably. Ontario brought many

Roman Catholic schools, which had been privately funded, into the public sector during 1985–1988.

Educational Funding

Canada is among the world leaders in terms of resources devoted to education. The provinces fund public education from their general revenues, which come from taxes and other sources, such as federal government transfer payments. The principles of education finance are based on intergovernmental responsibility for the equalization of the educational tax burden and opportunity, the preservation of local autonomy, and the stipulation of provincial control (Dibski, 1995). In general, there is provincial/local sharing of educational financing; the rationale is to minimize inequities that arise between poorer and richer localities. In most provinces, the ministries of education have the responsibility for establishing school districts, providing grants to school boards, developing educational goals and curricula, authorizing textbooks, certifying teachers, and controlling teacher-education programs. The provincial governments are involved, directly or indirectly, in collective bargaining with teachers' unions. School boards get provincial grants for offering their programs, busing students when necessary (e.g., in rural areas), and managing their sites. However, the school boards, along with the municipal governments, also raise revenue through local residential and business property taxes. Prince Edward Island and New Brunswick are the exceptions; their school boards receive full funding from the state and do not raise revenues locally.

Federal transfer payments also provide a major source of educational funding. The education of some groups (such as native students in the ten provinces and three territories and the children of armed forces personnel) is the responsibility of the federal government. The federal government also pays indirectly for education in the provinces through transfer payments to provinces from federal revenues. Of increasing importance, these federal equalization payments (section 36 of the Constitution Act, 1982) are preventing interprovincial disparities in public programs as well as in standard of living. The payments are designed to equalize provincial fiscal capacity by joint cost sharing of social programs, such as education, health, and welfare. The concept enables provinces to provide reasonably comparable levels of service, in spite of their differences in ability to pay, and provides an ongoing commitment to equality that is critical for public school education. The federal funds become part of the provincial budgets, and each province expends them according to its own priorities (Carter, 1988).

Standards

Eighty percent of Canada's working-age population has completed secondary school, and a significant proportion of this population has gone on to higher education (Council of Ministers of Education in Canada, 2000). Canadian students generally perform quite well in international test score comparisons, the Program for International Student Assessment (PISA) and the Third International Mathematics and Science Study (TIMSS), although there is concern about some students and subjects.

The Pan-Canadian Education Indicators Program, as well as provincial and territorial programs, provides data on Canadian education systems. In addition, the annual report card on Quebec's high schools, initiated in 2000, is a ranking guide that has sparked debate over its focus on test scores as the main criterion of school quality, and it is likely to affect discussions of issues such as the use of taxpayer-funded school vouchers. Its rating of public and private schools, based on test scores, parental income, and graduation rates, is designed as a guide for parents. However, the report card has been severely criticized for neglecting to take into account the selective entrance examinations now used by many private schools; the school rankings, therefore, are more an indicator of student selectivity than of educational quality.

Standardized tests are not used to determine students' promotion from grade to grade or their graduation from secondary school, and teachers are not held accountable for the test results. Moreover, most universities no longer require the Scholastic Aptitude Test (SAT) or other standardized admissions tests (although they do require the SAT from students applying with a high school diploma from the United

States). University admissions are based on students' academic records, references, and statements of purpose.

A type of voucher system exists in some provinces because their departments of education subsidize the cost of tuition at most private schools. These subsidies, which enable parents to send their children to private schools for reduced tuition rates, replace what otherwise would have been spent in the public sector. The provincial governments are helping, in effect, to maintain a two-tier system.

DEMOGRAPHIC TRENDS

A decline in fertility rates has changed the age structure in Canadian society from a broad base of young people to a rapidly increasing middle-aged and older population; Canada depends, therefore, on immigration as a source of population growth. Although the number of immigrants has varied widely over its history, Canada continues to be one of the world's major immigrant nations.

The history of Canadian immigration policy reflects the country's changing values and priorities. Early immigration was exclusionary in character and based mainly on immigration from Europe. In the 1970s the government under Prime Minister Pierre Trudeau undertook an extensive public review of Canadian immigration policy: The 1976 Immigration Act shifted immigration toward a much more diverse set of countries in Asia, Africa, and South America. Over the past twenty-eight years, therefore, Canada has evolved from a nation in which the population was composed primarily of Canada's original inhabitants (the First Nations people and the Inuit) and Europeans to a nation with immigration from around the world.

These changes in immigration and related policies are reshaping racial and ethnic relations in Canada. In 1867 Upper Canada (now the Province of Ontario) and Lower Canada (now the Province of Quebec) joined to form the Canadian Confederation; at that time, people of British and French origin (the original settlers) constituted 92 percent of the total population. By 1949 the other provinces and territories joined the Canadian Confederation without substantially changing the founding demographics. In contrast, the 1996 census showed dramatic differences in the reported origins of Canadians (Statistics Canada, 1996): Close to half of the total population belongs to ethnic groups other than British or French. Even in francophone Quebec, over one-quarter of the population consists of non-French groups.

The central fact of Canada's history has been the relations between the English and French charter groups, the First Nations and Inuit, and other ethnic groups (Elliot & Fleras, 1990). But these broad groups have not had equal status, and the English–French equation continues to dominate Canadian history.

Policy initiatives dealing with the changed demographic profile were largely a result of three factors: the development of French nationalism in Quebec during the early 1960s that threatened Canadian federalism, aggressive state intervention in social policy, and the assertive demands of minority ethnic groups (Anderson & Frideres, 1981). Quebec's volatile politics led to the establishment of the Royal Commission on Bilingualism and Biculturalism in 1963. Its 1969 report on ethnic groups pointed to a demographic transformation. Several ethnic groups, in addition to the French in Quebec, felt strongly about their cultures and were demanding to be recognized, despite the continuous linguistic assimilation of immigrant groups into the anglophone sector. The government responded with a policy on multiculturalism that recognized the new social reality. In 1971 Prime Minister Trudeau presented the nation with a new policy, "Bilingualism within a Multicultural Framework." It was the first official acknowledgment of the reality of pluralism in Canadian society.

It is interesting to note that in 1969 the Official Languages Act made English and French the two official languages at the federal level, although multiculturalism legislation was not federally enacted until 1988. Bilingualism, based on the concept of the "founding nations," granted special privileges to French and English groups because of their claim that they had "founded" Canada; the legislation ignored Canada's native population. Bilingualism became compulsory in federal offices across Canada. In 1983 the new Official Languages Act was passed to further strengthen the legislation, keeping English and French as the two official Canadian languages at the federal level. At the provincial level, eight of Canada's ten provinces use English as the official language; New Brunswick is bilingual, and French is the official language in Quebec, although most government services (including education) are accessible in English to the anglophone community. The other provinces, which are officially English, offer some services, particularly those pertaining to the judicial system, to the French minority. Five provinces have officially accepted multiculturalism in education, and Quebec has its own intercultural education perspective. Enrollment in French second-language programs has grown enormously. The federal government has given aid to various French-language teacher-training programs, as well as to students at all levels of education, in order to ensure the survival of French in Canada.

Multiculturalism has been defined in various ways in Canada and continues to be controversial. As a pattern of social organization, the "Canadian mosaic" was thought of as complementary to political federalism when the policy of multiculturalism was announced in the early 1970s.[4] Its aim was to legitimize the place of minority ethnic groups (along with the French and English) in Canadian society. As a political ideology, it has provided Canada with an identity. As a policy, multiculturalism implies consensus within the rhetoric of a "just" society where there is to be "unity within diversity." Its objectives are (1) to assist all cultural groups to grow and contribute to Canada; (2) to help minority groups overcome cultural barriers so that they can enjoy full participation in Canadian society; (3) to develop healthy intergroup relations, thereby reducing racial and ethnic tension and promoting national unity; and (4) to provide facilities to minority groups for language learning. The implementation of the third objective was quite weak until the Multiculturalism Act of 1988 and the more recent establishment of the Race Relations Directorate. The fourth objective received criticism for placing too much emphasis on the accommodations that minority groups need to make and not enough on adjustments required of the dominant culture.

The 1982 Charter of Rights and Freedoms (enacted by the Canada Act, sections 1-34) strengthened previous constitutional guarantees that protected the individual rights of women and ethnic group members while introducing legal provisions to prevent discrimination on the grounds of ethnicity or race. Multiculturalism is vaguely alluded to in section 27 of the 1982 Constitution Act (enacted by the Canada Act [U.K.], c.11-Schedule B)—"This Charter shall be interpreted in a manner consistent with the preservation and enhancement of the multicultural heritage of Canadians"—but multiculturalism is not the main point of the charter.

The concept of multiculturalism has changed over time from a recognition of diversity to the promotion of full and equitable participation of Canadians of all origins. Policy initiatives and legislation have strengthened this change by adding equity and antidiscrimination measures. The Multiculturalism Act of 1988, for example, calls on the government to foster equality and access for all Canadians. Eight of its nine principles address equity issues, and the ninth deals with culture. In addition, the Race Relations and Cross-Cultural Understanding Program is designed to eliminate racial discrimination at the individual and institutional levels, and the 1986 federal Employment Equity Act removes barriers that limit the participation of women and minorities, as well as native and disabled persons.

MULTICULTURAL EDUCATION

The Context

The application of federal multicultural policy to education is limited both because education is a provincial responsibility and because neither legal nor political remedies are available in the absence of a substantive rights guarantee. Although national legal protections to prevent discrimination on the grounds of ethnicity or race in the Charter of Rights and Freedoms do have implications for education, the vagueness of the multiculturalism clause inhibits its application. The exception is religion, the one component of multiculturalism that is an integral part of the education system.

The federal government assists multicultural programs and research in education through a department, originally set up as the Multiculturalism Directorate in 1972 under the secretary of state. But the lack of federal control over education and provincial legislation in general has limited federal ability to influence education in a multicultural direction to any meaningful degree. The education policies in the provinces have traditionally promoted an Anglo- or French-dominated culture, with little recognition of the unique requirements of an increasingly diverse society that is attracting immigrants from around the world. However, multicultural policies are slowly evolving, and the changes can be summarized in several stages (Ghosh & Tarrow, 1993).

In the *assimilation stage,* the assumption was that society represented a single culture and subordinate groups would relinquish their identities in favor of the existing, dominant mode. In education, the different needs of diverse groups were ignored; variations in learning styles or behavioral patterns were considered deficiencies. Thus, differences equaled inferiority, and the effort to overcome these deficiencies focused on molding all students to be part of the dominant culture.

The early multicultural programs began in the *adaptation stage.* Nondominant culture was perceived as exotic and an artifact; the resulting "sari, steel drum, and samosa approach" depoliticized culture and avoided issues of discrimination and race relations. It also permitted educators to continue to neglect other cultures by substituting, instead, the observance of "multicultural days." However, the emphasis on static and romantic representation neither created greater tolerance nor contributed to integration (Moodley, 1981). Moreover, the need to teach languages resulted in an emphasis on compensatory programs, which were used broadly in education as the method to achieve equal educational opportunity.

The *accommodation stage* in education was characterized by "multicultural education" programs, such as ethnic studies, comparative religion, studies of other cultures, and heritage language programs, along with attention to ethnic and gender representation in the curriculum. The goal was to avoid sins of commission and sins of omission: Publishers stressed both the inclusion of ethnic minorities in curriculum material and the removal of stereotypical portrayals. The assumption was that increasing ethnic representation in the curriculum and hiring a few teachers from minority groups would help students from these groups develop a sense of identity and a positive self-concept. Some provinces also offered heritage language classes to enable ethnic groups to maintain their languages. On the whole, however, minorities did not get the same life opportunities; the culture of their schools and the curriculum, which was still based on the dominant English or French tradition, marginalized them, as did the racism and discrimination they experienced in overt and covert forms in the school system and later in the job market.

In the current *incorporation stage,* there is a greater emphasis on intergroup relations and creating a "just" society through, for example, prejudice-reduction strategies and programs to increase equity in employment. Recently, immigration criteria have been changed to ensure the use of nonracial standards. The *integration stage* extends the previous stage by placing greater emphasis on formulating new "worldviews" through antiracist education, a respect for human rights, and more emphasis on a global perspective in the curriculum. Although antiracist education has been implemented for some time in England, these initiatives have been confined to only a few cities and provinces in Canada.

Multicultural Education in English Canada

The general policy of multiculturalism has been translated in different ways by Canadian provinces. Saskatchewan was the first to endorse the federal policy in 1975, and four other provinces have subsequently implemented it. Choices regarding the medium of instruction were offered to the Ukrainian, Russian, German, Jewish, and native Cree populations in the western provinces of Alberta, Manitoba, and Saskatchewan. Nova Scotia, on the extreme east of Canada, now has a strong policy of intercultural education even though its long-settled black population suffered segregation in schools until the 1950s. The two provinces distinctly ahead of the others with regard to a transition to multicultural education are British Columbia and Ontario, largely because they have the most diverse populations. British Columbia, which has the longest record of immigration from diverse societies, has a large Asian population, and it continues to be the province of choice for a substantial proportion of Asian immigrants. Overall, most immigrants go to Ontario, and about half of its population is composed of people who are not of British descent.

Ontario also has the largest number of racist incidents reported in Canada. In 1997 the Ontario provincial government endorsed multiculturalism as a policy, and it now has adopted an antiracist policy.

Although largely decentralized, the Ministry of Education encourages the teaching of English as a second language and focuses on the elimination of bias in textbooks. Although English is the language of instruction, it is also taught as a second language to the significant percentage of the population whose first language is not English. The 1992 amendments to the Education Act expanded earlier legislation and required provincial school boards to implement policies on antiracism and equity. School boards have responded with their own policies on curriculum, race relations, heritage languages (sixty-three languages in 1990–91), school and community relations, student placement, and teacher recruitment.

QUEBEC'S UNIQUE STATUS

Language Policy

Although Quebec is one of ten provinces, its position in Canada is unique. It is the only province to have rejected the federal policies of both bilingualism and multiculturalism. Quebec's official language is French, and it has its own intercultural policy. One-quarter of Canada's population resides in Quebec. Although close to three-quarters of the Quebec population trace their lineage to French ancestry, there is a small fraction (around 4 percent) who are of British stock, and the remaining population is composed of diverse ethnic groups (Statistics Canada, 1991).

Until the 1960s and the Quiet Revolution, the policy of the Quebec government, led by Premier Maurice Duplessis, was to discourage immigration.[5] The attitude toward immigration in Quebec, however, changed when the birthrate declined significantly. To facilitate increases in immigration, the Quebec government requested greater autonomy in the selection of immigrants, which was administered jointly by the federal and provincial governments. The McDougall Gagnon–Tremblay agreement granted the request, and Quebec became the only province to have its own immigration department.

The rise of French nationalism in the 1960s, which resulted in the Quiet Revolution, challenged Anglo supremacy in its attempt to end discrimination—both ethnic and linguistic—against French Canadians in their own region and to become *maître chez nous* (masters of our own house). At the same time, the Roman Catholic Church's role diminished greatly in Quebec, and language, rather than religion, became the distinguishing characteristic for the Quebec population.

The French in Quebec concluded that they required more than bilingualism to augment their socioeconomic status and power. The policy of multiculturalism, which implied equal status for all cultures, also was perceived as inconsistent with a French cultural revitalization. At a time of fervent nationalism, the classification of French culture as equal in status to other cultures was unacceptable. The rise of French nationalism was an offshoot of the reality that French Canadians constitute only 2 percent of the North American population and their linguistic survival is threatened within an English-speaking continent. Their main concern, therefore, was the survival of a distinctive identity in terms of language, society, and culture; it led to legislation in 1974 making French the official language in Quebec, and in 1977 it became obligatory for most children to be taught in French.[6] The legislation was controversial because it gave priority to the rights of Francophones as a group over the individual rights of non-Francophones. The repercussions have been far-reaching.

In 1978 La Politique Québécois du development culturelle (Policy of Cultural Development for the People of Quebec) formulated Quebec's policy, stressing the importance of diversity in the construction of a common society through the medium of the French language. In 1990 the government of Quebec issued a position statement on immigration, thereby acknowledging the importance of Quebec's diversity. Several factors led to the official endorsement of a policy that previously had been discouraged: (1) the continuous decline of the French population (the low birthrate was certain to decimate future generations, a possibility further aggravated by substantial outmigration because of concern about economic instability), (2) an aging population (current estimates are that 25 percent of the total will exceed sixty-five years of age in another decade), and (3) a need to stimulate the economy through the expansion of the labor market and increased consumption. As a result, large numbers of immigrants (notably Vietnamese, Haitian, Latin American, and Lebanese) arrived in Quebec and increasingly are perceived as posing a serious threat to the French language. It is ironic that the focus on the survival of the French language in Quebec coincided with the need to increase immigration significantly. In 1990–91 students whose first language was neither French nor English made up 35 percent of the total school-going population in the four Montreal school boards (McAndrew, 1993).

To safeguard the language, the government formulated three main objectives: (1) to facilitate easy access to French language teaching, (2) to foster a sense of belonging and participation among immigrant and ethnic groups, and (3) to develop intergroup relations among all residents of Quebec. These objectives resemble the federal multicultural policy, although they were initially developed for a different purpose.

Intercultural Education

Until the past generation, the philosophical approach toward education of both the French and the English has been that of assimilation, rather than integration. It has been only since the Quiet Revolution that the assimilation policy of the French and English sectors began changing. Quebec became the first Canadian province to offer legal guarantees for the educational rights of minorities through its Charter of Rights in 1975. Several more years elapsed, however, before the province could focus on the educational, social, and cultural needs of the new immigrants. Quebec developed the "Intercultural Education" policy to address these needs by facilitating the integration of the new arrivals. Under this policy, Quebec was to be pluralistic in outlook but francophone through its reliance on the French language.

Thus, education policy stresses, at least officially, "new efforts to integrate immigrant students and prepare the whole student population to participate in social integration in democratic, Francophone, pluralistic Quebec" (Ministère de l'Education, 1998, p. v). The schools are to reflect the francophone vision by preparing students from all cultural communities to use the French language as a means to develop a new, common identity.

In a recent policy document, the government's *Plan of Action* (Ministère de l'Education, 1998, p. 9), the francophone element must override all others to enable French Quebec's survival in an overwhelmingly anglophone North America. The French language, therefore, must be presented in a positive light by schools and other learning institutions (Ministère de l'Education, 1998). Along with changes in the demographic and linguistic landscape in the province, the Quebec Human Rights Charter underwent modifications in 1985, and, in the following year, a Declaration on Ethnic and Race Relations was announced; the Superior Council of Education in Quebec also issued several documents embodying the concept of intercultural education.

Historically, the school system developed by the Catholics has been linked with the French, and the much smaller system developed by the Protestants has been associated with the English. Moreover, the unambiguous preference of most immigrants to Quebec has been to send their children to English schools, for both economic and social prestige reasons. The Protestant schools, however, though admitting all ethnic, religious, and cultural communities, paid little attention to the special educational requirements of pluralism. The Catholic schools admitted only Catholics (mostly French); thus, there was no problem of dealing with heterogeneity. A Quebec government document, *Let's Build Quebec Together* (Ministère des Communautes Culturelles et de l'Immigration du Quebec, 1990), summarized the situation by stating that, until recently, Quebec society prescribed a model of cultural and ideological homogeneity for all those residing in Quebec, regardless of their origin.

The pluralistic nature of Quebec society was neither acknowledged by the English Protestant system nor faced by the French Catholic system until legislation in 1977. Law 101 forced children of many non-French-speaking groups into French medium schools by stipulating that attendance at those schools was obligatory for all students living in Quebec, including children of immigrants from commonwealth countries, immigrants from English-speaking countries, and former residents of English-speaking Canada; the only exceptions were temporary residents, native persons, or children with at least one parent who had attended English medium primary school in Quebec or who had a sibling currently registered in an English medium school.

This language policy had major consequences for education in Quebec. Immigrant students who were not French were compelled to join the French school system, which was totally unprepared to accommodate such vast numbers. Traditionally very homogeneous in composition, the French education system has had to cope with a significant proportion of diverse cultural groups since 1971. In contrast, the English schools had always been accustomed to having a mixed and varied student body and, until about fifteen years ago, had consistently implemented a policy of assimilation, deliberately overlooking the pluralistic reality. The declining birthrate of the "original" Quebec population (*Québécois de souche*), alongside the burgeoning presence of "Allophones" (as many as 90 percent in certain French schools) from as many as eighty-five ethnic and twenty religious groups, causes concern among many of the "originals."[7] Fear of racial tension is the least of their apprehensions. The real danger is perceived to be a threat to the French culture posed by the multiplicity and vigor of other cultural groups. Culture clearly is less amenable to legislative control than language; thus, the threat is not only more subtle but also more potent because of the implications for future generations.

The language policy also dramatically changed the linguistic composition of the school boards. In 1978–79 the French Catholic sector had 27.3 percent non-French students, and the English sector had 72.7 percent. Within a decade the numbers had changed to 65.19 percent in the French sector and 34.82 percent in the English sector.

School boards based on language (French and English) were established in 1996. School boards based on religion will be terminated, although four boards retain the right to remain religious within the linguistic organization. The overall impact will be to increase the importance of the French language and to attenuate the role of religion in education.

Some observers have argued that the government's policies on immigrant education have responded primarily to a concern that French Canadians are victims of a "linguistic menace" and, therefore, have neglected problems faced by new immigrant groups (McAndrew, 1985). The government has been criticized for giving insufficient attention to promoting the types of skills and intercultural understanding that would lead to educational success. Immigrant groups have been described as finding themselves caught between "two solitudes," a phrase taken from the book of that title by Hugh MacLennan (1945) and referring to the separate worlds of the French and English in Quebec. Initiatives have recently been proposed to address some of the earlier problems. Because of the nonnegotiable status of French, however, many immigrants are discouraged from moving to Quebec and choose Ontario or British Columbia instead.

As described previously, multicultural education in Quebec has gone through three stages: (1) a policy of *assimilation*, a "uniform cultural and ideological model" (Ministère des Communautes Culturelles et de l'Immigration du Quebec, 1990) for all Quebecers; (2) an *adaptation* stage focused on language classes to compensate for the "deficiencies" of non-French groups; and (3) *accommodation* to a diverse population in the context of continuing to build a francophone Quebec (exemplified by the document *Let's Build Quebec Together*). The current approach, therefore, is designed for a diverse society but places the responsibility on "cultural communities" and immigrants to familiarize themselves with the "cultural codes of the new society and redefine [their] identity to reconcile these values with those of [their] original culture" (Ministère des Communautes Culturelles et de l'Immigration du Quebec, 1990, p. 45)

Given Quebec's history, it was perhaps unavoidable that the sociopolitical discourse would center mainly on the French–English equation. Although many cultural communities make up Quebec's society, their urgent needs have been dealt with only within the context of nationalism and language, rather than on their own merits. Until this imbalance is recognized, attempts at intercultural education will remain peripheral to language learning (Ghosh & Ray, 1995). Even though language learning is an essential component of intercultural education, it is not sufficient. The policy issues are complex: Quebec's requirement that students be educated in French can hardly be questioned when education in English is not challenged in the rest of Canada. Policies to ensure equity for Quebec's cultural communities, however, still have a low priority both in the education system and in the broader society.

MULTICULTURAL POLICY
AND EQUALITY OF OPPORTUNITY

As a group, minorities in Canada are better educated than the majority population (de Silva, 1997; Hou & Balakrishnan, 1996), and their proportion of university graduates is about twice as high (de Silva, 1997). This results, at least in part, from immigration policy. In the 1960s, for example, certain minority groups responded to Canada's need for professionals. Current immigration policy uses the following point assignments: (1) education: 25; (2) official languages (English and/or French): 24; and (3) employment experience: 21. Quebec's immigration policy heavily favors knowledge of French, and the province, for example, has been turning away much-needed professionals (such as doctors) who are not proficient in French.

Despite their relatively high educational levels, however, minorities, especially immigrant youth, face discrimination in school (Canadian Council on Social Development, 2000; Davies & Guppy, 1998) and in the job market (Anisef et al., 1999). Moreover, the comparison of average educational level masks the problems faced by individual minority groups both in access to education and in employment and income (Baker & Benjamin, 1995; Canadian Race Relations Foundation, 2000; Frank, 1997; Henry et al., 1995; Pendakur & Pendakur, 1998). Racism remains a major problem, and different minority groups experience different levels of discrimination. Of all groups, native peoples have the greatest disadvantage in education, employment, and income; the black population, native or foreign born, faces the largest wage differential (Canadian Race Relations Foundation, 2000).

Differences among population groups are also visible in the composition of the government. Minority groups are underrepresented in official government positions and in political parties (Task Force on the Participation of Visible Minorities in the Federal Public Service, 2000). Moreover, the participation of minorities in "elite" groups generally remains limited, although certain minorities are "visible" in a number of professions and in higher education, an outcome that might be influenced by immigration patterns. Overall, however, Canadian society continues to be a hierarchy based on race and ethnicity, with a wide gap between reality and political discourse, despite multicultural policies that have been in effect for almost three decades.

The Vertical Mosaic (Porter, 1965) was the first significant study to depict Canada as a hierarchical society, based principally on ethnicity, class, and gender. Although there have been positive changes, this "vertical mosaic" continues.

CONCLUSION

One measure of a democracy's success is the way it treats its minorities. Yet, despite long-term efforts in many countries to promote equality of educational opportunity through legislation and multicultural education, racism—along with major gaps in education and employment—continues. As Canada becomes increasingly diverse, the country cannot afford to ignore the consequences of an education system that does not provide maximum opportunity for all its citizens. Canadians face the challenge of redefining the meaning of multiculturalism in order to sustain an equitable and high quality of life: The traditional definition—helping students retain their cultural identities—is too limited; it will be essential for schools to build on these identities to enable students to develop the skills and knowledge needed to be full participants in society.

Globalization has brought with it a new agenda that involves change in both ideology and policy. The elections held in Quebec in April 2003 returned the federalist Liberal Party of Quebec to office with a clear majority, after the separatist Parti Québécois had been in power for two terms. This result suggests that the younger generations are increasingly occupied with economic and global issues, multilateral trade agreements, and advances in communication and technology and that their aspirations are focused on developing the skills needed to participate effectively in a multicultural, international context.

NOTES

This chapter is adapted from a keynote address given at the Reddin Symposium on Canadian Studies, Canadian Studies Center, Bowling Green State University, Bowling Green, Ohio.

1. The Canadian Constitution was patriated from Britain in 1982 (i.e., the process of devolving full constitutional power to Canada from Britain was completed).

2. The report emphasizes that Canadians must not lose sight of the fact that they still lead privileged lives that are the envy of most of the world. The six countries include the United States, Japan, Germany, Australia, Sweden, and Norway.

3. "First Nations" refers to Canada's aboriginal populations, which are composed of four main groups, excluding the Inuit in the north (indigenous people of the Arctic) and Métis (people of mixed French/European and indigenous ancestry). "Band council" refers to a group of First Nations' representatives formed under the Indian Act or chosen according to the group's self-government customs.

4. "Canadian mosaic" stems from a book written by former governor-general Gibbon in 1938, in which Canadian differences from the American "melting pot" are discussed in romantic terms. Since then, the idea has referred to ethnic or cultural groups being allowed to retain their distinctive characteristics. More recently, the concept has been criticized for giving a static, rather than a dynamic, expression to multiculturalism.

5. Quebec went through a period of rapid social, political, and cultural change, a time the historians call the "Quiet Revolution." It was facilitated by the victory of a liberal government that championed comprehensive changes. Perhaps the most important was the loss of power of the Roman Catholic Church and the establishment of a more secular education system, along with changes in other institutions.

6. The Supreme Court of Canada declared in 1988 that Quebec's language laws were, in part, unconstitutional because they violated the rights of linguistic minorities. The Quebec government used the "notwithstanding" clause in the charter and enforced the language legislation.

7. "Allophone" refers to a person whose native language is neither French nor English.

REFERENCES CITED

Anderson, A. B., & Frideres, J. S. (1981). *Ethnicity in Canada: Theoretical perspectives*. Toronto: Butterworths.

Aniself, P., Sweet, R., James, C., & Lin, Z. (1999, August 16–17). Higher education, racial minorities, immigrants and labour market outcomes in Canada. Paper presented at the International Symposium on "Non-traditional" Students, University of British Columbia, Vancouver.

Baker, M., & Benjamin, D. (1995, May 25–27). Ethnicity, foreign birth and earnings: A Canada/US comparison. Paper presented at the conference on

Transition and Structural Change in the North American Labour Market, Kingston, Ontario.

Canadian Council on Social Development. (2000). *Immigrant youth in Canada*. Ottawa: Canadian Council on Social Development.

Canadian Race Relations Foundation. (2000). *Unequal access: A Canadian profile of racial differences in education, employment and income*. Toronto: Canadian Race Relations Foundation.

Carter, G. E. (1988). Taxation. In J. H. March (Ed.), *The Canadian encyclopedia, 4* (pp. 2112–14). Edmonton: Hurtig.

Conference Board of Canada. (2000). *Performance and potential: 2000 2001*. Ottawa: Conference Board of Canada.

Council of Ministers of Education in Canada. (2000, February). *Education indicators in Canada*. Report of the Pan-Canadian Education Indicators Program. Toronto: Council of Ministers of Education in Canada.

Davies, S., & Guppy, N. (1998). Race and Canadian education. In V. Satzewich (Ed.), *Racism and social inequality in Canada: Concepts, controversies and strategies of resistance* (pp. 131–56). Toronto: Thompson Educational.

de Silva, A. (1997). Wage discrimination against visible minority men in Canada. *Canadian Business Economics, 5* (4), 25–42.

Dibski, D. (1995). Financing education. In R. Ghosh & D. Ray (Eds.), *Social change and education in Canada* (pp. 66–81). Toronto: Harcourt Brace.

Elliot, J. L., & Fleras, A. (1990). Immigration and the Canadian ethnic mosaic. In P. S. Li (Ed.), *Race and ethnic relations in Canada* (pp. 51–76). Toronto: Oxford University Press.

Frank, J. (1997). Indicators of social inequality in Canada: Women, aboriginal peoples, and visible minorities. In A. Frizzell & J. H. Pammett (Eds.), *Social inequality in Canada*. Ottawa: Carleton University Press.

Ghosh, R., & Ray, D. (Eds.). (1995). *Social change and education in Canada*. Toronto: Harcourt Brace.

Ghosh, R., & Tarrow, N. (1993). Multiculturalism and teacher education: Views from Canada and USA. *Comparative Education, 29* (1), 81–92.

Gibbon, J. M. (1938). *Canadian mosaic: The making of a northern nation*. Toronto: McClelland and Stewart.

Henry, F., Tator, C., Mattis, W., & Rees, T. (1995). *The colour of democracy: Racism in Canadian society*. Toronto: Harcourt Brace.

Hou, F., & Balakrishnan, T. R. (1996). The integration of visible minorities in contemporary Canadian society. *Canadian Journal of Sociology, 21* (3), 307–26.

Livingston, D. W., & Hart, D. (1995). Popular beliefs about Canada's schools. In R. Ghosh & D. Ray (Eds.), *Social change and education in Canada* (pp. 16–44). Toronto: Harcourt Brace.

MacLennan, H. (1945). *The two solitudes*. Toronto: Collins.

McAndrew, M. (1985). Le traitement du racisme, de l'immigration et de la réalité multi-ethnique dans les manuels scolaires francophones au Québec [Racism, immigration, and multi-ethnic reality as portrayed in the school books in French Quebec]. In *Études ethniques au Canada/Canadian ethnic studies*. Montreal: McGill University; and Toronto: University of Toronto.

———. (1993). *The integration of ethnic minority students 15 years after Bill 101: Some issues confronting the Montreal Island French language public schools*. R. F. Harnie Program on Immigration and Ethnicity Papers. Toronto: University of Toronto.

Ministère de l'Education. (1998). *Plan of action for educational integration and intercultural education*. Montreal: Ministère de l'Education.

Ministère des Communautes Culturelles et de l'Immigration du Quebec. (1990). *Let's build Quebec together: A policy statement on immigration and integration*. Montreal: Ministère des Communautes Culturelles et de l'Immigration du Quebec.

Moodley, K. (1981). Canadian ethnicity in comparative perspective. In J. Dahlie & T. Fernando (Eds.), *Ethnicity, power and the politics of culture* (pp. 6–21). Toronto: Methuen.

Pendakur, K., & Pendakur, R. (1998). The colour of money: Earnings differentials among ethnic groups in Canada. *Canadian Journal of Economics, 31* (3), 518–48.

Porter, J. (1965). *The vertical mosaic: An analysis of social class and poverty in Canada*. Toronto: University of Toronto Press.

Statistics Canada. (1991). *Census of Canada*. Ottawa: Statistics Canada.

———. (1996). *Census of Canada*. Ottawa: Statistics Canada.

———. (2002). *Canada at a glance*. Ottawa: Statistics Canada.

Task Force on the Participation of Visible Minorities in the Federal Public Service. (2000). *Embracing change in the federal public service*. Catalogue No. BT22-67/2000. Ottawa: Supply and Services.

13

New Zealand: Empowering Teachers and Children

Terry J. Crooks

> Clear away the obstacles so you may see the path forward . . . turn your face to the world of light. The generations yet unborn are waiting there for you.
>
> —Maori proverb

New Zealand comprises two main islands and a number of smaller islands with a total area similar to that of Japan or the British Isles. It was settled by Maori explorers about 1,000 years ago and then by European settlers (predominantly from Britain) starting about 200 years ago. New Zealand became part of the British Empire when a representative of Queen Victoria signed a treaty with local Maori chiefs in 1840, and it became an independent state in 1907. It is a parliamentary democracy, with a single-house parliament.

New Zealand's population is approximately four million, with 85 percent of the population residing in urban areas, including close to 60 percent in the six largest urban areas. About three-quarters of the population are of European origin, predominantly from the British Isles. The indigenous Maori population makes up about 15 percent of the balance; people from other Pacific Islands, about 6 percent; and people of Asian origin, about 5 percent. Because of more youthful age profiles, the latter three groups contribute about 21 percent, 8 percent, and 6 percent, respectively, of the students in New Zealand schools.

NEW ZEALAND SCHOOLS

School attendance is compulsory in New Zealand from age six to sixteen. However, it is normal to enroll children in early childhood care and education well before their fifth birthday, to enter them into the school system on or soon after their fifth birthday, and to continue their formal education past their sixteenth birthday. About 55 percent of school-leavers proceed directly into some form of tertiary education.

New Zealand has about 2,700 schools and about 60,000 students per year entering school. Almost 4 percent of the students attend independent (private) schools, partly supported by state funding. The remaining students attend state or integrated schools (such as those established by religious denominations) that are largely state funded. About 11,000 students receive their education predominantly in Maori; the remainder, predominantly in English. Primary schooling (years zero to eight) usually starts at age five and lasts seven and a half to eight and a half years. Secondary schooling normally lasts for up to five additional years (years nine to thirteen). More than 80 percent of students remain until year twelve, and almost 60 percent remain until year thirteen.

Because much of New Zealand is sparsely populated, many schools are small. For instance, 34 percent of the 2,100 schools for year-four students have fewer than twelve students in year four, and 43 percent of the 1,500 schools for year-eight students have fewer than twelve students in year eight.

THE NEW ZEALAND SCHOOL SYSTEM IN THE 1980S

For thirty years after World War II, New Zealand enjoyed a high level of economic prosperity and full employment, based largely on guaranteed access for its agricultural exports to Great Britain and on the protection of its small-scale manufacturing industries with import controls and tariffs. Britain's decision to join the European Economic Community signaled the end of this period, putting New Zealand under greater pressure economically. For some years in the late 1970s and early 1980s, heavy borrowing disguised a declining economic position, but by the time a new government took office in 1984, urgent action was needed. The dramatic response was to float the New Zealand dollar and fully adopt free market policies, exposing New Zealand to the pressures and vagaries of the market without the protections that other countries continue to apply to key sectors of their economies. These changes enjoyed strong support from some leading politicians and key staff in the Treasury and some other government agencies.

Education had enjoyed a similar period of relative calm, prosperity, and growth, following a path announced by Minister of Education Peter Fraser in 1939:

> The government's objective, broadly expressed, is that every person, whatever his level of academic ability, whether he be rich or poor, whether he live in town or country, has a right, as a citizen, to a free education of the kind for which he is best fitted, and to the fullest extent of his powers. . . . It was necessary to convert a school system, constructed originally on a basis of selection and privilege, to a truly democratic form where it can cater for the needs of the whole population over as long a period of their lives as is found possible and desirable. (in Beeby, 1992)

The official who wrote these words for the minister, Dr. Clarence Beeby, became director general of education in 1940 and served in that role for twenty years, leading the Government Department of Education, which had controlling oversight over New Zealand schools. During his time in office, the standard school-leaving age became fifteen years, so that almost all children reached at least secondary school. A broader core curriculum was established, teacher training was enhanced, and school facilities and resources were considerably improved. Students who achieved well in secondary school could proceed to tertiary education and enjoy low tuition fees and good support for living costs.

Between 1940 and 1985 the selective nature of secondary education gradually softened, allowing a much higher proportion of students to reach the upper levels of secondary schooling. The last step in this process occurred in 1986, when the examination to award the university entrance qualification moved from the penultimate year of secondary school (year twelve) to the final year (thirteen). By then, economic conditions had declined, so it was much harder for students leaving school to find employment than had been the case in the 1950s, 1960s, and 1970s. The combined effect of the factors was a dramatic increase in the proportion of students staying a full five years in secondary school (less than 10 percent in 1960, up to about 20 percent by 1985, and about 40 percent by 1990). Schools therefore sought to provide alternative options in years twelve and thirteen, recognizing that programs designed to prepare the academic elite for university study were inappropriate for increasing percentages of their senior students.

While these changes were happening, the population mix in New Zealand was changing. The rate of increase of the Maori population was substantially higher than that of the population as a whole, approximately doubling the percentage of Maori in the population from 6 percent in 1951 to 12 percent in 1991. Over the same period, there was a dramatic influx of people from smaller Pacific Island communities, such as Western Samoa, Tonga, and the Cook Islands, raising their percentage of the population from 0.2 percent to almost 5 percent. Because these Maori and Pacific Island people had larger average family sizes and younger age structures than the majority European population, their contributions to the school population were proportionately larger (about one and a half times their overall percentage in the population). This placed added demands on the schools to deal with a greater variety of cultural and linguistic backgrounds, especially in Auckland (New Zealand's largest city).

CHANGES IN SCHOOL ADMINISTRATION

The ten years following 1987 were a period of revolutionary change in New Zealand education, contrasting strongly with the forty years of evolutionary change that preceded it. Several factors came together:

- politicians who wanted to have greater direct leadership of education and to rely less on the advice of educators and their officials;

- leaders of other government departments, such as the Treasury and State Services Commission, and prominent pressure groups, such as the Business Round Table, who saw free market approaches as suitable for government services such as health and education;
- politicians and other opinion leaders who argued that Department of Education officials, school principals, and teachers were not sufficiently responsive to their wishes or those of the communities in which they served (the term *provider capture* was a popular abbreviation for this view);
- substantial national debt, which was diverting taxation to pay for debt servicing and therefore constraining the growth of spending on services such as health and education; and
- a pattern of greater public criticism of the standard of education, following similar patterns overseas, such as the 1983 publication of *A Nation at Risk* in the United States and the rapid implementation of new centralized requirements and accountability measures by Margaret Thatcher's government in the United Kingdom in the late 1980s.

Having made major and rapid changes to New Zealand economic policies between 1984 and 1987, the government turned its attention to education. Again, change occurred very quickly, apparently because of a belief that the best way to overcome the inertia associated with provider capture was to move fast enough to outflank the protectors of the status quo before they could establish strong defensive positions. The initial focus was on the organization and administration of the education system. In mid-1987, a small working party of five (two businessmen, two tertiary educators, and a social researcher) began to review existing structures and practices. It reported publicly nine months later (Task Force to Review Educational Administration, 1988), and three months later the minister of education (who was also the prime minister) announced government decisions implementing most of the task force recommendations (Lange, 1988). Reforms of the administration of tertiary education were deferred for a further year until a new task force reported.

What follows here is necessarily a very condensed account of the changes, their impact, and the issues arising from them. Readers interested in a fuller account are referred to a book published by two American investigators who spent five months in New Zealand undertaking this task (Fiske & Ladd, 2000).

The effects of the changes have been different for primary and secondary schools and for state, integrated, and private schools. Before the changes, state primary and intermediate schools were administered largely by elected regional education boards, which in turn reported to the national Department of Education. Each had a school committee representing parents, but it had only a small role in the administration of the school (relating to the employment of nonteaching staff and some spending on supplies). The School Committee had no say over staffing, apart from a minor role in guiding the selection of a new principal. State secondary schools had an elected Board of Governors, which appointed the principal and staff, was responsible for the school's finances and buildings, had oversight over school programs, and reported directly to the national Department of Education. In addition, integrated schools, which previously were outside the state system, began to accept funding comparable to that for state schools in exchange for a large measure of state control over school practices and curricula. They retain some of their special character (such as special religious curriculum components), own their own buildings, and charge fees associated with their special character and buildings, but otherwise they are treated similarly to state schools. Private (or independent) schools, which do not fall under the constraints of the state system and which have large enrollment fees, have increasingly received some government funding for staffing and operational costs, in recognition that their existence reduces funding requirements for state schools. The government, however, has not accepted the arguments to implement a voucher system that would allow students to attend any school, bearing with them equal government funding.

In the administrative changes introduced in 1989, the national Department of Education was reconfigured into a Ministry of Education and several independent agencies. At the same time, governance of all state and integrated schools became the responsibility of newly established boards of trustees, one per school (but subsequently with provision for more than one school to share a board should they choose to do so). The board of each state school includes the principal, a staff member elected to represent the school staff, and several trustees elected by the parents of current students. Boards of state-funded integrated schools have additional members appointed to help preserve the special character of these schools (such as the religious heritage associated with the school). Boards of secondary schools also have a student member, elected by the students. Boards may co-opt additional members.

Each board of trustees is responsible for the operation of its school, within constraints imposed by its signed agreement (charter) with the national Ministry of Education. This agreement includes rules and guidelines that apply to all schools but also includes components to reflect the specific goals of each school. The Education Review Office, a state agency separate from the Ministry of Education, conducts external audits to review the performance of each school regularly (normally at about three-year intervals), to judge compliance with legal requirements and national education guidelines, and to specify issues that should receive attention. At its establishment in 1989, the focus of the Education Review Office was on accountability, with provision of advice discouraged because of potential confusion between the two roles. The mandate of the Education Review Office now includes providing advice while maintaining the audit function.

As mentioned earlier, before 1989 the administration of primary schools was much more centralized. Regional teams of school inspectors operated under the direction and leadership of the national Department of Education. They worked closely with regional education boards to control key decisions for each school, including the selection of the principal and teachers, the provision and maintenance of buildings and other resources, and professional development programs for school personnel. The inspectors monitored the work of principals and teachers, gave guidance and assistance, and guided the career development of school personnel through their advice, grading of teachers, control of professional development opportunities, and control of teacher movement between schools and positions of responsibility within schools. The current system devolves most of these responsibilities to individual boards of trustees, with school principals having a greatly enlarged role.

Consequences of These Changes for Schools and Students

School Choice

When the administrative changes were announced, it was proposed that schools would become much more responsive to their local communities (through the consultation and decisions of their boards of trustees) and therefore would develop distinctive characteristics, which might lead to students or their parents choosing schools because of their particular characteristics. This possibility, to be signaled in the locally developed school charters, was soon severely curtailed when the government placed its major emphasis on the nationally required components of the school charters, requiring the Education Review Office to focus predominantly on those national components when it reviewed schools (Codd, McAlpine, & Poskitt, 1995). Very recently, however, the government has allowed schools a greater role in goal setting and asked the Education Review Office, as part of its audit, to place a substantial focus on each school's own goals and self-evaluations.

Throughout most of the 1990s, under a government led by the National Party, advocates of free choice in schooling were in the ascendancy. The government relaxed some requirements on schools to accept students from their immediate vicinity and allowed them to accept a higher proportion of students from farther away. Particularly among secondary schools, which previously were required to take most of their students from a clearly defined zone, this led to substantial increases in targeted recruiting (for instance, for students with high academic or sporting achievements), to heavy advertising and other promotional activity, and, in some cases, to an unwillingness to enroll local students with weaker backgrounds or disabilities.

Over the same period, the government encouraged schools to take greater responsibility for their staffing by accepting direct responsibility for the teacher salaries component of their funding. In the initial reforms, school funding was divided into two components. Schools were entitled to certain numbers of teachers and leaders, based mainly on the numbers of students enrolled in the schools, but the Ministry of Education held the salary funding. Schools received funding directly for support staff, supplies, building maintenance, utilities, and other operating expenses and had to account for the use of that funding. Under the new model that schools could choose, given various official names but commonly called "bulk funding," schools received the funding component for teacher salaries directly. This allowed them greater flexibility. In theory, for instance, they could employ more teachers on lower salary levels (generally less qualified or experienced teachers) rather than fewer on higher salary levels. For these and other reasons, the teachers' unions bitterly opposed bulk finding, but more than one-quarter of all schools chose it, in most cases to gain the greater funding available to them (but not necessarily to other schools) under the formula used. The current government has, however, reverted to central funding of teacher salaries for all state and integrated schools.

From its inception in 1989 the Education Review Office has been required to make its reports on individual schools publicly available. The rationale behind this was to increase the public accountability of schools and allow parents access to information about school characteristics or performance that might influence their choice of schools for their children.

As Fiske and Ladd (2000) have documented, these factors apparently led to a notable increase in the stratification of the school system between 1989 and 1998. Many schools in poorer areas, particularly those with high proportions of Maori and Pacific Island children, experienced a significant degree of "white flight" or loss of children from more affluent or educated families, which made the task of educators in these schools harder. They had to cope with reduced funding and with redundancies of teachers because of falling rolls, reduced bases of parental experience to draw from for the board of trustees, reduced abilities to raise local funds for extra resources, and greater challenges in recruiting highly qualified and capable teachers. These challenges increased the risk of a spiral to failure and even school closure. The present government, led by the Labour Party, is committed to reducing social and economic disparities, and its policies for education reflect that. It has increased the differential funding

support for schools in poorer areas, restricted schools' ability to recruit outside of their own zone, and extended programs of school and
community development to increase the likelihood of good educational outcomes in the schools in poorer communities. How successful these strategies will be remains a matter of conjecture: Early evidence from the National Education Monitoring Project suggests that
disparities may be decreasing in some curriculum areas but that in
other areas they are proving resistant to change.

Another factor increasing stratification in some parts of the country
has been a rapid inflow of immigrants, particularly from South Africa
and parts of Asia. Many of these immigrants have chosen to live close
together in selected suburbs of Auckland, with the result that there
are numerous Auckland schools that have more than one-third of
their students drawn from families of recent immigrants. In general,
these families place a high priority on the education of their children,
and the children rapidly become successful in their New Zealand
schools.

The students (4 percent of all students) who attend independent
(private) schools come predominantly from high-socioeconomic-
status families who are able to afford the tuition fees. Substantial proportions of the students attending many independent secondary
schools are from families (often farming families) living in rural areas,
where small enrollments in the local state schools often restrict the
range of academic, sporting, and cultural opportunities available. Because 96 percent of all students attend state and integrated schools,
however, collectively these include a very broad sample of the population, with little socioeconomic bias in any region of the country.

One special area of school choice and stratification encouraged by
the reforms has been the considerable expansion of Maori-immersion
education, and, in particular, Kura Kaupapa Maori (KKM) schools,
over the past fifteen years. Maori-immersion education involves students learning for much or all of the school day in the Maori language.
There has been a major push to expand Maori-immersion education,
both to help preserve Maori language and culture and to provide a
more effective form of education for some Maori students. By the end
of 2002, New Zealand had ninety Maori-immersion schools and ninety
other schools where some students enrolled in classes that used Maori

immersion for 80 percent or more of the school week. About 7.5 percent of Maori students attended these immersion schools or classes. Just under half of these attended one of the sixty-one KKM schools: schools initiated by their local Maori community and substantially governed by it, within the boundaries allowed for integrated schools. KKM schools involve a special curriculum recognized in legislation and 100 percent Maori language immersion, perhaps varied by the inclusion of some teaching of English as a subject in the last year or two before the students graduate and move to the next level of schooling, conducted in English. The results achieved by KKM schools are promising, with impressive achievement in Maori language and culture often coupled with levels of achievement in other curriculum areas that are comparable to those achieved by Maori students learning in English in mainstream schools. There is evidence starting to emerge of the long-term benefits from education in KKM.

Local Control of Schools

As indicated earlier, the initial suggestion that the new administrative arrangements would represent a major shift of control of schools to local communities was not realized fully. The government shifted the balance back to the center by placing emphasis on national requirements and giving less emphasis to local goals and preferences. Furthermore, the government continued to control both the staffing entitlements of the schools and their operational funding. All schools do some local fund-raising, but for most state and integrated schools this represents only a moderate percentage of their total funding and thus provides limited scope for local initiatives beyond that already available from the operational funding allocated to boards (most of which is committed to unavoidable requirements such as nonteaching staff, building and equipment maintenance, photocopying, curriculum resources, and utilities).

The most significant new element of local control through boards of trustees has involved the staffing of primary and intermediate schools. Before 1989 these schools and the families associated with them had little direct control over the appointments of their principals and staff. Local inspectors of schools consulted a little with school committees about the appointment of a new principal and with principals about the appointment of their teachers, but the inspectors made final appointment decisions, and their inspection and grading of teachers also largely determined the positions for which teachers would be eligible. Teachers' unions were represented in the appointment process and also had negotiated contracts with the Department of Education that gave higher-graded teachers priority over lower-graded teachers and gave teachers who were no longer needed in one school priority for appointments in other schools within the same education board district (and in some cases nationally). Beginning in 1989, in contrast, the board of trustees of each school had full control over who was appointed as its principal, and principals, in consultation with their boards of trustees, then appointed their own teaching staff. This is one of the most valued aspects of the new arrangements: Surveys of principals and trustees have indicated that few would want to return to the former appointment procedures (Wylie, 1997). Nevertheless, there have been significant concerns expressed about the capabilities of boards of trustees to make appropriate judgments about the professional attributes of applicants, particularly when appointing principals.

The Role of Principals

The main change in the role of secondary principals has been an increase in marketing activity. With schools in greater competition with each other for market share, it has become important for principals to build an appropriate image for their school and to persuade prospective students and their families to enroll there.

An associated development has been the rapid increase in New Zealand of fee-paying foreign students, predominantly from Asia, whose families are keen for them to have advanced educational opportunities beyond their own country and in particular to learn English in a setting where it is the language in common use. Many schools, and again particularly secondary schools, have found that this extra income gives them opportunities for expansion and enhancement that are irresistible. Consequently, many principals are devoting substantial time and effort to overseas recruitment activities, including travel to meet prospective students and their families.

For primary and intermediate school principals, the largest change has arisen from the abolition of regional education boards and the associated groups of school inspectors. As a result, large proportions of the school administration workload have shifted from education boards to schools: building maintenance, teacher appointments, budgeting and accounting, staff professional development, teaching resource selection and purchase, and many other functions. This has often required the appointment of other support staff and therefore their supervision. More than ever, these responsibilities have divided principals' efforts between the professional leadership of their teachers and the administrative management of their schools. Some principals have addressed this challenge by becoming administrators and passing much of the professional leadership responsibility on to other staff; some have preferred to delegate most of the administration to an executive officer or a deputy principal; and others have tried to do everything, at the risk of burnout or ineffectiveness in one or both roles. The problem is especially severe for principals in schools that are so small that the principal is also expected to be a classroom teacher. More than half of New Zealand's 2,000 primary schools are staffed on the assumption that their principals will spend at least part of their week teaching. In the smallest schools, principals can have 80 percent of a full teaching load.

Because of these new demands on principals, and particularly primary school principals, the role has become less attractive. Larger proportions than in the 1980s appear to be suffering stress-related illnesses, retiring early, resigning to return to classroom teaching, or moving into other occupations.

CHANGES IN SCHOOL CURRICULA

School curricula also have undergone extensive restructuring since the late 1980s. Before 1990 curricula evolved slowly, led by experienced specialists in the Department of Education and with extensive involvement of the teachers' unions and classroom teachers. Major changes usually involved several years of exploration, during which a substantial number of teachers experimented with and commented on them. The syllabi that resulted from this process were not highly prescriptive, but the Department of Education often supported and promoted their implementation through the publication of resources for teacher or student use.

In 1991 the Ministry of Education, in a newly elected government led by the National Party, introduced sweeping changes. The plans, called the "Achievement Initiative," had been widely reported and promoted over the previous two years, when the National Party was in opposition. They were largely modeled on the curriculum and assessment changes made in England and Wales by Margaret Thatcher's government in the late 1980s. The stated rationale for these changes was to improve student learning through better-designed and more focused teaching and assessment programs and through greater continuity of learning programs when students moved from one school to another. Many in the education community, however, felt that the changes reflected a lack of trust in teachers and a wish to restrict their freedom through tighter specification of what they would teach.

Operating under considerable time pressure, working groups of curriculum experts and teachers identified several strands for each curriculum and, within each strand, a substantial number of achievement objectives. The objectives, placed into eight levels, represented the planned progress of students over their years of primary and secondary education. The first five levels were spaced approximately two years apart, with each of the last three levels intended to represent one year of average progress.

In each curriculum area, a draft version was released first, with a few months allowed for feedback before the final form was decided on and the document was published, becoming a mandatory part of the school curriculum a year or so later. The final versions for mathematics, science, English, and technology (a brand new subject) were published in 1992, 1993, 1994, and 1995. As anticipated by many educators as early as 1991, by 1995 primary school teachers were agitated about the pace of curriculum change with which they were being asked to cope. The plan to proceed rapidly with the remaining three curriculum documents was abandoned, helped by controversy about the social studies curriculum, for which a second consultation draft was published. The final version for social studies was published in 1997; health and physical education in 1999; and the arts in 2000.

A key factor in the slowdown of new documents was the need to fit in professional development for teachers as each document appeared. This did not receive adequate consideration in 1992 and 1993, but politicians and officials soon realized that the new curricula would have little worthwhile impact until teachers had time to understand and assimilate them into their teaching practice. In time, many teachers had two or three days of professional development for each of the new curricula. Whether this was sufficient for most teachers to understand and internalize the thinking underlying the new curricula is highly doubtful, but on the surface, at least, most teachers began to implement the new teaching programs. One constraint on the coherence and quality of the professional development was the decision of the ministry to arrange the professional development regionally through a contract-tendering process. This, combined with the lack of sufficient time for coordinated planning and resource development, often seemed to result in poor coordination of what was offered in different regions and much "reinventing of the wheel."

By 1997 educators and researchers had become increasingly concerned about curriculum overload and fragmentation associated with teachers trying to implement (and be held accountable for) all the strands of all the curricula. This led to changes in the national education guidelines for schools, offering schools greater flexibility in curriculum implementation, particularly for the first four years of schooling where renewed priority was given to literacy and numeracy.

The curriculum changes of the last ten years have seen a considerable tightening of expectations for schools and teachers. Pressure to implement the fairly detailed progressive structures of the new curricula, with their strands, levels, and achievement objectives, largely has come through the reviews of schools conducted by the Education Review Office, supplemented by the nationally funded but regionally implemented professional development contracts. Paradoxically, as curriculum expectations became stronger, teachers initially received few resources to support their implementation of the new curricula. This placed very heavy demands on teachers, most of whom were expected to refocus or significantly extend the range of their teaching while simultaneously discovering or creating the resources they would need to achieve these changes. More recently, increasing numbers of resources have been prepared and distributed.

There is significant debate about the merits of these curriculum changes. On the one hand, they are seen as helping teachers by offering them more structured guidance, for their teaching, protecting students from teachers who are not very capable of planning good programs without detailed guidance, and increasing the continuity of learning programs for students moving between schools. Counterarguments are that many teachers feel that they and their students are on a treadmill of curriculum requirements, that the large list of achievement objectives encourages shallow rather than deep learning, and that the loss of the trust and creative freedom that teachers previously enjoyed has undermined their sense of professionalism (Locke, 2001; O'Neill, 2002).

Over the last two years the Ministry of Education, under the new government led by the Labour Party, has conducted a "Curriculum Stocktake" to review the appropriateness of the overall curriculum structure, the nature of the individual curriculum documents, and the implementation requirements and guidance for schools. Arising out of that is a three-year project that may influence the shape of the curriculum for the coming years. We will need to wait to see what the result of that process is, but probably there will be some reduction in the number (and therefore level of detail) of achievement objectives and an increase in professional flexibility for teachers.

The curriculum changes brought with them major changes in how primary and intermediate school teachers were expected to assess and report on the progress of their students. The nature of those changes and the issues associated with them have been fully discussed in a recent article (Crooks, 2002) and will not be repeated here. In the next section, however, I will look at assessments for qualifications in the final years of secondary schooling because these assessments dominate the work and accountability of secondary schools, and the approach now being introduced represents a quantum change that is highly contentious.

CHANGES IN SECONDARY SCHOOL QUALIFICATIONS

For more than forty years the majority of students in years eleven to thirteen (the final three years of secondary school) have been attempting national qualifications, through national end-of-year exams, moderated school-based assessments, or a combination of both. The precise form of these assessments has been adjusted several times over the last fifty years, and the percentage of students remaining in school until years twelve and thirteen has risen dramatically.

The community places high importance on these qualifications because they are traditional indicators used to make or influence important decisions that affect career options and access to tertiary education. For many (perhaps even the majority) of the older members of the community, their highest formal academic qualification is one they obtained in secondary school. With much higher proportions of secondary school students now proceeding to tertiary education, the real importance of secondary school qualifications is fading, but it will probably take many years before community perceptions reflect that change. In the meantime, these are clearly high-stakes assessments.

A reasonably detailed account of the progressive changes in the nature of these qualifications and how they have been awarded is given in Crooks (2002), with fuller historical accounts available in Lee (1991) and Strachan (2002). I offer a concise summary here, in order to highlight the magnitude and nature of the changes of the last fifteen years.

Forty years ago, when I was in secondary school, the last three years of secondary school were highly selective, with national examinations for qualifications as the filtering devices. Most students who remained in secondary school for three years took nationally marked three-hour school certificate examinations in four or more subjects. These examinations were marked on a percentage-correct basis. The marks for different subjects were then statistically scaled against each other, so that the total group of students taking any pair of subjects should have similar mark distributions in the two subjects. Marks in all subjects were then scaled so that the mean mark was about 50 percent and a desired spread of marks was obtained. To pass school certificate (i.e., obtain the qualification) and therefore be able to progress to the next higher level of secondary school, students needed to obtain at least 200 marks in their four best subjects. About half of those taking the examinations met that requirement. The next higher level applied a similar procedure, with passes at 50 percent or better required in four subjects to gain the "university entrance qualification." As the title suggests, this permitted students to enroll in a university, but most students intending to undertake university study returned to secondary school for one more year. At the end of that final year, they could take national examinations for the university bursaries examination and the entrance scholarships examination. Performing well cumulatively in five subjects, relative to the total pool of students who took the examinations, resulted in the award of a scholarship, "A" bursary or "B" bursary. These provided varying levels of additional financial support for those holding them who pursued tertiary study.

As noted earlier, the filtering process provided by this normative qualifications structure, combined with a school-leaving age of fifteen years and very low levels of unemployment, led to low levels of retention of students to the final year of secondary education. Forty years ago fewer than 30 percent of students reached the penultimate level of secondary education, and fewer than 10 percent reached the final level.

By 1989 this qualifications structure underwent major changes that progressively softened these barriers to students progressing through secondary schooling. The school certificate examinations still existed, with similar intersubject and overall scaling, but many subjects now included a mark component for school-based assessment of skills or knowledge not suited for assessment in a written national examination. Examples are project work, laboratory work, and oral performance in foreign languages. Each school determined the ranking of its students in these components, but the level and range of marks were statistically adjusted to reflect the results that each school's students achieved in the written national examination component. Students could progress to the next level of schooling subject by subject, based on standards set by their own school, or could continue to study at the lower level in their weaker subjects. The university entrance examinations no longer existed. Instead, year twelve contained the sixth-form certificate qualification. This was awarded on the basis of assessment activities within each school, followed by interclass and intersubject statistical moderation within the school, and then the mix of grades available to each school was controlled by the school certificate marks obtained by its students the previous year. Students gaining adequate grades (as judged by their school) in a subject at year-twelve level were free to proceed to year-thirteen study in that subject or a related subject. Year thirteen offered the university bursaries and scholarships examination, still with a five subject aggregate needed to gain a tertiary study bursary or scholarship, but by 1990 this was also the main route for admission to university (requiring adequate performance in four subjects). As described for the school certificate, many of these subjects included statistically adjusted components from work done in school during the year.

By this point, more than 90 percent of students were staying in secondary school to year eleven; about 70 percent, to year twelve; and about 35 percent, to year thirteen. The employment market was much less buoyant than in the 1960s, and the government was keen to encourage students to remain in the education system longer. As a result, a substantial proportion of year-thirteen students did not intend to proceed on to university study, making the university bursaries examination inappropriate for many of them. Schools were developing alternative programs for these students, but the programs had no status nationally as qualifications.

At postschool level, the seven universities controlled their own degrees and other qualifications, but a number of weakly coordinated national bodies administered other postschool qualifications. Students who had demonstrated particular skills and knowledge through one of these bodies, or within a school or tertiary institution, would often find that they could not obtain credit for that work toward a qualification offered by another body, school, or institution. There seemed to be an urgent need for coordination and rationalization. The administrative reforms of 1989 addressed this issue through the establishment, in 1990, of the New Zealand Qualifications Authority (NZQA). The NZQA's mandate was to increase the coherence of qualification systems, so that there were sensible and varied pathways toward appropriate qualifications for as many students as possible and so that skills and knowledge gained and assessed in one context could receive credit, where required, in any other context. Thus, it had oversight or responsibility for all qualifications, whether based on work done in secondary schools, tertiary institutions, workplaces, or community agencies. This was clearly a huge task, given the well-established but incompatible systems and practices of the many education providers involved (over 400 schools providing secondary education and many institutions or agencies providing tertiary education and training).

The NZQA was established at a time when the majority view among New Zealand educators was that norm-referenced assessments, with quotas for the number passing based on the number of students attempting the qualification, should be replaced by criterion-referenced or "standards-based" assessments. The latter approaches compare students' work to predescribed levels of performance, with no limitations on the proportions of students who can achieve each performance level. Official documents about desirable assessment practices in schools and tertiary education in New Zealand almost universally endorse standards-based assessment, but many teachers and some assessment experts are skeptical about its feasibility. Whereas norm referencing, based on ranking, is easy to accomplish, standards-based assessment requires considerable clarity about the skills and knowledge to be assessed and the standards to be achieved. The transition to standards-based assessment, like most large transitions from well-established practices, is proving very demanding: There are still strong pockets of support for norm referencing, and many teachers who have found the arguments for standards-based assessment convincing have struggled to develop practices consistent with the goal.

In 1991 the NZQA adopted a single "Qualifications Framework" for academic and vocational qualifications covering the whole expanse of education and training from year eleven in secondary school through the doctoral degree (NZQA, 1991). This was seen as a brave and risky move, given the tradition in most countries of treating separately academic qualifications and trade and vocational qualifications. The NZQA then made its task even more difficult by deciding in 1992 to move toward a single, standards-based approach for all components of all qualifications. This approach was based essentially on a mastery-learning model, with required learning outcomes grouped into "unit standards" representing relatively small clusters of related requirements, with associated performance standards. Students attempting unit standards would either pass or fail (gain credit or not gain credit), with no distinctions recorded for degrees of excellence beyond passing. Students would be permitted multiple attempts to pass unit standards without undue delays between attempts. Also, students who already had appropriate knowledge and skills were to be awarded relevant unit standards without being required to attend the learning program prepared for other students, through a process of recognition of prior learning. Although the unit standards approach gained substantial and quite rapid acceptance in many areas of trade and vocational education, where its mastery approach seemed a very suitable choice, it was soon under strong attack from many other educators, including teachers of most secondary school subjects and many programs in tertiary education. The lack of provision to recognize degrees of excellence was a major concern, as was the apparent fragmentation of qualifications that would arise from assessing a large number of unit standards. NZQA personnel pointed out that unit standards did not require that learning be broken into modules to match the unit standards—they were collections of knowledge and skills that could be assessed at appropriate points in an integrated teaching program. However, in many educators' minds, the unit standard model appeared to require or strongly encourage a modular teaching model. The workload and interteacher moderation requirements (to help ensure consistency of standards among teachers) arising from abandoning traditional national examinations also worried many teachers, and they and others in the community were concerned about the loss of the standardization that had been associated with these examinations.

Since 1998 the assessment model has been modified: The new approach reaffirms the goal of standards-based assessment, offers two grade levels higher than bare pass where this is deemed appropriate, and uses national examinations where the knowledge and skills to be assessed suit such examinations. Although unit standards will still be available for some secondary school subjects, notably ones that have not been included in the school certificate or university bursaries awards, most secondary school subjects are now to be assessed using "achievement standards." Achievement standards have four associated grades: not achieved, achieved, merit, and excellence. They will be available for year eleven (Level 1 standards), year twelve (Level 2), and year thirteen (Level 3). In most subjects, half or more of the achievement standards will be assessed through national examinations (usually forming separate sections of a longer examination), with the others assessed within schools and subject to interschool moderation processes. Thus, national examinations will continue to play a central role in the new qualifications, but there will be greater opportunity to assess goals that evade assessment through written examinations.

Students are able to earn "National Certificates of Educational Achievement" (NCEAs) by earning enough credits at appropriate levels. Credits are earned by passing achievement or unit standards. Because there will be great diversity in the options available to students, the meaning of an NCEA at a given level is going to be quite limited. Employers and educational institutions wanting to understand and evaluate a student's achievements usually will need to see the student's "record of learning," which lists all credits by title and indicates the standard achieved.

Achievement standards replaced the school certificate examination in 2002, with sixth-form certificate being replaced in 2003 for most students and in 2004 for the rest (the choice at the discretion of schools). The university bursaries qualification will be phased out beginning in 2004.

The NCEA had a rocky start in 2002, when Level 1 NCEA assessments replaced the school certificate. As was entirely predictable, most teachers were nervous about the new approaches required (setting tasks, marking against described standards, and participating in moderating processes among teachers and schools) and found them very time consuming. They did not always see sample assessment tasks made available by the NZQA as helpful or appropriate. But preliminary evidence (Hipkins & Vaughan, 2002) suggests that the NCEA assessments are perceived by schools to be more motivating for lower-achieving students and yet to have the potential to maintain or even raise performance levels for the top students.

A major complication in implementation was that the national union award for secondary teachers was renegotiated during the year, and the added work and responsibility associated with the NCEA implementation became, very publicly, a bargaining factor in the negotiations. This came close to destabilizing NCEA implementation, with temporary embargoes on some of the required activities. Once the union award was settled, however, and teachers had a few months' experience with the new processes, the controversy settled down and did not resurface in 2003, even though most schools are implementing Level 2 while continuing with Level 1.

In the longer term, an important issue will be to find an appropriate balance between the pressure to ensure that all students nationally are assessed using the same standards and the added cost and workload that are associated with interschool and interteacher moderation processes to help achieve this. It is not realistic that the setting and marking of every task by every teacher will be checked and approved. As teachers become more used to the achievement standards they are involved in assessing, over a period of several years, they will begin to internalize the standards and gain confidence in implementing them; this should allow moderation requirements to be eased, to a level designed to reassure rather than assure. Because these are human processes, involving difficult judgments from thousands of different judges, there will always be scope for news media stories that undermine public trust in the NCEA awards. Indeed, issues of public trust may have more influence on the future of the NCEA than technical considerations such as its reliability and validity (Lee & Lee, 2001). The fact that assessment of about half of the achievement standards takes place through national written examinations is intended, however, to help reassure teachers and the community that the potential for unfairness and inconsistency is being kept under adequate control.

Two fundamental issues associated with the new standards-based approach to assessment for qualifications continue to concern some of New Zealand's assessment scholars. The first concern, mentioned previously, is that the modular approach to the assessment of unit standards and achievement standards will lead teachers into a modular approach to their teaching, thus fragmenting learning and making it more difficult for students to build strong and integrated conceptual maps of the subjects they are learning. That this is a possibility is self-evident, but how pervasive it turns out to be is not. The second concern is that the descriptive standards and associated examples will prove insufficient guides to allow teachers to develop reasonable consistency in their assessment, thus requiring extensive, cumbersome, and expensive systems of moderation on a continuing basis (Hall, 1998). Some feel that the alternative of statistical moderation of school assessments, using national examinations as benchmarks, is a more practical and appropriate approach; but part of the reason for the school-based assessment components is that they are learning components that are distinctive from those that are nationally examined (e.g., oral performance in languages, as opposed to reading and writing skills), so using the latter to adjust the former statistically is somewhat questionable.

It will be some years before the impact of these qualifications changes can be properly evaluated. The outcome of New Zealand's experiences will almost certainly be of considerable interest to other countries that are considering changes in their qualification systems.

Changes in the qualifications achieved by different ethnic and socioeconomic subgroups will be of particular interest. In 2001, 53.5 percent of Asian school-leavers had met the requirements for university entrance and perhaps also obtained a university bursaries award, compared with 9.8 percent of Pacific Island school-leavers, 7.4 percent of Maori school-leavers, and 29.8 percent of all other students. These figures changed less than 1 percent from eight years earlier, except for a 6.5 percent increase for Asian students. Similar major differences in achievement are found for students from different socioeconomic groups. Disparities of this magnitude clearly have important implications for subsequent career directions and opportunities. It is interesting to note, however, that the participation rates in tertiary education of these different ethnic groups are much more similar than the school-leaving qualifications would suggest, but their patterns of enrollment are quite different. Maori participants, for instance, currently are more likely than other participants to enroll at a later age (midtwenties or beyond), to undertake studies for certificates or diplomas rather than degrees, and to enroll in private providers or one of the three *wananga* (tertiary institutions with a specific focus on Maori education).

CHANGES IN SCHOOL ACCOUNTABILITY PROCESSES

As noted earlier, two government agencies play major roles in overseeing the work of schools. The Ministry of Education defines the resources available to schools, the curriculum taught, and the boundaries of acceptable practice. There is also a more specific arrangement with each school, both through the school charter and through a new requirement for school target setting and annual reporting on progress toward those targets. The Education Review Office is independent from the ministry and has the role of evaluating and reporting publicly on individual schools.

The ministry has three key roles in monitoring and responding to school performance. First, to obtain a national picture of student achievement, it has participated in international studies of student achievement such as the Third International Mathematics and Science Study (TIMSS), Progress in Reading Literacy (PIRLS), and the Program for International Student Assessment (PISA); and it has commissioned the Educational Assessment Research Unit at the University of Otago, which I codirect, to conduct regular national monitoring of the achievement of primary school students through the National Education Monitoring Project (NEMP). Since 1995 NEMP has provided detailed national assessments of the knowledge, skills, and attitudes of primary and intermediate school students at two levels: year four (ages eight to nine) and year eight (ages twelve to thirteen).

NEMP operates similarly to the National Assessment of Educational Progress in the United States. Small, nationally representative samples of students attempt each assessment task. Fifteen different areas of the national curriculum are covered over a four-year assessment cycle (Crooks & Flockton, 1993; Flockton, 1999). About 40 percent of the assessment tasks remain constant from one cycle to the next, so that trends in achievement across a four-year interval can be observed and reported. The remaining tasks are released, making them available for teacher use and allowing detailed and clear reporting of students' responses. Many of the tasks are performance tasks, and heavy use is made of videotaping to record student responses.

NEMP's purpose is system-level accountability. It identifies which aspects are improving, staying constant, or declining nationally, allowing successes to be celebrated and priorities for curriculum change and teacher development to be debated. No information is provided about individual students or schools, so this is not a high-stakes accountability mechanism, but increasing attention is being paid to the trends and performance patterns that are being revealed by NEMP, and these are influencing both educational practices in schools and the development of national education policy.

Second, the ministry has developed a new planning and reporting policy for schools, required of schools by the Education Standards Act (2001). It requires schools to set specific targets for school performance and report them to the ministry. These targets will be expressed, commonly but not exclusively, in terms of student achievement outcomes (assessed in a variety of ways including, in some schools, the use of standardized tests). The school charter includes a long-term strategic plan and an annually updated section spelling out annual targets and priorities, aimed at raising achievement and reducing disparities for particular groups of students. Because of existing patterns of disparity for Maori and Pacific Islander students, the plan must give attention to their needs and to instruction relating to Maori language and culture. Each school is to monitor performance against its charter and report annually to its community and the ministry, including in its report "an analysis of any variance between the school's performance and the relevant aims, objectives, directions, priorities or targets set out in the school charter" (Education Standards Act, section 87, clause 2).

This regime has just come into full operation in 2004, so the specifics of implementation and its longer-term effects are matters of speculation at present. Key issues will be the extent to which the policy builds trust and an optimal motivational environment and the weight given to schools' own priorities, relative to government priorities. There is no doubt that there is merit in schools establishing goals for improvement, finding ways to monitor progress toward these goals, and reviewing their success or lack of success in making the desired improvements. A key point, though, is that these strategies will be more effective if people feel a sense of ownership—if they adopt them because they believe in their value, rather than because they were required to adopt them. At present, most school personnel have little sense of ownership of the new policy and see it as another bureaucratic requirement that represents a threat rather than a promise of help.

Third, although it is the role of the Education Review Office to visit schools and evaluate their work, that office has no power to require schools to change. That power rests with the Ministry of Education, which can close schools, suspend their boards of trustees and replace them with commissioners, or impose requirements on how a particular school operates. Though not used a great deal, this is accountability in its most obvious form.

The Education Review Office has changed in very significant ways since its establishment fourteen years ago, partly because of three government-requested reviews of its role and functioning. I will comment briefly on some of the history and then outline its current approach to the evaluation of schools, which is the accountability mechanism that has the greatest influence on most New Zealand primary schools (the national qualifications structure almost certainly has a stronger influence on most or all secondary schools).

The Education Review Office, established in 1989, replaced the Inspectors of Schools from the former Department of Education—but with a substantially narrower focus. It was initially conceived of as an audit agency, and the name initially proposed for it was "the Review and Audit Agency." A central idea in its design is that an agency responsible for school evaluation should not provide advice to schools about how to resolve concerns identified by the agency, for this would mean that its next review of that school would include evaluating the effects of its own advice, and this would compromise its audit role. (Recent problems experienced by major accounting firms in the United States involved a similar issue.)

One of the consequences of this design idea was that many schools saw the Education Review Office as an agency that posed a threat and offered no help, a view exacerbated by the first model of review adopted: accountability (compliance) audits. These focused on checking whether features required by legislation or school charters were present in the schools. Using a checklist approach, reviewers focused on relatively easily checked features, ranging from the display of fire exit signs to the development of school policies and evidence of paperwork related to the government's curriculum and assessment requirements. Schools had little role in defining what features would be looked at and valued. The tone of the reports seemed to schools largely negative: Positive features were treated as expected, and negative features were highlighted. Thus, even schools with mostly good results received reports that had a negative tinge, and what varied was the volume of negative comment. Although there was justification for many of the features checked, the accountability audit model had severe failings: There often was little trust, little sense of ownership of the results within schools, and too much attention given to surface aspects in the work of schools at the expense of deeper aspects. The availability of the reports to news media and the public made them high-stakes evaluations. An unfortunate side effect was that schools often perceived staff of the Education Review Office as adversaries, rather than valuable experienced colleagues and influential education leaders (as most of the school inspectors had been). This reduced the ability of the office to recruit successful, experienced teachers and principals.

After about four years the Education Review Office added effectiveness reviews to the mix. These came closer to addressing the core of the educational enterprise because they focused on what schools were helping their students to achieve. Educational effectiveness is, however, extraordinarily difficult to judge. Brief visits by reviewers, usually involving less than an hour looking at each class, provide a very limited platform for judging the effectiveness of school programs. The expertise of reviewers is critical in this sort of work, and it is hard to escape the view that, on average, the reviewers were less well equipped to make these judgments than the school inspectors of a few years earlier had been.

Many of the public comments made in connection with these reviews during the 1990s had a negative effect on teacher trust in the process and on the public's trust in teachers and schools. Those picked up by the news media had a strong negative focus, usually criticizing yet another aspect of the education system and seemingly suggesting that remarkably low proportions of teachers and schools were doing a good job. This had an adverse effect on teachers, even though it may have gained favor for the Education Review Office with some politicians, agencies, and interest groups. Some of the comments did lead to worthwhile action, notably in areas of the country where poor socioeconomic conditions appeared to have demoralized some schools, although even these gains could, I believe, have been achieved with less public pain for teachers and schools. There are appropriate ways to stir remedial action without public derogation and without punishing all for the deficiencies of some—good teachers use such ways all of the time!

The situation is steadily improving with the adoption of a new review model, "Review and Assist," which focuses on factors directly related to educational outcomes for students. Assistance is limited to guidance and suggestions of alternative approaches to consider, provided at the time of review. Most important, schools conduct a self-review, and the external review places significant emphasis on the school's own targets and priorities while not neglecting to draw attention to government goals that appear to be receiving too little priority. There is much more of a sense of negotiation in this model, and compliance has become a smaller component, with the focus more on quality of teaching and learning programs. The main concern remaining is the quality of reviewers: Very high-caliber reviewers are needed, and the office has to overcome aspects of its previous reputation in order to attract staff with such capabilities.

Using assessment results in making judgments about the performance of teachers and schools remains a hot issue in New Zealand. In the final years of secondary school, where the national examination results are available, some newspapers have published tables comparing the results for different schools in their region. Often these comparisons have taken no account of different school circumstances, such as the socioeconomic resources of the families of the children attending each school, but in some cases, more selective comparison groups have been chosen. Some political parties and interest groups have argued strongly for national testing in primary and intermediate schools to permit such comparisons at those levels, but to date this has been resisted strongly and effectively by teachers and others concerned about the direct and indirect effects of such high-stakes testing. Currently, no nationwide use of standardized tests occurs until the national examinations for NCEA in year eleven of secondary school.

CONCLUSION

The last fifteen years have not been a settled period for the staff and students of New Zealand schools. Major changes in school administration and accountability appear to be on the verge of settling down and working satisfactorily, although a change of government could result in the reintroduction of policies designed to promote further competition and choice among schools. Changes in school curricula, which have predominantly affected primary schools, are not yet fully established and are under study. Very substantial changes in secondary school qualifications are being implemented over several years, and it will be quite some time before their effectiveness can start to be evaluated.

This fifteen-year period has, I believe, seen a significant transfer of influence from experienced education leaders to politicians and managers and a reduction in perceptions of professional ownership of their practices for classroom teachers (Locke, 2001). Change has been imposed, rather than owned, and at a frenetic pace. If this trend continues, there appears to be a considerable risk of decision making that is less educationally sound, centrally and within schools, accompanied by a significant loss of the intrinsic motivation that persuades people to invest the very substantial effort required to become and remain excellent teachers.

Few in the community would disagree with the government's desire to reduce disparities in the educational achievement of different ethnic groups or the need to provide an extra measure of support for some schools and students to help achieve that. Many, however, are skeptical about how readily the goal can be achieved. It seems unlikely that the answer lies solely with teachers and schools because the interrelated effects of poverty and factors in families and the wider community clearly play a large part in influencing the motivation, learning approaches and opportunities, and relevant learning experiences beyond school that students bring to their learning in school. This suggests that community development will have to play as big a part as school development before much higher proportions of our students approach the goal set out by the minister of education in 1939: education to the fullest extent of their powers.

NOTE

Internet resources consulted include the following: www.minedu.govt.nz, the Ministry of Education Web site, with wide-ranging information about ed ucation in New Zealand; www.nzqa.govt.nz, the New Zealand Qualifications Authority Web site, with information about qualifications in the secondary and tertiary sectors; and www.ero.govt.nz, the Education Review Office Web site, with information about reviewing the performance of schools.

REFERENCES CITED

Beeby, C. E. (1992). *The biography of an idea: Beeby on education.* Wellington: New Zealand Council for Educational Research.

Codd, J., McAlpine, D., & Poskitt, J. (1995). Assessment policies in New Zealand: Educational reform or political agenda. In R. Peddie & B. Tuck (Eds.), *Setting the standards* (pp. 32–58). Palmerston North, New Zealand: Dunmore Press.

Crooks, T. J. (2002). Educational assessment in New Zealand schools. *Assessment in Education, 9,* 237–53.

Crooks, T. J., & Flockton, L. C. (1993). *The design and implementation of national monitoring of educational outcomes in New Zealand primary schools.* Dunedin: Higher Education Development Centre.

Fiske, E. B., & Ladd, H. F. (2000). *When schools compete: A cautionary tale.* Washington, DC: Brookings Institution Press.

Flockton, L. C. (1999). *School-wide assessment: National Education Monitoring Project.* Wellington: New Zealand Council for Educational Research.

Hall, C. (1998). The National Qualifications Framework green paper: What future for the framework? *New Zealand Annual Review of Education, 7,* 29–57.

Hipkins, R., & Vaughan, K. (2002). *Learning curves: Meeting student needs in an evolving qualifications regime: From cabbages to kings; A first report.* Wellington: New Zealand Council for Educational Research.

Lange, D. (1988). *Tomorrow's schools.* Wellington: Government Printer.

Lee, H. (1991). The credentialed society: A history of New Zealand public school examinations. Unpublished Ph.D. thesis, University of Otago, Dunedin.

Lee, H., & Lee, G. (2001). The National Certificate of Educational Achievement (NCEA): Fragile—handle with care. *New Zealand Annual Review of Education, 10,* 5–38.

Locke, T. (2001). Curriculum, assessment and the erosion of professionalism. *New Zealand Journal of Educational Studies, 36,* 5–23.

National Commission on Excellence in Education. (1983). *A nation at risk.* Washington, DC: U.S. Government Printing Office.

New Zealand Qualifications Authority. (1991). *Developing the National Qualifications Framework.* Wellington: New Zealand Qualifications Authority.

O'Neill, O. (2002). *A question of trust.* BBC Reith Lectures 2002. London: BBC.

Strachan, J. (2002). Assessment in change: Some reflections on the local and international background to the National Certificate of Educational Achievement (NCEA). *New Zealand Annual Review of Education, 11,* 245–73.

Task Force to Review Education Administration. (1988). *Administering for excellence.* Wellington: Task Force to Review Education Administration.

Wylie, C. (1997). *Self-managing schools seven years on: What have we learned?* Wellington: New Zealand Council for Educational Research.

14

England: New Governments, New Policies

Alison Wolf

> But 'tis the talent of our English nation,
> Still to be plotting some new reformation.
>
> —John Dryden (1631 1700)

The world's views of English society and English education are formed largely by a mixture of BBC costume drama, Hollywood, and the classics of English literature (most recently *Harry Potter*). So the images that spring to mind are of boarding schools and quaint uniforms, of young "gentlemen" (and royal princes) on the playing fields of Eton, and of Oxbridge quadrangles and dreaming spires.

Eton remains a great school, but it and, indeed, the other great "public" boarding schools have long ago lost the inside track to political success and thus their dominance in society. The last four leaders of the right-wing Conservative Party have been a small shopkeeper's daughter, a man who left school at sixteen to be a bank clerk, a small-town Yorkshireman who retained his regional accent, and a nongraduate army officer. The last of these is also the only one of the four to have attended any sort of private school at all (although, ironically, Tony Blair, a member of the Labour Party, was entirely privately educated). The percentage of English schoolchildren who attend private schools is about 8 percent—less, for example, than the U.S. percentage. What is true, however, is that the private or, as they are now usually called, independent schools dominate entry to the most prestigious, most competitive university courses by virtue of their students' performance in public examinations. This is especially true for the big private day schools of London, Birmingham, and Manchester—England's three largest cities.[1]

This chapter focuses on the past fifteen years of frenetic school reform and on the social and economic reasons that education policy has been so high on the political agenda. However, in order to understand the context of reform, and also because outsiders' views of the English system are often formed by very partial media images, it is first of all worth outlining the structure of English education today.

THE SCHOOL SYSTEM

With a few exceptions, English schoolchildren attend first a primary and then a secondary school from which they may leave full-time education or move on, at age sixteen or eighteen. Most attend a neighborhood primary school and then move to a large, nonselective secondary "comprehensive" school serving the full eleven to eighteen age range. However, at age sixteen, following important and high-stakes public examinations (the General Certificate in Secondary Education [GCSE], normally taken in nine or more subjects), some will leave school for the job market or apprenticeship and others will move to a college (which in the United Kingdom is not a term applied to universities). This may be a "sixth-form college," which specializes in education for sixteen to eighteen year olds and offers both academic and vocational options. Alternatively, it may be a "further education college," an institution that resembles an American community college but also offers courses, both academic and vocational, to sixteen to eighteen year olds. For those who remain in secondary school, the most important and highest-recruiting courses are those leading to academic examinations: namely, A levels, the "General Certificate of Education (Advanced level)," normally taken in three or four subjects.

A levels, like the GCSEs, are public examinations with very high stakes for the individual candidate. Students' GCSE results determine which course they will follow after age sixteen and, in particular, whether they will be among the 40 percent or so who enter A-level classes. A-level results, in turn, determine which course at which university a student will enter. Although it is entirely possible to enter some form of higher education without A levels, they form the gateway to desirable courses in high-status universities.

Most of the younger students who move into further education do so in order to follow a vocational or semivocational program, of which schools tend to offer only a limited selection. However, a good number of college students also work toward A levels. Either way, age sixteen marks a critical selection point, when students are steered toward very different options. Until then, there is very little formal selection or sorting in the state system, and promotion is effectively automatic and age dependent. The lack of selection or tracking before age sixteen makes the current school system very different from that of the postwar period. It was in 1945, after World War II, that England finally moved to universal secondary education. It did so by establishing a system that assigned eleven year olds to either academic "grammar schools" or nonacademic "secondary modern schools" on the basis of an academic examination taken in the final year of primary school, the "11-plus."[2] Between 1965 and 1980 that system was swept away in favor of the nonselective comprehensive secondary school.

Funding for state schools in England (and indeed the whole United Kingdom) comes almost entirely from the central government, but between it and the schools lies the administrative tier of local education authorities (LEAs). Although, as discussed later, the LEAs have lost a great many of their powers in recent years, they have ultimate responsibility for the way schools are organized in their area, including, notably, whether secondary schools have a "sixth form" of sixteen to eighteen year olds or whether these students will be consolidated in a few schools or a sixth-form college. There are also local differences in the extent to which an LEA shares its powers and responsibilities—notably in the cases of "aided" schools with a religious character and origin. As in much of Europe (and unlike the case in the United States), a good number of English schools are church schools in the broadest sense—Catholic and Church of England but also Jewish and, most recently, Muslim. These schools are entirely non-fee-paying; are subject to all the same curriculum, admissions, and other policies as any state schools; and may admit pupils of other faiths. However, they retain a religious character; they may give preference in admissions to pupils of the relevant faith; and the churches are involved in their governance. This situation dates back to the origins of mass education in the nineteenth century, which was largely the creation of the churches (West, 1970), and to the compromises with the latter that heralded the nationalization of elementary education in 1870. The existence of religious schools within the state system is not a major area of controversy, and their reputation with parents is usually high (Dennis, 2001; Gordon, Aldrich, & Dean, 1991; Jenkins, 1995).

This chapter focuses on school reform, but it is also important to be aware of how much English higher education has changed in recent years. The country now has one of the highest participation rates in Europe and the highest graduation rate (measured in terms of proportion of the population achieving full bachelor's degrees). Over 40 percent of an age cohort now moves more or less directly into some form of higher education, and the government's target is for 50 percent to do so in the near future (Department for Education and Skills, 2003; Organization for Economic Cooperation and Development, 2002). The university sector is extremely hierarchical, with very competitive entry for the top institutions. The rapid expansion of higher education has had a direct effect on schools because it means that a large and growing proportion of the population is concerned directly with how well schools perform, in the sense of producing students with good A-level grades and, therefore, the likelihood of progressing to "good" universities. Although the private schools enroll only about 8 percent of students overall, they produce a far higher proportion of the country's A-level candidates and, especially, of candidates who obtain good A-level grades in traditional academic subjects.

Finally, in understanding the English educational (and indeed political and social) scene, it is critical to grasp the enormous power of central government. The fact that fundamental reforms of secondary education, established in 1945, could be swept away almost entirely within thirty years, underlines this point: The successive changes to be discussed later reflect the same phenomenon. Britain has no written constitution. It has a first-past-the-post election system, which awards legislative seats to the constituency candidate with the most votes cast (very often a minority of the total), with no element of proportional representation.[3] This system tends to produce large parliamentary majorities for a single party, rather than the coalitions common in many other countries. Party discipline is strong, and the upper house (the House of Lords) has few powers. All this means that a British government has been able to pass whatever laws it likes, provided the members of its own party will accept them. Although these powers are now circumscribed in many areas by the treaties of the European Union, in others—including education—there are no such restraints. The result is that governments can be, and frequently are, extraordinarily radical in the changes they introduce and very often inspired by clear ideological principles. The veneer of age and tradition overlaying English life often conceals this not only from foreigners but from the English themselves, who tend to see themselves as mired in the past and as practical, moderate, nonideological people. In education, at least, the facts suggest otherwise.

DIAGNOSING THE SCHOOL SYSTEM: EDUCATION AS PROBLEM AND CURE

For fifteen years English schooling has been in a state of more or less constant change. Moreover, other enormous upheavals preceded these by only a couple of decades. The reforms that shape today's schools started under the Conservative administrations of Thatcher but reached their apogee (or possibly their nadir) in the early years of the Labour administration headed by Tony Blair, when an average of one new directive or policy paper *a day* issued forth from the national ministry of education. Underlying this ferment was a conviction among politicians, shared by the national media, that state education was failing.

This section is concerned with the origins of this view. The response to it, again under major political parties, has been informed by two basic principles, which are also in tension. The first is a commitment to centrally driven reform (as the only way for revolutionaries or reformers to realize their objectives in, as they see it, the face of local obduracy and self-interested opposition). The second is a belief in choice, variety, and, to varying degrees, the efficiency of market principles. These two principles, and their translation into education policy, are discussed later.

Concerns over the quality of education emerged first and most starkly with respect to primary schools and the teaching of reading and mathematics. In the 1950s and 1960s preparation for the 11-plus examination dominated the upper years of primary education. There was a general feeling that the result was often narrow and stultifying and failed to encourage the full intellectual or creative development of pupils. A major governmental review, chaired by Bridget Plowden (1967), led to a report titled *Children and Their Primary Schools* that became synonymous in policy discussion with a general "progressivism," a belief in unstructured classrooms and individualized learning, and opposition to any form of testing. In fact, read today, the Plowden Report seems entirely moderate, full of common sense, and very different from its popular reputation. However, it was contemporaneous not just with a general revulsion against categorizing children permanently at the age of ten or eleven, which led to the abolition of selective secondary schooling in favor of comprehensives, but also with the emergence of an influential set of "progressive" ideas that went far beyond anything advocated by Plowden as national policy. These, in turn, were attacked aggressively by conservative-leaning writers, whose "black papers," linking progressive ideas to a decline in educational standards, received widespread publicity (see, e.g., Aldrich, 2002).

The establishment of comprehensives started in earnest in 1965 under a Labour government. Many Conservatives were strongly against the abolition of grammar schools, but although they were in power from 1970 to 1974, the process continued unabated. The actual organization of schools was the responsibility of the country's LEAs, most of which had well-advanced plans by 1970, with, often, a great deal of bipartisan support. In some localities, grammar schools were "saved," but Thatcher, in her period as a Conservative minister of education (1970–74), signed off on more local reorganizations (into comprehensive schools) than any other minister before or since.

In much of the country, meanwhile, primary teachers continued, throughout both the 1970s and the 1980s, to operate in a fairly traditional style, albeit much less examination oriented than in the past, and with a general reluctance to measure children formally and compare them with any national or external yardstick. In some schools and districts, however, there was a genuine and enthusiastic commitment to "exploratory" or informal methods; the teaching of formal spelling or times tables was effectively (though not legally) abandoned in favor of having children explore writing and number bonds for themselves, and any form of whole-class didactic teaching became anathema. Significantly for the future, many of the most committed of these schools were in inner London, home not only to politicians but also to England's enormously influential national press and broadcasting. One particularly high-profile case, in 1976, pitted working-class parents against "progressive" and highly politicized teachers at William Tyndale School in London (Aldrich, 2002). The school was a primary school in a fairly poor area of London, where the head and the majority of teachers were highly committed to a more or less totally unstructured regime, underpinned by left-wing politics that were seen as implying such an approach and as something they wanted to pass on to the children. The parents, however, felt that their children were not being taught anything. The LEA was in conflict with the school governors (who had appointed and supported the head); there was almost a year of protests, demonstrations, and strikes before the head left and the school staff was (in large part) reconstituted.

The Tyndale case was the immediate pretext for a seminal speech by the Labour prime minister of the time, James Callaghan. Foreshadowing change to come, he stated that "during my travels around the country in recent months, I have had many discussions that show concern" (1976, p. 333) about the state of education and educational standards. In the advice showered on him in anticipation of what was a much-heralded speech, he noted, it was

> almost as though some people would wish that the subject matter and purpose of education should not have public attention focused on it; nor that profane hands should touch it. I cannot believe that this is a considered reaction. . . . Public interest is strong and legitimate and will be satisfied. . . . I have been very impressed in the schools I have visited by the enthusiasm and dedication of the teaching profession, by

the variety of courses that are offered. . . . But I am concerned on my journeys to find complaints from industry that new recruits from the schools sometimes do not have the basic tools to do the job that is required. . . . On another aspect there is the unease felt by parents and others about the new informal methods of teaching which seem to produce excellent results when they are in well-qualified hands but are much more dubious when they are not. . . . There is now widespread recognition of the need to cater for a child's personality, to let it flower in the fullest possible way. The balance was wrong in the past. [But] we have a responsibility now to see that we do not get it wrong in the other direction. There is no virtue in producing socially well-adjusted members of society who are unemployed because they do not have the skills. (1976, p. 333)

The sentiments and concerns expressed in that speech would be applauded by key figures in every single government that has followed, even though the actual policies used in response to the problems Callaghan perceived have been modified and changed continuously. However, major changes to the education system were delayed by economic crises—of which the United Kingdom experienced plenty in the late 1970s and early 1980s. Callaghan's government had to grapple with a "winter of discontent," when major public sector strikes led to power cuts that forced the country onto a three-day week, rubbish lay uncollected, hospitals could not function properly, unemployment soared, and the International Monetary Fund forced humiliating economic and fiscal changes on the government.

None of this altered the public's perception of educational failure. On the contrary, in the quest for explanations of the country's then-evident economic failure, education became a favored candidate for blame, with some influential commentators citing a long-standing tradition of classical and humanistic education and antipathy to science, technology, and commerce and others emphasizing the superiority of current European (especially German and French) education (Barnett, 1986; Prais, 1995; Sanderson, 1999). These arguments had a major influence on politicians, civil servants, and the media; the results of international comparative surveys received widespread coverage and were seen as confirming the negative effects of "progressive" education. For example, those run by the International Association for the Evaluation of Educational Achievement showed English children performing badly on, in particular, traditional mathematics and computational questions. Then and now, England's performance in science tended to be rather good, but this finding never received comparable coverage. The widespread belief that educational standards were low and falling received added impetus from the conviction—not peculiar to England—that education was the key to economic success in the modern world (Wolf, 2002a).

During the 1970s and 1980s concern about educational standards focused on the primary schools. More recently, political reformers have been increasingly concerned with secondary education. This is partly because it has taken time for the mixed effects of the move to comprehensive schools to become clear and for responses to crystallize among politicians and commentators. In the suburbs, small towns, and countryside, the system bedded down with no great problems. In the cities, however, the result was as much to strengthen as to overcome class-linked barriers to opportunity.

Throughout the world, cities exhibit extremes of wealth and poverty, and the refusal of their middle classes to use large, nonselective secondary schools is far from a purely English phenomenon. However, the effect of comprehensive education on city education, and its impact on the relative academic performance of state and independent sectors, was especially rapid and visible in England because of its educational history. The grammar schools of the post-1945 selective system included many state-operated institutions but also included a number of ancient and independent institutions that opted into the state system as "direct grant" schools, accepting all or most of their students on the basis of the 11-plus examinations, with their fees paid by the state.[4] When required to be nonselective, almost all of these schools opted to become independent and fee paying once again and, so, largely the preserve of an urban middle class that was increasingly preoccupied with its children's educational future. As direct grant schools, they had also been largely middle class—but with a significant proportion of high-achieving working-class students. Meanwhile, the cities' other "state" grammar schools, along with the secondary moderns, became comprehensive schools. However, many of them (because of their geographical location) recruited overwhelmingly from low-income areas and lacked any significant middle-class enrollment.

The problems of working-class concentration in the comprehensive schools were, and continue to be, compounded by enormous social changes. In the last decades of the twentieth century England experienced unprecedented levels of immigration (so that its foreign-born population is now at close to U.S. levels and, in London, higher than in New York). Immigrants concentrate in the big cities, and soaring rates of family breakdown and births to single young mothers increase the pressures this creates. Although many city schools manage, nonetheless, to provide reasonable or indeed good education, a significant number became institutions to which no caring parent would willingly send a child with any academic bent or ambition. Of course, this had been true of a good many of the older secondary moderns too, but it was (and is) a far cry from the original promise of equal educational opportunity within the comprehensive system. This promise of equality was articulated by Michael Stewart, the first minister of education in the 1964 Labour government: "No child will be put in a position of being sent to a school which is accepted from the start as not possessing as good facilities as some other schools for advanced academic education" (Kogan, 1971, p. 7).

The cities' increasing educational polarization fed through into the increasing academic dominance of the independent sector, as the grammar schools' success in, for example, sending pupils to Oxbridge faded into history. Nothing in the last fifteen years of frenetic reform has had any impact here: The proportion of state-educated students entering Oxford and Cambridge was around two-thirds throughout the 1960s and 1970s (e.g., 64 percent in 1978) without there being any overt policies to encourage this. By 2000 the proportion was remaining stubbornly below 50 percent, despite active "outreach" programs by the universities and tongue-lashings from government. Those who do enter from state schools are overwhelmingly from suburbs and university towns and are middle class themselves. The picture is the same in other top-ranked universities. Recent data indicating declines in social mobility since the 1970s reflect this development (Blanden et al., in press).

Different parts of the political and media establishments might vary in how much they worried about the education system's supposed economic failings, as compared with its failure to promote equal opportunity or its failure to preserve high standards and culture. Over-all, however, by the time Thatcher became prime minister, dissatis-faction was widespread, and blame was frequently directed toward the teaching profession and the LEAs. By contrast, both then and throughout the period I am about to describe, most parents have tended to express general satisfaction with their children's own teach-ers. They have also become ever more concerned about their chil-dren's educational success and prospects. As noted earlier, there has been a sustained and enormous expansion of university education in Britain, and a degree has become a prerequisite for an increasing proportion of middle-class occupations. The ever-greater importance of education in determining life chances (Wolf, 2002a), allied to the competitive nature of upper secondary school examinations and uni-versity entrance, ensures that education remains a high-profile con-cern, whichever party is in power. Moreover, the fact that school funding comes almost entirely from central government taxes makes the cost and efficiency of education of direct and abiding interest to the Treasury, itself by far the most important and powerful of the de-partments of state.

THE CENTRALIZATION SOLUTION

Margaret Thatcher came to power in 1979. A sustained period of rela-tive economic decline for the United Kingdom had come to a head with the "winter of discontent," during which the (Labour) government ap-peared to have lost all authority over public sector unions. The self-confidence of much of the British elite had never been lower, with talk not of a positive future but simply of "managing decline." How much the events of the Thatcher years are a cause for celebration or excoria-tion and how much they were her personal achievement are matters on which there is no consensus at all within the United Kingdom, for Thatcher divided public opinion in a way unequalled by any other twentieth-century prime minister. On one thing, however, observers are agreed. Hers was the most centralizing government in several hun-dred years, and education was one of the prime objects of its zeal. What is also clear is that, as with many other aspects of the Thatcher legacy, her successor governments—Conservative and Labour—have chosen to consolidate, rather than reverse, her approach.

In 1979 most of the important operational decisions about both primary and secondary schools were made by the LEAs. Today, these bodies, though they still exist, have virtually no independent authority, and in a few cases private contractors appointed by central government run them directly. In 1979 there was no national curriculum; today, all children from five to sixteen in state-funded schools follow a highly prescriptive, uniform curriculum that covers the full timetable. In 1979 the first formal and publicly reported testing experienced by most state-educated children (and for many the first formal testing of any sort) came at age sixteen, when they took examinations marking the end of compulsory schooling.[5] Today, English children are among the most tested in the world, with external tests, developed by public bodies, used at ages five, seven, eleven, fourteen, sixteen, seventeen, and eighteen—and sometimes in between as well.

This happened partly because, as we have seen, politicians and opinion makers had become convinced that education was in a perilous state and partly because British society had become so politically polarized. Education had been a local function since the coming of compulsory schooling. Over the years there had been a gradual move away from independently elected local school boards and distinct funding streams for education (including substantial amounts of locally raised revenue) toward relatively few large local authorities, whose funding for education came largely through a general grant from central government for local services, in which education was just one of a number of functions. Localities also experienced the progressive reduction of their power to supplement central funding during the postwar years in the cause of expenditure equalization. Thus, in most areas, the LEA was coterminous with the other local authorities, namely, the borough or county councils responsible for other local government services, and run by elected councils. Consequently, they were seen as very much a department of those councils.

However, the substantive powers of LEAs were enormous in the postwar decades. Although the central ministry (then known as the Department for Education and Science) distributed the vast bulk of the funds for state education, the ministry did not employ any teachers or run any schools and had no direct control over either the curriculum or the examinations taken by students leaving school for the job market or higher education. Harold Wilson, a Labour prime minister of the 1960s, regarded the department as "little more than a postbox" between the LEAs and the powerful teachers' unions, which conducted their national pay bargaining directly with the employer representatives—that is, the LEAs (Sharp, 2002, p. 105).

The LEAs of the early Thatcher years included some run by ideologically committed left-wing councils, reflecting the polarized politics of the period.[6] These councils were a prime target of a central government whose campaign platform had included curbing their powers (including their tax-raising powers). The major way in which councils could raise additional funds for local initiatives, including educational ones, was "rates," a form of property tax. In the mid-1980s the government moved to cap the degree to which councils could increase rates. Thatcher's views on property taxes were clear: "I had always disliked the rates intensely. Any property tax is essentially a tax on improving one's own home. It was manifestly unfair and un-Conservative" (1993, p. 644). Curbing councils' powers meant that education spending levels became, in effect, something decided entirely by central government, which remains the case, even though there has been a series of further changes to local tax mechanisms.

In the specifically educational context, numerous LEAs, along with the teachers' unions (some of them also, at this time, dominated by left-wing caucuses), were perceived by the government as aiding and abetting a decline in education standards, denying children a proper education, and undermining national prosperity in pursuit of misguided "progressive" ideals. Although opposition to Thatcher was at all times strong and vocal, local authorities also found rather few passionate defenders of their educational powers. As noted earlier, the conviction that there was something seriously wrong with England's schools, especially in the teaching of basic elementary-level skills, was widely shared across the political spectrum. The fact that London teachers were particularly militant over pay and conditions (partly on ideological grounds and partly because of the sheer cost of living in the capital) fueled the determination of a London-based government to seize power for itself.

The policies that demolished LEA powers also included, as the next section will discuss, far greater independence for schools themselves, but the most dramatic and visible educational changes of the Thatcher years were those that enlarged the powers of central government and of the secretary of state for education. In the past, LEAs had been free to undertake major curriculum innovation; the Inner London Education Authority, for example, developed a distinctive and entirely individualized secondary mathematics program, which was used throughout its schools and nowhere else in the country. The County of Kent (covering London suburbs, Dover, Canterbury, and the southern Thames estuary) was another LEA with its own secondary mathematics scheme, again quite distinct from that used in most of the rest of the country. LEAs ran their own large inspection services, which had a major influence on teaching content and pedagogy in their schools. Of course, what schools taught was not completely random: Most offered the "normal" collections of mathematics and science, languages, social sciences, and vocational options. In the upper secondary years, the need for sixteen- and eighteen-year-old pupils to pass the externally set public examinations, each with its own syllabus, structured teaching tightly. Nonetheless, the not-for-profit examining bodies that ran these exams offered a wide range of syllabus options, and LEAs with their own curriculum initiatives could arrange to have them examined specially.[7] All this was to change with the introduction of a compulsory national curriculum.

It was James Callaghan, the Labour prime minister, who first signaled central control over the curriculum, in the 1976 Ruskin College speech quoted earlier, which expressed disquiet over "progressive" methods and indicated that a mandated core curriculum might be a necessary way of ensuring a basic equality in provision (and standards) in all schools. Like Callaghan, however, the early Thatcher governments were largely preoccupied with the economy, and the major curriculum reform of those years was, in fact, one generally welcomed by the education establishment. As already noted, the important public examinations that English (and, indeed, all British) pupils take at sixteen or eighteen play a central role in both labor market entry and university selection. The introduction of the GCSE in the 1980s meant that there was now a single set of public examinations offered at age sixteen, where previously there had been two, one less academic (and so less respected or valuable) than the other.

Other actions, however, signaled an increasingly interventionist approach to the curriculum. Two new centrally appointed bodies were established—one to advise on curriculum and one, on examinations. In an attempt to counteract what was seen as a deeply embedded prejudice against technical skills and against business, money was poured into a "Technical and Vocational Education Initiative" and into "Enterprise" activities that encouraged pupils to carry out small-scale business ventures. In both cases, money went directly into participating schools, bypassing the LEAs, a practice that has continued ever since, with schools receiving ever-increasing portions of their funding through special, centrally run, and often short-lived "initiatives."

Then, in 1987, a full-blown national curriculum was launched. In the space of a year English schools moved from a situation where there was less governmental control of the curriculum than anywhere else in Europe to having one of the most tightly and minutely defined curricula on the Continent. Callaghan, and, indeed, Thatcher herself, had been concerned largely to ensure that the core subjects—English, mathematics, and science—were taught to guaranteed standards throughout the primary and secondary years. Offered a taste of power, the civil servants and political advisers of the central ministry and the new government advisory bodies staged a complete takeover of the curriculum, urged on by then–Secretary of State Kenneth Baker.

Alongside the three original foundation subjects (mathematics, English, science) came seven other compulsory ones: history, geography, technology, music, art, physical education, and a foreign language. In every single one of these, for the years of compulsory education (ages five to sixteen), the government prescribed detailed "attainment targets," specifying exactly what must be achieved by each pupil through ten levels of attainment and doing so at a level of detail that encompassed content as well as skills. The result effectively absorbed the entire school timetable, and options pretty much vanished. The 1988 Education Reform Act, which enacted this into law for all state (though not for independent) schools, also established a National Curriculum Council, with the authority to oversee implementation and revise the curriculum as and when requested to do so by central government, and a School Examinations and Assessment Council, to ensure that the new curriculum was adequately assessed and examined. The latter requirement produced an explosion in the amount of testing within schools.

National Curriculum and Testing

The introduction of a national curriculum was not without supporters in the education world, though there were few enthusiasts for anything as detailed and prescriptive as the final product, which arrived accompanied by (literally) truckloads of "guidance," instruction, and regulation. For the accompanying testing regime, it was hard to find anyone within the schools who had a single kind word. This was not something that bothered the government, for the purpose of the new testing regime was assuredly not to please schools and teachers— quite the contrary. On the one hand (as the next section discusses), it was intended to empower parents and establish a sort of market- driven virtuous circle leading to higher standards everywhere. On the other—and this was the aspect that has become increasingly dominant—it was meant to assert central control over the whole school system and to identify failing and backsliding schools that could then be targeted for improvement.

The new national curriculum divided the years of compulsory schooling into four "Key Stages": Stage 1 (ages five to seven), Stage 2 (ages seven to eleven—that is, through the end of primary school), Stage 3 (ages eleven to fourteen), and Stage 4 (ages fourteen to six- teen). There were to be new tests at the end of Key Stages 1, 2, and 3; Key Stage 4, covering the final two years of compulsory school, changed the least because it was already structured and driven by the demands of the subject-based public examinations, the GCSE, which is now taken by virtually all English sixteen-year-olds. Although GCSEs were and are extremely high stakes for the individual pupil taking them, the new Key Stage tests had far more to do with holding schools and teachers accountable. These tests were not intended to select or sort children in any formal sense. Rather, the results were for the use of parents, so that they could judge their children's progress, and they were also to be collated and, along with the results of the

GCSE examinations, published, on a school-by-school and LEA-by-LEA basis. The resulting "league tables" showed the relative attainment of every state school's pupils across the land; the press also compiles comparable tables showing independent schools' GCSE and A-level performance. Fifteen years on, the league tables are firmly established, unpopular with schools, and as controversial as ever.

The first years of the reform were deeply unhappy ones for the primary schools, and there is some convincing evidence to suggest that standards actually declined rather than rose at this time, as teachers struggled to master and implement the new requirements (see, e.g., Phillips & Furlong, 2001). The testing regime, especially for seven-year-olds, hovered between tragedy and farce. The Department of Education gave the early contracts for test development to university-led consortia, which were determined that the tests should be "authentic," that is, they should reflect the full curriculum, provide rich information on individual children's development that could be used by teachers to inform their teaching, and be nonthreatening to the children concerned. The result was completely unmanageable. Test administration stretched over a full six-week period; while the class teacher was observing and recording one or two children's interpretations of why a piece of wood did or did not float in a basin of water, the other twenty-eight or so seven-year-olds in the class were either more or less unsupervised (and, one hopes, still inside the classroom) or in the care of the resentful and overburdened teachers of the six- or eight-year-olds' classes. Only a credible national threat to boycott the next round of tests, supported not just by the teachers' unions but also by the full administrative hierarchy of the LEAs, secured change. Tests became, instead, the short, conventional, pencil-and-paper operations that were what Prime Minister Thatcher had envisaged in the first place.

In this form, the tests continue, and they function well enough from a narrow administrative perspective. Tests for eleven-year-olds are the most high profile, and those for fourteen-year-olds, the least; both cover mathematics, English, and science. The two separate curriculum and assessment authorities established in 1988 (and placed in different parts of the country) soon merged into a single, large London-based agency, the Qualifications and Curriculum Authority. This body, supposedly at arm's length from government but in fact its operational arm, devises and administers the seven-, eleven-, and fourteen-year-olds' tests—sometimes in-house, sometimes through contractors. The test results indicate which level of the ten-level national curriculum an individual child has reached in each of the subjects taken. Children take them, under formal test conditions, on a given date; the papers are collected and marked externally but returned to the schools for checking and for use in the classroom. The Department of Education collates and publishes the results (electronically and alphabetically) on an LEA-by-LEA basis, and the national press immediately publishes in hard copy the list of school results in rank order by LEA.

Although the tests now roll out quite smoothly year by year, they remain highly controversial. (The independent sector, which has voluntarily adopted most of the substance of the national curriculum, has shown no enthusiasm whatsoever for the seven-, eleven-, and fourteen-year-olds' testing regime. The vast majority of its schools do not enter pupils for any of them.) The most generally unpopular tests are those for seven-year-olds, for parents tend to share with teachers an unease over anything that labels children at this young an age and are very aware that children's early learning, particularly in reading and writing, progresses at very different speeds. Moreover, as the tests have become regular, well known, and in some ways routine, so they have also become a greater source of strain for children. Although their most important function is to judge school performance, children are nonetheless increasingly aware that the exam at age seven is the first of many times when they will be assessed and appraised and that performance in these areas matters for their futures.

In spite of the opposition, successive ministers have been convinced of the need to retain a centrally imposed requirement, one that, they believe, ensures that children who are slipping badly behind their peers—and schools that are failing them—are identified early on. This perspective reflects the origins of the reform movement in worries over the teaching of basic skills at the elementary level. One concession was made, in 2003, to allow schools to select their own date for testing seven-year-olds, rather than giving the test on set dates systemwide. It is not yet evident how this local selection can be reconciled with the need to keep papers (and answers) secure, for the Key Stage tests (as with all of England's public examination papers) are intentionally made available after the event, and children's results are fed back to schools, to provide formative input into teaching and to make the standards and content of the various levels explicit and clear.

The tests for eleven-year-olds are, if anything, even more unpopular with teachers—but not with parents. In understanding the persistence of the testing and league table regime beyond the Thatcher years, it is important to remember that both the unease over standards expressed by (Labour's) Callaghan and the commitment to reform of the Thatcher governments found ready echoes in the voting public at large. People might express positive sentiments about their own children's teachers and schools, but they shared the politicians' and media's fears about falling standards and were also (rightly) convinced of the growing importance of education for their children's futures. The eleven-year-olds' tests provide parents with a clear measure of how well their children are progressing, and opinion polls consistently show that this is welcomed. Between the general disappearance of the 11-plus and the advent of Key Stage testing, many (possibly most) parents received no such nationally benchmarked feedback until their children took GCSE examinations at sixteen—by which time it was too late to take any major remedial action.

For teachers and schools, however, the eleven-year-olds' tests are threatening and high stakes because it is on these test results that high-profile league tables are based. Children worry about them, of course, but once they are taken, they move on quickly to secondary schools that actually make little direct use of the results, preferring, in almost every case, to retest incoming pupils using their own measures. Their teachers, however, stay behind.

League tables, for primary and also for secondary schools, have become a battleground between those who regard them as reflecting, for the most part, nothing but the social origins of the student body and those who see them as a necessary part of a successful program of school improvement. For many decades English schools have been subject to regular inspections by Her Majesty's Inspectorate of Schools. Another component of the recent school reform drive has involved the enhancement of inspectors' powers, along with a new government bureaucracy, the Office for Standards in Education, which is empowered to identify "failing schools" that need to be put under "special measures." One of the indicators used to judge and grade schools is, inevitably, their performance on the Key Stage tests. Critics of the tests, and of the league tables, point to the fact that a very high proportion of the primary schools that fail inspections do indeed have poor Key Stage 2 test results but also score very highly on indexes of social disadvantage and of numbers of children for whom English is a second language. To a large extent, therefore, poor results simply reflect the school's socioeconomic situation. The only fair way to measure school performance, the critics continue, is on a value-added measure, which looks at whether a school performs better or worse than one would predict given the characteristics of its student body and other resources. Measuring, judging, and reporting performance on the basis of "raw" test scores is misleading and unjust to the schools.[8]

The response from governmental agencies and their supporters is that good numbers of schools with disadvantaged students perform very well and that, for too long, social disadvantage has served as an alibi for poor-quality schooling. The critics have now won the intellectual argument, to the extent that recent governments have made efforts to find robust and simple ways of measuring value-added—and have been largely defeated in the attempt. The testing and the league tables, meanwhile, continue as before and became even more important when Labour took over from the Conservatives in 1997. One of the retained policies was that of setting numerical targets for public sector agencies and the country as a whole (e.g., 50 percent participation in higher education, mentioned earlier). Under Labour, a precise numerical target was added, to the effect that at least 80 percent of eleven-year-olds should, by 2004, reach a particular level of attainment in mathematics and English.[9] Moreover, to help ensure this, the government intervened yet more directly in the classroom. The Thatcher reforms had set a national curriculum and defined levels and objectives through externally set tests. To this, Labour added the "numeracy hour" and the "literacy hour," which set out, for primary teachers, exactly how they should teach, from the nature of the materials to the percentage of time to be spent on whole-class direct exposition as compared with other methods. Though never legally compulsory, it was only a very brave and confident head teacher who could hold out against implementation; and while novelists and writers railed against the mechanistic view of language teaching this implied, politicians could, again, point to general public support for reforms that emphasized getting the "basics" right for everyone. At the secondary level, meanwhile, the compulsory Key Stage 3 tests have retained a fairly low profile, with attention, and teacher anxiety, centered on the league tables that rank schools by pupil success in the GCSE examinations.

These reforms have certainly revolutionized the governance of English education and the orientation and practice of the classroom teacher, but have they done anything for the quality of children's learning? There has been clearly rising performance on some tests (but also a lot of teaching to the test), similarly rising performance in international surveys, and more time in primary schools spent on basic skills, but there is also evidence from some regional/local data of far more modest improvements than the government tests imply and sometimes no change at all. My own judgment is that there has been some genuine improvement in eleven year olds' reading and math skills, though less than the official statistics imply and with some real costs. The effects are clearest in the primary schools, where there are now no traces left of old-style "progressivism" and where the final years, in particular, are almost entirely directed toward preparing for the Key Stage 2 tests taken in year six. Teachers study the content of past papers obsessively and drill children on particular types of questions. When the Qualifications and Curriculum Authority announced that it had developed national curriculum–calibrated tests applicable in years three, four, and five (i.e., the years between the two formal testing years), almost every school in the country requested a set. Key Stage 2 results show an enormous increase in the proportion of children achieving a given level. Some of this improvement is probably genuine—but much of it almost certainly reflects the familiar, well-known syndrome of teaching to the test. Old-style "progressivism" has vanished.

At the secondary school level, the effects have been less dramatic but possibly more insidious, in the sense that particular groups of students have been adversely affected. The importance, for English pupils, of public examinations at ages sixteen and eighteen predates by decades the school reforms discussed here. There has been a steady and continuing upsurge, throughout the past half century, in the number of entries and certificates obtained by young people, but this has happened everywhere. It can be accounted for easily enough by the expansion of universities and the growing importance of education in the labor market, with no need to invoke the government's centralizing drive for school reform.

What is true, however, is that the publicity afforded to a school's examination performance puts a low-performing school in a spotlight that can make it extraordinarily difficult for the school to attract a balanced intake of pupils and very easy for it to spiral even further downward. Parents may fully understand that a school's performance is not in any obvious way its "fault," but they are also quite clear that they want their own children to attend high-achieving schools that are relatively trouble free. Some schools can and do reverse an apparent downward trend, but many are unable to, and their staff become increasingly demoralized. In recent years influential voices in central government have argued that any school can succeed and that it is simply a matter of "leadership." This belief led to a policy of parachuting "super-heads" into "failing" schools, a policy that demonstrably, and sometimes dramatically, failed on virtually every occasion it was tried.

Another more general problem attaches to the way in which league table statistics are calculated. Labour, a party addicted to numerical targets in every area of public policy, has placed special emphasis on increasing the number of pupils obtaining at least five GCSE passes at grades A–C. (Although a GCSE pass grade runs from A through E, the labor market and universities—and indeed pupils themselves—draw a clear distinction between A–C and D–E.) The result has been to focus school attention on pupils for whom this is a viable goal (Gillborn & Youdell, 2000). The proportion of the cohort attaining at least five A–C grades has increased (and is now around 50 percent), and the proportion attaining only three or four A–C passes has decreased. Conversely and significantly, the proportion of pupils who attain only very low grades (Ds and Es) has not shrunk at all, indicating the lack of incentive for schools to concentrate efforts on this group. The same pressures have encouraged schools to enter pupils for syllabi that are relatively easy; hence, the most academic mathematics syllabus has seen its numbers of entrants reduced by half in favor of an easier option, which precludes an A grade but offers a B or C and so meets the league table requirements (Tikly & Wolf, 2000).

If one interrogates senior policy makers—whether politicians, advisers, commentators, or senior officials—many will, today, express a belief that centralization, targets, and league tables have run their course as a means to improvement and that more independence must be restored to schools. However, there is no sign, to date, of any genuine relaxation of central control over the content of the curriculum or its assessment. Instead, central government continues to pronounce on the smallest details of curriculum and examining while still embracing the principles of school autonomy and parental choice, to which we now turn.

Parental Choice, School Autonomy, and Competition in the Context of Centralization

One of the most intriguing and curious aspects of English school reform over the last fifteen years is that it has combined an enormous faith in the ability of central government to safeguard and raise education standards with a very different approach to improving quality: parental choice, school autonomy, and competition. Whereas both major political parties have been equally enthusiastic about the centralization of the curriculum and the use of targets and testing for accountability, this second strand of reform is more associated with the Conservative governments of the 1980s and 1990s. However, the Labour governments that followed have not reversed these reforms to any significant degree and, indeed, recently have become increasingly sympathetic toward their underlying premise.

The themes of "markets" and "choice," notably in the privatization of public utilities, were characteristic of much of the Conservative public sector policy in the Thatcher years. The ideology was then generalized to education, though with some specific additions. Most members of the Conservative Party had never been convinced that the grammar schools should be abolished and, as we have seen, viewed much of local government as irresponsible, extremist, determined to undermine economic recovery, and an obstacle to raising standards in education. A variant of the privatization being implemented in other public sector activities could, they concluded, bypass LEAs and improve standards across the whole system. If parents could choose their schools and if funds followed the pupils, then good schools would reap rewards, but there also would be immediate pressure brought to bear on less well-performing schools to raise their standards. The very worst might close, but overall a virtuous circle would be established. As long as local authorities controlled school entry, however, and told parents where they might send their children, there was no incentive for standards to rise. On the contrary, tax money was maintaining a classic wasteful monopoly, as evidenced by the perilous state of pupils' performance.

English schools have always been relatively autonomous by European (and indeed global) standards, in that most major administrative decisions lie with the head teacher and the school's "governing body," which operates rather like a company board or university council. However, by the 1970s governing bodies were dominated increasingly by members nominated by, and answerable to, local councils and the local authority bureaucracy. The first moves to reverse this came, as with so much of the reform movement, during the Callaghan (Labour) government of the mid-1970s. It commissioned a report (the Taylor Report) that suggested that governing bodies should in future give equal weight to representatives of the LEA, parents, staff, and the local community, a recommendation that was welcome to none of the local authorities or local government party caucuses. Labour offered a watered-down version of the proposals, lost office before they could be enacted, and was succeeded by the first Thatcher government, which duly and quickly moved to reorganize governing bodies on Taylor Report lines (Sharp, 2002).

The change was very popular with schools themselves; even more so were the changes that followed, which devolved ever-increasing parts of the education budget directly to schools. Devolved budgets have also been accepted, and indeed taken yet further, by recent Labour ministers, so that English schools now control more of their budgets directly than those of almost any other developed country.

This part of the reforms has remained popular and appears to be successful. In spite of fears to the contrary, schools manage their finances with very few serious problems.

The powers of LEAs have, commensurately, shrunk. By the late 1980s legislation made it clear that the governing body, and not the LEA, is the senior partner in relation to the individual school. The areas where LEAs retain major independent responsibilities have shrunk to dealing with "special needs" (including pupils excluded for disruptive behavior), major building works (including building new schools and, occasionally, closing failed ones), and a few cross-school programs such as library and music services. In the final days of the pre-1997 Conservative governments, individual schools were being strongly encouraged to opt out of LEA control altogether and become "grant maintained," with their funding coming directly from the center and bypassing LEAs altogether.[10] The days when an LEA could develop a new syllabus and negotiate its public examination and certification are gone. The examination boards themselves are regulated and controlled by central agencies to an unprecedented degree and are allowed to offer only a limited number of options, all of which must comply with national curriculum requirements.

In addition to reducing the powers of the local authorities, successive governments have also taken repeated steps to break up the uniform nature of secondary education, reflecting the conviction that a (uniform) comprehensive model had failed. The first steps in this direction were taken in 1980, when the Thatcher government introduced the "Assisted Places" scheme to enable pupils to benefit from education in independent schools at state expense. The size of the scheme was limited mostly by the cash available and, to a limited degree, by the willingness of independent schools to receive state-educated pupils; but in essence, the idea was to make it possible for academically able children from poor families to attend selective, fee-charging secondary schools. The scheme was, not surprisingly, much disliked by state schools that lost high-achieving pupils and was loathed by much of the Labour Party. Evaluations of the scheme indicated that many of the beneficiaries were from rather well-educated backgrounds and, in a good number of cases, were the children of divorced parents who had managed to get the child's eligibility assessed on the basis of one parental income only (Edwards, Fitz, & Whitty, 1989). The scheme was abolished by the incoming Labour government in 1997, but the Conservatives' underlying hostility to uniform standardized secondary provision was one that much of the Labour government now shares.

Another Conservative innovation that Labour retained was the City Technology Colleges (CTCs). Again, the idea was to create distinctive and highly desirable secondary schools, this time within the state sector. The CTCs, established with a national administrative office completely outside the LEA structure, could select their student body on the grounds of interest but not ability and were originally expected to attract large amounts of private business funding. In effect, most of their (preferential) funding came from the state, and their numbers remain small. But they are very oversubscribed, and their symbolic importance, as a clear break with the idea of the universal, neighborhood comprehensive, has been enormous (Walford, 2000). CTCs do appear to produce somewhat better academic results than other schools with students from similar backgrounds in terms of family income and prior attainment.

Although the Labour Party has officially opposed any form of academic selection, it not only shares the school reform movement's general antipathy to LEAs and belief in parental choice but also is increasingly determined to create greater diversity at the secondary level. To date, this has been accompanied by only very small changes in national curriculum requirements, which effectively dictate and standardize teaching content up to age sixteen. However, Labour has widened the general philosophy of CTCs by introducing the idea of "specialist schools," which again attract additional funding on the basis of a successful bid—of course, to central government—to specialize in a particular area such as languages, music, science, or technology. The purpose is to offer something more than what one former Labour minister, in a widely reported speech, dubbed the "bog-standard comprehensive."[11]

All these changes were expected to improve education because of the virtuous circle of parental choice outlined earlier. Parents, it was emphasized again and again, were entitled to know about their children's schools and performance; they were entitled to choose a school that would suit their children; and by exerting that choice they would reward and encourage success. The proponents of this argument were (for the most part) perfectly sincere, but they also displayed a remarkable reluctance to think through how this would actually operate in practice. Schools, after all, are made of expensive and inflexible bricks and mortar, with teaching forces, classes, and timetables that cannot expand and contract continually on a year-by-year basis. Right there, the analogy with most marketplace goods breaks down.

Parents have certainly availed themselves of the right to choose a school and, especially in urban areas, spend enormous amounts of time and energy considering their selection and worrying about what they will actually be offered. Although geographical proximity continues to play some role in school admissions, it is now quite tightly circumscribed; moreover, a sibling in the school does not guarantee admission. Schools are not allowed to select on ability, but they are allowed to use criteria related to interest and affinity to the school's culture (which can include religion). Many parents suspect that, in practice, a child's academic ability does play a role.

Because success breeds success, some schools are enormously oversubscribed, and others are shunned by parents—and, because funding is related to enrollment, schools with low enrollment find it ever harder to provide an adequate program or retain good staff. A very few "failing" schools have closed, but most limp on. Appeals against admissions decisions have soared. Many commentators predicted that school choice would enormously benefit the middle classes, that they would be the ones to avail themselves of it (at the expense of poorer and less educated families), and that social segregation in schools would increase as a result (see, e.g., Ball, 2003). The evidence suggests nothing quite so clear-cut. Although the right to choose is a national one, in a good many places it remains a hypothetical option; there is only one school within reach, particularly at the secondary level. Conversely, in urban areas, poorer and immigrant parents also take the choice of schools very seriously and refer to the league tables in doing so. The degree to which social segregation has actually increased is hotly debated, but on balance the evidence suggests that there has been some increase—but less than many predicted and not in all areas (see, e.g., Gorard, Fitz, & Taylor, 2001; Noden, 2000.) Whether choice has done anything for overall standards is anyone's guess, but in the present climate *choice* and *variety* seem likely to remain the watchwords of government education policy, at least until the next ideological upheaval among the English policy-making classes.

CONCLUSION

In some respects, notably its concern with "choice," England's school reform movement reflects more general ideological trends apparent not just in the English-speaking world but more generally.[12] The major changes, however, have been associated less with parental choice than with wholesale and continuing centralization of powers. Because "school choice" reforms all imply decentralization, the two general reform strands might seem diametrically opposed to each other. There is, however, a common theme that unites the two: namely, the undermining of local authorities, and indeed of any formal institutions set between individual schools and parents on the one hand and central government on the other.

It is also worth emphasizing that reform has been driven far more by concerns over the country's economic performance than by recent social changes, even though these have been profound. All political parties are preoccupied with the contribution of education to the economy and the need for skills. It is in this context that a cross-party consensus developed to the effect that standards of education were poor and wide-scale reform was necessary. In recent years, emphasis has moved from all children in primary schools to lower-achieving students at the secondary level. But the basic concerns and, therefore, the forces underlying school reform remain intact. Indeed, the next target has been identified in the form of yet another wholesale change.[13]

NOTES

1. This chapter is about England and not about the United Kingdom. Scotland's education system has always been different from England's, and, since the first Blair government-enacted devolution and the first Scottish Parliament since the 1707 Act of Union was elected, it has been diverging even further. The education system of Northern Ireland has also, historically, been somewhat different from that of England. It has, until now, retained selection

at age eleven and in effect runs two parallel systems of state-funded Catholic and state-funded Protestant schools. Finally, Wales, until recently, operated a system that was more or less identical to England's, with the exception that Welsh-medium or bilingual schooling is provided in Welsh-speaking areas of the country. Here, too, devolution is leading to a widening gap, which is as much about asserting national identity as it is about differences over school reform.

2. Before the war, a large proportion of pupils remained in upper elementary classes until they left school altogether at age fourteen, as opposed to moving to a separate secondary school. The system introduced in 1945 was in principle tripartite, with grammar, technical, and modern schools; but only a few technical schools were ever opened, and most of these had, by the 1960s, either closed or been absorbed into further education colleges and shed their classes for eleven- to sixteen-year-olds (Sanderson, 1994; Stanton & Richardson, 1997).

3. The exception is in elections to the new Scottish Parliament, which has a complex proportional representation plus "list" system (whereby some members of a party obtain seats on the basis of and in proportion to the total number of votes cast for that party by the whole electorate; these seats are allocated in the order in which candidates appear on the party's list).

4. A few state-operated institutions do still survive and are the focus of continued political controversy.

5. At this period, the examinations were O levels or Certificates in Secondary Education, the precursors of today's GCSEs.

6. As noted earlier, LEAs are now coterminous with general local authorities and under the authority of their elected councilors, though this was not always the case. One major exception, until its abolition by the Conservatives, was the Inner London Education Authority, which covered the whole area of the old London County Council, before the latter's replacement postwar with separate borough councils (e.g., Southwark, Westminster, Hackney). However, these boroughs did not run education, and a directly elected Inner London Education Authority remained; following its abolition, the boroughs became LEAs.

7. For a history of these distinctive organizations, see Petch (1953) and Wolf (2002b).

8. There is a considerable literature both on the intellectual case for "value added" and on the technical issues associated with it. The technical literature emphasizes that estimates of value added must be reported with standard errors, showing that the precise value lies within a range; once this is done, it becomes clear that, for many schools, the apparent differences do not in fact reach statistical significance. Within a school there also may be major differences among classes, teachers, and subjects in the amount of value added found. (The way in which a school's position in a league table

may fluctuate widely from year to year—especially those with quite small numbers of students per class—has made English schools increasingly aware, at a practical level, of some of the basic aspects of statistical sampling!) These findings emphasize the need for individual pupil–level data (with attainment scores from at least two points in time). For an overview of the issues, both substantive and technical, a good starting point is the work of Harvey Goldstein; see, e.g., Goldstein & Sammons (1997), Goldstein & Spiegelhalter (1996), Goldstein & Thomas (1995, 1996), and Goldstein et al. (2000). See also Goldstein's home page for a regularly updated discussion of the issues (go to www.ioe.ac.uk and follow links).

9. The level of attainment is level 4 of the national curriculum, which was originally set as the average (median) attainment level for eleven-year-olds. The Key Stage tests are, as noted earlier, marked and reported in terms of attainment of a particular level, typically at age seven (Key Stage 1) and at age eleven (Key Stages 3, 4, or 5).

10. The number of schools that had actually opted out in this way was fairly small at the time that the incoming Labour government reversed the policy. It is unclear how many of those opting out did so out of a strong desire for yet more independence; there also were strong financial benefits to opting out. The policy created particular problems for LEAs with overcapacity because schools that felt that they might be merged, be closed down, or lose their sixth forms (sixteen- to eighteen-year-olds) were especially likely to start the process of obtaining "grant-maintained" status.

11. The speaker was Estelle Morris, in a 2002 speech that met with widespread criticism. She resigned from office later that year, for unrelated reasons.

12. Sweden, for example, has been strongly influenced by such arguments.

13. A major government inquiry under Mike Tomlinson is currently examining ways to move to a new system. For information, see the Department for Education and Skills Web site (http://dfes.gov.uk).

REFERENCES CITED

Aldrich, R. (Ed.). (2002). *A century of education*. London: RoutledgeFalmer.

Ball, S. (2003). *Class stratification and the education market: The middle class and social advantage*. London: RoutledgeFalmer.

Barnett, C. (1986). *The audit of war: The illusion and reality of Britain as a great nation*. London: Macmillan.

Blanden, J., Goodman, A., Gregg, P., & Machin, S. (In press). Changes in intergenerational mobility in Britain. In M. Corak (Ed.), *Generational income mobility in North America and Europe*. Cambridge: Cambridge University Press.

Callaghan, J. (1976, October 22). Towards a national debate (the prime minister's Ruskin speech). *Education, 332–33.*

Dennis, N. (2001). *The uncertain trumpet: A history of Church of England school education to AD 2001.* London: Civitas.

Department for Education and Skills. (2003). *The future of higher education.* London: Department for Education and Skills.

Edwards, T., Fitz, J., & Whitty, G. (1989). *The state and private education: An evaluation of the assisted places scheme.* London: Falmer.

Gillborn, D., & Youdell, D. (2000). *Rationing education: Policy, practice, reforms and equity.* Buckingham: Open University Press.

Goldstein, H., Huiqi, P., Rath, T., & Hill, N. (2000). *The use of value added information in judging school performance.* Perspectives on Education Policy No. 40. London: Institute of Education.

Goldstein, H., & Sammons, P. (1997). The influence of secondary and junior schools on sixteen year examination performance: A cross-classified multilevel analysis. *School Effectiveness and School Improvement, 8* (2), 219–30.

Goldstein, H., & Spiegelhalter, D. (1996). League tables and their limitations: Statistical issues in comparisons of institutional performance. *Journal of Royal Statistical Society, 159* (3), 385–443.

Goldstein, H., & Thomas, S. (1995). School effectiveness and "value-added" analysis. *Forum, 37* (2), 36–38.

———. (1996). Using examination results as indicators of school and college performance. *Journal of Royal Statistical Society, 159* (1), 149–63.

Gorard, S., Fitz, J., & Taylor, C. (2001). School choice impacts: What do we know? *Educational Researcher, 30* (7), 18–23.

Gordon, P., Aldrich, R., & Dean, D. (1991). *Education and policy in England in the twentieth century.* London: Woburn Press.

Jenkins, E. W. (Ed.). (1995). *Studies in the history of education: Essays presented to Peter Gosden.* Leeds: Leeds University Press.

Kogan, M. (1971). *The politics of education.* Harmondsworth: Penguin.

Noden, P. (2000). Rediscovering the impact of marketisation. *British Journal of Sociology of Education, 21* (3), 371–90.

Organization for Economic Cooperation and Development. (2002). *Education at a glance.* Paris: Organization for Economic Cooperation and Development.

Petch, J. A. (1953). *Fifty years of examining.* London: Harrap.

Phillips, R., & Furlong, J. (2001). Education, reform and the state: Twenty-five years of politics, policy and practice. London: RoutledgeFalmer.

Plowden, B. (1967). *Children and their primary schools.* London: HMSO.

Prais, S. J. (1995). *Productivity, education and training: An international perspective.* Cambridge: Cambridge University Press.

Sanderson, M. (1994). *The missing stratum: Technical school education in England, 1900–1990s.* London: Atholone Press.

————. (1999). *Education and economic decline in Britain, 1870 to the 1990s*. Cambridge: Cambridge University Press.

Sharp, P. (2002). Central and local government. In R. Aldrich (Ed.), *A century of education* (pp. 93–116). London: RoutledgeFalmer.

Stanton, G., & Richardson, W. (Eds.). (1997). *Qualifications for the future*. London: Further Education Development Agency.

Thatcher, M. (1993). *The Downing Street years*. London: HarperCollins.

Tikly, C., & Wolf, A. (2000). *The mathematics we need now: Demands, deficits and remedies*. London: Institute of Education.

Walford, G. (2000). From City Technology Colleges to sponsored grant-maintained schools. *Oxford Review of Education, 26* (2), 145–58.

West, E. (1970). *Education and the state*. London: Institute of Economic Affairs.

Wolf, A. (2002a). *Does education matter? Myths about education and economic growth*. London: Penguin.

————. (2002b). Qualifications and assessment. In R. Aldrich (Ed.), *A century of education* (pp. 206–27). London: RoutledgeFalmer.

15

Australia: The Challenges of Poverty, Pedagogy, and Pathways

Allan Luke

> I forget what I was taught. I only remember what I have learnt.
>
> —Patrick White (1912–90)

THE STATE OF AUSTRALIAN EDUCATION

This discussion analyzes the state of Australian education, with illustrations drawn from the context of Queensland state education. In so doing, I want to develop three broad claims about the challenges facing Australian education, which roughly focus on the early, middle, and senior years of schooling:

1. The principal problems facing educators and systems in the early years are the powerful effects of *poverty,* in both its most historically persistent forms and those that are emergent in communities experiencing both structural economic change and increasing diversity of the population, in what we could term the new Australia, for want of better words.
2. As the consequential effects of poverty wash through schools and systems at all levels, the principal challenge in the middle years is that of *pedagogy,* the building of new educational practices that

might begin to turn around the educational performance of the
significant percentage of youth who begin to disaffiliate with formal education and other social institutions in these years.
3. The major issue facing the secondary school is that of *pathways,*
   where the state at large is struggling to articulate and enable new
   pathways from school to work and further education in the face
   of the very new economic conditions and forms of cultural identity, practice, and affiliation noted earlier.

I will make the polemical claim that Australian schools are in effect
serving the social and economic interests of slightly more than half of
all Australian youth—despite over a decade of major and costly attempts at policy and curriculum revision, market-based reform, and attempts to apply business-management techniques to school systems.

My purpose is to ask how education systems can respond to conditions "after the marketplace." I believe that we can now assess the
legacy of the last decade of neoliberal and liberal reforms: The sum total of reforms has left us all dressed up with multiple outcomes, volu-
minous new curriculum documents, a de facto national testing system,
and school-based management—but without a strong normative vision
or set of criteria based on principles that are fundamental to a just and
powerful education system in new economic and social conditions.

It is important to begin by acknowledging the many educators envisioning and driving reform across Australian education: teachers
strongly focused on pedagogy in classrooms; civil servants and education bureaucrats working across the education system in what are difficult conditions for many—because their work is invisible to those
outside civil service culture, largely disrespected by the teaching workforce and unions, and rarely acknowledged in education research; and
those politicians who are deeply committed to understanding these
dilemmas, generating innovative responses to the problems, and in effect reinventing Australian education. In most Australian states, the
major policy settings for "reform" have been in place for some years.
These consist of (1) standardized achievement testing in literacy and
numeracy at key junctures in schooling; (2) the ongoing updating and
implementation of curriculum documents; and (3) school-based management, whereby principals can make semiautonomous decisions

about school programming, structures, and procedures, ostensibly to ensure the improvement of (1) and the better implementation of (2). The effects of this approach are compounded and, perhaps, confounded by the emergence of powerful market forces, with the Catholic and independent sectors differentially funded but less explicitly regulated in terms of testing performance and curriculum compliance. Though on different timelines in various states, this general suite of reforms has evolved for a decade. Let me return to the three propositions about the state of Australian education.

On Poverty in Early Childhood

My first claim is that there is no general basic skills crisis in early childhood. Rather, family material conditions, social relations, and communication patterns are in historical transition. That transition is strongly influenced by both residual and emergent forms of poverty—both those persistent forms of class and cultural inequality that have plagued us throughout our history among indigenous, migrant, and working-class communities and those that are arising in the new Australian economy.

By recent estimates, 20 percent of Queensland children are from families living at or below the nominal Henderson poverty line (Education Queensland, 1999). Poverty is increasingly concentrated in new migrant communities, indigenous communities, and emergent "edge-cities," the cheap mortgage belts surrounding capital and provincial cities. As early as the preliminary studies for *Education 2010* (Education Queensland, 1999), it was clear that specific zones of concentrated poverty required urgent cross-governmental action and, moreover, much stronger coordination of community-based capital, the reconstruction of social infrastructure, and the enlistment of private sector resources. At the same time, the new suburban poor have high degrees of mobility and transience, with families shifting residence in search of work. One edge-city, predominantly white school that I visited had successfully implemented an early intervention reading/literacy program, only to have a 60 percent turnover between years three and six. This hindered the establishment of sustainable effects through any "single-shot" grade-level intervention.

Moreover, the school system itself is becoming more stratified because of a significant movement of students from state to nonstate schools, a trend that has been encouraged by increased federal government subsidies to the nonstate sector. If the current trend continues, the risk is that by 2010 we will have a state school system in which as few as 50 percent of Queensland children are enrolled, and these children will come primarily from working-class or poor families who cannot afford independent or private schooling.

In this demographic reality, there have been some gains in average test scores. According to the face-to-face individual diagnostics undertaken by year-two teachers, 72 percent of this same student cohort was experiencing some difficulty with early reading and language (Education Queensland, 2002). Nonetheless, by later in year three, 90 percent of these same children have achieved the state "benchmark" for functional decoding in the year-three testing system (Ministerial Council on Education, Employment, Training and Youth Affairs, 2001). Both of these instruments have their limitations. The former has reasonable levels of contextual and content validity, but overall validity is only as good as that which can be achieved through loose systems of teacher diagnosis. The latter is based on an arbitrary "cut point" for establishing the benchmark. If we disaggregate the data by location, we find that the concentration of reading failure is in those specific zones noted earlier. This finding again demonstrates the powerful connection between early achievement differentials and concentrated poverty.

As part of a richer analysis, this would suggest that although a simple testing/phonics emphasis might push some specific test-score achievement up, as it has in some states, it is at best only a partial strategy. Certainly, this has been the experience in Tasmania and other states. At worst, it may be a misgauged response in a system where teachers are actually moving 90 percent of the student population to what are nominally basic reading levels in the first three years of instruction but where those skills contribute very little to subsequent achievement as the demands become more complex. Basic skills levels and instructional efficacy—as much as they might appeal to the "back to basics" advocates—may not be the problem, or the solution, to sustainable gains for the lower quartile of the student cohort.

We could triangulate these data with the largest-scale analytic study of early home/school transitions for lower socioeconomic and ethnic minority children in Queensland. Freebody, Ludwig, and Gunn (1996), who observed home literacy and classroom events over an extended period and found that the problem was more complex than the typical attribution of school achievement problems to "deficit parenting." Their finding confirms aspects of the now classical match/mismatch hypothesis: Successful students who come from English-as-a-first language, school-like interactional environments are better primed to succeed in school-based interaction. But they also offer a startling and extremely unsettling finding: Early school instruction tends to be intellectually trivial and cognitively low level—more focused on classroom management of behavior and body, on teaching children procedural routines for school and lesson work, including worksheets, than on in-depth knowledge and skill development. Their point is that the curricular and interactional norms of schools where benchmarks of "success" were being defined and assessed were of dubious educational value.

Taken together, using both quantitative and qualitative methodology, blending teacher judgment data, psychometric (testing) data, and large-scale analytic work, we can set the grounds for a very different analysis and a potentially more powerful policy approach than blanket test-driven endorsements of standardized programs. First, this suggests the need for a community-targeted government strategy for intervening in concentrated poverty—one that would attempt to coordinate a range of available capital in communities (Luke, 2003). Second, it suggests that effective pedagogical reform may not reside primarily in the need for packaged, standardized commodities for the teaching of basic skills. Indeed, such an approach might misdirect scarce resources. This is especially the case if the problem in achieving cognitive depth is in fact exacerbated by a basic skills orientation. It is this latter concern that turns up again in studies of the middle years.

On Pedagogy in the Middle Years

There are other key findings in the 2001 round of literacy testing. First, there is evidence that year-five performance is lower in absolute terms than current year-three performance. Although we have no longitudinal cohort data, which makes "value-added" studies difficult and problematic, we could hypothesize that this is an instance of a trend, the fifth grade slump that has been broadly depicted in reading surveys in the United States. That is, early gains in reading and literacy established through intervention tend to decline as we move toward the middle years of schooling.

There is a range of possible explanations for "slump" data. The Freebody, Ludwig, and Gunn (1996) study was broadly corroborated by the Queensland School Longitudinal Restructuring Study (Lingard et al., 2002). That study was the largest observational study of classroom practice in Australian educational history, with the coding of 1,000 classrooms at key junctures of schooling. Among other results, it found that levels of "productive pedagogies" were low, with a visible slump in the categories of intellectual demand in the middle years. Lingard and colleagues argue that this is a major impediment to educational achievement and outcomes, particularly among lower-achieving students. Both studies, then, suggest a very different policy challenge than the remediation of basic skills and its common companion, the standardization of teacher behavior as a means to ensure basic skill delivery (Luke, 2004). The policy challenge highlighted by these accounts is to develop forms of pedagogy that encourage in-depth knowledge, complex technical skills, and an understanding of substantive disciplines that can generate sustainable improvement in student achievement.

In a recent national study of literacy and numeracy in the middle years of schooling (Luke et al., 2003), we also see that there are unresolved issues in pedagogical depth and quality. This problem appears to create the single biggest impediment to the translation of many of the significant gains of the middle years reforms (e.g., better social and psychological ethics of care, higher retention and student motivation, more relevant curriculum) into improved achievement and different life pathways, especially among the lower-performing groups and cohorts. Yet even if we succeed modestly at changing the quality of pedagogy in the middle years, serious questions have been raised about the continued relevance and longitudinal effects of senior schooling for many students.

On Pathways from School to the New Economy

In the last five years, all Australian states have conducted various studies on pathways from school into further education and work. The secondary school retention rates of students generally have been in decline nationally. The overall percentage of Queenslanders who complete twelve years of schooling is 67 percent, with an apparent retention of about 74 percent from years eight to twelve (Education Queensland, 2002). Roughly one-quarter of the potential school-completion cohort, therefore, has left school, and governments generally have very limited tracking data on the life pathways of these students. Many of these students simply "disappear from the screen" of social analysis, turning up variously in data sets maintained by health, police services, unemployment, and social welfare agencies. However, governments, much less education systems, have very little rigorous empirical sense of who these youth are, how they get from institution to institution, or how and when they depart from these systems altogether.

My interpretation of the data on those who remain suggests that between one-fifth and one-third are struggling to reach levels of achievement that would secure ready pathways to further education or employment. In the case of Queensland, this situation has led to two major reports by Pitman (2003) and Gardner (2002) and a series of proposed training reforms that extend the mandatory age of schooling, a move also announced in South Australia. The Pitman study in particular calls for a fundamental rethinking of the senior school. The senior system remains strongly geared to binary tracks that lead to traditional university entry on the one hand, and vocational education on the other. Yet we could ask whether this system has become dysfunctional, with almost half of the overall cohort either underprovided for or leaving.

Beginning from these data, and considering the case-based work on youth of Pitman and others, I would offer a broader interpretation: The institutions of schooling are struggling to adjust to the new multiple pathways from school, not only to further study and work but to unemployment, poverty, and marginalization as well. There is, of course, considerable infrastructure and investment in the current system, in curriculum reform, and in high-stakes examinations and matriculation assessment. Yet to begin to redevelop systems of secondary assessment and high-stakes pathways also requires high-profile public leadership.

From the data that we do have available, though, it appears that the education system maintains a dual route from school to work that was designed for a more stable employment market, with traditional, separate pathways through high-stakes assessment systems to university studies and to vocational training. At the same time, there is evidence that the school/further education/work pathways are becoming more flexible, with up to half the entering cohorts of many universities composed of students who have not followed traditional routes, a considerable number of university graduates engaged in vocational training, and many retrenched workers increasingly seeking to meet retraining requirements. In that process, somewhere between one-quarter and one-half of the cohort is "lost," with systems lacking a definitive sense of how, where, and to what ends. This is not exclusively an Australian phenomenon but, instead, reflects broader trends among the developed workforces in Organization for Economic Cooperation and Development countries.

THE NEW AUSTRALIA

The narrative that I have developed here is partial, raising many areas for further research and development. It suggests that schooling is struggling to come to grips with the new Australia, with its culturally and linguistically diverse population, with its volatile economy characterized by new and concentrated stratifications of wealth and poverty, and with new pathways from school to work, community, and civic life. This is a troubling and complex picture. But I believe that it belies, rather than reinforces, the capacity of the quick fixes offered by the testing, basic skills, and accountability models advocated in the approaches to education policy I have critiqued here. Just as medical models are limited in their power to analyze and treat complex social, cultural, and economic problems, hypodermic models of educational treatment ultimately have only limited medium- to long-term efficacy.

To find productive policy alternatives would require that we anticipate the limits of particular interventions (e.g., early intervention models, phonics programs) when their articulation is not related to a broader set of systemic approaches to social policy. An education project will work only if it is conceptualized within a broader social policy that brings together government and community-based resources systematically to address issues of changing demographic patterns and available community capital of all kinds—social, economic, and ecological. This broader agenda would direct us toward professional interventions that could begin to have an impact on achievement gains through a focus on pedagogy and curriculum within the school. It will demand the reinvention of relations among educational institutions that heretofore have operated autonomously, from child care, to schools, to adult education. And it will require a sociological imagination capable of envisioning, designing, and realizing new student pathways that are facilitated by these institutions and are designed to meet the needs of the new economy. We need to move toward a richer, more multidisciplinary approach to educational analysis and policy development—something beyond the crude league tables and single-dimension test-score analyses.

At present, most Australian states are "aligning their curricula"— mapping *existing* instructional materials against national "benchmarks" and "competencies." That approach is comparable to putting a 1980s Holden engine in a 1990s Falcon body, with a mid-1970s Nissan chassis; it cannot address the new economics, new skills, and new cultural contingencies that confront educators, parents, and systems. We need to think five to ten years out. We need to align—from scratch if necessary—curriculum, pedagogy, and assessment/reporting, to do the job in a way that will allow teachers, students, and communities to get on with the job.

The orientation of piling on a lot of tests and asking teachers to do more and more is becoming quite dysfunctional. Though few educators and researchers would disagree with the need for interstate curricular coherence, public accountability, and systems of assessment, the descriptions of literacy curriculum benchmarks to date are at best problematic in their capacity to encompass the broad range of curriculum reforms undertaken by Australian educators. At the same time, there is little international evidence that national or statewide testing systems per se will lead to improvements in instructional effectiveness, innovation, or student achievement. The point is that the translation of the former into the latter—benchmarks into testing—puts at risk innovations in instruction, curriculum, and assessment.

There is also a risk that the limitations of the benchmarks will become major liabilities for the education system—that minimum requirements will become maximum expectations. Teachers, for example, who at present might be observing students for a range of language competencies and practices (problem solving, higher-order thinking, use of critical reading as a resource for writing) might find themselves testing and teaching for simple proficiency with conjunctions and prepositions. That is the case in many jurisdictions in the United States, where "what can be tested" has become the major driving force in determining what counts as literacy in classrooms and communities. Where this is the case, benchmarks and affiliated assessment practices could narrow and limit the capacity of teachers and school communities to adjust to the challenges of new workplaces and new technologies. It would be a tragedy if twenty years of innovation in curriculum, instruction, and assessment were discarded in favor of national benchmarks and standardized testing.

We are about to have the largest generational change in our education system since World War II: Between 2005 and 2010, 50 percent of our teachers and 70 percent of education administrators will be leaving the school system. We have to ask ourselves if we want to rely on a state-of-the-art 1980s system, a set of curriculum documents that takes students and prepares them for an economy that does not exist anymore, and a lot of American-style tests, or if we are going to have the debate needed about the old and new educational experiences that our children will require, not for the 1980s but, instead, for 2010 and beyond.

Our education systems have struggled for over a decade to define coherent policy directions other than neoliberal competition, proliferation of outcomes and tests, and piecemeal responses to cultural and linguistic diversity that have created a welter of "add-on" and "pull-out" programs. In policy making, the evidence about changed contexts and conditions facing communities and schools, state systems, and bureaucracies needs to be placed on the table. And it is in the context of this evidence—about poverty, about new demographics and cultures, about available capital in social fields, about life pathways, about fair and unfair patterns of access and employment, about changing economies and institutions—that education reform needs to be made and assessed.

At the same time, we should talk about our commitments to inclusion, to bringing voice and identity into classrooms and institutions. But strategies of educational inclusion must aim toward changed material conditions and consequences. Looking back at the postwar period, A. H. Halsey (1986) commented, "Exhortation alone is futile, whether to altruism or to tolerance or to the recognition of the equal claim of others to share in the bounty afforded by society" (p. 173). The challenge is to rebuild institutions in ways that enable changed material and social relations.

NOTE

This chapter is adapted, in part, from sections of an article published in the *Australian Educational Researcher,* 4 (2003). It also draws on discussions in *Curriculum Issues* (1998) and on Australian Broadcasting Corporation's *Lateline* (2001).

REFERENCES CITED

Education Queensland. (1999). *Education 2010.* Brisbane: Education Queensland.
———. (2002). *Destination 2010.* Brisbane: Education Queensland.
Freebody, P., Ludwig, C., & Gunn, S. (1996). *Everyday literacy practices in and out of school in low socioeconomic communities.* Brisbane: Griffith University/Department of Employment, Education and Training.
Gardner, M. (2002). *The review of pathways articulation.* Brisbane: Queensland Government.
Halsey, A. H. (1986). *Change in British society* (3d ed.). Oxford: Oxford University Press.
Lingard, R., Ladwig, J., Mills, M., Hayes, D., Bahr, M., & Chant, D. (2002). *Queensland School Longitudinal Restructuring Study.* Brisbane: Education Queensland.
Luke, A. (2003). Literacy and the other: A sociological approach to literacy research and policy in multilingual societies. *Reading Research Quarterly, 38* (1), 132–41.

————. (2004). Teaching after the market: From commodity to cosmopolitanism. *Teachers College Record.*

Luke, A., Weir, K., Dole, S., Land, R., Carrington, V., Elkins, J., Vankraayenord, C., Moni, K., Pendergast, D., Kapitzke, C., & Mayer, D. (2003). *Beyond the middle: Literacy and numeracy for at risk students in the middle years of schooling.* Canberra: DETYA.

Ministerial Council on Education, Employment, Training and Youth Affairs. (2001). *National report on schools in Australia.* Canberra: Ministerial Council on Education, Employment, Training and Youth Affairs.

Pitman, J. (2003). *The senior certificate: A new deal.* Brisbane: Queensland Government.

16

United States: America's Orgy of Reform

Peter Schrag

> Every government degenerates when trusted to the rulers of the
> people alone. The people themselves, therefore, are its only safe
> depositories, and to render even them safe, their minds must be
> improved. . . .
>
> —Thomas Jefferson (1743–1826)

"No other people ever demanded so much of schools and of education [as did the Americans]," wrote the highly regarded American historian Henry Steele Commager a half century ago: "None other was
ever so well served by its schools and its educators" ([1951]1964,
p. 546). Despite that success, and partly because of it, as Commager
also noted, the schools "have been, and are, under continuous pressure and attack" ([1951]1964, p. 548). American schools have been
charged with creating unity out of a nation of immigrants from a hun-
dred different cultures and languages and thus to perfect democracy;
to mitigate, if not eliminate, economic and social inequity; to teach safe
sex, safe driving, and the evils of alcohol, tobacco, and drugs; to provide recreation for children and sports and other entertainment for local communities; to provide first-line social services in a society whose
public health and welfare system lags far behind those of most other
industrialized nations; and now, of course, to educate children from
that great diversity of backgrounds—all of them—to a high degree of

technical and academic competence. Given the almost unbounded expectations, the attacks are hardly surprising. Two respected Stanford University scholars, David Tyack and Larry Cuban (1995), called it "tinkering toward utopia."

The great burdens of literacy, unity, and equity have been part of the schools' task since the mid-nineteenth century. But for the past two generations, and particularly in the present conservative national climate, the conventional political rhetoric has been loading virtually all social problems on the schools, as if there were no other social institutions and no need to provide them. Beneath those burdens, Americans are deeply divided about the best way to raise and educate children: between strict discipline and permissiveness; between conservative direct instruction—an emphasis on, and much drill in, phonics and math "facts" on the one hand and learning by exploration, discovery, and deduction on the other; between unforgiving high school graduation policies based on test scores and flexible approaches emphasizing continuous opportunities; and between race-blind college admission policies and race-conscious affirmative action implicitly recognizing the obstacles that poor and minority children must overcome.

It should not be surprising, therefore, that the phrase "school reform" has become a constant in the politics and policy making of American education. In 1957, after the Soviet Union beat the United States into space with the launching of the Sputnik satellite, the schools were widely attacked for their failure to train students adequately in math and science. Admiral Hyman Rickover, "the father" of the atomic submarine, and other national figures issued warnings that if the schools did not toughen their curricula, the Russians would win the Cold War. Rudolph Flesch's *Why Johnny Can't Read,* published in 1955, became a best-seller (it is still in print).[1] A generation later, in 1983, during a difficult economic stretch for the United States, a presidential commission issued a grim report, *A Nation at Risk,* warning the country that if the schools did not shape up, the Germans and the Japanese would beat America's economic brains out: "If an unfriendly foreign power had attempted to impose on America the mediocre educational performance that exists today, we might well have viewed it as an act of war. As it stands, we have allowed this to happen to ourselves. . . . We have, in effect, been committing an act of unthinking, unilateral educational disarmament" (National Commission on Excellence in Education, 1983).

These attacks, and many others, were accompanied by reports from public colleges and universities that large percentages of their entering students required remedial work they should have had in high school or before, as well as data that appeared to show the declining performance and standards of the schools—sliding scores on college admissions tests like the Scholastic Aptitude Test; on the National Assessment of Educational Progress, which has been sampling student performance since the early 1970s; on the Third International Math and Science Study (TIMSS); and on other international comparisons of academic achievement. The public rhetoric rarely mentioned the dramatic increase in college attendance and, therefore, in the test-taking population or the serious sampling flaws in the international comparisons. Each round of attacks presumed, instead, that sometime in the past there was a golden age when the schools were academically rigorous and serving both children and the larger society as they were supposed to.

No one, of course, has ever described that golden age, nor is it possible. American schools have always been ladders to opportunity in an open society, but whereas a century ago, when the economy provided countless semiskilled jobs in smokestack industries, and in the construction of railroads and urban infrastructure, they were measured by their successes—the children of immigrant tailors or butchers who became lawyers and doctors—now they are measured by their failures: dropout rates, the percentage of students who take less than three years of math or four years of language and literature in high school, those who *do not* go to college or are not adequately prepared when they get there.

The conclusion, widely echoed by legislators, businesspeople, and the media, that the schools are failing—in recent years often said in so many words—has driven almost two generations of reform—and particularly intense reform since *A Nation at Risk* in 1983. The overall tenor of those reforms has been traditional-conservative: a greater emphasis on drilling students in "the basics" in math and reading and on multiple-choice tests and so-called high-stakes accountability systems; the denial of promotion or diplomas to students who do not pass the prescribed tests; and monetary rewards for schools and teachers that raise student test scores and sanctions, including reassignment and "reconstitution," of schools that fail to do so. It has produced programs for increased "professional development"—and particularly the retraining of teachers in the new, often narrowly scripted teaching systems in reading and math that the states and many local districts have mandated. It has also generated increasing pressure on colleges of education and other teacher-training institutions to revise their own orientation to conform with the newly mandated curricula and (often paradoxically) a call for creating more routes into the profession that bypass teachers' colleges altogether.

Because the American constitutional system assigns the prime responsibility for education to the states (and, in turn, to local school districts), most of those reforms, including prescriptions of higher academic standards, have been mandated by state legislatures, state boards of education, and university admissions policies. Common among them are a minimum of four years of high school English; three years (instead of two) of math, including at least one year of algebra; three years of science; two, and preferably three, years of a foreign language; and history and government. But in the past few years, and particularly since the passage of President George W. Bush's "No Child Left Behind" (NCLB) Act in 2001, a revision of federal education legislation first enacted in the 1960s, there is now (for the first time in U.S. history) also a federal mandate requiring all states to test all children in grades three to eight in reading and math and to show annual yearly progress toward the achievement of the states' own proficiency standards. In a provision taken from similar requirements in Texas, where George W. Bush was governor before moving to the White House, such progress has to be measured not only by the scores of the school's total enrollment but by the achievement of specified economic and ethnic subgroups: Latinos, blacks, poor children, English language learners, and others. It thus seeks to force schools to pay attention to students who were often neglected before or written off as being too "disadvantaged" to achieve at a high level.

The law provides that children in schools not making such progress be allowed to transfer to any other public school at the expense (including transportation) of the child's home district; specifies that all schools serving poor children have only "highly qualified" teachers by the year 2005–6 or lose the federal funding designated for schools serving poor children; and, in the interim, requires schools to notify parents if their child's teacher is not credentialed. The law also provides federal funding for materials and teacher training in improving student reading in low-performing schools.

The requirements of NCLB, needless to say, are controversial, and their full implementation, assuming it comes, is still years off. But because the law leaves it to states to set their own definitions of proficiency toward which schools and their students must progress, the law has a powerful incentive for states to lower their own standards and avoid the costly and controversial requirement of finding places for children attending schools deemed not to be meeting their annual progress targets. And because schools have to show annual progress for all subgroups, the system faces growing criticism from local schools that the criteria unfairly penalize schools where most groups improve but one slips back, perhaps because of an influx of immigrants. Indeed, because the law requires that schools show progress for each succeeding year—not the growth of students over time—schools that get new groups of immigrants every year will find it nearly impossible to meet the standards (Winerip, 2003). More important, the federal government has not provided the funding promised in the original bill, and virtually all states are themselves facing severe budgetary crises in the early years of the new century. Therefore, the chances of complete implementation of the law become even more uncertain, especially the very expensive mandate of getting "highly qualified teachers" in every classroom serving poor children or reasonably defining what such teachers need.

Yet, long before the federal law was enacted, the states themselves, responding to *A Nation at Risk,* the apparent decline in test scores in the 1970s, and complaints from businesspeople and others about the gaps in the skills and knowledge of high school graduates, enacted reform after reform: the tests; the increased course requirements needed to graduate from high school; the pressure to require more homework; the attempts to phase out the practice of "social promotion," which moved students from grade to grade with only minimal attention to their ability to do the required work; the pressure to raise standards for teacher training and licensing; and the continual introduction of new education programs. Inevitably, those reforms produced intense academic and political controversies—which in the United States often reach a high pitch of emotion—that echoed old debates about the best way to teach reading or math; about whether so-called high-stakes testing increases cheating, narrows the curriculum to the material that can be tested, and raises the pressure either to hold back students who might lower scores or to cause them to drop out of school altogether; and about whether testing works at all to raise performance (Amrein & Berliner, 2002; Greene, Winters, & Forster, 2003).

INCREASING DEMANDS

As might be expected, the sweeping reforms of the past decade or so, most of them imposed from the top, by legislatures, state boards of education, or local boards, and often in rapid and sometimes unrelated succession, have also had a wide impact in the field—on teachers, on school administrators, and, of course, on students and parents. Among most Americans, the opinion surveys reveal satisfaction with schools close to home, including the schools that respondents' own children attend, but considerable dissatisfaction with the education system generally. Thus, with the exception of scattered complaints, and occasional test boycotts by students and parents (as in Massachusetts, e.g., beginning in 2000 [Schrag, 2000]), there has been, if not enthusiastic acceptance, at least acquiescence in the testing and accountability systems imposed by the states.

One of the things that characterizes the American education system, in comparison to those in most other nations, is the degree of access for virtually all students to some institution of higher education: community (two-year) college, state four-year college, and state university, as well as a wide variety of private colleges and universities, trade schools, and other institutions. That access—often at relatively little real cost for tuition—is one of the glories of the American system, and Americans continue to respect and support it, though sometimes with reservations. (The success of that system is highlighted by the huge numbers of foreign students it continues to attract.) At the same time, however, politicians, editorial writers, and, very probably, a large segment of the public react strongly to reports that high percentages of students admitted to the nation's public universities are required to take heavy doses of remedial courses in the first two years (which greatly decreases their chances of graduating) and, more generally, to complaints from employers and leading business representatives that the average high school graduate cannot read well enough and has not learned enough math to qualify for jobs in what is said to be an increasingly technological and demanding job market. The diploma, it is often said, should not merely reflect seat time but have real meaning in educational substance. At the same time, some students are suing schools for denying them diplomas solely because they were unable to pass the state-mandated test, charging that they have completed the required work and thus are entitled to graduate. If they failed to pass the mandatory examination, they charge, it is because they were denied the qualified teachers, the books, or the facilities necessary to learn the material. As more students face the possibility that they will be denied their diplomas, there is a strong chance that states, fearing such suits and responding to mounting pressure from the affected parents and schools, will soften the requirements, postpone them, or, as at least one state has done, create alternative assessments.

There are intense disputes, as there are elsewhere, about what the economy will really require in the coming years: Labor market projections suggest that the largest growth will be in relatively low-skill, and low-paying, service jobs, but the general public belief—at least the staple of public rhetoric—is that there will be fewer and fewer jobs for people who do not have a strong educational background, often at least two years beyond high school. But among many teachers and their unions, both the assumption that all students must be qualified for higher education and the large series of new mandates showering down on them have begun to create a significant backlash. The traditional scope of collective bargaining in American education— in theory at least—covers only compensation, hours, and working conditions, which include such things as seniority and tenure rights. But in 2002 California's largest teachers' union, the California

Teachers Association, with some 200,000 members, nearly succeeded in securing passage in the state legislature of a major bill that would have made everything from the selection of textbooks to the creation and role of school-site parent committees into issues subject to the collective bargaining process. That would not necessarily mean that local teacher organizations would have taken control of these things, but they could have used them as leverage on wages and other issues.

The complaint underlying the pressure for the bill was that the reforms handed down from the top not only put increasing pressure on teachers but imposed on them materials, teaching strategies, and curricula that they had no role in choosing and over which they had no control, in which many did not believe but for whose success they were nonetheless going to be held accountable. And because one part of the California reforms, like those in other states, strongly encouraged local districts, especially those serving the state's poor, black, and Latino children, to adopt highly scripted reading and math programs—programs that in some cases mandated virtually everything the teachers were supposed to do—they generated particular frustration and restiveness among veteran teachers who believed that their experience entitled them to more trust and credit, if not honor, than those scripted programs bestowed on them. With those kinds of narrowly prescriptive programs, said California Assemblywoman Jackie Goldberg, "we might as well hire robots" (personal communication, February 10, 2003).

TESTS, RESOURCES, AND CHOICE

As already indicated, the American school reform movement of the past two decades was based on the premise that even the country's ablest students were, in many cases, not performing as well as they should or as well as their peers in other countries. Among the most troubling data on those international comparisons is the relative apparent decline in the scores of U.S. students between elementary and secondary school. As the National Center for Education Statistics (2001) summarizes one of those measures, "The 1995 TIMSS assessments revealed that U.S. 4th-graders performed well in both mathematics and science in comparison to students in other nations and U.S. twelfth-graders scored below the international average and among the lowest of the TIMSS nations in mathematics and science general knowledge." Though scholars like Gerald W. Bracey (2001) and Iris C. Rotberg (1998) have raised major questions about sampling and other methodological flaws in the international comparisons, those comparisons continue to serve as a starting point for discussions about the perceived problems in U.S. education.[2]

All manner of reasons have been adduced for these problems—from the contention that U.S. schools are so bad that they actually cause students to get less proficient as they move through the system to the belief that although the reform-driven "basics" programs in the early grades have taught children low-level decoding and arithmetic skills, they have not prepared them for problem solving, analysis, and other higher-order skills. Equally plausible are the wide cultural differences among nations: Because the U.S. system provides so many second chances and such generous access to training and higher education, American high school students in general have fewer incentives driving them to high levels of achievement—and a great many more negative peer pressures—than students in societies where test scores at the age of thirteen, or seventeen, or nineteen are often irreversible determinants of students' academic and vocational futures.

Although U.S. students are constantly warned both by their schools and, in many cases, by their parents that if they do not get high grades in high school, they will not get into the more competitive colleges, and although thousands of students, most of them middle class, are enrolled in private after-school "rat race" tutoring and college admissions test–preparation programs, many more expect to go to institutions that are either only marginally selective or not selective at all. In addition, the system struggles with the particular problems of many black students in a peer culture that disparages academic effort as "acting white" and with the more general (but similar) problem of an adolescent culture that tends to tease and often abuse any student—white, black, or Latino—perceived as too much of an intellectual (Bishop, 2003; Ogbu, 2003; Steele, 1997, 1999; Steele & Aronson, 1998).

But far and away the most dramatic gaps are not those between Americans and Koreans, or Finns, or Czechs but, rather, among the major economic and ethnic groups within the United States. In graduation rates, in college attendance, in test scores, and in other generally accepted measures of educational outcomes, the gap between whites and Asians on the one hand and blacks and Hispanics on the other is substantial. The achievement gap is not surprising, given the uneven playing field: the large numbers of children in the United States who live in poverty, the increasing income gap between rich and poor, and the unequal distribution of resources for education. Although increased educational and economic access in the past forty years has led to dramatic gains in educational achievement for many African Americans and Hispanics, others continue to live in high-poverty communities with resource-poor schools. The historic American hope had always been that schools would become the great democratic equalizers in economic and social conditions, that education, in the words of Horace Mann, who, in the 1830s and 1840s, was the great promoter of public schools, would do better "than to disarm the poor of their hostility toward the rich; it prevents being poor" (1848, cited in Commager, [1951]1964, p. 568). But the gaps, which go back to the beginnings of the nation's school system, almost perfectly reflect not merely the relative economic and social conditions of the respective groups but also the conditions of the schools they attend. Schools serving America's poorest children—many of them in the inner cities, some in small farm towns—have several times the rate of underqualified teachers: teachers lacking credentials, teachers who have neither majored nor minored in college in the subjects they now teach in high school, teachers who ranked low in their college classes, and teachers who attended colleges that are not nearly as academically rigorous as those attended by teachers in the affluent suburbs. There are similar differences in the availability of textbooks, in materials, and in the condition of school facilities.

States and school districts provide most of the funding for primary and secondary education in the United States, with the federal government contributing less than 7 percent of the total. As a result, the levels of education funding differ enormously, both among and within states. In the 1970s constitutional lawsuits seeking equity in per-pupil school funding between rich and poor school districts succeeded in forcing some states to level funding between districts that had high local property tax bases—still the primary source of school funding in most districts—and those that did not. But even where those suits were successful, the resulting reforms had little if any impact on the education of poor and minority children.[3] Many of them did not go to school in low-wealth districts, yet the least-qualified (and the lowest-paid) teachers were still concentrated in schools serving the neediest children, with the oldest, most crowded, and most rundown schools located in the inner cities. Thus, resource disparities among schools within districts were often much larger than the disparities among districts (see Roza & Miles, 2002; and *Serrano v. Priest* [1971, 1976]). Because the U.S. Supreme Court rejected the contention that education is a federal constitutional right, huge disparities also remain in education funding and school quality among the fifty states (see *San Antonio Independent School District v. Rodriguez*, 411 U.S. 1 [1973]).

In the past decade, a new, and perhaps unique, fiscal strategy has been evolving to replace the search for equity. In a series of state constitutional lawsuits, many of them leading to favorable court decisions, school districts and organizations representing poor and minority children, who now make up nearly 40 percent of U.S. school enrollment, are demanding that states, rather than equalize nominal funding, calculate what is required to adequately educate different groups of children—which in many cases means more than dollar equity for poor and at-risk students—and then provide the teachers and other resources necessary. Some courts have ordered their states to provide preschool programs for all low-income children—something that is common for all children in nations like France but is new in the United States. The definition of adequacy, of course, is subject to much professional, philosophical, and judicial dispute, even on the most basic issues: Does constitutional adequacy, for example, mean a high-quality education preparing students for college or postsecondary training, as a trial judge ruled in New York State, or does it mean, as an appellate court held in overruling the trial judge, that, in effect, an eighth grade education is enough?[4] (That ruling itself was later overturned by the state's highest court, which upheld the trial judge's high standard.)

Even where a court or legislature agrees on a specific meaning of adequacy in a particular state, there is no certainty that it can be effectively provided, in part because funds are scarce; in part because legislatures, jealous of their own powers and prerogatives, delay and evade judicial orders; and in part because teachers' union contracts, with their seniority rights and their determined resistance to differential pay, make it difficult to assign the most able and experienced teachers to low-performing inner-city schools, much less keep them there. Nonetheless, the legislatively enacted standards, testing and accountability programs, and mandates of the past twenty years have generated increasing political, legal, and moral pressure for adequacy in resources. If the state requires students to meet what are widely advertised as high academic standards in reading and literature, math, science, history, and other fields and to pass high-stakes tests for advancement and graduation, and if local schools are in some way measured and held accountable for their success, the state presumably has a commensurate responsibility to provide the resources to give students the opportunity to learn the appropriate material and schools the means to teach it. It is that link that has driven the adequacy argument in lawsuits and even in legislatures where suits were unsuccessful or never filed. In Florida, it also energized a costly voter referendum, passed in 2002, mandating a sharp reduction in class sizes (and thus in student–teacher ratios) and requiring the state to fund it.

The same implicit bargain also helped secure the wide bipartisan support for the Bush "No Child Left Behind" Act cited earlier. NCLB, Bush's prime (and much ballyhooed) domestic initiative in his first year in office, got the very strong and public support of two of Congress's leading liberals, Sen. Edward Kennedy of Massachusetts and Rep. George Miller of California, and wide backing from a large number of other Democrats. At the time of its passage, Miller lauded the bill for its "historic increases in funding and better targeting [of that funding] to schools with high percentages of low-income children."[5]

But (perhaps characteristically when such commitments are made) a large part of the administration and Congress have never provided most of the additional federal school funding that was authorized by NCLB. That has generated increasingly sharp criticism from both Kennedy and Miller, particularly after Bush included a $300 million appropriation for private school vouchers—public money that children could use for tuition at private and religious schools—in his proposed budget for the

2003–4 fiscal year. It has also produced increasing backlash among state legislatures, even those dominated by Republicans, complaining about unfunded intrusions on their constitutional prerogatives.

Bush's highly controversial voucher proposal, though officially limited to pilot programs, including one in the long-troubled Washington, D.C., schools, touched on one of the most divisive education issues in America—one regarded by many people, and by the public school establishment generally, as the H-bomb of education reform, something that would drain both funds and motivated parents from public schools and make those schools the default system for the most dysfunctional students and families. In his 2000 campaign and his original proposals for NCLB, Bush advocated limited private and religious school vouchers for children in officially designated "failing" schools—schools with chronically low test scores. One state, Florida, and two cities, Cleveland and Milwaukee, now have limited tax-funded private school vouchers for poor children. But the Bush proposal was blocked in Congress, just as a series of broad voucher proposals have been rejected by voters, fearing a crippling drain of public funds from public schools, in California (twice), Michigan, Colorado, and other states. (Recently, however, the Colorado legislature approved a voucher program.) In the affluent suburbs, where the schools have strong local support, there is no support for vouchers. The U.S. Supreme Court's decision in 2002 to uphold the constitutionality of vouchers for religious schools, however, appeared to provide new encouragement for voucher advocates and may generate yet another round of voucher campaigns in coming years.

In any case, the pressure for vouchers continues, especially for poor children in troubled inner-city schools, where the idea gets substantial support from some parents and community leaders. The voucher idea, first promoted by economist Milton Friedman in the 1960s, was originally an economic idea—to promote competition and thus quality and accountability through market forces. For obvious reasons, it was quickly taken up by parents who send their children—and pay tuition—to religious schools because they offer a moral and religious climate that they believe they cannot get in a scrupulously secular public system that, under America's tradition of sharp separation of church and state (and by virtue of a series of Supreme Court decisions), prohibits school-sponsored Bible reading and prayer, teaches Darwinian evolution, and generally (though not always) excludes religious creation stories from its science classes. The issue of vouchers thus brought together two major wings of political conservatism—economic conservatives and religious conservatives.

But in the past decade the voucher movement has transformed its rationale into an equity and quasi–civil rights argument: If the wealthy have choice, through either their financial ability to move into communities with good schools or their ability to pay private school tuition, why shouldn't the poor? How can anyone, the Left particularly, justify keeping the poorest children in the worst schools (Coons & Sugarman, 1992; Schrag, 1999)? The proposed voucher amounts would not begin to cover the tuition of many private schools, nor is there any indication that the private schools would accept significant numbers of children from the most troubled public schools. Nonetheless, the voucher idea has strong conservative support, leading many teachers' union leaders and other public school defenders to regard high-stakes testing and accountability systems as part of a larger strategy to undermine support for public schools. In the view of the Left, if the tests show that schools are failing, the Right would be creating a climate favorable to a market-based education system.

More immediately, the demand for more choice has produced a classically American compromise, charter schools—publicly funded schools chartered by states or local districts to groups of parents or teachers who commit themselves to specified education programs and objectives (specialized science or arts schools, schools with extended days or intensive instruction in the basics, or progressive discovery-oriented education or home schooling charters)—in return for freedom from many, though not all, state school regulations. By 2002–3 there were an estimated 2,700 charter schools enrolling some 700,000 students, a very small proportion of America's total school enrollment (of some 50 million) and thus more useful (so far at least) as a safety valve than as the major movement that many of its advocates had hoped (or its opponents feared) it would become ("Basic National Statistics," 2002).

Because the movement is barely a decade old, outcomes are hard to measure. What outcomes there are—in test scores and other assessments—are mixed, with some charter schools producing high-achieving students and some doing no better or even worse than traditional public schools. And because many of the state laws authorizing charters are themselves of recent vintage and are reflective of the deeper American ambivalence between regulation and unfettered experimentation, there have been widely publicized scandals—reports of maladministered funds and sometimes of outright theft and corruption (Miron & Nelson, 2002; SRI International, 1997).

STANDARDS VERSUS BUDGETS

As suggested earlier, there has been a classic American pattern in school reform, a generational struggle between traditionalism and progressivism, which itself reflects divisions in national attitudes and values. Americans celebrate merit and consequences, but they also want second chances and third chances. We understand, or think we understand, the need for well-trained workers and well educated citizens, but we also have a long history of anti-intellectualism and democratic egalitarianism that disparages intellectual pretension, "eggheads," and elitism and that honors self-educated, practical people. In addition, despite the official rhetoric and policies of recent years, there is a deeper uncertainty about whether the fundamental gaps can be closed by the schools, whether they will depend on poverty reduction and other social programs that address the broader needs of children, or, indeed, whether they can be closed at all (Howe, 1993). That uncertainty has been part of the educational ethos for much of American history, resting in part on historical racism and, more recently, on a long list of studies indicating that between 75 and 80 percent of test-score variation among schools is determined by the economic and educational backgrounds of students and that schools contribute no more than 25 percent. The official mythology is that all children can learn at a high level regardless of the terrible conditions that they come from and that when they do not, the schools are at fault. But many teachers do not believe it, and chances are good that most other Americans do not either. Bush, in perhaps the most powerful phrase of his campaign, called it "the soft bigotry of low expectations."

In the past two decades, the conservative, meritocratic side of our nature has dominated American school policies. In state after state, curricula have emphasized the "basics" in math and reading, emphasizing mastery of computational skills and decoding of words and sentences over the creative and the analytical; fact-based multiple-choice tests over so-called authentic assessment based on wider and more creative portfolios of student work—essays, projects, open-ended problem solving, and analysis; and (in theory) standards that emphasize academic work over practical vocational training.

But there is growing evidence that this era may soon end or at least give way to a widespread diminution of the standards and requirements that were enacted in the 1990s. In part, the standards, enacted by legislators and other policy makers seeking to prove how "tough" they can be, set a great many benchmarks too high, which itself helped spark the backlash among teachers and now legislators, mentioned earlier. And as more children begin to bump up against the high-stakes consequences of those requirements, a growing number of parents are likely to join them. As in previous generations of high-stakes testing, it will be unrealistic politically to support a system that fails to promote and graduate large numbers of students.

In many parts of the country, particularly the Southwest, there is, in addition, the growing political power of Latinos, who now constitute America's largest ethnic minority and whose children, in places like California, are already close to a majority in school enrollment. That power, exercised primarily through ethnic and civil rights organizations and through the growing Hispanic caucuses in state legislatures, is putting increasing pressure on the system to make special accommodations for the large number of children (25 percent in California) who come to school speaking some language other than English at home. That pressure, too, touches on deeper American social issues—immigration policy, the debates between cultural "melting pot" assimilation and multiculturalism in absorbing new residents from widely different origins, exemplified particularly by the political and pedagogical debate over bilingual education—meaning primary instruction in the native language of students who come to school speaking some language other than English. In the years since 1998 voters in California, Arizona, and Massachusetts have passed initiatives prohibiting most bilingual instruction and requiring students with limited English proficiency to be put into English "immersion" programs, except where parents specifically request bilingual classes. But that has not ended the controversy or the political pressure from educators, legislators, and scholars who contend that trying to teach children to read (or teach them math or science) in a language they do not understand is pointless.[6]

But the most important element in the impending swing away from the reform zeal of the 1990s, and the likely watering down of the standards and requirements it imposed, is the simple lack of money. Beginning in the year 2000, and increasingly in the succeeding years, recession sharply reduced state and local revenues and created large deficits. Combined with the reductions in federal spending associated with the tax cuts of 2001–3, the recession, and the mounting costs, foreign and domestic, of the American war against terrorism, those financial constraints will almost certainly undermine the reforms and reduce the ability of states to withstand the counterpressures. It would have been nearly impossible, in any case, to attract and retain the "highly qualified" teachers that the federal law requires by 2006, despite the claims by some jurisdictions that they were succeeding. (In some cases, as in California, where 45,000 teachers who were not even fully licensed were relisted overnight as fully qualified, the success was based entirely on an official redefinition of what *highly qualified* means. In New York City, increased beginning salaries and a sharp reduction in the required qualifications for new teachers likewise produced a sudden spurt in new hires who were deemed fully qualified.) But the budget cuts that began in 2002 made the idea of having nothing but highly qualified teachers in the poorest and most difficult-to-staff schools even more unrealistic.

More broadly, the promise of additional resources to implement the great rush of reforms of the 1990s was a kind of quid pro quo, a force to sustain morale in the trenches and dampen the natural restiveness of professionals who had often been overlooked in the development of the accountability systems, the new curricular standards, and the reform regulations to implement them. As those resources get scarcer, resistance will almost certainly increase.

EDUCATION AND THE "CULTURE WARS"

Because of the enormous range of responsibilities that Americans charge their schools with, the public education system inevitably gets enmeshed in America's larger culture wars: about the role of religion in public life, about sex education and gender roles, and about racial and ethnic pride. The conventional criticism of America's "failing schools" holds the school establishment, and particularly school bureaucracies and teachers' unions, responsible for school success. But there are a great many other issues that distract schools from their mission. In the 1980s, when billionaire Ross Perot led a campaign in Texas to prevent students who had less than a C average from participating in high school sports, it was not the teachers or bureaucrats who resisted but in fact parents and local boosters who regarded such policies as discriminatory: Winning the Friday night football games came first; academic stardom came later, if at all.

Local protests about the inclusion of one or another book in a course or even on school library shelves are not uncommon. There are recurring fights about the teaching of evolution and demands by religious fundamentalists that creationism be given equal time with Darwin; attacks by some parent groups on the use of Mark Twain's classic novel *Huckleberry Finn* because it includes dialogue with the word *nigger*, and challenges by conservatives to a whole range of other books because they include talk about sex or depictions of gay relationships as normal or because they are suffused with what fundamentalists call "secular humanism." In Alabama, state law, enacted in response to pressure from fundamentalists, requires each biology textbook to include a label stating that evolution is only a theory and that students are advised to make their own judgments about it. In Kansas, in 1999 the state school board ordered Darwinian evolution stricken from the state's science standards. Two years later, after the resulting uproar led to the election of three new board members, the board reversed itself (Blair & Hoff, 2001; Hill, 1996).

Not surprisingly, the nation's culture wars have also led to a pervasive fear among school boards and state authorities that one or another passage or picture in an approved textbook will be found offensive by some group, leading in turn to the creation of official state committees to screen books to ensure that texts and illustrations are balanced by ethnicity and gender, politically unobjectionable, and conducive to correct nutritional and health practices (see Ravitch, 2003). Not surprisingly, that often leads to widespread criticism about the nation's bland, passively written history and social studies books, texts that are devoid of drama, tension, and voice and, often, of the remotest interest (Fitzgerald, 1979; Zimmerman, 2002). Each of these concerns tends to make teaching more cautious and to divert attention from the high standards the schools are supposed to uphold.

CONCLUSION

Unlike most other Western nations, the United States, with its 50 million schoolchildren, has no single national education system. It has fifty state systems operated by thousands of local semiautonomous districts. The local property tax is still a major funding source, although gradual shifts toward more state funding during the past decade, the accumulating state mandates discussed earlier—the new course and testing requirements, the graduation standards—and the passage of the federal "No Child Left Behind" Act have begun to centralize American education in unprecedented ways.

Those new mandates rest on two basic, currently dominant, assumptions:

- that for much of the twentieth century, American schools have been too flabby in their demands, too much under the sway of the progressive disciples of people like John Dewey and A. S. Neill, too disrespectful of high academic demands, too taken up with fostering students' self-esteem, and, thus, too much given to fuzzy standards and criteria: life adjustment courses, tolerance, creativity, and discovery learning (Ravitch, 2000)
- that the schools, pretty much alone, can not only eliminate all the academic inadequacies of American youth but also ameliorate a whole range of other social ills from teenage pregnancy, to drug abuse, to poverty

But it is not certain to what extent Americans fully believe either one.

The pendulum, of course, has not always swung to the right. In the 1960s, as in the first three decades of the twentieth century, there was a whole range of progressive voices—Paul Goodman, John Holt, Herb Kohl, Edgar Friedenberg—arguing for more educational flexibility, for child-centered programs, and for choice and "open" schools, some of them even supporting vouchers to give children and parents more freedom from what they regarded as lockstep schools. Their closest contemporary successor is Alfie Kohn (1999), who argues, along with a considerable group of academics, teachers, and organizations (exemplified by groups like FairTest in Cambridge), that the new regimen and the high-stakes tests associated with it are stultifying and destructive of children's intellectual and personal development. There also remains the widespread, though currently muted, belief—a belief backed by a great deal of research—that children's backgrounds, including economic status and parental education, are the most powerful determinants of school success. At its fringes it borders on social determinism—a position articulated most recently by Richard Herrenstein and Charles Murray (1994), that culture is the most important driver of test scores and will trump almost anything the schools can do. It is this view that many believe leads to low expectations for poor children and inadequate resources for their schools—thus creating a self-fulfilling prophecy.

There are also intensively divisive questions about tracking. Because not all children go to college and most jobs call for a good deal less than high-level academic training, many policy makers and educators stress the need for better vocational high school programs and for better school-to-career programs—educational opportunities for students not going to college. But there is also serious criticism from people who fear that vocational education programs will once again track minority students into dead-end courses and low-wage jobs. For the moment, the call to prepare all students for college remains official policy—though often not the actual practice—in the great majority of states.

Finally—and touching on all these issues—there is the great debate and uncertainty about how much difference money makes. Conservative economists like Eric Hanushek (1989, 1997) of the Hoover Institution at Stanford argue that even as the nation's real spending on schools has been rising in the past thirty years, test scores have stayed flat in some fields and declined in others. Others have tried to show that on international measures, America spends more per pupil in real terms than nations with higher scores. But the comparisons are subject to great doubt, in part because other nations provide far broader preschool and more generous social welfare programs and in part because of the larger difficulties in comparing different societies. Yet even Hanushek shows that good teachers can make a large difference in the success of students and often can overcome the disadvantages students come to school with (Rivkin, Hanushek, & Kain, 2002). And good teachers, especially teachers willing to teach in schools serving disadvantaged children, have to be paid commensurately and require support and working conditions that also cost money.

Perhaps the greatest paradox is that few of the most dogged reformers recognize the progress that the nation has made in the past thirty years: the increase in math (and, on some measures, reading) scores; the greatly increased proportion of students going to, and graduating from, college; the integration of learning disabled students into mainstream classes (and thus, often, into test-score averages); and the absorption of a century-high influx of immigrant students. But these factors have not deterred much of the conservative reform movement of the past generation. Paul Peterson (2003), a professor at Harvard, a supporter of vouchers, and one of the most emphatic voices of the movement, has written: "Many areas of American life have changed for the better [since the release of *A Nation at Risk* in 1983] except, it appears, the K–12 education system . . . despite 20 years of agitation and reform . . . student achievement has at best stagnated, if not declined" (p. 40).

The great mystery in that observation is how, if the schools are and have been so bad, American life—in health care, in technological development, in income, and in general quality of life—could have changed so much for the better. Peterson says it was technology that did it, but for the most part, of course, it was American industry and technicians (albeit bolstered by a large group of Asian Silicon Valley immigrants) who developed the technology and manage it.

Though no one will ever claim that American schools are as good as they ought to be, especially not the schools serving the country's poor and disadvantaged students, the conventional wisdom about failure has generally drowned out both the good news and the more balanced assessments, which in turn often leads to excessive expectations (Berliner, 1996; Berliner & Biddle, 1998; Schrag, 2000). But as the reforms of the past two decades pile up on the schools, as pressure from civil rights groups is brought to bear on what they regard as tests and standards that discriminate against minority children, as education funding is rolled back, and as terrorism, recession, oil shortages, and other issues overwhelm education in the nation's political debates and in the public mind, fatigue is likely to combine with backlash to produce, if not another swing of the pendulum, a rollback in the demands and standards.

Indeed, it has already begun. California, which has been spending nearly $2 billion annually to maintain classes in grades K–3 of twenty students or less—a rigid formula that has not yet produced any demonstrable improvements in student performance—is in the process of creating more flexible rules for local districts. Some districts, unable to afford the lower class sizes even with the extra state funding, are giving up the class size–reduction program at least in some grades; some, strapped for funds, are considering giving it up altogether. More important, budget cuts will force districts to lay off many good young teachers. Some states, including California, are on the verge of deferring the effective date of their high school exit exam—the date when students who fail will no longer be allowed to get a diploma—or of permitting students deemed to be doing well to graduate even if they do not pass it. Many more are revising their tests. None of this is likely to involve much conscious, systematic reexamination of the overall reform policies of the past generation, but it will produce a gradual attrition toward a more pragmatic, less utopian mean. That, too, has always been the American way.

NOTES

1. Rickover famously warned (in 1963) that if U.S. schools did not improve, "the Russians will bury us." See Rickover (1963) and Flesch (1955).

2. Methodological flaws cited include, e.g., differences in the proportion of low-income students in the test-taking population; differences in student

selectivity (overrepresentation in the sample of the highest-achieving students); differences in the ages of students tested (a range of seventeen to twenty-one in the secondary school study); and the country's practice with respect to the inclusion or exclusion of low-achieving students, language-minority students, students with disabilities, vocational or apprenticeship programs, and entire regions of the country (Rotberg, 1998).

3. The most influential of those cases were *Serrano v. Priest,* 5 Cal. 3d 584 (1971) and *Serrano v. Priest,* 18 Cal. 3d 728 (1976). But in California, where the courts ordered the state to equalize funding, the ultimate outcome, after a major voter revolt against state property taxes, was to level funding *down* compared with other states.

4. For a fuller picture of the status of the adequacy suits, see "Litigation Update," at www.accessednetwork.org. See also Schrag (2003).

5. See Miller's Web site, at www.house.gov/georgemiller/eseainfo.html.

6. There is a huge amount of literature touching on this debate. See, among others, August & Hakuta (1997). For the case for it, see Crawford ([1991]1993); for the case against, see "English for the Children," at www.proenglish.org/issues/be-prop227.html.

REFERENCES CITED

Amrein, A. L., & Berliner, D. C. (2002). *An analysis of some unintended and negative consequences of high stakes testing.* Tempe: Educational Policy Research Unit, College of Education, Arizona State University. Available at www.greatlakescenter.org/pub/H-S%20Analysis%20finalExec%20Summary.pdf (accessed May 18, 2003).

August, D., & Hakuta, K. (Eds.). (1997). *Improving schooling for language-minority children: A research agenda.* Washington, DC: National Academies Press.

Basic national statistics. (2002). Available at www.uscharterschools.org/pub/uscs_docs/o/index.htm#national (accessed May 19, 2003).

Berliner, D. C. (1996). *The manufactured crisis: Myths, fraud, and the attack on America's public schools.* New York: Harper Collins.

Berliner, D. C., & Biddle, B. I. (1998). The lamentable alliance between the media and school critics. In G. I. Maeroff (Ed.), *Imaging education: The media and schools in America* (pp. 26–45). New York: Teachers College Press. Draft available at http://courses.ed.asu.edu/berliner/readings/alliancew.htm (accessed May 19, 2003).

Bishop, J. H. (2003). *Nerds and freaks: A theory of student culture and norms.* Brookings Papers on Education Policy. Washington, DC: Brookings Institution.

Blair, J., & Hoff, D. (2001, February 21). Evolution restored to Kansas standards, but called "controversial" in Alabama's. *Education Week*, 13.

Bracey, G. W. (2001, October). The 11th Bracey report on the condition of public education. *Phi Delta Kappan*, 151–69.

Commager, H. S. ([1951]1964). *Living ideas in America*. New York: Harper & Row.

Coons, J. E., & Sugarman, S. D. (1992). *Scholarships for children*. Berkeley: Institute of Governmental Studies, University of California.

Crawford, J. ([1991]1993). *Bilingual education: History, politics, theory and practice*. Los Angeles: Bilingual Educational Services.

Fitzgerald, F. (1979). *America revised*. New York: Vintage.

Flesch, R. (1955). *Why Johnny can't read—And what you can do about it*. New York: Harper & Row.

Greene, J. P., Winters, M. A., & Forster, G. (2003). *Testing high stakes tests: Can we believe the results of accountability tests?* New York: Manhattan Institute. Available at www.manhattan-institute.org/html/cr_33.htm (accessed May 18, 2003).

Hanushek, E. A. (1989). The impact of differential expenditures on school performance. *Educational Researcher, 18* (4), 49.

———. (1997). Assessing the effects of school resources on student performance: An update. *Educational Evaluation and Policy Analysis*, 141–64.

Herrenstein, R., & Murray, C. (1994). *The bell curve: Intelligence and class structure in American life*. New York: Free Press.

Hill, D. (1996, November 20). Counter evolutionary. *Education Week*, 1.

Howe, H., II. (1993). *Thinking about our kids: An agenda for American education*. New York: Free Press.

Kohn, A. (1999). *The schools our children deserve*. Boston: Houghton Mifflin.

Mann, H. (1848). Education is the balance wheel of the social machinery. Twelfth annual report as secretary of the Massachusetts Board of Education. In H. S. Commager ([1951]1964), *Living ideas in America* (p. 568). New York: Harper & Row.

Miron, G., & Nelson, C. (2002, May 15). What's public about charter schools? *Education Week*, 38–39.

National Center for Education Statistics. (2001). International comparisons of education. In *Digest of Education Statistics*, chap. 6. Available at the U.S. Department of Education Web site, http://nces.ed.gov/pubs2002/2002130f.pdf (accessed May 19, 2003).

National Commission on Excellence in Education. (1983, April). *A nation at risk*. Available at the U.S. Department of Education Web site, www.ed.gov/pubs/NatAtRisk/risk.html (accessed May 18, 2003).

Ogbu, J. U. (2003). *Black students in an affluent suburb: A study of academic disengagement*. Mahwah, NJ: Lawrence Erlbaum.

Peterson, P. (2003). Ticket to nowhere: In the wake of "A Nation at Risk," educators pledged to focus anew on student achievement. Two decades later, little progress has been made. *Education Next* (Spring), 39–46.

Ravitch, D. (2000). *Left back: A century of failed school reforms.* New York: Simon and Schuster.

———. (2003). *The language police: How pressure groups restrict what students learn.* New York: Alfred A. Knopf.

Rickover, H. (1963). *American education: A national failure.* New York: Dutton.

Rivkin, S. G., Hanushek, E. A., &. Kain, J. F. (2002, July). Teachers, schools and academic achievement. Paper prepared for the National Bureau of Economic Research, Cambridge, MA.

Rotberg, I. C. (1998). Interpretation of international test score comparisons. *Science, 280,* 1030–31.

Roza, M., & Miles, K. H. (2002). *A new look at inequalities in school funding: A presentation on the resource variations within districts.* Seattle: Center on Reinventing Education, University of Washington.

Schrag, P. (1999, November 23). The voucher seduction. *American Prospect,* 46–52.

———. (2000, March). High stakes are for tomatoes. *The Atlantic,* 19–22.

———. (2003). *Final test: The struggle for adequacy in America's schools.* New York: New Press.

SRI International. (1997, December). *Evaluation of charter school effectiveness.* Available at www.lao.ca.gov/1997/121197_charter_schools/sri_charter_schools_1297-part1.html (accessed May 19, 2003).

Steele, C. (1997). A threat in the air. How stereotypes shape the intellectual identities and performance of women and African Americans. *American Psychologist, 52,* 613–29.

———. (1999, August). Thin ice: "Stereotype threat" and black college students. *The Atlantic,* 44.

Steele, C., & Aronson, J. (1998). Stereotype threat and the test performance of academically successful African Americans. In C. Jencks & M. Phillips (Eds.), *The black–white test score gap.* Washington, DC: Brookings Institution.

Tyack, D., & Cuban, L. (1995). *Tinkering toward utopia: A century of educational reform.* Cambridge: Harvard University Press.

Winerip, M. (2003, February 19). A school left behind by new federal standards. *The New York Times,* 7.

Zimmerman, J. (2002). *Whose America? Culture wars in the public schools.* Cambridge: Harvard University Press.

Concluding Thoughts:
On Change, Tradition, and Choices

Iris C. Rotberg

> He that will not apply new remedies must expect new evils; for time is the greatest innovator; and if time of course alter things to the worse, and wisdom and counsel shall not alter them to the better, what shall be the end?
>
> —Francis Bacon (1561–1626)

I am frequently asked which country has the best education system—certainly, a reasonable question to pose to the editor of a book on international education policy. But the question is meaningless without further specificity, particularly in defining "best" and for what purpose. I can only respond, and even then with many caveats, if I know which aspects of the education system are most important to the questioner: High test scores in mathematics and science? If so, for 10 percent of the population? For 50 percent? For 90 percent? A high proportion of children completing secondary school? Access to higher education? If so, for what percentage of the population?

For some, it is not the outcome measures of an education system that are important but, rather, the processes at work in the system: Do classes have a mix of student achievement levels? Does the system track students to ensure that those who are higher achieving receive an elite academic education? Is there individualized instruction for both the higher-achieving students and those with special needs?

Does the system keep upper-middle-class children in public, not private, schools? Is there a wide selection of courses and extracurricular activities? Is the system fully integrated by socioeconomic status? Are educational resources distributed equitably across the system? Is there meaningful school choice? Is there accountability—rewards and sanctions for teachers and principals based on student performance? Are there national curricula and tests? Do students' test scores determine promotion and graduation? Each of these questions represents a fundamental issue that defines a quality education system in many people's minds. It is typically assumed that the processes used will lead to favorable outcomes—often unspecified—which are consistent with the questioner's underlying values about the way a society should be educated or even structured.

The fact is that there is no answer to the question of which country has the best education system because it almost always comes down to core values about how a society should work—issues that have been debated by philosophers and social thinkers for centuries. What is clear is that some of the core values are, as a matter of economic feasibility, impossible to achieve, and others are inconsistent not only with each other but also with the basic traditions of the country itself. It is, in my view, unrealistic and probably counterproductive to argue that a country can have it all. The best we can do is articulate, if possible, where we are coming from and what our goals are.

There remains, even then, the question of how we get there. Even if we know where we want to go and why, there are constraints and ironies that make the articulated goals difficult to implement. This book, in country after country, describes those constraints and ironies, some of which are couched in terms of the financial or political environment; others, related to national tradition; and still others, the result of socioeconomic factors—all of which are outside the capacity of education policy makers to influence. The chapters also describe instances of dramatic educational change that have occurred in a relatively short period—sometimes in response to major political and economic upheavals—as well as more gradual progress in access, innovation, and response to the educational needs of increasingly diverse populations. All of the countries represented in the book have decided that retaining the status quo is unacceptable in the context of national and global change. At the same time, the reforms both reflect, and are constrained by, each country's societal context, its priorities, and its basic value system.

Thus, irrespective of a country's decisions about educational access, equalization of school finance, tracking, school choice, and the myriad policies that define an "education system," there remains the issue of how a society facilitates the growth potential of its citizens—after the conclusion of their formal schooling. The customs and practices of a nation may be consistent or at odds with policies that define the education system. For example, no matter how egalitarian or "fair" the education system, these advantages will be diminished if graduates are chosen for powerful or prestigious positions based primarily on graduation from a very few elitist schools. It will not be sufficient to guarantee equitable admissions standards for minorities and women if there is discrimination in the job market or if these groups, in practice, are excluded from high-ranking positions in government and the private sector. A nation's policies on tracking or school choice matter little if university tuition is simply unaffordable for many students. And, conversely, even in those countries where there is inequity in the financial resources available to rich and poor school districts or regions, the pernicious effects may be somewhat moderated if the society and economy are geared to providing and encouraging second and third chances, mobility of labor, or entrepreneurial opportunities. The education system is but one of many variables that affect the future of a nation and its diverse population.

This chapter pulls together some of the themes experienced across countries. To set the context, it begins with an overview of the major societal pressures that motivated the school reforms, citing as examples the experiences of the countries represented in the book. It then analyzes the major trends in school reform, the conflicting goals and policy choices that countries face as they attempt to implement reform, and the societal constraints that limit it. The chapter concludes with a discussion of the challenge of balancing change and tradition, in particular the role that values and political structures play in facilitating or limiting change and thus in the likelihood that a school reform, whether "homegrown" or borrowed from another country, can be successfully implemented.

SOCIETAL PRESSURES FOR EDUCATION REFORM

Significant Political/Economic Change

The most dramatic examples of school reforms have been in response to the major political/economic changes that have occurred in China, Russia, and South Africa in the past ten to twenty years. The changes have been so extensive that the education systems have been fundamentally restructured.

In China, the restructuring has "opened up" the school system to innovative educational practices but has also led to increased inequalities among different regions of the country. As economic differences in China have grown, so, too, have gaps in innovation and in education funding, which is no longer centralized but now comes largely from local resources.

The political and economic changes in Russia have contributed to both increasing inequalities in educational resources and access and a potential for educational innovation that would not previously have been possible. As certain areas, or sectors of the society, have become more affluent, they have been able to invest in schools that can specialize or innovate; schools in less affluent areas or sectors have fallen further behind. As in China, equality of educational resources has given way to the increasing economic disparities in the broader society.

South Africa, on the other hand, has moved in the opposite direction. In the past ten years political and ideological changes have led to a redistribution of educational resources that is among the most significant ever attempted: Under apartheid, per-pupil expenditures for whites were ten times greater than those for blacks, who attended schools designed to perpetuate apartheid by providing students with only a minimal education and by employing a curriculum that advocated separatist policies. That system was considered intolerable; as a result, the education system has been transformed into one that distributes resources based on student enrollment rather than on race and also provides additional funding to high-poverty areas. At the same time, South Africa faces the challenge of modernizing curriculum and teaching, implementing fundamental changes in the education system's administrative structure, and maintaining support of the middle class—both black and white—for public education. The country strives to maintain a public integrated school system—even if it means permitting middle-class families to subsidize their schools.

Chile and Germany have also made significant, though perhaps less dramatic, changes in their education systems in connection with political upheavals. Under the military regime (1973–90), Chile instituted one of the world's most comprehensive voucher systems with the advice of economists trained at the University of Chicago, who based the system on Milton Friedman's free market economic theories. It is perhaps ironic that a plan established by the military regime—a regime under which many teachers experienced tragic human rights violations—remains in place today and is generally accepted by teachers, even after fourteen years of democratic government.

After the reunification of Germany in 1990, East Germany's education system, which was highly ideological but less stratified than that of West Germany, was totally replaced by the West German model. Although many of the changes in East German education have been positive, West Germany lost the opportunity in the transition period to re-examine its own education system, particularly the problems in academic achievement created by early student tracking—problems that have recently become quite visible as a result of the Program for International Student Assessment (PISA) test-score comparisons (Organization for Economic Cooperation and Development [OECD] PISA, 2001). Thus, West Germany retained a system that was highly stratified by student achievement levels and transferred it to East Germany, where it replaced a system that previously had not tracked students.

More Subtle Changes in Political Philosophy

Less dramatic political changes have also contributed to school reform initiatives. Israel, for example, now questions its long-standing assumption that central government can ensure equal educational opportunity for large numbers of immigrants from diverse backgrounds. Sweden questions some of the basic assumptions of its welfare state and, like Israel, has become disillusioned about the ability of centralized, "rational" education planning to ensure social equity. Both countries, therefore, have weakened central control and encouraged increased school choice. In the United States, the federal government questions its historic reliance on state and local jurisdictions to hold school systems accountable for student performance and has mandated testing requirements that go far beyond any the country previously experienced.

Changing Demographics

In many countries, immigration has led to increasingly diverse student populations, who are often concentrated in center cities or in the suburbs immediately surrounding them. The dramatic increase in immigration (and, therefore, in the mix of racial/ethnic groups, cultures, and languages) has occurred in only a few decades. Even a country like the United States, with its long tradition of immigration and diversity, continues to have a significant increase in the proportion of students from minority populations. Indeed, in many parts of the country, the term *minority* is a misnomer.

The increasing diversity places new demands on school systems, which are often blamed for educational problems. Many school systems respond by attempting to reverse traditional practices, which are perceived as ineffective in serving new student populations. Thus, countries with highly centralized education systems have sought to relax central control in order to make schools more responsive to the diverse student population. Countries with a tradition of local control, on the other hand, have moved in the opposite direction and have increased central oversight—all in response to the perception that changing demographics require a shift from the status quo, whatever it was.

For example, education reforms in France—a country with a highly centralized education system—reflect a concern that schools are not meeting students' individual needs because the curriculum is highly standardized nationally (and even internationally) and because teacher education has emphasized subject matter at the expense of pedagogy. Sweden's disillusionment with central planning also reflects a concern, described earlier, that its education system has not succeeded in narrowing the gaps among different socioeconomic groups.

During the same period, England moved in the opposite direction and transformed a system with the most decentralized curriculum in Europe to a system with one of the most highly prescriptive national curricula. New Zealand also responded to perceived educational problems by centralizing curriculum and increasing testing requirements. In the United States, the federal government is playing a substantially larger role in determining how often children should be tested (every year in grades three through eight), the use of the test scores to measure the performance of schools, and sanctions for schools if their progress is defined as "inadequate." Because of the tradition of local control in the United States, however, there is no national curriculum, and states choose their own tests, which often are not based on a specific curriculum; the result is that the tests themselves are increasingly shaping the content and focus of children's educational experiences.

Over the past thirty years Canadian education policy has also responded to substantial increases in the diversity of the student body because of changes in immigration patterns. For example, Quebec, with declining birthrates, needs immigration to maintain its population level and in recent years has encouraged it. But Quebec has also established policies mandating the dominance of the French language, and the goal of maintaining French language and culture remains central—a goal that both discourages many immigrants from choosing Quebec (over, for example, Ontario or British Columbia) and strongly influences the education of those who do.

As the situation in Quebec demonstrates, changes in birthrates can also have a major influence on the educational environment. In Japan, small family size is perceived as weakening the extended family network and the role models it provides, thereby decreasing the opportunities children have to "experience nature and a range of human relationships" and to "integrate knowledge gained in school with 'real-life' situations." In response, schools have initiated a program of "integrated studies," an interdisciplinary curriculum that encourages experiential learning and problem solving, designed to help children realize the practical value of knowledge. At the same time, declining student enrollment has resulted in a surplus of teachers and reduced competition to attend universities—a trend that has the potential to reduce the pressure of admissions examinations, although the competition to enter the most prestigious universities can be expected to remain intense.

Turkey, on the other hand, is experiencing major population increases because of high birthrates; thus, education policies must balance the need to serve large numbers of new students (estimated at a minimum of 1.2 million additional children each year) with the simultaneous need to strengthen educational quality—and accomplish both objectives with limited resources. The population growth also means that the increasing demand for higher education far exceeds university spaces—a situation contributing to what the author describes as "some of the world's worst 'exam anxiety' for young people applying to university."

Changes in the Global Economy

Globalization has become a major factor in motivating countries to reform their education systems and in their choice of specific reforms. They are concerned about the loss of jobs in traditional industries and recognize that competitiveness will depend increasingly on a highly skilled workforce that can meet the demands of knowledge and high-technology industries. *A Nation at Risk,* issued by the United States in 1983, was one of the early reports that linked education and economic strength, and that theme recurs frequently throughout this book.

Singapore, to a unique degree, links its education system to perceived economic pressures, and, as the global economy changes, the country attempts to change its education program so that its students will be trained to meet new demands. In the past twenty years Singapore has experienced two recessions, which have served as the impetus for new reforms that require the country to balance a highly competitive, examination-oriented education system, based on traditional teaching practices, with a system that encourages students to be creative, solve problems, and develop the entrepreneurial skills needed to compete internationally.

Although Singapore links economic and educational goals more explicitly than elsewhere, other countries also share a concern about providing students with the skills needed to compete in the global economy. China designs education policies, for example, to ensure that the regions of the country with the most advanced economies also have the most advanced education systems. The government, therefore, has set different educational growth targets for different regions of the country. Australian policy makers are also beginning to reassess the country's education policies because of a concern that existing policies are geared to a job market that no longer exists, and, at the same time, Sweden's "welfare state" faces new challenges in a global economy that makes it more difficult to raise the taxes required to finance reforms in education and other social programs. Turkey faces a need to restructure its education system as it attempts to gain membership in the European Union and strengthen its economy. In the United States, the increased emphasis on testing is linked to a concern that the education system is not meeting international academic standards and that, as a result, its students will fall behind in global competition. In all of these examples, a concern about global competition—about jobs—provides a major incentive for school reform.

The difficulty, however, is that the identification of the problem does not necessarily lead to school reform that is relevant to that problem. Indeed, some countries, as seen previously, adopt reforms that are opposite from each other in addressing similar problems, as each country seeks to change its past practice. In other cases, countries apply similar "solutions" to quite different problems, as shown in the discussion of decentralization.

TRENDS IN SCHOOL REFORM

Decentralization

Although many countries relax central control in an attempt to respond to educational problems, the specific problem to which they are responding varies considerably among them. Some countries decentralize in order to respond more effectively to a diverse student population or because of disappointment in the ability of well-intentioned central plans to close the achievement gap between children of high and low socioeconomic status (SES). In other cases, decentralization is a response to a more general disillusionment about cumbersome bureaucracies or the quality of public schools. Countries also decentralize in the aftermath of political or economic upheaval, when national resources are scarce.

Decentralization is a generic label describing decreased central control, but the word tells us little about who retains responsibility and for what purpose. In some cases, the responsibility is delegated to a state or province; in others, to a local authority (e.g., a school district); and, in still others, to schools or to parents through school choice plans. Moreover, the specific responsibilities that are delegated differ from country to country and might include responsibilities for any, or all, of the following: resources; curriculum; tests; accountability plans; and teacher selection, salaries, and credentials.

Consider, for example, England and the United States, both examples of countries that are partially decentralized. In England, funding comes primarily from the central government; the responsibility for curriculum and tests is also highly centralized. Local education authorities have little power. But individual schools do have the authority to make certain decisions, for example, about budget allocations, and families have the right to choose their schools.

The allocation of responsibilities is very different in the United States. Most school funding comes from state and local jurisdictions. Although both the federal government and states set testing and accountability requirements, the states have the responsibility for selecting the specific tests that will be used to meet those requirements and for setting policy on whether and how standardized tests will be used to determine student promotion and graduation. States, school districts, schools, and teachers generally all play a role in curriculum decisions, although the level of involvement varies across school districts. Budget allocations are typically controlled by school districts but sometimes by schools. Parental choice options can be broad or limited, depending on the school district.

Each of these decisions makes a difference. In England, for example, funding is quite equally distributed across the country; in the United States, the distribution of resources is highly unequal. The difference in these funding patterns, in turn, has major implications for educational quality and opportunity.

Accountability

Several of the countries represented in this collection place increased emphasis on teacher accountability. This trend is a by-product of decentralization: As central governments delegate responsibilities to local jurisdictions, they require these jurisdictions to demonstrate that they are using their new independence effectively. The most visible method of implementing accountability plans is through student testing requirements; the test scores, in turn, are used as indicators of school quality. The United States has the most demanding test-based accountability requirements, but other countries—England, Australia, and New Zealand, for example—also are placing greater emphasis on testing, sometimes in combination with publicly disseminated school rankings and increased reporting requirements.

Of course, "standardized" or "national" tests are administered in most countries, but these tests typically are used for purposes of student selection into academic secondary schools or universities. What is unique about the current trend is that the tests are used to assess the quality of schools—an application that is questionable because of the methodological problems inherent in making that link. Test-score rankings of schools (or nations) provide little information about the quality of education because they are influenced by other factors that are difficult to control: for example, the poverty levels of students taking the test and student selectivity (overrepresentation of the higher-achieving students in the test-taking population). Not surprisingly, the increased emphasis on testing is quite controversial in most countries because of a concern that it will lead to unfair school evaluations and will also diminish the learning environment for students and make schools a less attractive place to work for teachers.

Flexible Learning Environments

Many countries are attempting to move from a strict reliance on didactic teaching and rote learning to learning environments that encourage student participation, problem solving, and critical analysis. In some countries, the transition is motivated by concern about children's overall cognitive and emotional development. The chapter on

Japan describes the purpose of increased flexibility as "cultivating Japanese people with 'rich humanity' and 'rich creativity by letting individual abilities grow.'" The chapter on China describes the process as "return[ing] the time to the students" and encouraging "multiple solutions to a problem."

Singapore's education reforms also reflect a concern about developing students' problem-solving and analytical capabilities—a concern reflected in the slogan "Thinking Schools, Learning Nation." South Africa, which has made enormous progress in redistributing resources, still must confront the even more demanding task of implementing "large-scale reforms in curriculum and teaching methods (in a country that has eleven national languages), both to remove apartheid content and ideology and for the sake of pedagogical modernization." The chapter on Turkey describes the challenge of modernizing curricula and teaching methods and the "inherent difficulties in moving from a reform idea to implementing it in practice."

Attempts to revise curricula and teaching methods also are limited by testing practices. Parents, students, and teachers do not accept changes that are perceived to be inconsistent with high test scores, particularly when the scores determine students' admission to universities or teachers' perceived performance under accountability plans. China, which has recently been successful in implementing innovative education programs in some schools, has also revised its university entrance examinations to support changes in classroom practice that encourage students to integrate knowledge from diverse fields, rather than simply memorizing facts. A recent university entrance examination, for example, included a question on the increase of private cars in China; the response required students to draw on knowledge of statistics, comparative analysis, supply and production, urban traffic, pollution, and social studies.

Many families and teachers, however, remain concerned about changing the type of test questions. Success in university entrance examinations has traditionally been the main route out of poverty in China. High scores seem more attainable if they depend primarily on hard work and memorization: It is more difficult to prepare for test questions that require analysis—particularly when the new teaching approaches have not yet reached the majority of Chinese schools.

That, in turn, increases the gap between the affluent and poorer areas of the country.

As many countries throughout the world struggle to make a transition from rote learning to school environments that emphasize a broader set of skills, the United States—which has a reputation for flexible teaching practices—appears to be moving in the opposite direction. There is an increasing emphasis on testing, more pressure on schools to raise scores, and strong incentives to "teach to the test" by narrowing the curriculum and encouraging rote learning.

Access

Countries throughout the world have experienced a dramatic increase in educational access, although there is still a long way to go in order to achieve universal access to primary and secondary school and reduce disparities in opportunity. The author on China describes the "spectacular achievements in the expansion of basic education," along with increased enrollment in junior secondary education. In Turkey, the extension of compulsory education from five to eight years has increased school attendance and reduced the gap in school enrollment between boys and girls, which has been a particularly serious problem in rural areas. In South Africa, the average grade-level achievement has increased from approximately seven to ten grades in less than a generation.

Most countries have also made substantial progress in expanding access to upper secondary schools and universities. France, for example, has added a vocational *baccalauréat* in order to increase the number of students eligible to attend universities. England, which formerly provided advanced academic education to only a small proportion of young people, has now opened up its education system. The United States, with relatively high attendance rates in higher education, has made major gains over the past thirty years in increasing the diversity of the student body.

Difficulties remain: Access to higher education has not always kept pace with rising expectations; the quality of education sometimes suffers because funding limitations make it difficult to support the faculty and infrastructure needed to serve the increased numbers of students; students from lower SES backgrounds continue to have very limited access to certain "elite" universities; and some countries' economies are unable to provide adequate jobs for university graduates. In general, however, increased access has opened up societies in ways that were not thought possible even a generation ago.

CHOICES, TRADE-OFFS, AND IRONIES

Conflicting Goals and Policy Choices

Every country's reforms—whether explicitly or by default—require difficult policy choices among conflicting goals. The chapters in this book are replete with discussions of the resulting trade-offs, the "costs," and the ironies. The following examples are typical of some of the choices countries face.

Public Schools and Equity

Middle- and upper-class families sometimes make financial contributions to their children's public schools as a price for foregoing private education. Thus, the public school system is preserved—but at the cost of creating disparities between schools serving affluent and low-income students. Many countries, in one way or another, reach an accommodation, but that compromise is often painful because it requires trade-offs between deeply held value systems.

That trade-off was perhaps most difficult in South Africa, which has focused its postapartheid reforms on rebuilding what was one of the world's most inequitable education systems. The school funding formula is now designed to equalize expenditures generally and also to provide additional funding to low-income areas; this redistribution, in turn, requires the withdrawal of funds from affluent schools—an action that many feared would cause middle-class families (now increasingly both black and white) to leave the public school system. To prevent that from happening, a decision was made to permit families to make private contributions to their public schools, thereby enabling those schools to have facilities and services not available in less affluent neighborhoods.

The concern about the inequity of this arrangement was balanced by the even more troublesome concern that, if private contributions were not permitted, middle-class families would leave the public school system, which would then lose both the participation of these families and their advocacy for high public expenditures on education—along with the resources and influence to do something about it. The decision, therefore, to permit private contributions to public schools was based on the expectation that the loss of the middle-class constituency from the public school system would, almost inevitably, have adverse consequences for the education of all children.

The type of decision that South Africa faced is repeated in different guises in countries throughout the world. The "best" option, of course, differs depending on the specific situation, but the choice is never easy.

In the United States, for example, affluent parents in some communities wish to make substantial private contributions to their children's public schools, in order to provide services or equipment that otherwise would not be available. As in South Africa, school superintendents are faced with a difficult choice between maintaining an equitable distribution of resources across schools and, instead, encouraging middle-class families to remain in the public school system by permitting them to fund their schools.

Both school choice and student-tracking plans raise similar issues. Most countries use some version of these arrangements—even countries where schools generally are nonselective. School systems that offer an elite academic track, for example, might provide an incentive for affluent parents to remain in the public school system—but often at a "cost" to children in the lower tracks. The question continues to be debated, especially in cities with high concentrations of poverty, where middle-class families are most likely to leave the public school system.

There are many variations on this theme. Over the past generation, England has moved to a comprehensive (nonselective) school system in place of its earlier reliance on "grammar schools," which were selective, served high-achieving children from both middle- and working-class families, and were successful in sending students to prestigious universities. The grammar schools, however, were abolished in an attempt to make the education system less stratified, yet many question whether that hope has been fulfilled. Education in England's cities is increasingly polarized, as middle-class families choose private schools, and the proportion of children from state schools attending prestigious universities has declined since the 1970s.

There have been, of course, societal changes as well as changes in school structure during this time period: England has experienced high rates of immigration over the past thirty years, and the proportion of the population that is foreign born is now higher in London than it is in New York. Therefore, we cannot identify with any certainty whether the transition to comprehensive schools or increased immigration was the driving force that has contributed to the current stratification of education, nor can we ignore the problems of early tracking that occurred under the grammar school system. The point is that well-intentioned "solutions" to perceived problems sometimes provide incentives (in this case, the incentive for increased private school attendance) that undermine the reform's initial purpose.

The trade-offs implicit in the South African and English examples are repeated in other countries. Cities in the United States, as in England, have education systems that are polarized, with many middle- and upper-class students (of all racial-ethnic groups) attending private schools. Although comprehensive schools have been the norm in the United States, there are many exceptions: schools that select by achievement levels or special interests, charter schools, and schools that are part of a voucher program. Moreover, students attending comprehensive schools are often tracked into different courses or programs within the school, depending on their achievement level. Some of these approaches have been developed in order to prevent an exodus to private schools, but they have only limited effectiveness in achieving that goal; they do, however, create considerable concern about the potential for relegating the children "left behind" to mediocre schools and tracks and for increasing social stratification.

Germany also provides an interesting example. A country in which most students attend public schools, Germany tracks children into three separate types of schools beginning in grade five: an academic track (*Gymnasium*), which is the major route to university; a middle track (*Realschule*), which provides a less intensive education and generally leads to technical or vocational training and sometimes to university; and a third track (*Hauptschule*) for the lowest-achieving students, which is intended to lead to vocational training but has high dropout rates, with many of its students unable to find either vocational training or employment.

Because SES is highly correlated with academic achievement, middle- and upper-class students are disproportionately represented in the academic track, with the *Hauptschule* enrolling the highest proportion of migrant workers' children. By magnifying the effects of SES, the tracking system is consistent with the PISA finding that the performance of German students correlates more strongly with SES than the performance of students in almost any other participating country (OECD PISA, 2001). However, this apparent link should be interpreted with caution because the effects of stratification in the education system cannot be separated from the effects of stratification in the broader society.

Overall, Germany ranks in the average or lower-than-average range for most of the tested areas. Despite this finding, the three-tier system in Germany continues. That outcome is not surprising: There were earlier attempts to develop comprehensive schools in those states governed by the Social Democratic Party, and most of these schools had difficulty surviving over the years. Apparently, there is considerable public support for a differentiated school system (at least, we can assume, among families whose children are in the academic track).

Ironies of Decentralization

As described previously, countries often decentralize in order to increase educational opportunities for diverse student populations. The hope is that by decreasing central control of curriculum and teaching practices, local communities will be able to tailor education programs to match their students' needs. The difficulty occurs, however, when education funding also becomes a local responsibility, as it has in China, or when funding from all levels of government is inadequate and unpredictable, as in Russia, where the issue of "who pays for what" and "who owes what to whom" is unsettled. The lowest-income communities and children are inevitably at the greatest disadvantage in the competition for scarce funds.

In some cases, school choice—another component of decentralization—also has contributed to inequalities. In Chile, for example, vouchers have led to some increase in stratification because schools play a role in selecting students, even if government policy discourages it; transportation and school fees are a problem for low-income families; and fewer private schools open in the lowest-income communities. New Zealand's school choice program makes it possible for secondary schools actively to recruit students with high academic or athletic achievement and to discourage lower-achieving students or those with disabilities from attending.

Central governments often give local jurisdictions greater freedom in one domain while tightening control in another. The United States allows states and school districts increased flexibility in the use of federal funds but, at the same time, institutes highly prescriptive accountability requirements based on standardized test results. Indeed, local jurisdictions in many countries must balance the freedom that they have been given to make programmatic decisions against the testing requirements. Teachers in all countries are under pressure to teach to the tests, whether the tests are given in third grade or in thirteenth—and even when tests are administered in later grades, they influence curriculum and teaching practices many years in advance.

The chapter on Israel uses the term *protective bureaucracy* to describe attempts by the central bureaucracy to contain the perceived negative effects of decentralization, which are described as increased politicization, increased societal divisions, and decreased egalitarianism. As families are offered greater school choice, and schools become more independent of central control, the number of schools that represent political positions and ideologies increases. The bureaucracy responds by tightening control in an attempt to mitigate that trend: "The irony, however, is that the ministry might become even more powerful, with all the disadvantages of a highly centralized education system. As a bureaucracy, it will return to the familiar and attempt to prevent any real structural change or the use of new teaching methods."

The tension between decentralization and the increased risk of ideological influence is not unique to Israel. The chapter on Turkey, for example, describes the concern that "decentralization might weaken national control so that local religious and separatist factions would have a 'golden opportunity' to gain control of schools—an outcome, it is feared, that would eventually lead to the disintegration of Turkey's national identity and the unity of the country."

The chapter on Russia describes the challenge of balancing central and local control this way: "In the mid–eighteenth century, Catherine the Great, writing about legal reform in Russia, noted that the most intractable issue was getting right the relationship between the center and the regions." Most countries continue the struggle to get that balance right.

Societal Constraints

The potential effectiveness of education reform is seriously limited by poverty and by a broad range of other societal problems, such as health concerns and inadequate resources for education—all factors that are outside the control of schools. No country has found that educational practices alone have solved the broader problems of society or eliminated the gap in educational performance between children of high and low SES, although educational practices can contribute to reducing or magnifying that gap. Although this point seems obvious, it apparently has not led to realistic expectations about what the education system can and cannot accomplish, nor has it reduced the level of disillusionment, blame, and rhetoric that occurs when expectations are not met.

The incidence of poverty varies widely among the countries represented in this book. In a few of the countries, a large proportion of children live in poverty. Even in countries with a high gross domestic product (GDP), where poverty affects fewer children, the amount of poverty varies considerably (Blackburn, 1997), and it has an adverse effect on student achievement (OECD PISA, 2001). As shown by a wide array of evidence, poverty is a major predictor of low educational achievement (Grissmer et al., 1994); thus, differences in poverty levels account for a significant portion of achievement variation both among and within countries. To a greater or lesser degree, all countries face an achievement gap based on SES, and many of the school reforms have been initiated in an attempt to reduce that gap.

Poverty's central role is often overlooked in interpretations of test-score rankings, which are assumed to indicate the "quality" of education. Whether nations or schools are compared, however, the test scores are strongly influenced by the SES of the children taking the test and, therefore, are not a simple reflection of school characteristics. The rhetoric surrounding test-score rankings ignores that reality and, in doing so, leads to "quick fixes" that are not designed to address basic societal problems.

In addition to poverty, other societal problems constrain education reform: Two of the book's chapters, for example, describe the impact of current health crises. In South Africa, the education system faces enormous human and financial problems arising from the high rates of HIV/AIDS among students, their parents, and their teachers. In Russia, chronic illness among children is a major contributor to low academic achievement; it is estimated that as many as one-third to one-half of primary school children in some parts of the country have "incapacitating" physical or mental conditions.

The impact of poverty and poor health on achievement is magnified by inadequate educational resources. In some cases, resources are scarce because of a low GDP or even temporary economic recessions; in others, the problem arises from unequal resource distribution—typically, it is the low-income population groups and regions of the country that have the least spent on their education. Moreover, these funding shortfalls are closely related to shortages in the supply and distribution of qualified teachers—shortages that affect most countries. The problems show up in different ways. In the United States, for example, schools in high-poverty communities often have to resort to "out-of-field" teaching because of teacher shortages resulting, in part, from high attrition rates. In Russia, young people are discouraged from entering the teaching profession because of extremely low salaries—payment of which sometimes has been delayed as much as nine months to a year—as well as difficult working conditions in some regions associated with poor facilities, inadequate textbooks, and uncertainties about the availability of even basic amenities such as heat and electricity. France attempts to address the problem of teachers' preference for affluent communities—Paris and the French Riviera—by assigning teachers to regions and schools; the approach clearly alleviates, but does not totally eliminate, the distribution problem because the more experienced teachers—those with seniority and, therefore, choice—are disproportionately represented in middle- and upper-income communities.

Each of these factors—poverty, societal problems, and inadequate resources—presents a major constraint on education reform. Their effect in combination can be overwhelming. Some countries—China, Russia, South Africa, and Turkey, for example—attempt to initiate a complex set of school reforms while meeting the challenges arising from extensive child poverty and scarce resources for education, often exacerbated by large inequalities in resource distribution and extensive, competing societal needs.

The countries with high GDP can invest heavily in education and have less poverty, but large differences exist even among these countries, in the distribution of educational resources, in the income and wealth gap between rich and poor families, and in poverty rates. The chapter on Australia describes the link between poverty and achievement this way: "The principal problems facing educators and systems in the early years are the powerful effects of *poverty*, in both its most historically persistent forms and those that are emergent in communities experiencing both structural economic change and increasing diversity of the population."

In comparison with many other industrialized countries, the United States has a high rate of relative poverty—defined as a low income compared with the country's average (Blackburn, 1997)—and a highly unequal distribution of resources, which results from the fact that most education funding comes from states and localities (Barro, 1996). These gaps in family income and educational resources are exacerbated, on the one hand, by the lack of social support systems often found in other industrialized countries but are mitigated, on the other, by a wide range of higher education options—along with second, and third, chances for students—that have increased opportunities for low-income and minority students. The basic problem remains, however: The combined effects of poverty and inadequate resources in many of the schools serving low-income communities have led to a substantial gap in educational achievement.

In contrast, Sweden has a smaller achievement gap (OECD PISA, 2001). Although causation cannot be established with certainty, a reasonable hypothesis is that Sweden's relatively "flat" distribution of income and wealth, its social support system, and its equitable distribution of educational resources have made a positive difference. They have not, however, eliminated the gap; indeed, the chapter on Sweden concludes that "social background remained the best predictor of educational attainment."

In short, public policies that increase educational access for low-income students are now indispensable given the pressures caused by poverty and the increased demand for an educated workforce in a global economy. These policies have made—and will continue to make—an important difference for low-income students and an even greater difference for future generations.

BALANCING CHANGE AND TRADITION

Values and Political Structure

Countries' traditional values and political structures play a major role in determining whether education reforms are implemented. In some cases, these traditions serve as facilitators; in others, they limit, or prevent, the reform initiatives.

Some countries have been able to make rapid change, as demonstrated most vividly in South Africa, where dramatic transformations in political leadership and values have been supported by what the author describes as an "extremely deliberative" process, "based on legislation and regulation to a degree perhaps unusual around the world":

> The system is attempting a set of reforms that is much larger in scope than what was attempted in, say, the desegregation of school systems in the United States, in that it is starting from a much greater level of inequality, where the poor and disadvantaged are the majority rather than the minority, where there is a simultaneous modernization and quality agenda at the same time as an equity and justice agenda, and while attempting to prevent, for the country as a whole, the sort of white-flight privatization of education common in American cities.

Thus, a country that still struggles with widespread poverty attempts to reform its education system to redress the past injustices suffered by a large majority of the population while, at the same time, maintaining the participation and support of all South Africans.

Major increases in innovative practices in China—for example, in classroom instruction and the examination system—have also occurred within an exceptionally short time. The author contrasts the relatively rapid changes in China with the slow pace of change in many other countries and attributes the difference to the fact that the Chinese reforms have built on traditional culture, for example, the general belief of Chinese teachers that there is a "best method"; the Chinese tradition of launching mass movements; and the high level of societal organization, which enables classroom changes to be supported by far-reaching and consistent school inspections, teacher training and development, and curriculum.

The changes in China, of course, have not always gone smoothly. There was some skepticism about the reforms in teaching methods, and, at first, only "lip service" was paid to recommendations to reform the examination system, which was based on a tradition of more than 1,000 years and still remains an integral part of Chinese education. As mentioned previously, concerns continue to be voiced about the new examination format: Teachers were used to preparing students to give "model" answers, and some parents and students correctly fear that memorization alone will no longer ensure high examination scores. In general, however, China appears to have been unusually successful in implementing change by building on traditional culture—or "holding new wine with the old bottle."

"For fifteen years," the chapter on England notes, "English schooling has been in a state of more or less constant change. . . . The reforms that shape today's schools started under the Conservative administrations of Thatcher but reached their apogee (or possibly their nadir) in the early years of the Labour administration headed by Tony Blair, when an average of one new directive or policy paper *a day* issued forth from the national ministry of education." The author attributes the country's ability to make rapid change (despite its "veneer of age and tradition") to its highly centralized government, based on a system in which seats in Parliament go to the candidates who receive the most votes in their constituencies, even if those votes represent only a minority of the total. Thus, a single party tends to receive large majorities in Parliament, party members often vote as a bloc, and governments can quickly mandate radical changes based on the ideological principles of the party in power. In short, "a British government has been able to pass whatever laws it likes, provided the members of its own party will accept them."

England's political structure is in sharp contrast to that of the United States, where change is much slower as a result of the "checks and balances" intrinsic to the three branches of the federal government and the fact that education is primarily a state and local responsibility. Moreover, unlike China, the United States does not easily translate a reform idea into practice because the system is not designed to encourage alignment between the reform and the support systems required to implement it. Indeed, the multiplicity of attempted reforms in the United States often results in reforms that conflict with each other. The outcome is that large-scale implementation of a new teaching practice, for example, has proved to be a slow process, despite the fact that innovation is considered basic to the American system. Innovation in the United States, more often than not, is local, at least initially: It is not easy to transfer the "best practice" across the country in the short term, although some reforms have been implemented nationally over a period of many years.

Moreover, even when the federal government attempts to centralize control (e.g., by increasing testing requirements through the "No Child Left Behind" Act in 2001), the requirements are implemented in very different ways across the country: The curricula and tests differ; the definition of a passing score differs; and the decisions about which students do and do not take the test differ. The chapter on the United States describes a likely outcome:

> As the reforms of the past two decades pile up on the schools, as pressure from civil rights groups is brought to bear on what they regard as tests and standards that discriminate against minority children, as education funding is rolled back, and as terrorism, recession, oil shortages, and other issues overwhelm education in the nation's political debates and in the public mind, fatigue is likely to combine with backlash to produce, if not another swing of the pendulum, a rollback in the demands and standards. . . . None of this is likely to involve much conscious, systematic reexamination of the overall reform policies of the past genera-

tion, but it will produce a gradual attrition toward a more pragmatic, less utopian mean. That, too, has always been the American way.

The challenge of balancing education reform with long-standing traditions, exemplified in South Africa, China, England, and the United States, is faced by all countries that seek to change existing policies and practices.

Some countries that have experienced major political and ideological transitions, for example, continue their former education policies, and others struggle to reform their education systems but are constrained by conflicting values. Chile made a transition from an authoritarian to a democratic government but maintained the education policies—decentralization, vouchers, and testing—begun under the military regime. After initial attempts to reverse these policies with the establishment of democratic government in 1990, the teachers now generally accept them, perhaps in part because of generous benefits they received in recent years under a policy of *reivindicación* (reclaiming the right to be repaid) for human rights abuses they suffered during the military regime. After reunification, Germany faced an ideological conflict reflected in its two different education systems. The East German system, based on a Communist ideology, was centrally controlled, and students attended comprehensive schools. West Germany, on the other hand, was a pluralistic society with a decentralized education system, and schools were stratified by student achievement levels. The conflict between the two traditions was resolved by transferring the West German system to the east. Russia, on the other hand, is still coping with a conflict, rooted in practices from the Soviet era, between a highly intellectual academic tradition and a tradition that emphasizes rote learning and narrow vocational training. That conflict continues to constrain attempts to implement Russia's current centers of academic excellence and innovation on a large scale.

Even countries that have not experienced major political and ideological change find that proposed reform initiatives sometimes conflict with the public's values and expectations. France currently attempts to balance the public's strong support for the "national character" of education with attempts to move toward decentralization in a system that for centuries has concentrated power in Paris.

The decentralization process proceeds slowly: "It exists on paper; all the rules and regulations to implement it have been published. Yet in practice less has happened than was aimed for." Traditional values and political structures in Turkey also limit change: Turkey's attempt, for example, to move from rote learning and test-based instruction to more "progressive" teaching practices is constrained by scarce resources; a huge bureaucracy that is resistant to change; and resistance from some teachers, parents, and students who believe that the reform efforts are inconsistent with their values and beliefs. On the other hand, these constraints are offset by the strong support for reform that exists among many business, intellectual, and political leaders because of their belief that change is required for Turkey's successful participation in the global economy and full membership in the European Union. Educational change in Japan and Australia, too, is limited by the public's values and expectations. Although Japan's reforms attempt to change educational practice by allowing "children to use their individuality," these reforms must contend with the country's strong desire to maintain its traditional cultural and community values, which emphasize cooperation and consensus. Australia's traditional vocational/apprenticeship training system historically has had wide public participation and support. Now, however, it confronts the changing needs of the global economy and a concern that many students undergo preparation for jobs that no longer exist.

In some countries, the established bureaucracy resists reforms instituted by political leaders because of a concern that the reforms might erode egalitarian traditions or weaken the quality of education. In Israel, for example, as political leaders relax central control of education and give more power to local communities, the education bureaucracy becomes concerned about the increasing segmentation of the education system based on families' ideological, religious, or political views. In Sweden, too, a school choice strategy has raised concern that the education system is becoming more segregated by ethnicity and achievement, thereby increasing status differentials among schools and diminishing the egalitarian traditions of the country. New Zealand, like many other countries, has responded to disappointment about the education system's inability to solve societal problems by giving politicians and managers more power to set policy and weakening the traditional role of educators—a trend that the author believes will result in decisions that are educationally unsound.

Finally, inconsistency or tension occurs because a national or provincial government attempts to balance two very different objectives. Reform in Singapore, for example, is designed to link education goals with the perceived needs of the global economy by giving students the broad set of educational experiences needed for the country to be competitive in that economy. Yet the reform "takes place in a society that exerts a level of political and social control unique among wealthy nations. That control might be inconsistent with an education environment that encourages critical thinking and flexibility." In Canada, the Province of Quebec gives priority to maintaining French language and culture—a position that, in practice, often conflicts with its attempts to encourage immigration and a school environment that supports a multicultural student body.

Perhaps the issue can best be summarized by a quote from the chapter on Turkey: "It doesn't come easily." Although in most cases change is occurring, the translation of a reform proposal from theory into practice often proceeds at a slower pace than was initially envisioned.

Building on the Experience of Others

When a country is dissatisfied with the outcomes of its education system, it often turns to other countries perceived to be more successful and seeks to identify the educational practices that led to their success. It is not surprising that many of the attempted reforms described in this book are "borrowed" from countries around the world. Educators, public officials, and researchers from different countries face similar issues and attend similar conferences; they are knowledgeable about reforms in other countries (although it is less clear that the results of these reforms are widely known). Moreover, as noted previously, the ease with which a reform—whether borrowed or homegrown—can be implemented depends on its consistency with the country's traditions and values, the extent to which the political structure encourages or inhibits change, and a set of societal conditions—for example, the economic environment, poverty levels, children's health status—that can facilitate or constrain change.

Successful school reform also depends on an accurate analysis of the problem to be addressed and its relevance to the proposed reform. It does little good to implement a reform if that reform is unrelated, or marginal, to the problem. It is not unusual for countries to choose, and oversell, school reforms—"quick fixes"—that have little logical connection to the problem at hand. In the United States, for example, test-based accountability is based on the assumption that sanctioning teachers and schools for students' low scores on standardized tests will somehow close the achievement gap. That is not a given. Indeed, there is early evidence that it might be having the opposite effect by narrowing students' learning experience, increasing dropout rates, and discouraging qualified educators from remaining in the profession or choosing to teach in low-income communities. That mismatch between a reform and the hoped-for positive consequences is not limited to the United States.

Despite the uncertainty about the efficacy of some reforms and their unintended consequences, there are positive developments. Countries are focusing on issues of equity, access, globalization, and the necessity for providing a broad-based education for their diverse populations. Each country in the book recognizes the problems it faces. Each, without exception, makes difficult choices. Each is faced with expectations by political leaders that the reforms it initiates—often with scarce resources—will work and will be accepted by educators, parents, students, and the general public.

Educators know that achievement measures inevitably reflect factors that are far more powerful than any reforms and that they will be held accountable for results over which they have only uncertain influence. They know too that schools, directly or indirectly, will be held accountable for societal and economic problems that are outside their control and indeed will be expected to solve those problems. These continuing challenges, however, should not detract from the enormous increase in educational access that has occurred over the past generation, as well as the increased attention to educational innovation and the needs of diverse student populations. Thus, despite the challenges of poverty and globalization and unrealistic expectations, educators throughout the world institute reforms, consider trade-offs, and make difficult choices—all in an effort to ensure equity, access, and a decent education for children.

NOTE

I have highlighted key themes in this chapter, using examples from the countries represented in the book, but do not attempt to summarize each chapter. The contributing authors have described the political, economic, and social context for education policy, along with the school reform issues in each of their countries, much more comprehensively than I could paraphrase here. The quotations in this chapter come from the other chapters in the book and, therefore, are not referenced.

REFERENCES CITED

Barro, S. M. (1996). *How countries pay for schools: An international comparison of systems for financing primary and secondary education.* Paper prepared for the Finance Center of the Consortium for Policy Research in Education. Washington, DC: SMB Economic Research, Inc.

Blackburn, M. L. (1997). *Comparing poverty: The United States and other industrial nations.* AEI Studies on Understanding Economic Inequality. Washington, DC: American Enterprise Institute for Public Policy Research.

Grissmer, D. W., Kirby, S. N., Berends, M., & Williamson, S. (1994). *Student achievement and the changing American family.* Washington, DC: RAND Institute on Education and Training.

Organization for Economic Cooperation and Development Program for International Student Assessment. (2001). *Knowledge and skills for life: First results from PISA 2000.* Paris: Organization for Economic Cooperation and Development Program for International Student Assessment.

Index

About the Contributors

Gérard Bonnet is in charge of European and international relations at the French Ministry of Education's Department of Assessment and Forecasting in Paris. He is responsible for promoting and organizing international cooperation in the field of quality education systems. He is also a visiting fellow at the Institute of Education's Bedford Group for Statistical and Lifecourse Studies at the University of London. His publications include articles on teacher training, assessment methodology, and comparative evaluation published in French and in international journals.

Mary Canning is lead education specialist in the Europe and Central Asia region of the World Bank, specializing in the education system of Russia, where she leads the bank's education policy dialogue and sector analysis. She also works on education reform in those countries of Central and Eastern Europe that joined the European Union in May 2004. Her reports and papers on Russia have appeared in the World Bank series, as well as in edited collections in Europe, such as *Crossroads in Russia: Experiences in Educational Cooperation.*

Kai-ming Cheng is the pro-vice chancellor, chair, and a professor of education at the University of Hong Kong. He is also a visiting professor at the Harvard Graduate School of Education and the Graduate

School of Education, Peking University, and serves as a member of Hong Kong's Education Commission. His publications focus on education planning, finance, and policy making in China, India, Japan, and other Asian systems of education and reflect his fundamental interest in the process of policy making and the notion of legitimacy in such a process.

Phyllis Ghim-Lian Chew is on the faculty of the National Institute of Education in Singapore. Her books and articles address a wide range of topics, including pragmatic strategies in business, gender studies, English as an international language, contemporary linguistics, and language and culture in an educational context.

Terry J. Crooks is a professor of education and the codirector of the Educational Assessment Research Unit at the University of Otago in New Zealand. He codirects the National Education Monitoring Project, which assesses the capabilities of fourth and eighth grade students in all curriculum areas, and is a past president of the New Zealand Association for Research in Education. His publications focus on educational assessment and the teaching and learning process.

Luis Crouch is a lead education economist for the World Bank's Human Development Network and was an economist at RTI International (Research Triangle Institute) in North Carolina, where he specialized in education planning, the measurement of performance indicators, and education finance. He has been a technical adviser to South Africa's Department of Education during the period 1995 to the present.

Eva Forsberg is an assistant professor and postdoctoral fellow of education at Uppsala University in Sweden. She has served as an expert consultant to Sweden's National Agency for Education and the Ministry of Education and Science. Her publications focus on issues of educational leadership and student participation in the policy process.

Mary Hatwood Futrell is the dean of the Graduate School of Education and Human Development and a professor of education policy at The George Washington University, Washington, D.C. She is a former president of the National Education Association, Education International, and the World Confederation of Organizations of the Teaching Profession and has served on the boards of the Carnegie Foundation for the Advancement of Teaching, the Kettering Foundation, and the Institute for Educational Leadership. Her publications focus on the teaching profession, the education of diverse student populations, standards and accountability, urban education, and higher education.

Ratna Ghosh is the James McGill Professor at McGill University in Montreal, where she also holds the position of William C. Macdonald Professor of Education. She recently completed her term as the dean of the Faculty of Education. She has engaged in research, training, and development work in Canada, the United States, Latin America, Asia, and Africa. She has also served as the resident director and president of the Shastri Indo-Canadian Institute, as an adviser to the Canadian government, and in several positions on the Canadian Human Rights Foundation. Her publications focus on issues of intercultural and international education and gender studies.

Batia P. Horsky is an art historian and educator. She is on the faculty of Nanyang Technological University in Singapore and has worked for Singapore's Ministry of Education. Her research focuses on museum education, management of arts programs, curriculum development, and creativity.

Dan Inbar is a professor of education policy and administration at Hebrew University and formerly was the dean of the School of Education. He has served on several committees of Israel's Ministry of Education and held appointments as a visiting fellow at European, Australian, Canadian, and U.S. universities. His research has focused on policy, educational choice, management, leadership, and diversity. His current research addresses issues of social capital and ethics in leadership.

Barbara M. Kehm is a professor of social sciences at the University of Kassel in Germany, where she is the director of the Center for Research on Higher Education and Work. Her publications focus on

German and international higher education. She recently contributed an overview of German universities and research institutions for a publication, *Trends in American and German Higher Education*, published by the American Academy of Arts and Sciences and its German counterpart, the Berlin-Brandenburg Academy of Sciences and Humanities.

Stephen T. Kerr is a professor of education and the associate dean for Academic Programs in the College of Education at the University of Washington in Seattle, where he also holds an adjunct appointment in the University's Program in Russian, East European, and Central Asian Studies. His articles and book chapters on Russia and the former Soviet Union have dealt with problems of change in educational institutions under conditions of rapid economic and social development.

Allan Luke is a professor and the dean of the Centre for Research in Pedagogy and Practice at the National Institute of Education in Singapore. He has served as the dean at the University of Queensland in Australia and the deputy director general of Education for Queensland Schools. His early work focused on the sociological and political significance of literacy, and his current work addresses issues of education in the context of globalization and the implications of global changes for pedagogy and research. His most recent book is *Struggles over Difference: Texts, Curriculum and Pedagogy in the Asia Pacific*.

Ulf P. Lundgren is a professor of education at Uppsala University in Sweden. From 1990 to 1999 he was the director general of the Swedish National Agency for Education. He has also served as an expert consultant to the Ministries of Education in Sweden and Portugal, to international organizations, and to various education committees within the European Union. His publications address issues of educational governance, policy, and philosophy.

Robert W. McMeekin is an associated researcher with the Centro de Investigación y Desarrollo de la Educación (Center for Education Research and Development) in Santiago, Chile. He has worked for the Ford Foundation and other employers on education and development issues in countries in Asia, Africa, and Latin America. He served as a human resources economist at the World Bank until his retirement. He also serves as a consultant to the UNESCO Regional Office for Education in Latin America and other organizations. His most recent book, *Incentives to Improve Education: A New Perspective,* applies new institutional economics concepts to study incentives in the education sector.

Adam Nir is the chairperson of the Department of Policy and Administration in Education at Hebrew University in Jerusalem and a member of the Board of Directors of the International Society for Educational Planning. His articles address issues of educational planning and administration, leadership, and school-based management.

Peter Schrag is the former editorial page editor of *The Sacramento Bee* in California and a longtime columnist on American politics and education. His articles, which address a wide range of issues related to societal trends, education, and politics, have appeared in publications such as *The American Prospect, The Atlantic Monthly,* and *The New Republic.* His most recent book, *Final Test: The Battle for Adequacy in America's Schools,* presents an analysis of school finance reform cases.

Hasan Simsek is a professor of education and the chairperson of the Department of Educational Sciences at Middle East Technical University in Ankara, Turkey. His research focuses on educational administration, higher education, and teacher education. Simsek and Ali Yildirim recently coauthored *Qualitative Research Methods in Social Sciences,* as well as articles on education policy in Turkey. Simsek has also served as a consultant to the World Bank and the Turkish Higher Education Council.

Ryo Watanabe is the director of the Department for International Research and Cooperation at the National Institute for Educational Policy Research in Japan and a visiting professor at the Tokyo Institute of Technology. He has published work in both English and Japanese on educational technology, comparative education, assessment of student performance, and educational cooperation. Most recently,

Watanabe served as coeditor and author of the *International Handbook of Educational Research in the Asia-Pacific Region*.

Alison Wolf is a professor of management at King's College, University of London, and previously was a professor of education at the Institute of Education, University of London. She has been an adviser to British government agencies, the Organization for Economic Cooperation and Development, the European Commission, and the New Zealand, French, and South African governments and has conducted program evaluations for the U.S. Congress. Her publications focus on education and the labor market and on assessment, qualifications, and skills. Her most recent book is *Does Education Matter? Myths about Education and Economic Growth*.

Ali Yildirim is a professor of education at Middle East Technical University in Ankara, Turkey, where he specializes in curriculum and instruction, teacher education, and qualitative research methods. Yildirim and Hasan Simsek recently coauthored *Qualitative Research Methods in Social Sciences*, as well as articles on education policy in Turkey. Yildirim has also served as a consultant to the World Bank and the Turkish Higher Education Council.

About the Editor

Iris C. Rotberg is a research professor of education policy at the Graduate School of Education and Human Development at The George Washington University, Washington, D.C. After beginning her career as a research psychologist, she entered the field of public policy research, holding positions with the National Science Foundation, RAND, the National Institute of Education, and the U.S. House of Representatives Committee on Science, Space, and Technology. Her research reports, articles, and commentaries address issues of school reform, testing and accountability, international education, science education, and federal policy for financing education. She has conducted research for the U.S. Congress on policy options for improving the education of low-income students, technology and human resources, and the outcomes of federal education programs. Her articles and commentaries appear in such publications as *Science, Brookings Papers on Education Policy, Phi Delta Kappan, The Bridge, Harvard Educational Review,* the *Washington Post,* and *Education Week.*